From Far Away™

Vol. 6

Story and Art by
Kyoko Hikawa

彼方から
FROM FAR AWAY

CAST OF CHARACTERS:

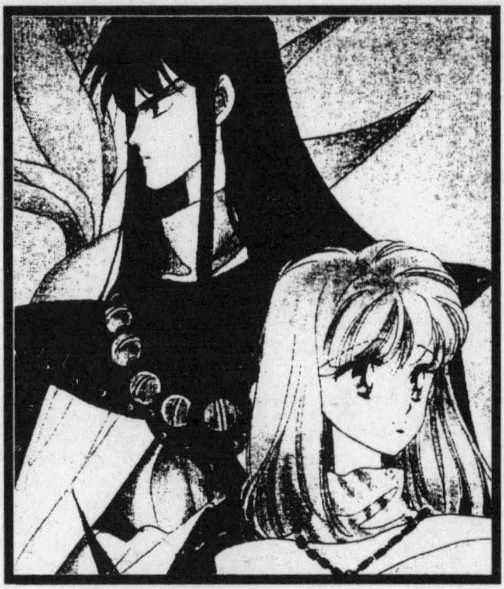

IZARK KIA TAJ (LEFT)
A TRAVELING WARRIOR. HE'S ACTUALLY THE SKY DEMON, BUT NOBODY KNOWS IT YET.

NORIKO TACHIKI (RIGHT)
NORIKO WAS AN ORDINARY HIGH SCHOOL GIRL BEFORE SHE WAS MYSTERIOUSLY TRANSPORTED INTO ANOTHER WORLD. SHE IS THE AWAKENING, BUT ONLY IZARK KNOWS THIS.

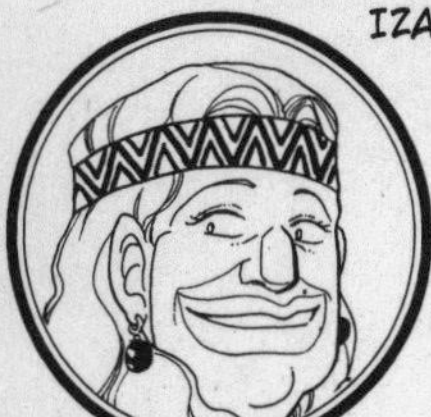

GAYA
A WARRIOR OF THE GRAY BIRD TRIBE WHO HAS KNOWN IZARK FOR MANY YEARS.

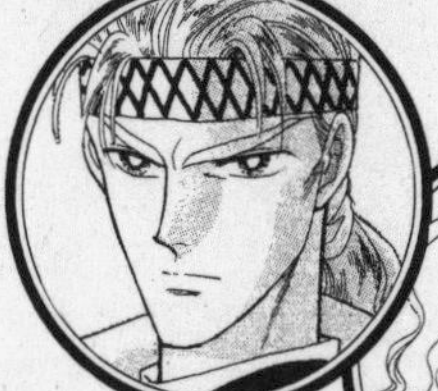

AGOL DENA ORFA
GEENA'S FATHER. HE LEFT HIS MASTER, LORD RACHEF AND JOINED NORIKO AND IZARK'S GROUP.

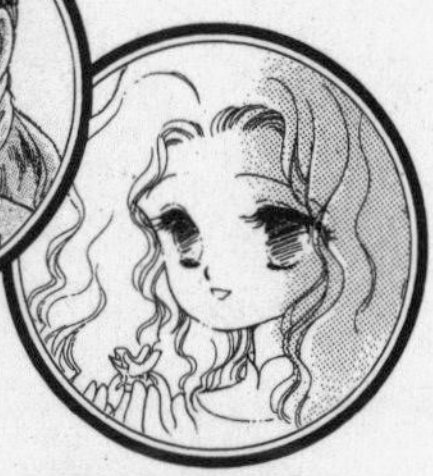

GEENA HAAS
A BLIND SEER. SHE IS VAGUELY AWARE OF IZARK AND NORIKO'S AS YET UNDISCLOSED IDENTITIES.

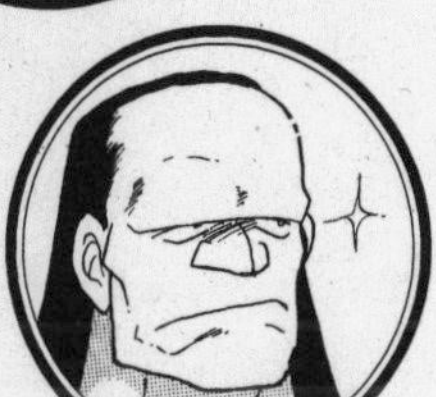

BARAGO
A WARRIOR WHO ONCE FOUGHT AGAINST IZARK, BUT NOW IZARK'S GOOD FRIEND.

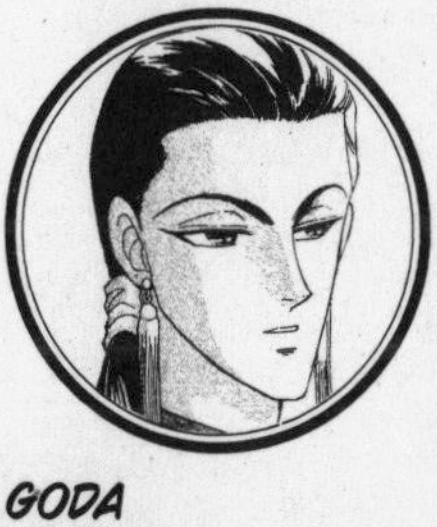

RACHEF
FROM THE SHADOWS, HE CONTROLS THE FREE CITY OF RIENKA. HE SEEKS THE AWAKENING, BUT HE DOESN'T KNOW WHO IT IS.

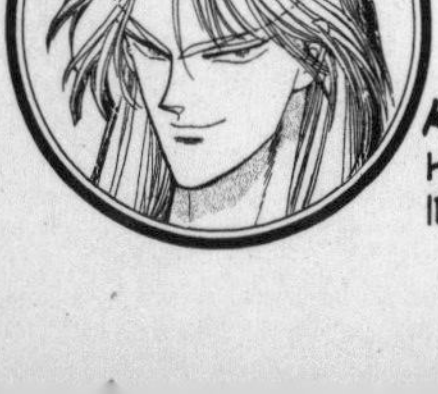

KEIMOS LEE GODA
HE IS OBSESSED WITH THE IDEA OF DEFEATING IZARK.

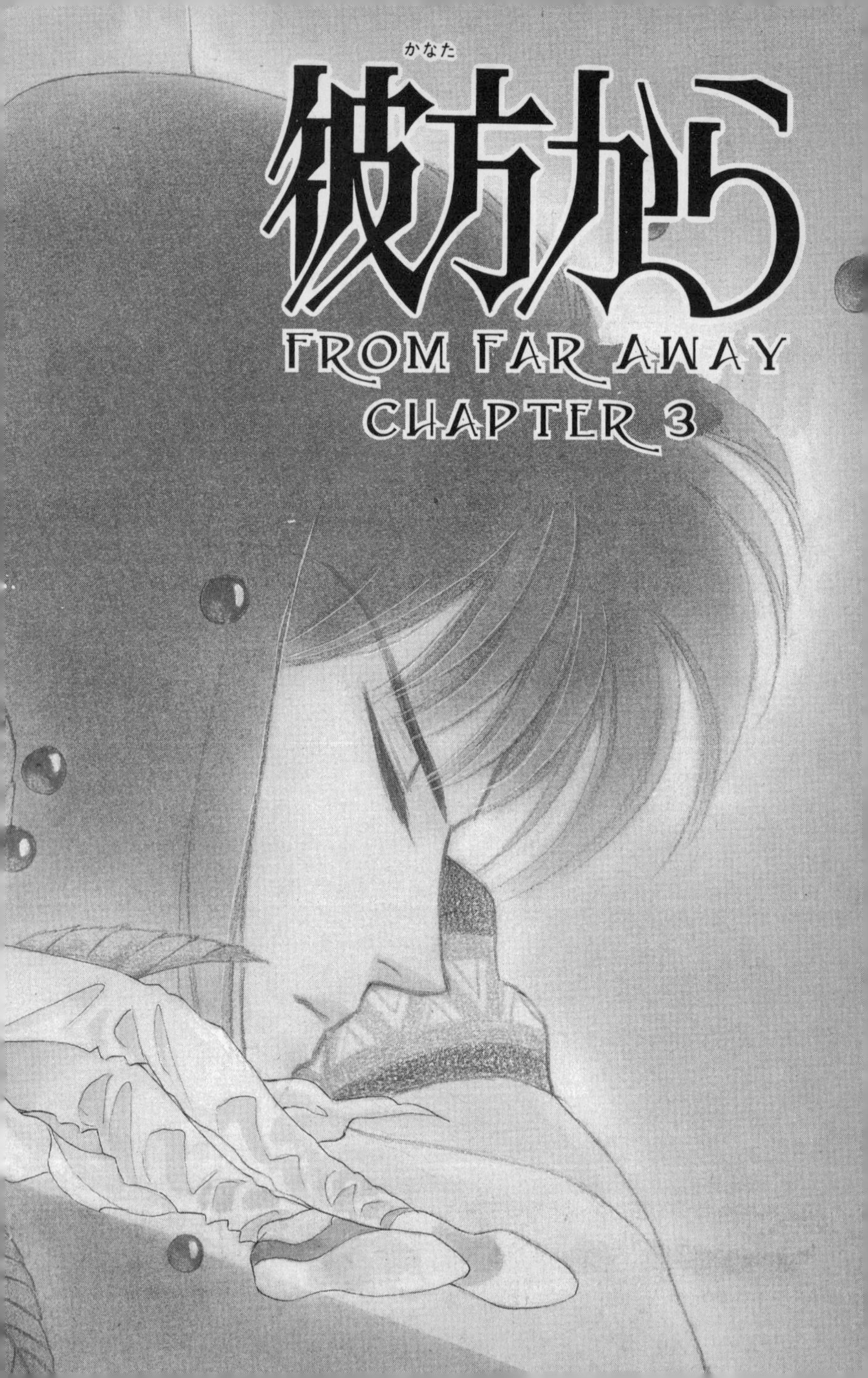
かなた
彼方から
FROM FAR AWAY
CHAPTER 3

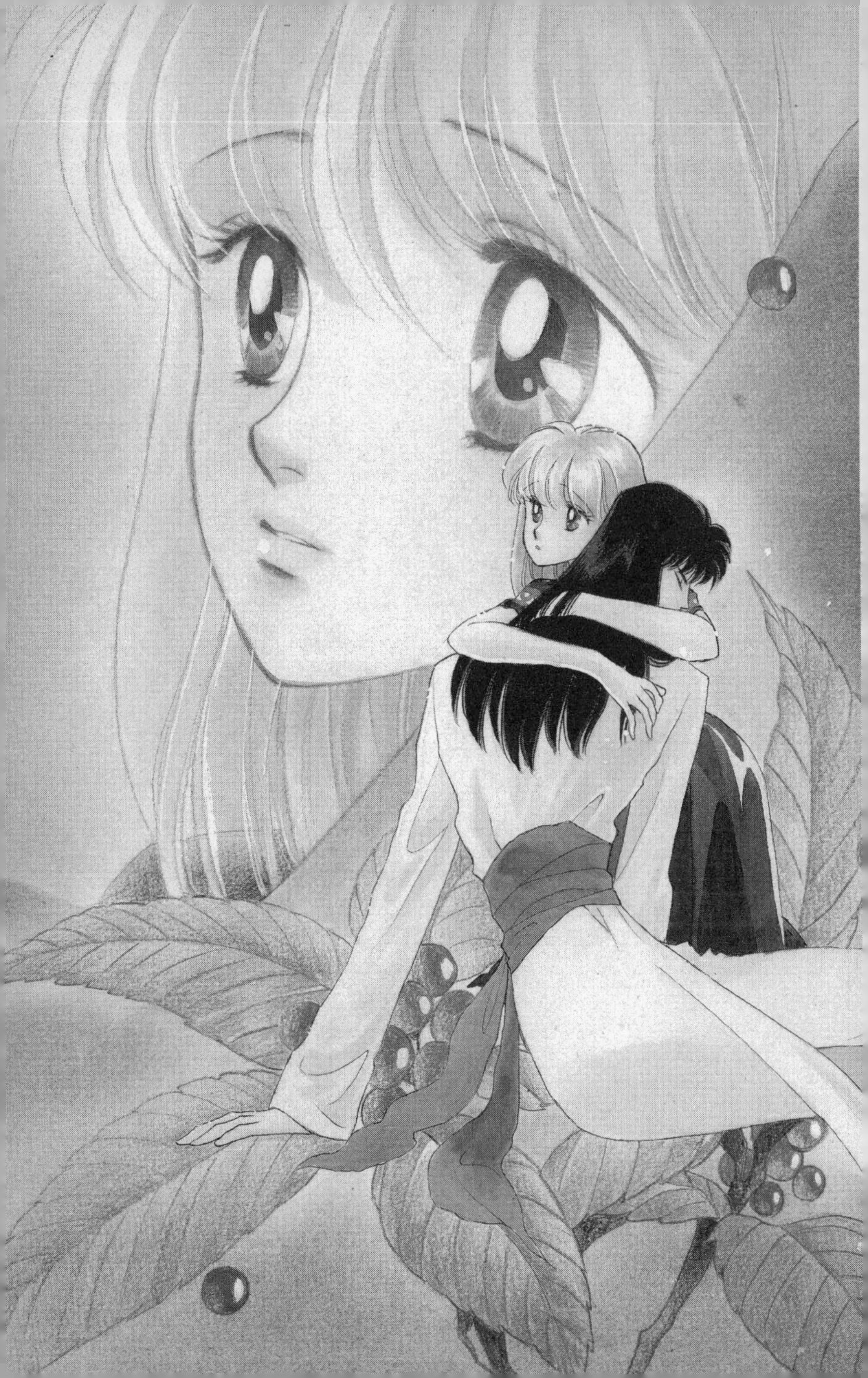

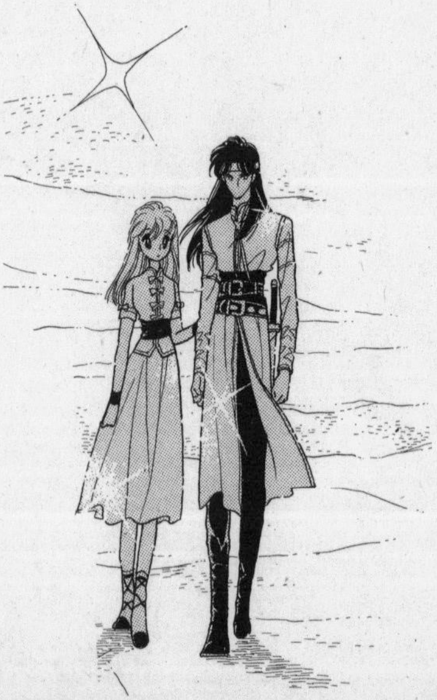

Thank you all for your fan letters.
I apologize for not being able to write you back.

Today, I want to pass along some of what I have learned from my readers.

First, here's a list of the most popular characters:

First place – Izark

Second – Noriko

Third – Gaya and Barago

Fourth – Other characters

Banadam has been not very popular lately.

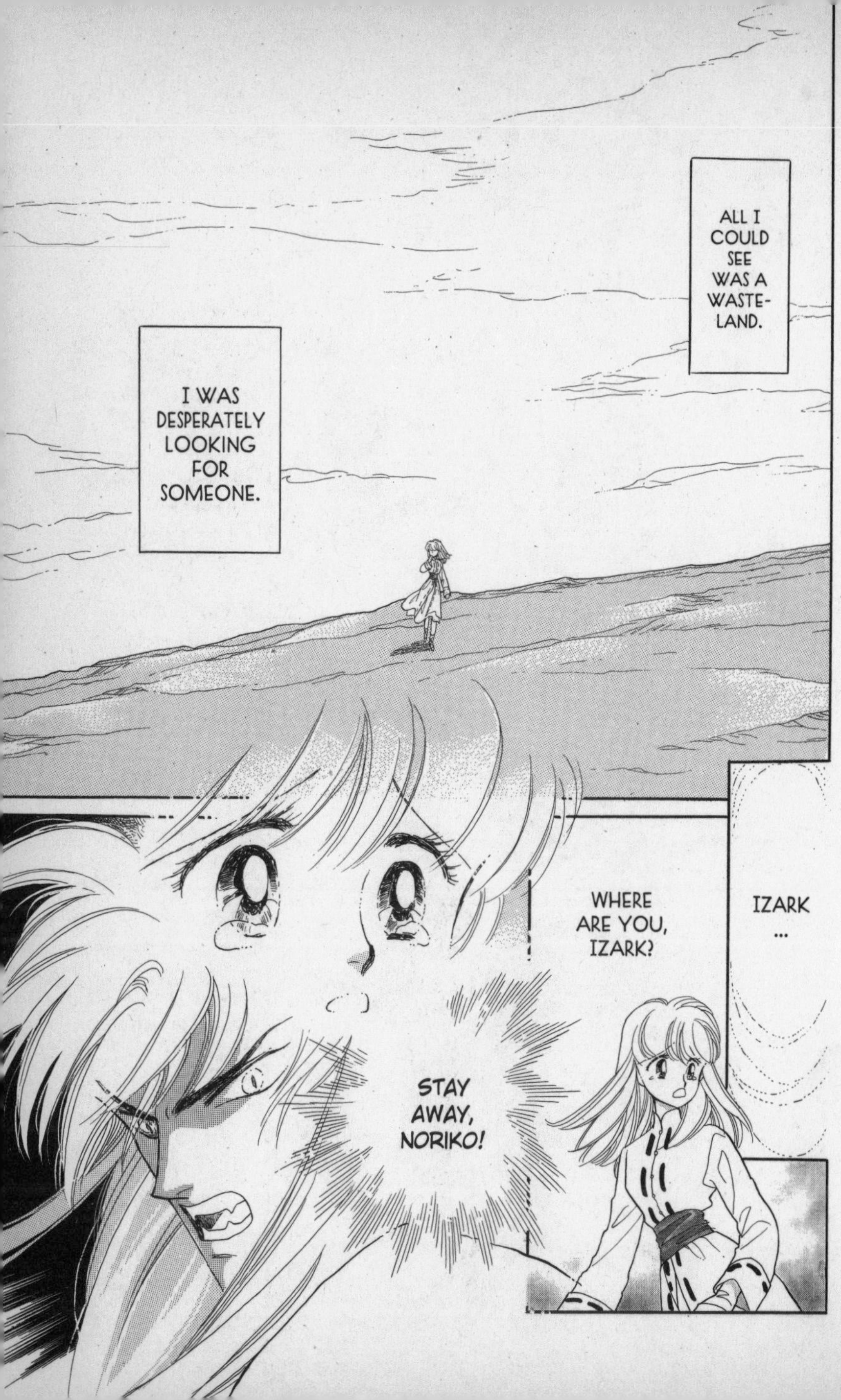
ALL I COULD SEE WAS A WASTE-LAND.
I WAS DESPERATELY LOOKING FOR SOMEONE.
IZARK ...
WHERE ARE YOU, IZARK?
STAY AWAY, NORIKO!

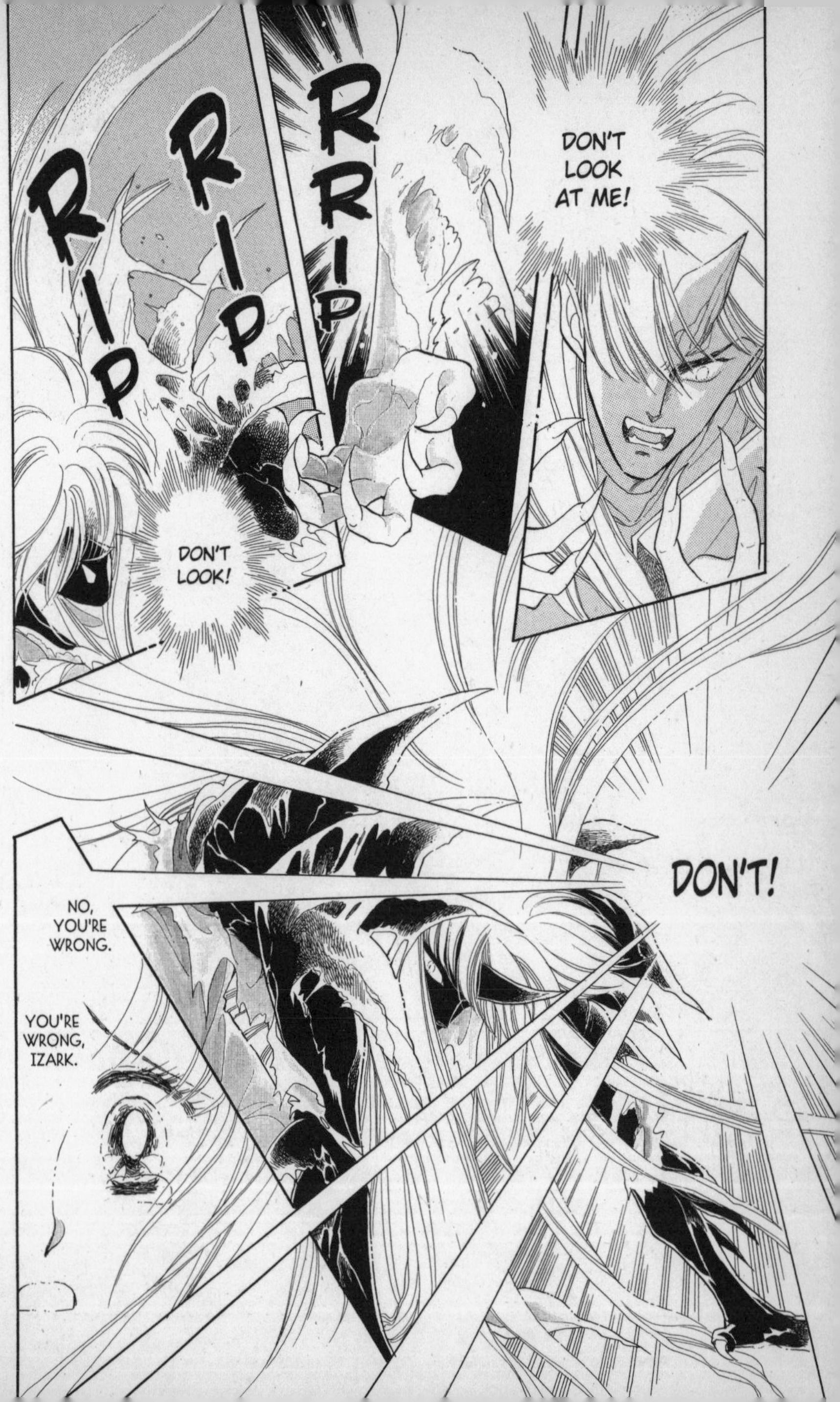
DON'T LOOK AT ME!
RRIP
RIP
RIP
DON'T LOOK!
DON'T!
NO, YOU'RE WRONG.
YOU'RE WRONG, IZARK.

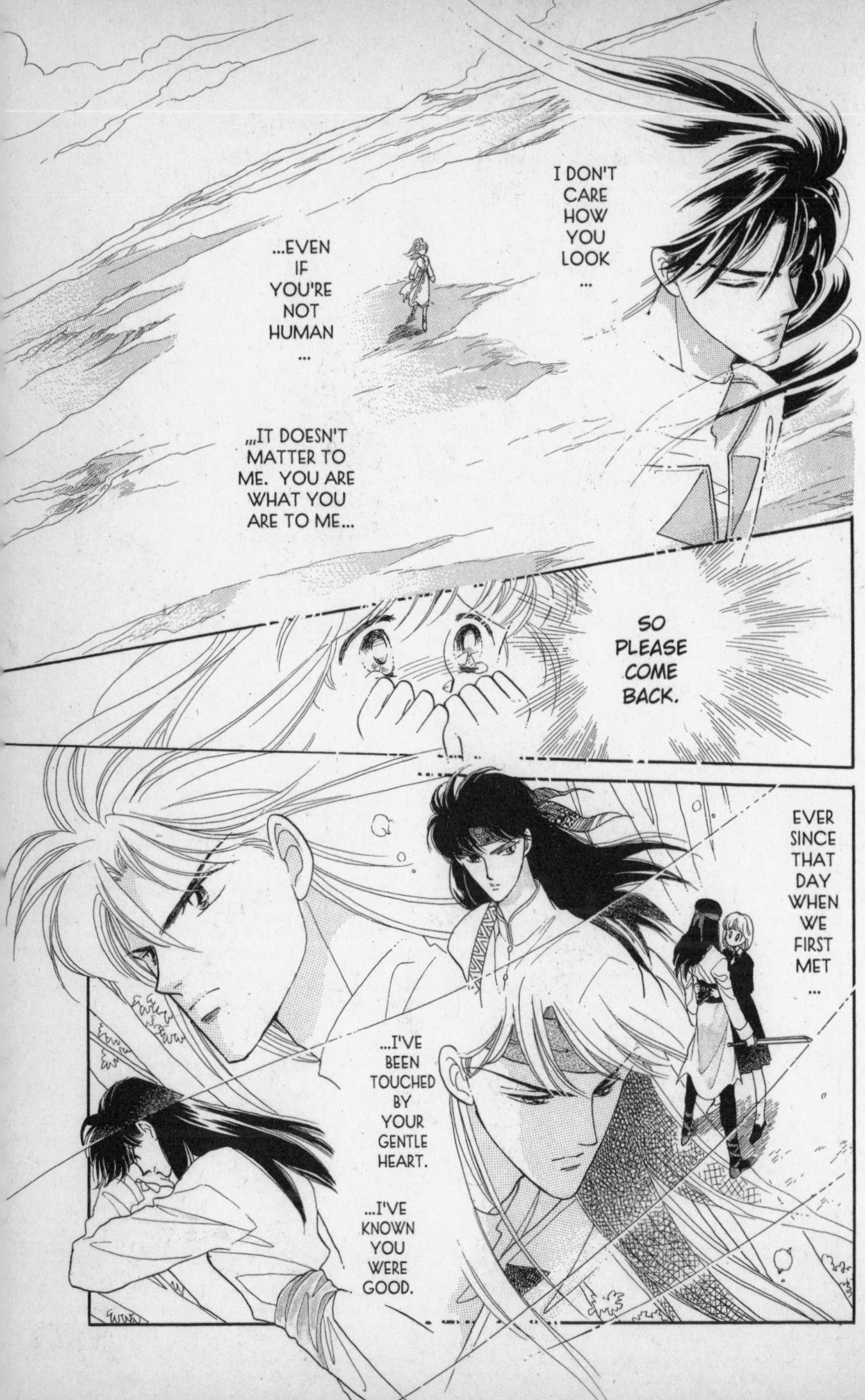
I DON'T CARE HOW YOU LOOK...
...EVEN IF YOU'RE NOT HUMAN...
...IT DOESN'T MATTER TO ME. YOU ARE WHAT YOU ARE TO ME...
SO PLEASE COME BACK.
EVER SINCE THAT DAY WHEN WE FIRST MET...
...I'VE BEEN TOUCHED BY YOUR GENTLE HEART.
...I'VE KNOWN YOU WERE GOOD.

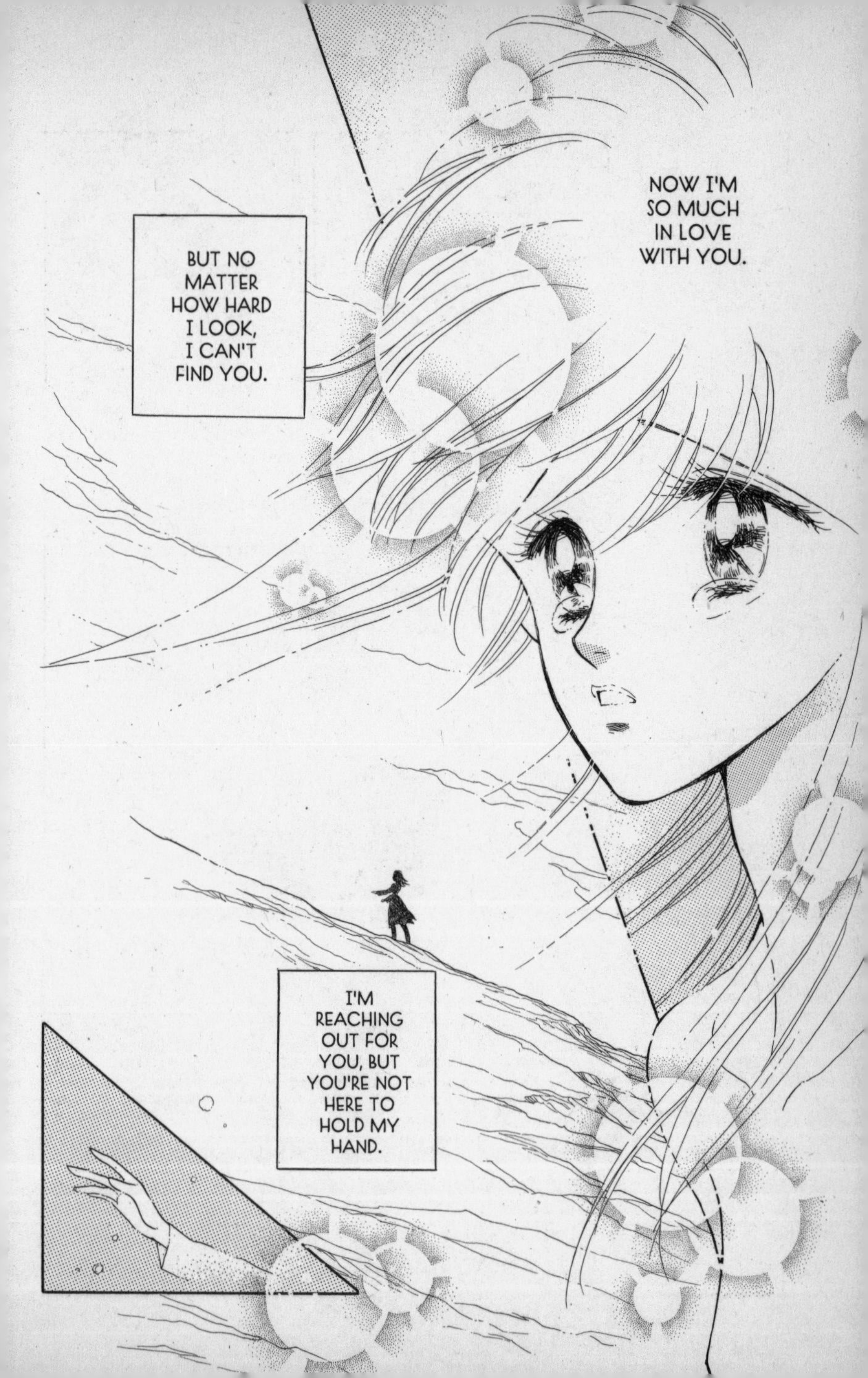
NOW I'M SO MUCH IN LOVE WITH YOU.
BUT NO MATTER HOW HARD I LOOK, I CAN'T FIND YOU.
I'M REACHING OUT FOR YOU, BUT YOU'RE NOT HERE TO HOLD MY HAND.

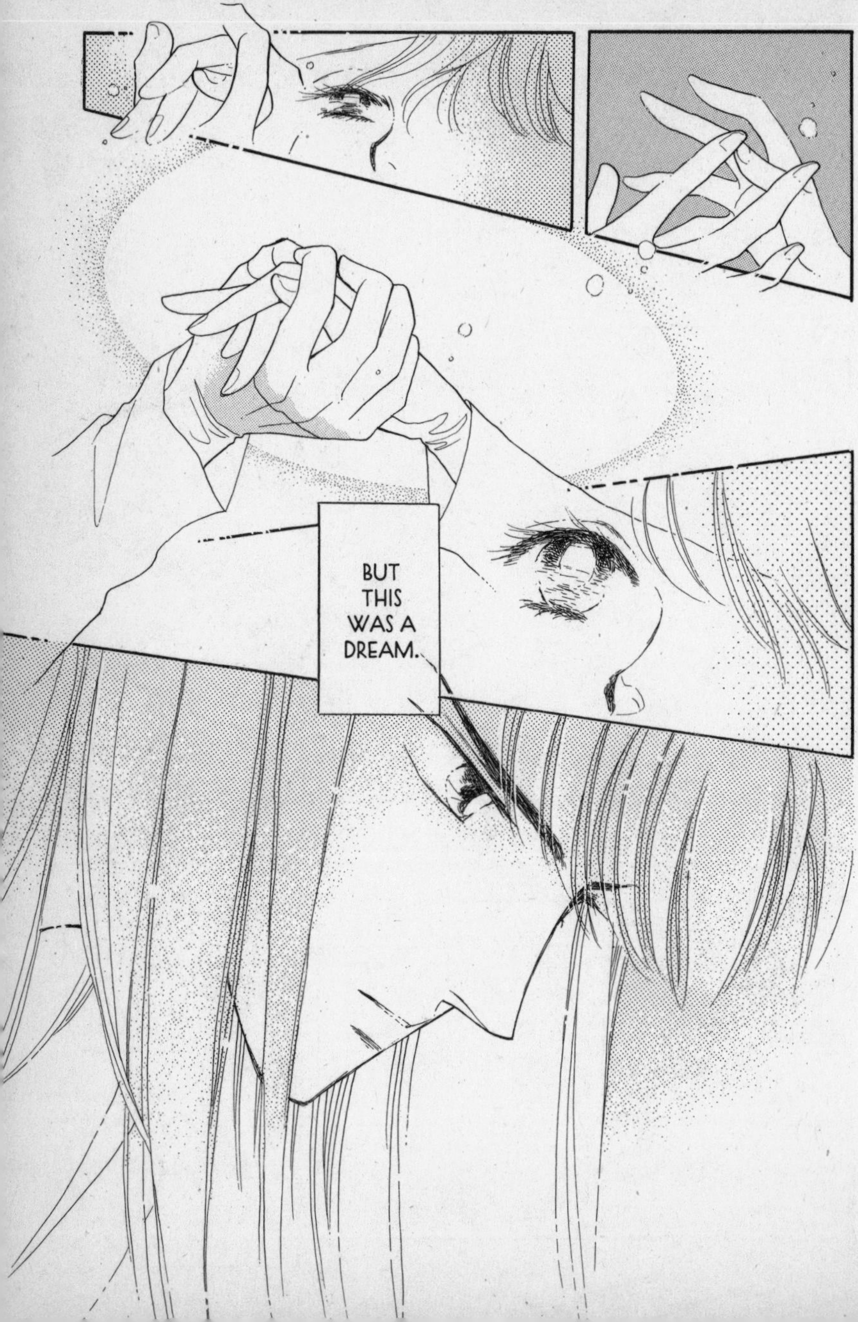
BUT THIS WAS A DREAM.

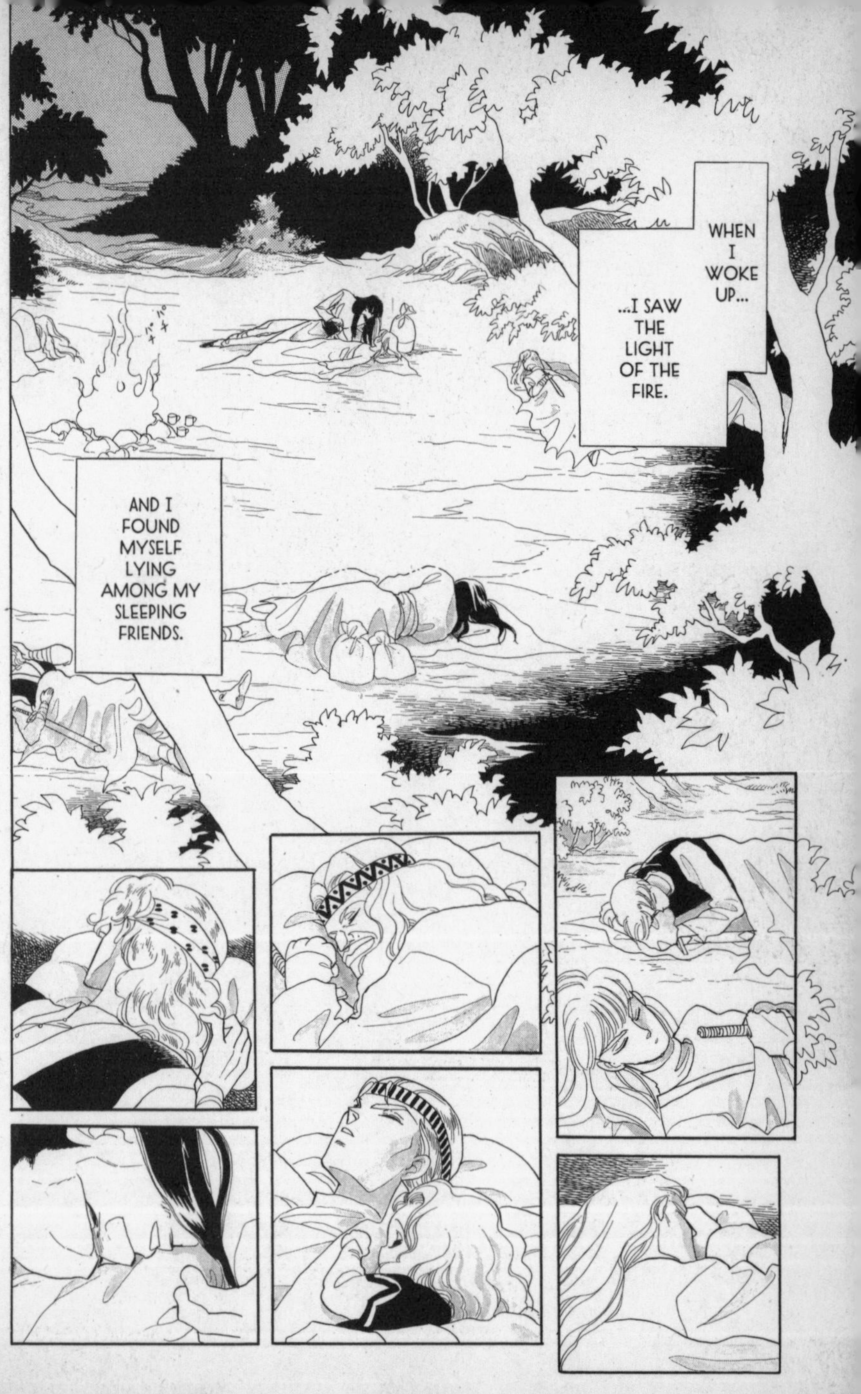
WHEN I WOKE UP...
...I SAW THE LIGHT OF THE FIRE.
AND I FOUND MYSELF LYING AMONG MY SLEEPING FRIENDS.

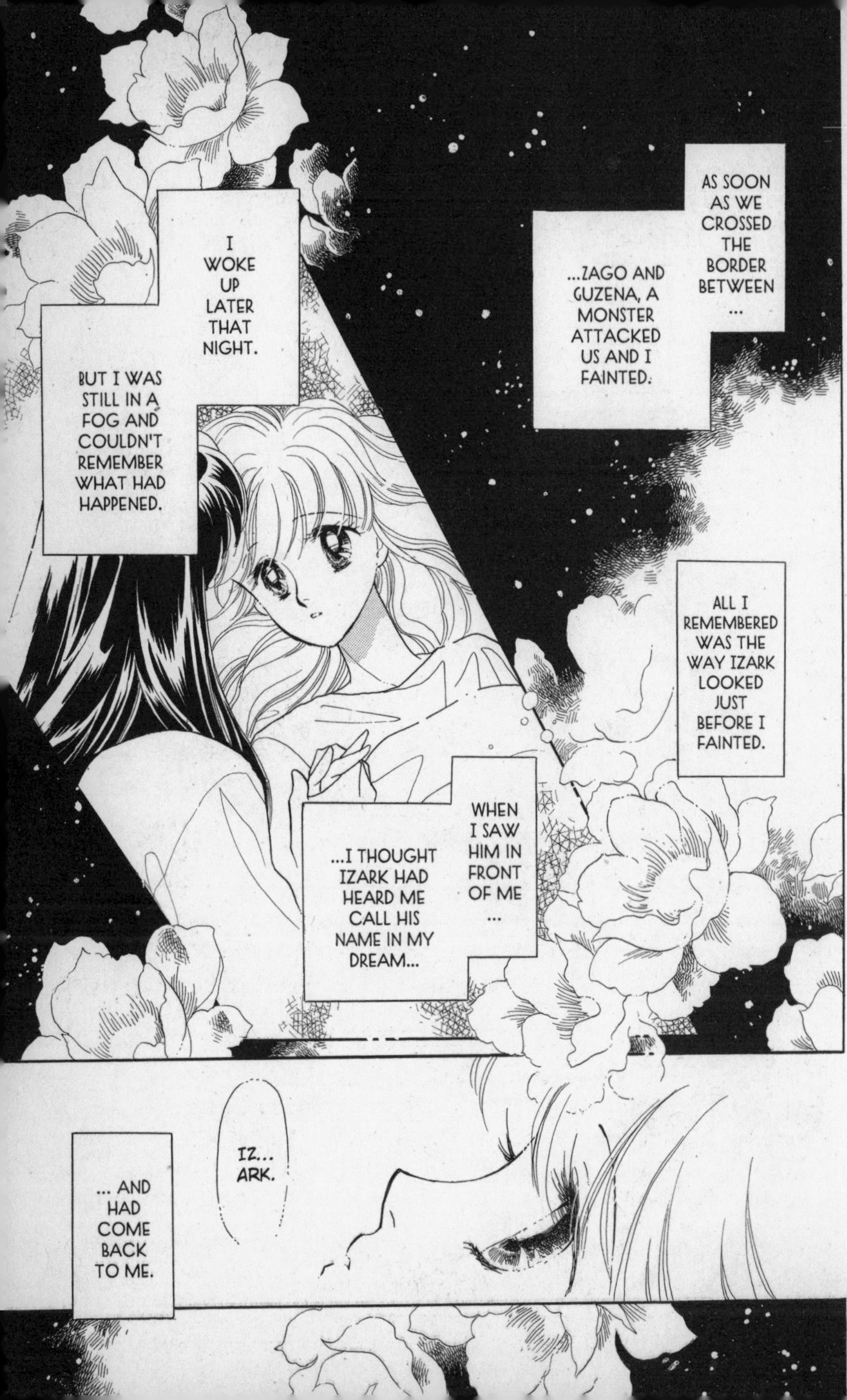
AS SOON AS WE CROSSED THE BORDER BETWEEN ...
...ZAGO AND GUZENA, A MONSTER ATTACKED US AND I FAINTED.
I WOKE UP LATER THAT NIGHT.
BUT I WAS STILL IN A FOG AND COULDN'T REMEMBER WHAT HAD HAPPENED.
ALL I REMEMBERED WAS THE WAY IZARK LOOKED JUST BEFORE I FAINTED.
WHEN I SAW HIM IN FRONT OF ME ...
...I THOUGHT IZARK HAD HEARD ME CALL HIS NAME IN MY DREAM...
IZ... ARK.
... AND HAD COME BACK TO ME.

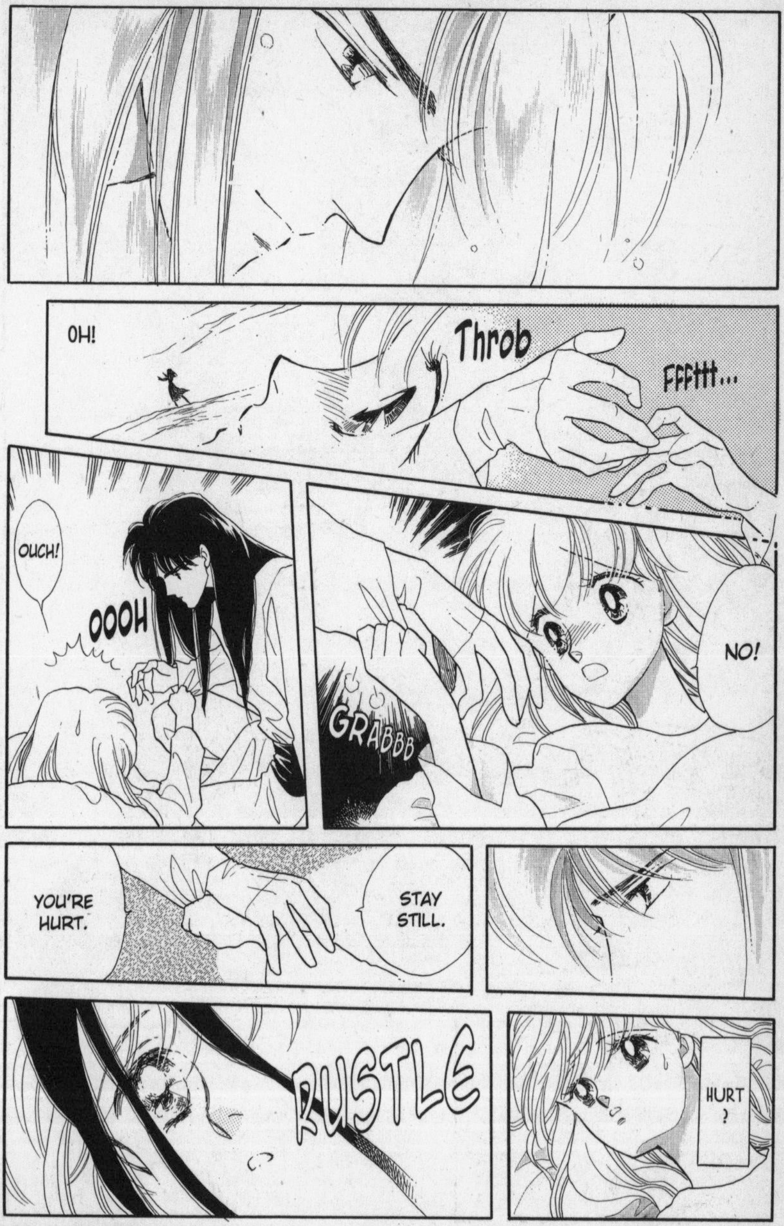
FFFttt...
Throb
OH!
NO!
GRABBB
OUCH!
OOOH
STAY STILL.
YOU'RE HURT.
HURT ?
RUSTLE

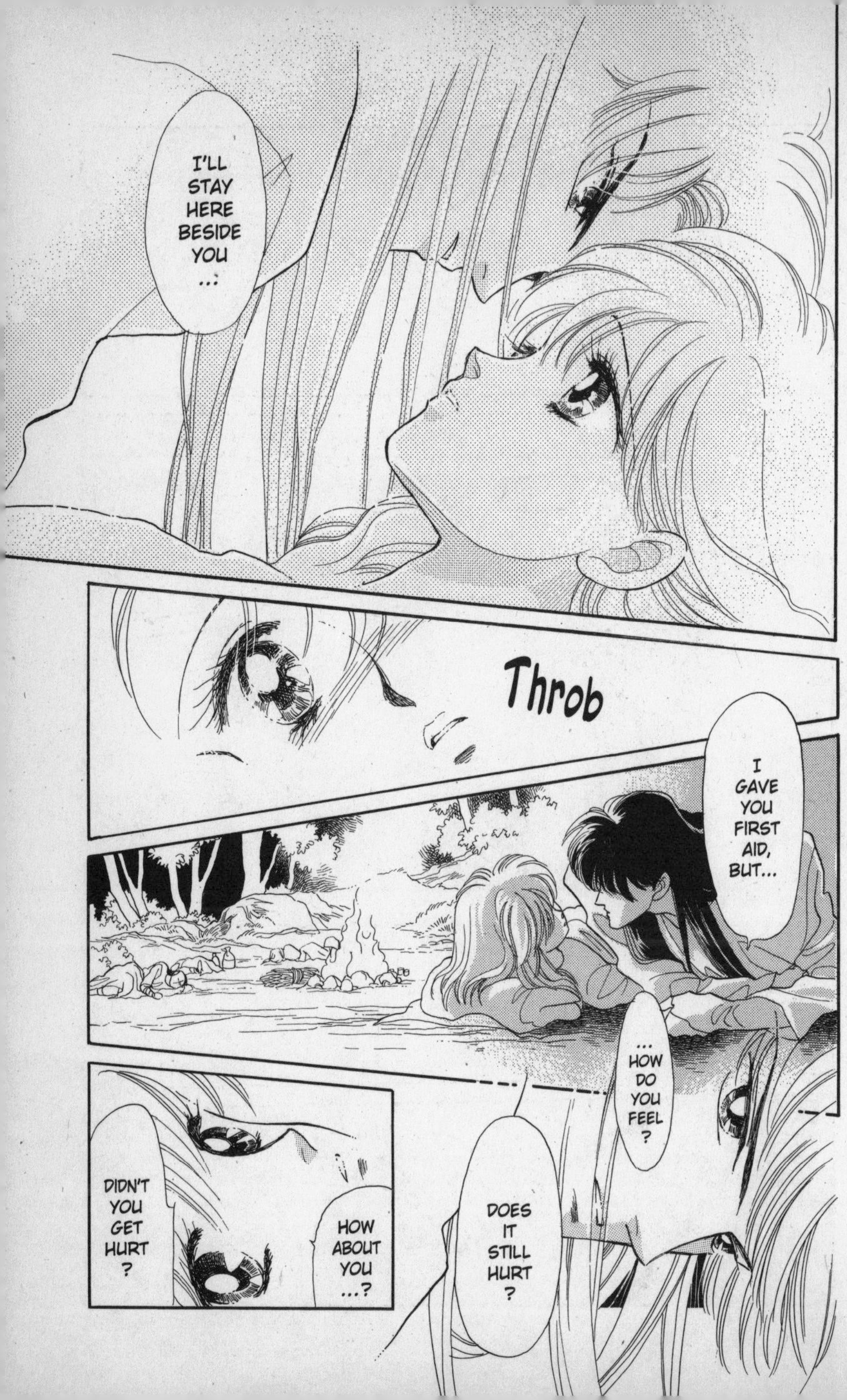
I'LL STAY HERE BESIDE YOU ...
Throb
I GAVE YOU FIRST AID, BUT...
... HOW DO YOU FEEL ?
DOES IT STILL HURT ?
HOW ABOUT YOU ...?
DIDN'T YOU GET HURT ?

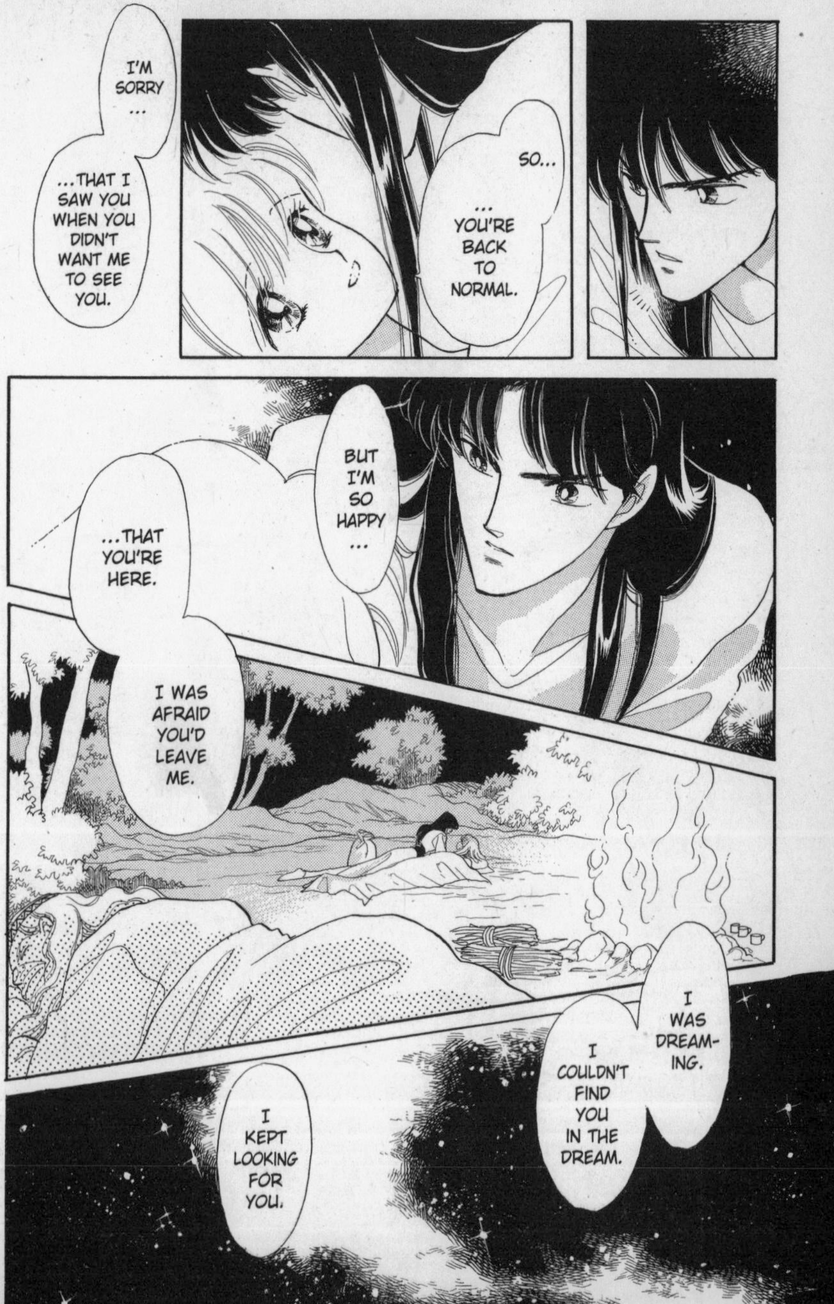
SO...
...YOU'RE BACK TO NORMAL.
I'M SORRY...
...THAT I SAW YOU WHEN YOU DIDN'T WANT ME TO SEE YOU.
BUT I'M SO HAPPY...
...THAT YOU'RE HERE.
I WAS AFRAID YOU'D LEAVE ME.
I WAS DREAM-ING.
I COULDN'T FIND YOU IN THE DREAM.
I KEPT LOOKING FOR YOU.

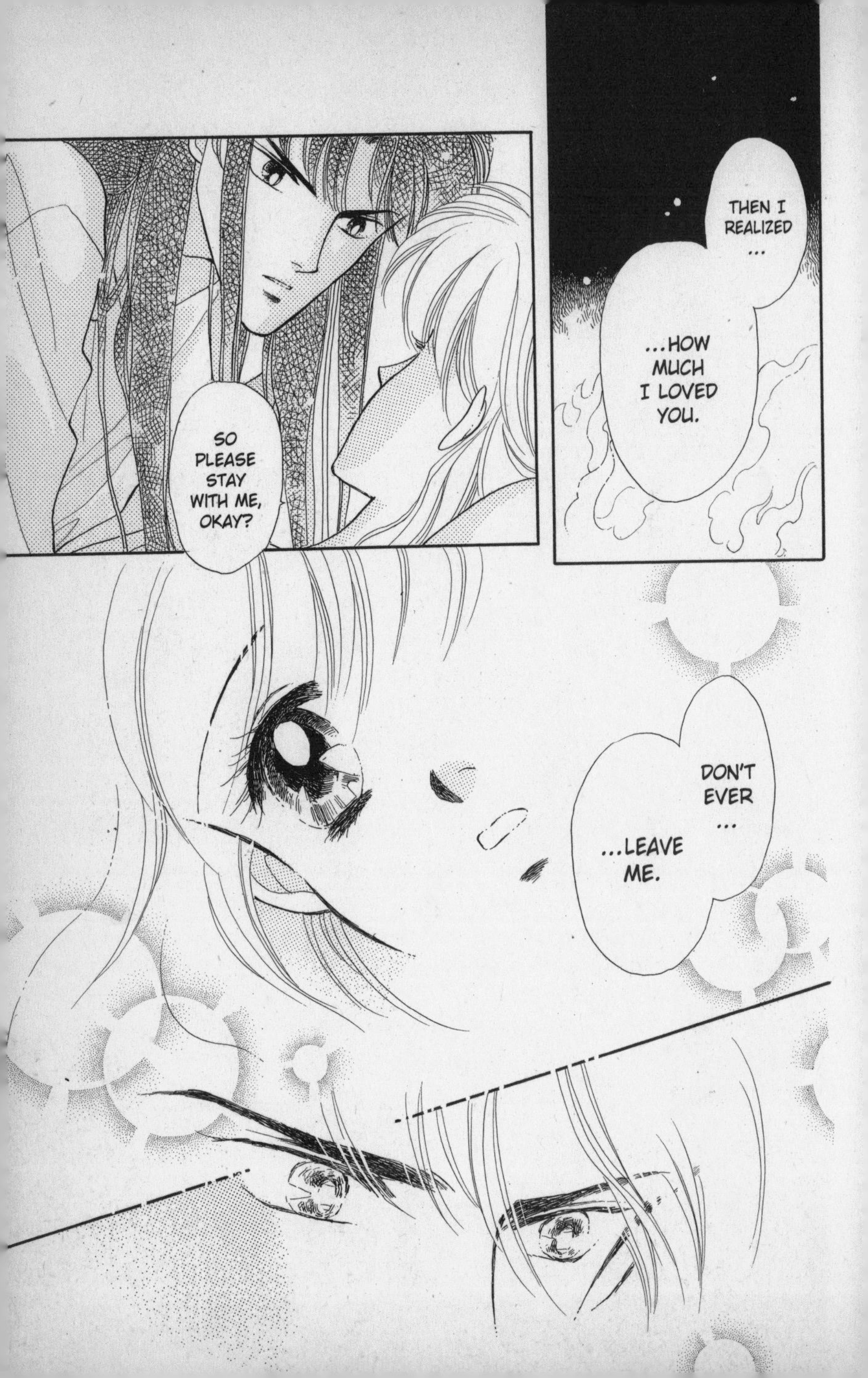
THEN I REALIZED ...
...HOW MUCH I LOVED YOU.
SO PLEASE STAY WITH ME, OKAY?
DON'T EVER ...
...LEAVE ME.

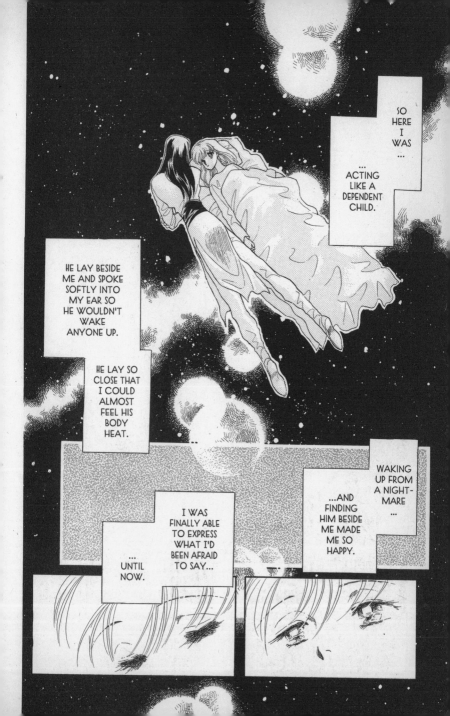

SO HERE I WAS ...

... ACTING LIKE A DEPENDENT CHILD.

HE LAY BESIDE ME AND SPOKE SOFTLY INTO MY EAR SO HE WOULDN'T WAKE ANYONE UP.

HE LAY SO CLOSE THAT I COULD ALMOST FEEL HIS BODY HEAT.

WAKING UP FROM A NIGHT-MARE ...

...AND FINDING HIM BESIDE ME MADE ME SO HAPPY.

I WAS FINALLY ABLE TO EXPRESS WHAT I'D BEEN AFRAID TO SAY...

... UNTIL NOW.

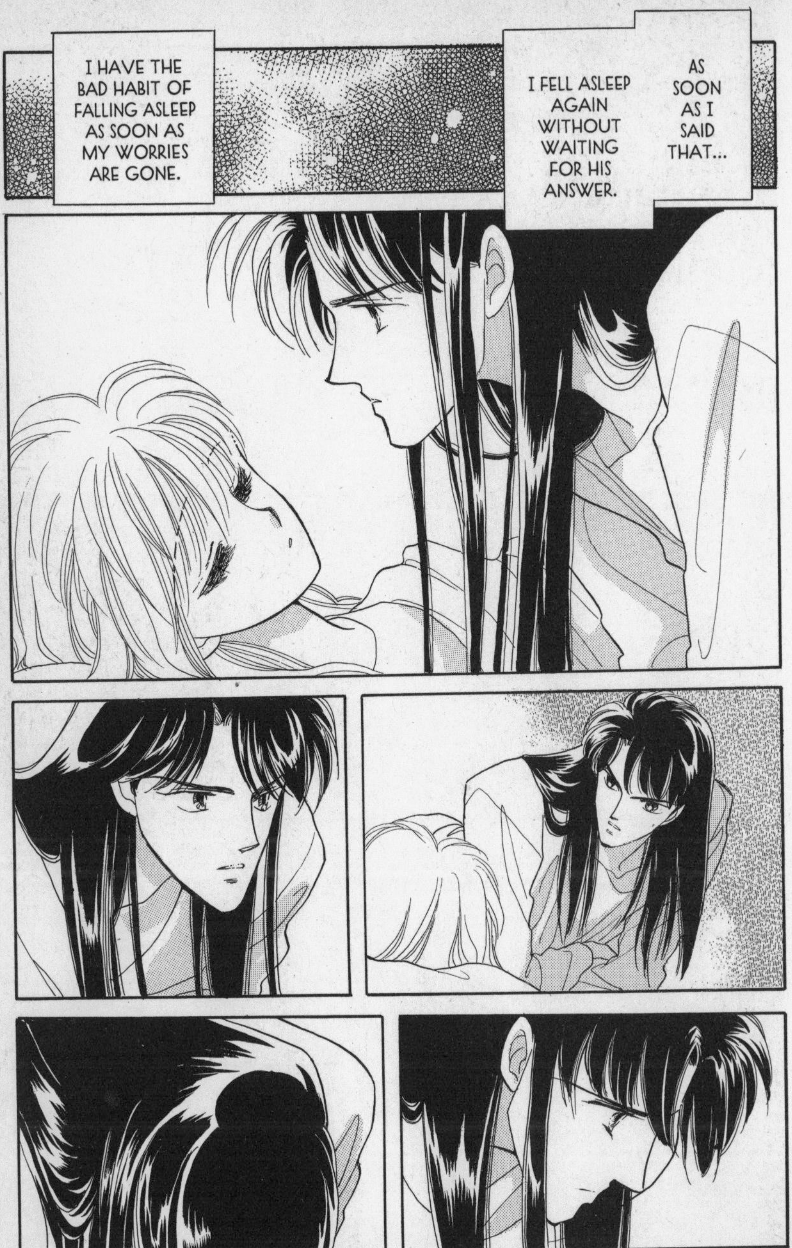
AS SOON AS I SAID THAT...
I FELL ASLEEP AGAIN WITHOUT WAITING FOR HIS ANSWER.
I HAVE THE BAD HABIT OF FALLING ASLEEP AS SOON AS MY WORRIES ARE GONE.

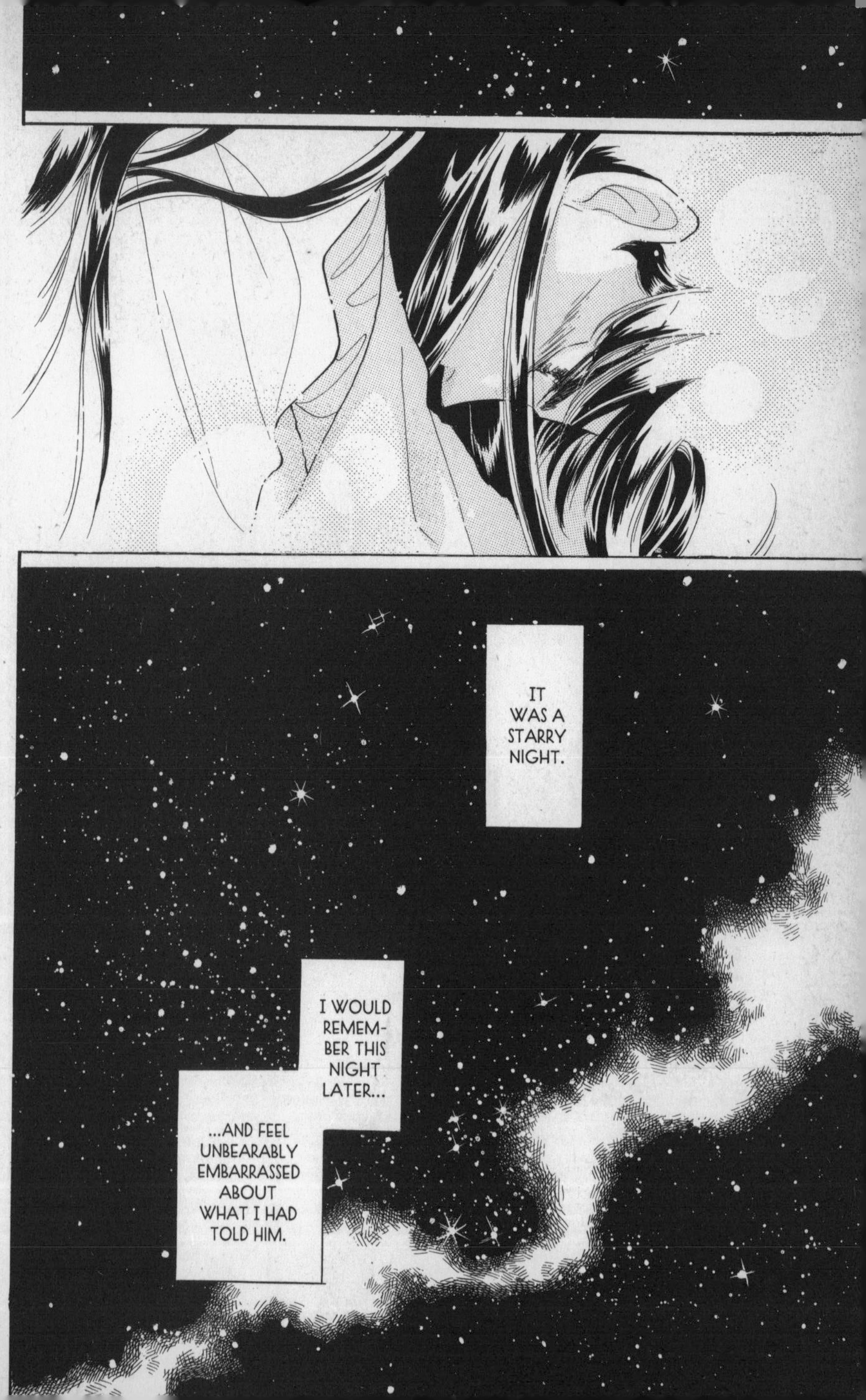
IT WAS A STARRY NIGHT.
I WOULD REMEMBER THIS NIGHT LATER...
...AND FEEL UNBEARABLY EMBARRASSED ABOUT WHAT I HAD TOLD HIM.

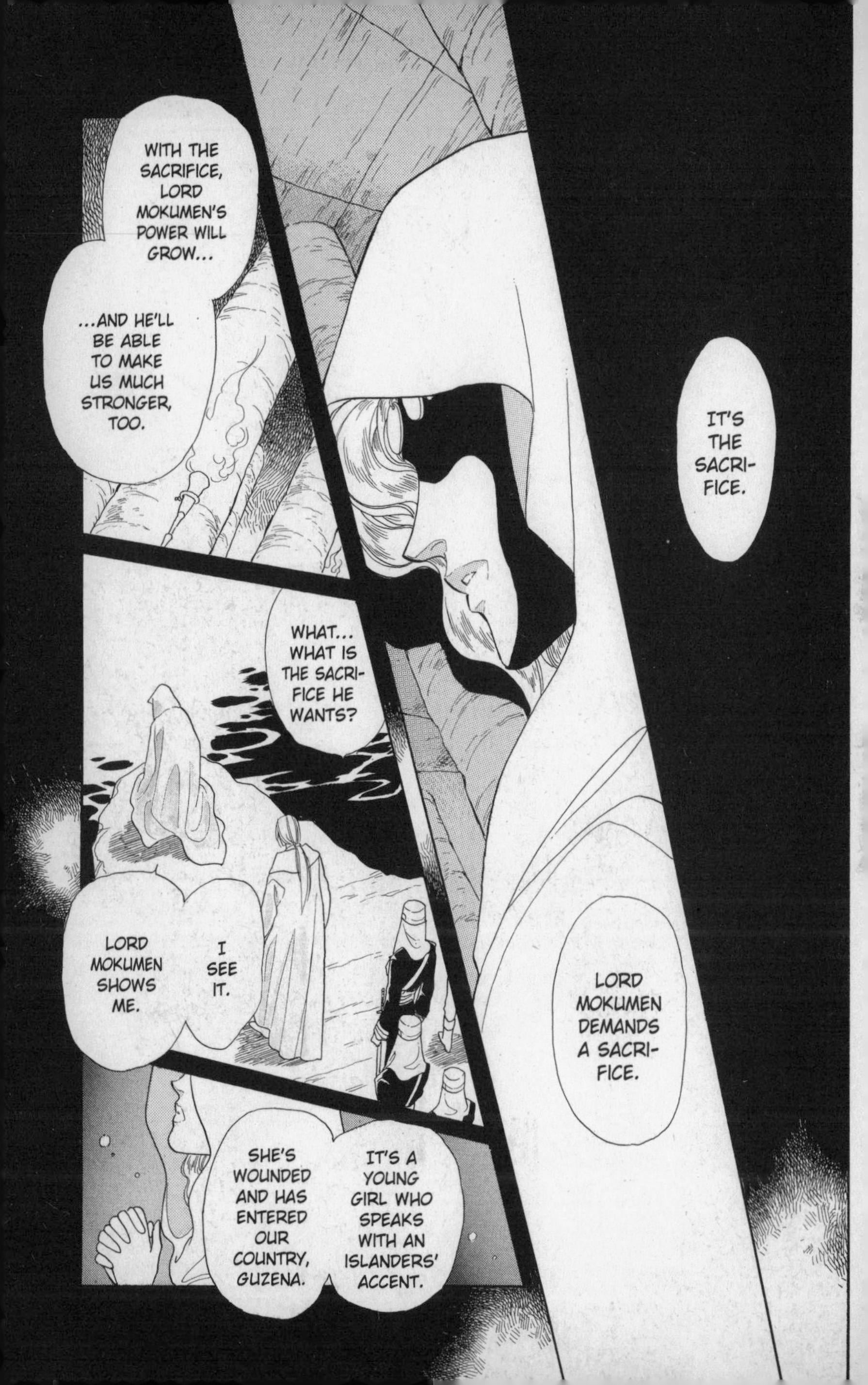
IT'S THE SACRIFICE.
LORD MOKUMEN DEMANDS A SACRIFICE.
WITH THE SACRIFICE, LORD MOKUMEN'S POWER WILL GROW...
...AND HE'LL BE ABLE TO MAKE US MUCH STRONGER, TOO.
WHAT... WHAT IS THE SACRIFICE HE WANTS?
I SEE IT.
LORD MOKUMEN SHOWS ME.
IT'S A YOUNG GIRL WHO SPEAKS WITH AN ISLANDERS' ACCENT.
SHE'S WOUNDED AND HAS ENTERED OUR COUNTRY, GUZENA.

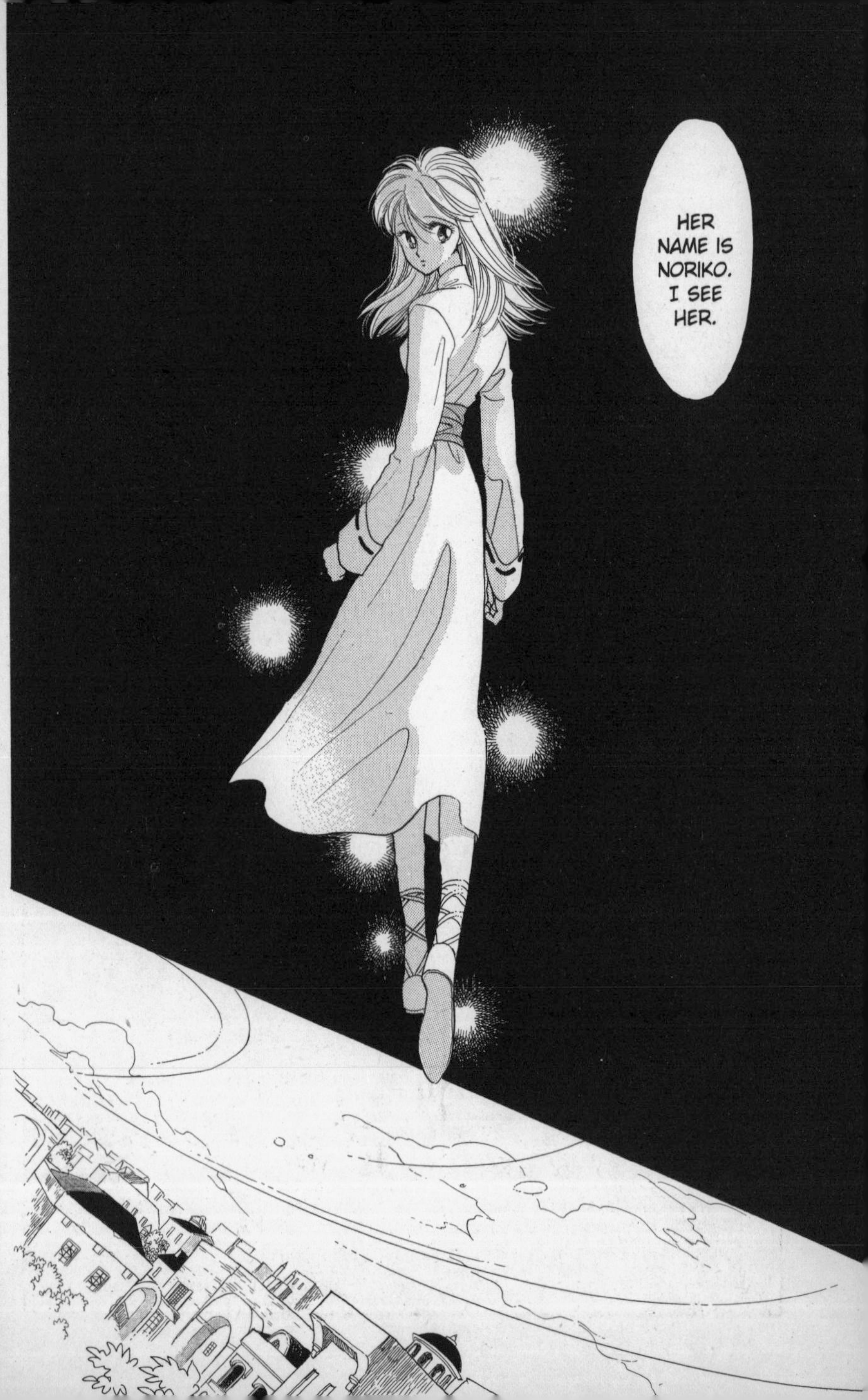
HER NAME IS NORIKO. I SEE HER.

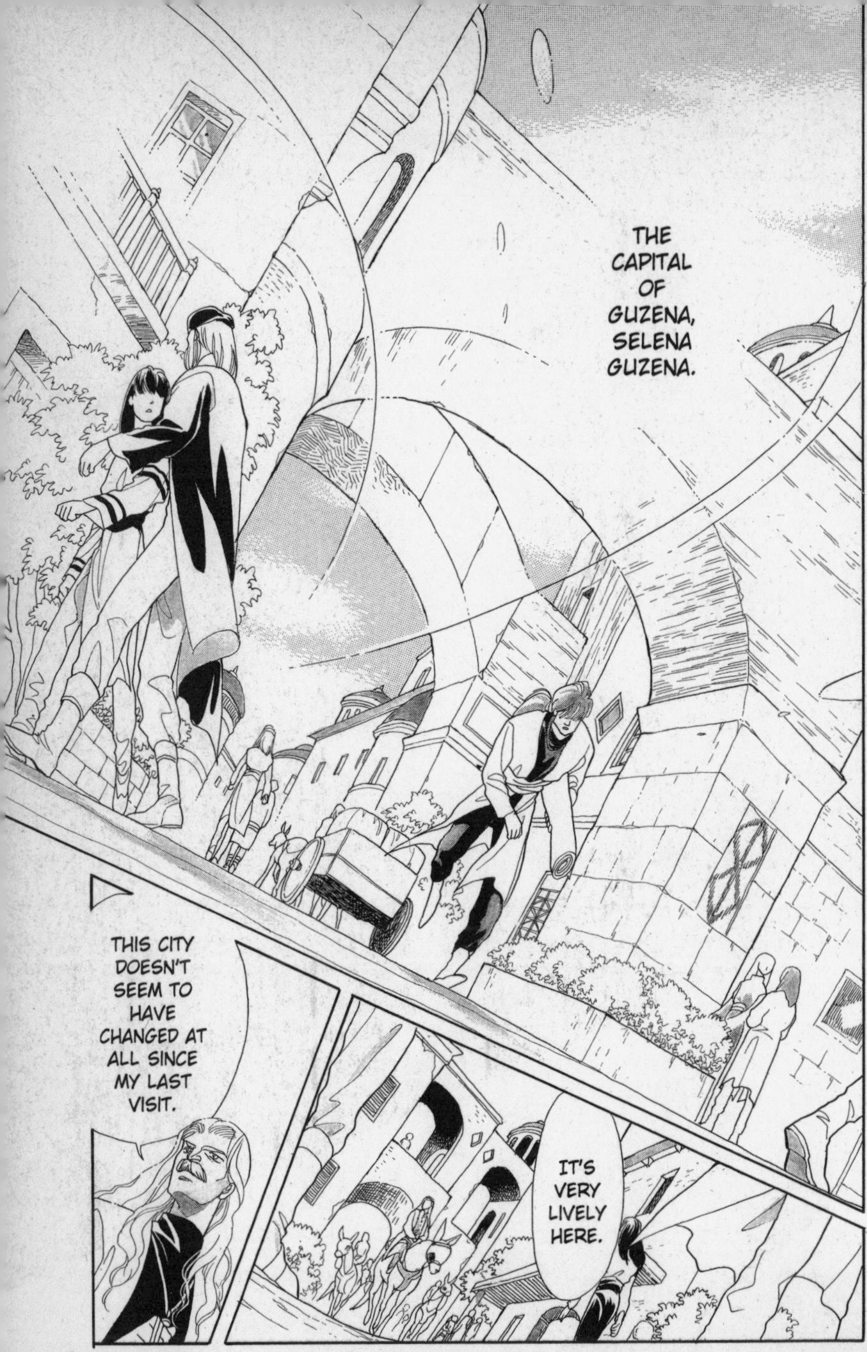
THE CAPITAL OF GUZENA, SELENA GUZENA.
IT'S VERY LIVELY HERE.
THIS CITY DOESN'T SEEM TO HAVE CHANGED AT ALL SINCE MY LAST VISIT.

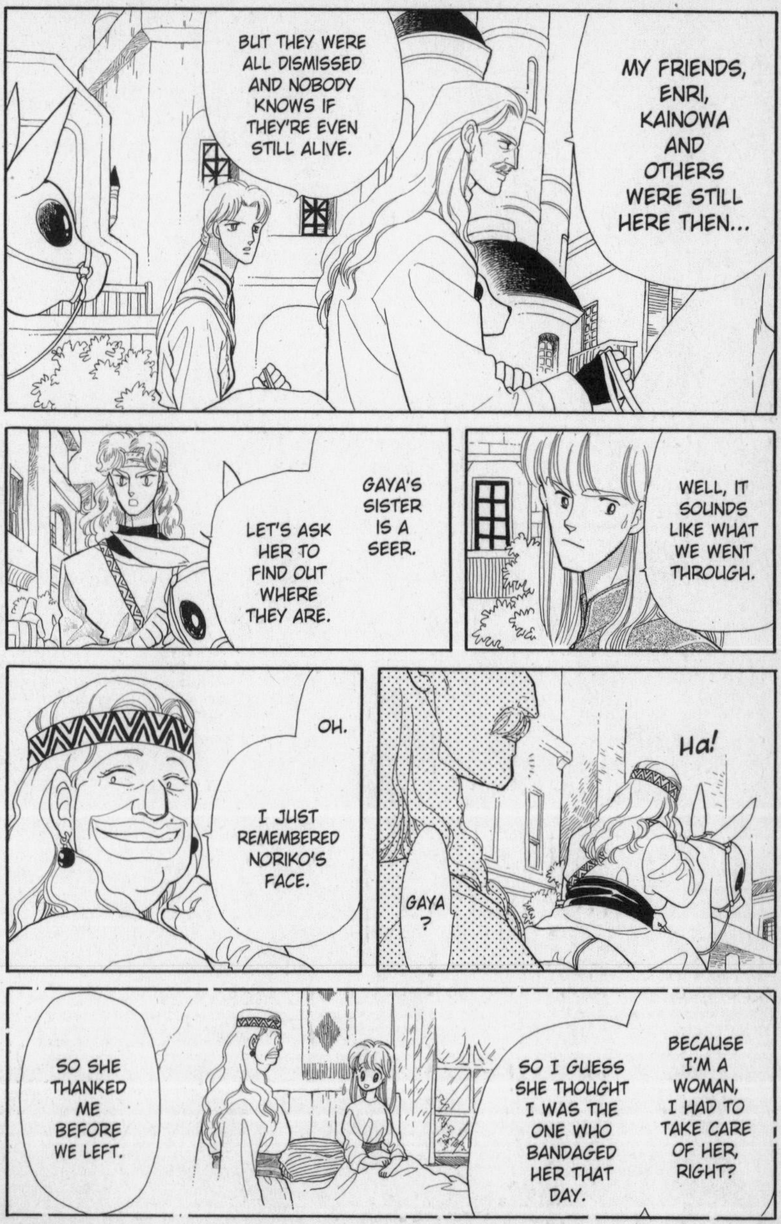
MY FRIENDS, ENRI, KAINOWA AND OTHERS WERE STILL HERE THEN...
BUT THEY WERE ALL DISMISSED AND NOBODY KNOWS IF THEY'RE EVEN STILL ALIVE.
WELL, IT SOUNDS LIKE WHAT WE WENT THROUGH.
GAYA'S SISTER IS A SEER.
LET'S ASK HER TO FIND OUT WHERE THEY ARE.
Ha!
GAYA?
OH.
I JUST REMEMBERED NORIKO'S FACE.
BECAUSE I'M A WOMAN, I HAD TO TAKE CARE OF HER, RIGHT?
SO I GUESS SHE THOUGHT I WAS THE ONE WHO BANDAGED HER THAT DAY.
SO SHE THANKED ME BEFORE WE LEFT.

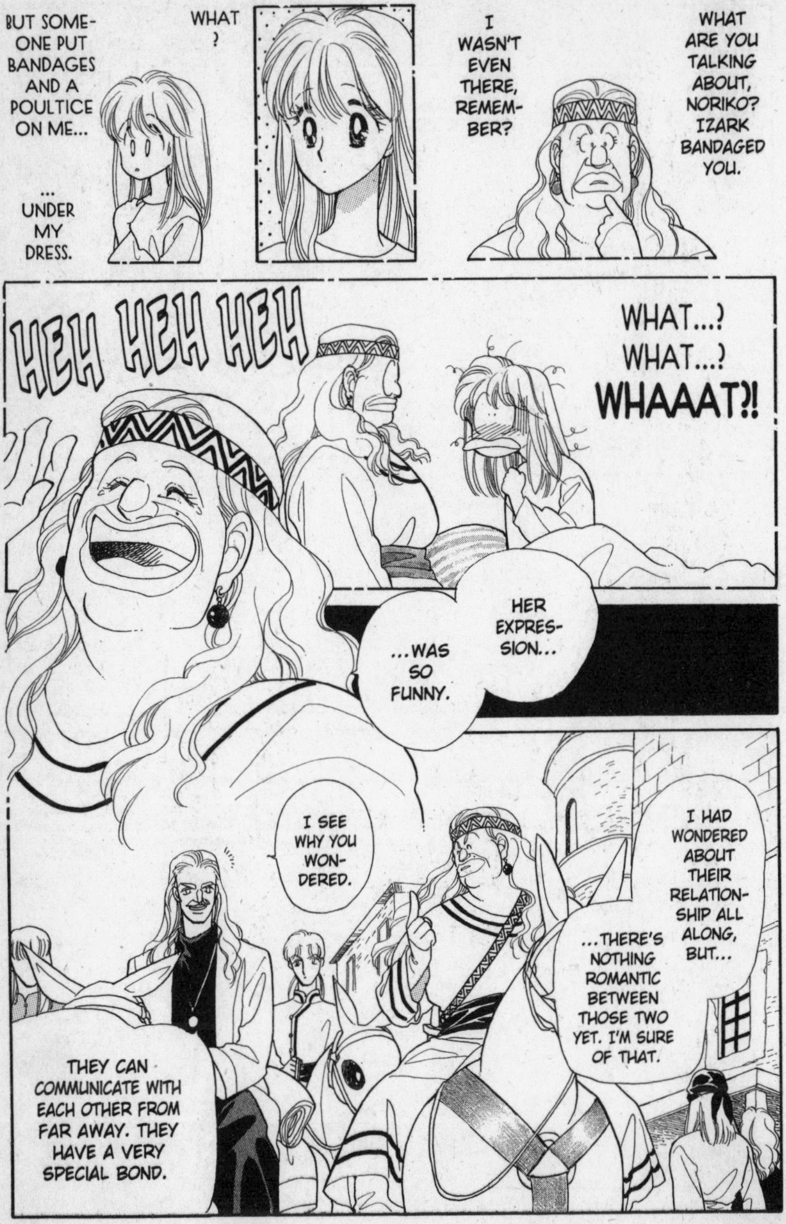
WHAT ARE YOU TALKING ABOUT, NORIKO? IZARK BANDAGED YOU.
I WASN'T EVEN THERE, REMEMBER?
WHAT ?
BUT SOME-ONE PUT BANDAGES AND A POULTICE ON ME...
... UNDER MY DRESS.
WHAT...? WHAT...? WHAAAT?!
HEH HEH HEH
HER EXPRES-SION...
...WAS SO FUNNY.
I HAD WONDERED ABOUT THEIR RELATION-SHIP ALL ALONG, BUT...
...THERE'S NOTHING ROMANTIC BETWEEN THOSE TWO YET. I'M SURE OF THAT.
I SEE WHY YOU WON-DERED.
THEY CAN COMMUNICATE WITH EACH OTHER FROM FAR AWAY. THEY HAVE A VERY SPECIAL BOND.

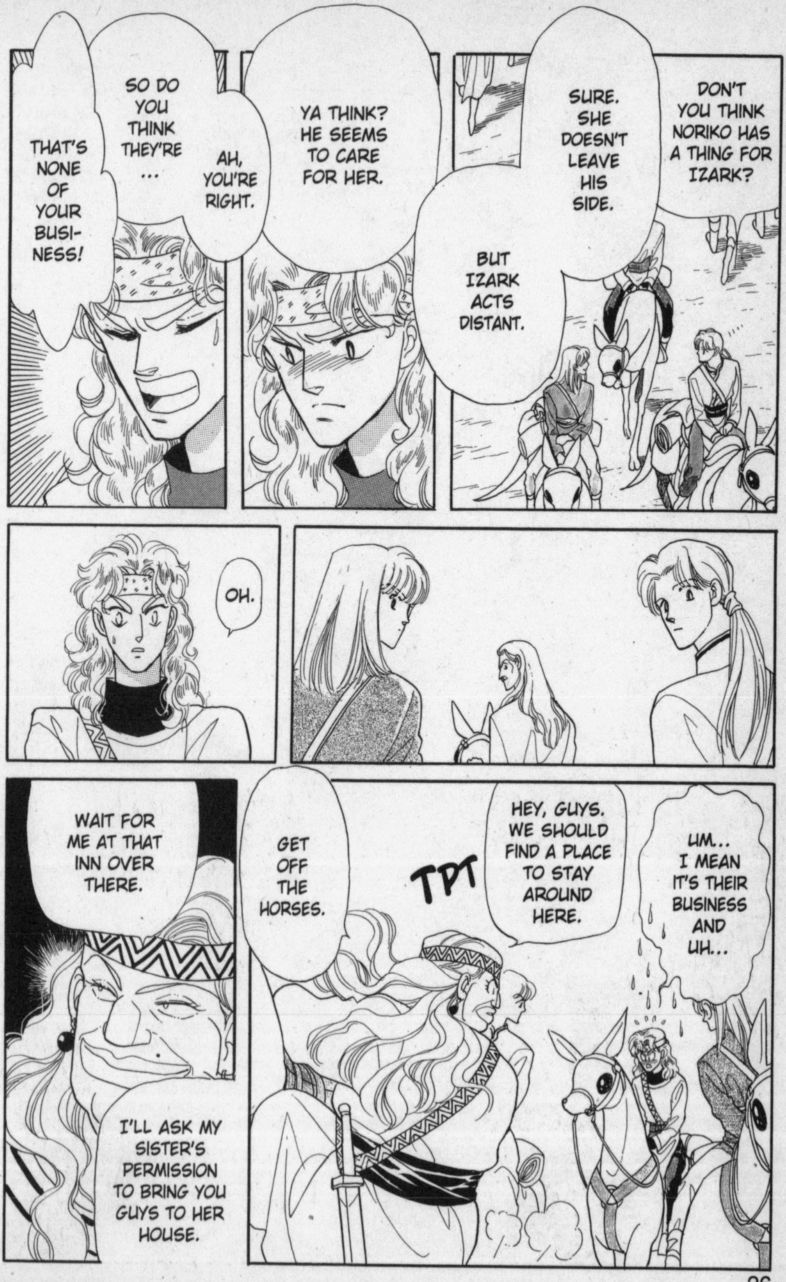
DON'T YOU THINK NORIKO HAS A THING FOR IZARK?
SURE. SHE DOESN'T LEAVE HIS SIDE.
BUT IZARK ACTS DISTANT.
YA THINK? HE SEEMS TO CARE FOR HER.
AH, YOU'RE RIGHT.
SO DO YOU THINK THEY'RE ...
THAT'S NONE OF YOUR BUSI-NESS!
OH.
UM... I MEAN IT'S THEIR BUSINESS AND UH...
HEY, GUYS. WE SHOULD FIND A PLACE TO STAY AROUND HERE.
TPT
GET OFF THE HORSES.
WAIT FOR ME AT THAT INN OVER THERE.
I'LL ASK MY SISTER'S PERMISSION TO BRING YOU GUYS TO HER HOUSE.

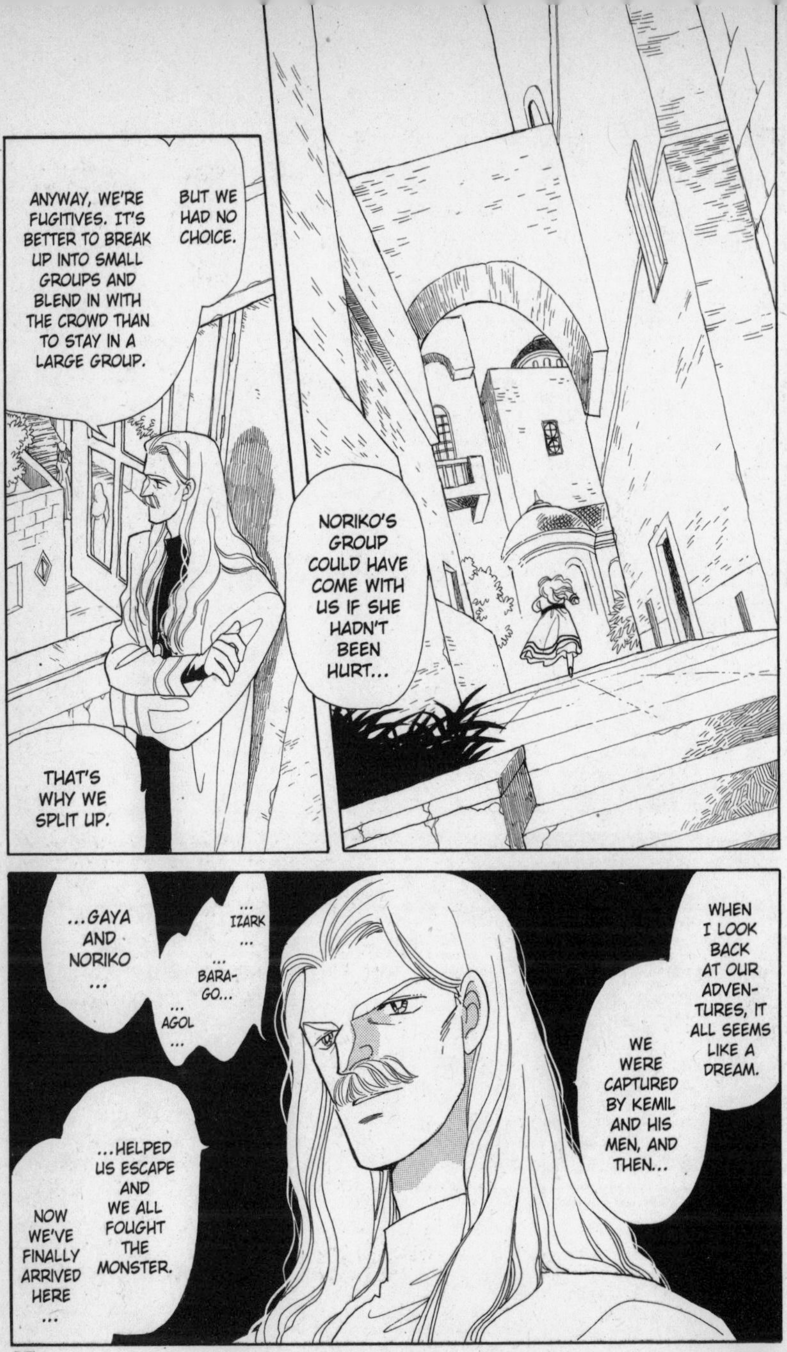
NORIKO'S GROUP COULD HAVE COME WITH US IF SHE HADN'T BEEN HURT...
BUT WE HAD NO CHOICE.
ANYWAY, WE'RE FUGITIVES. IT'S BETTER TO BREAK UP INTO SMALL GROUPS AND BLEND IN WITH THE CROWD THAN TO STAY IN A LARGE GROUP.
THAT'S WHY WE SPLIT UP.
WHEN I LOOK BACK AT OUR ADVENTURES, IT ALL SEEMS LIKE A DREAM.
WE WERE CAPTURED BY KEMIL AND HIS MEN, AND THEN...
...IZARK...
...BARAGO...
...GAYA AND NORIKO...
...AGOL...
...HELPED US ESCAPE AND WE ALL FOUGHT THE MONSTER.
NOW WE'VE FINALLY ARRIVED HERE...

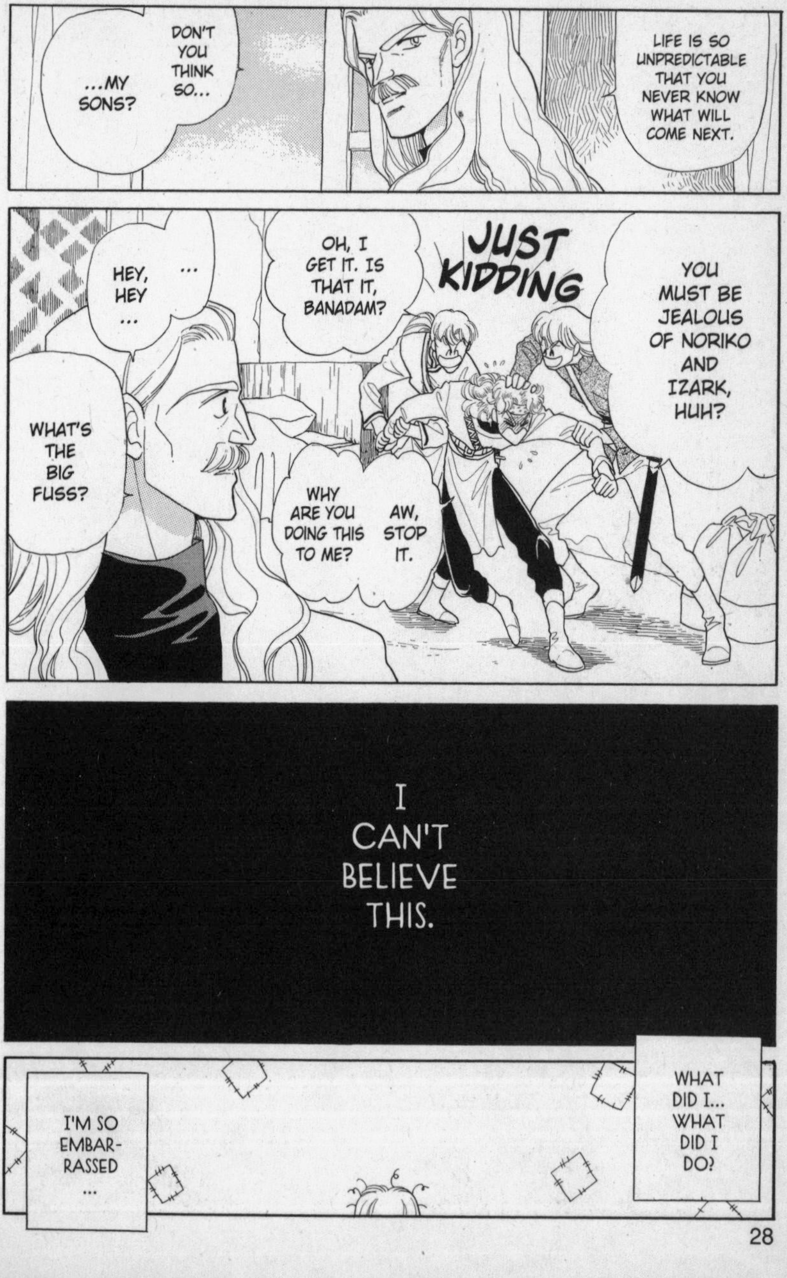
LIFE IS SO UNPREDICTABLE THAT YOU NEVER KNOW WHAT WILL COME NEXT.
DON'T YOU THINK SO...
...MY SONS?
YOU MUST BE JEALOUS OF NORIKO AND IZARK, HUH?
JUST KIDDING
OH, I GET IT. IS THAT IT, BANADAM?
AW, STOP IT.
WHY ARE YOU DOING THIS TO ME?
...
HEY, HEY ...
WHAT'S THE BIG FUSS?
I CAN'T BELIEVE THIS.
WHAT DID I... WHAT DID I DO?
I'M SO EMBARRASSED ...

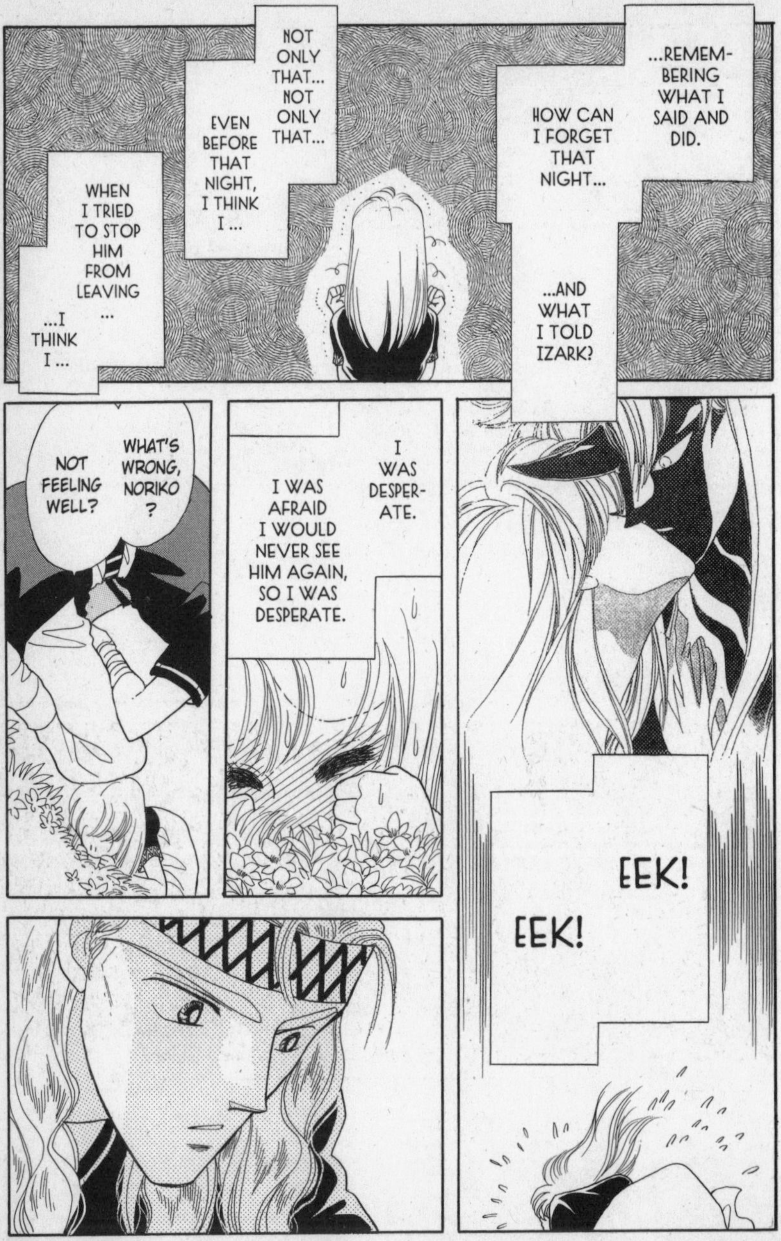
...REMEMBERING WHAT I SAID AND DID.
HOW CAN I FORGET THAT NIGHT...
...AND WHAT I TOLD IZARK?
NOT ONLY THAT... NOT ONLY THAT...
EVEN BEFORE THAT NIGHT, I THINK I...
WHEN I TRIED TO STOP HIM FROM LEAVING...
...I THINK I...
EEK!
EEK!
I WAS DESPERATE.
I WAS AFRAID I WOULD NEVER SEE HIM AGAIN, SO I WAS DESPERATE.
WHAT'S WRONG, NORIKO?
NOT FEELING WELL?

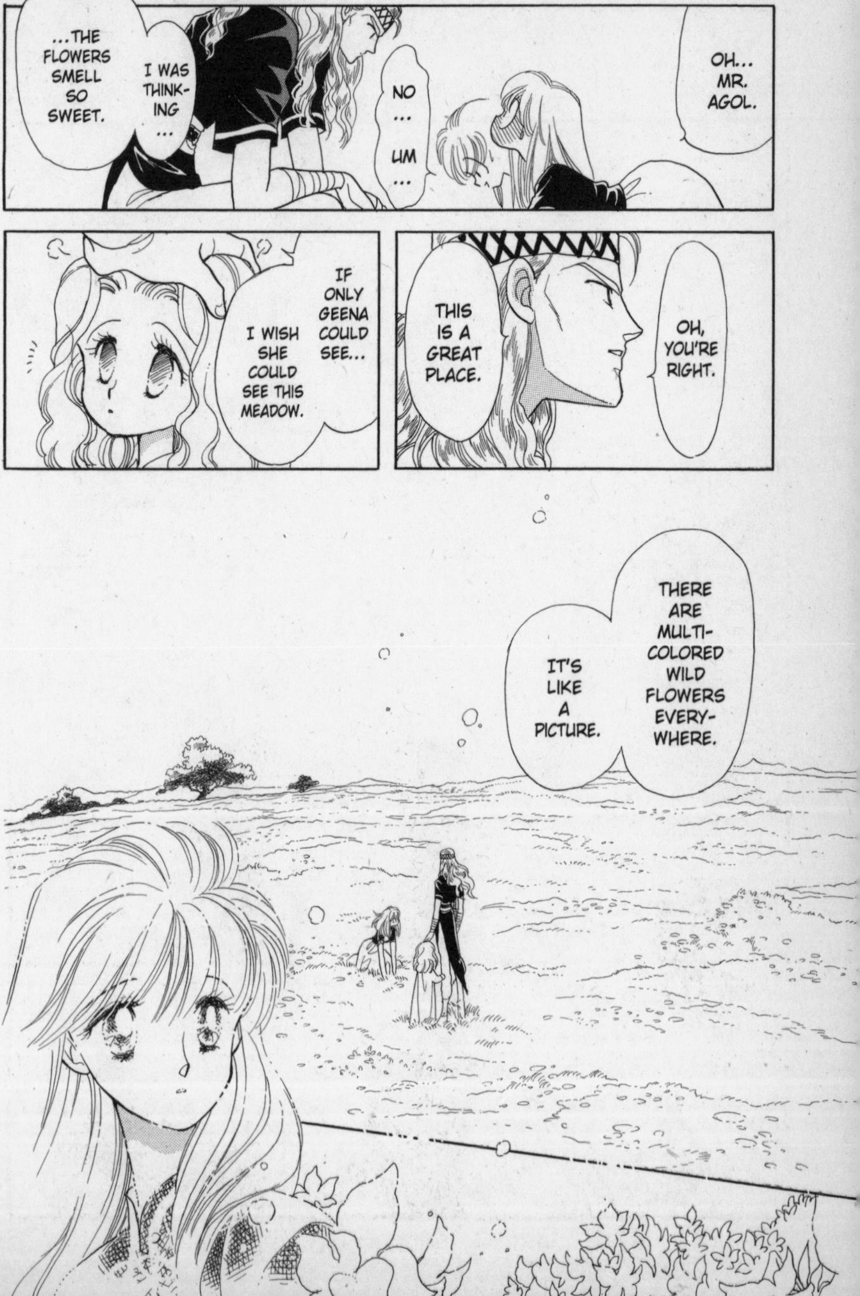
OH... MR. AGOL.
NO... UM...
I WAS THINKING...
...THE FLOWERS SMELL SO SWEET.
OH, YOU'RE RIGHT.
THIS IS A GREAT PLACE.
IF ONLY GEENA COULD SEE...
I WISH SHE COULD SEE THIS MEADOW.
THERE ARE MULTICOLORED WILD FLOWERS EVERYWHERE.
IT'S LIKE A PICTURE.

My readers most often want to know my characters' birthdays, blood types, height and weight. Unfortunately, even the author does not know the answer to these questions...

All I can say is that Noriko is around 155 cm tall (a little over 5 ft tall). Maybe that way you can guess how tall the other characters are.

Sorry for my vague answers to your questions.

The author's height is about 160 cm (about 5 ft 3 in).

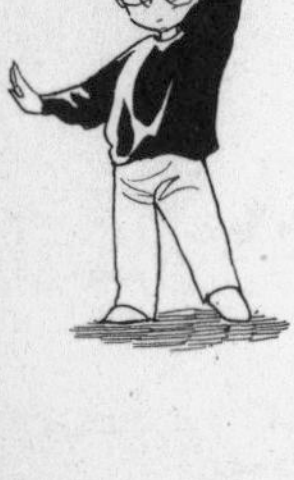

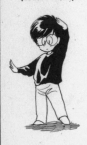

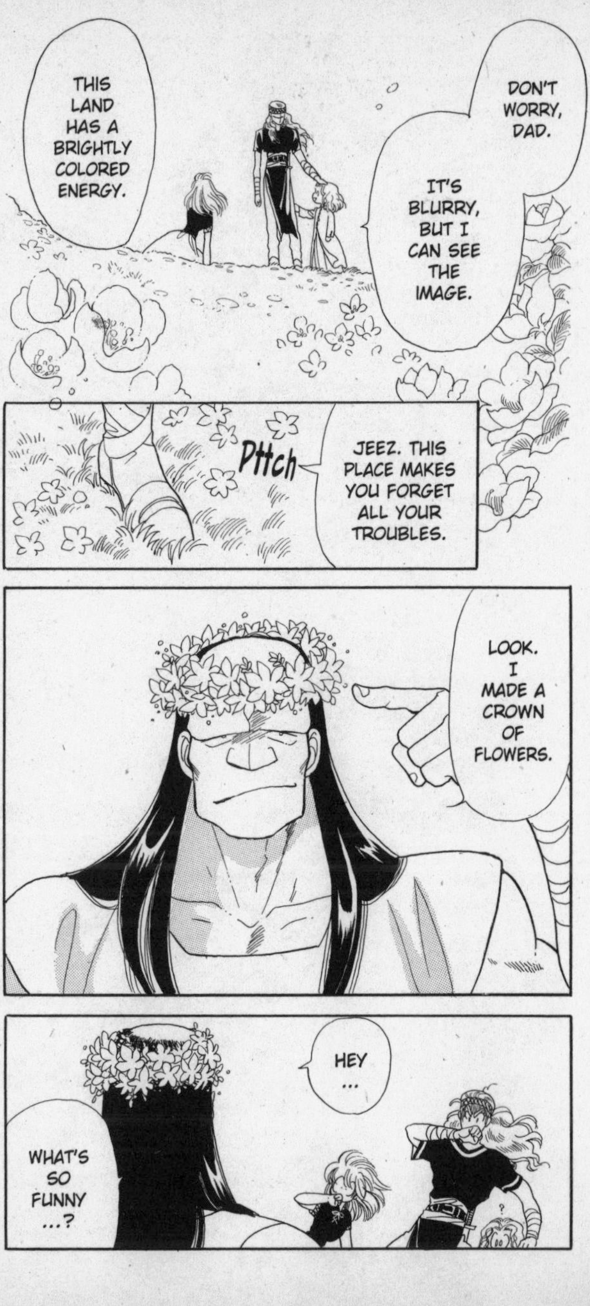
DON'T WORRY, DAD.
IT'S BLURRY, BUT I CAN SEE THE IMAGE.
THIS LAND HAS A BRIGHTLY COLORED ENERGY.
JEEZ. THIS PLACE MAKES YOU FORGET ALL YOUR TROUBLES.
Pttch
LOOK. I MADE A CROWN OF FLOWERS.
HEY ...
WHAT'S SO FUNNY ...?
?

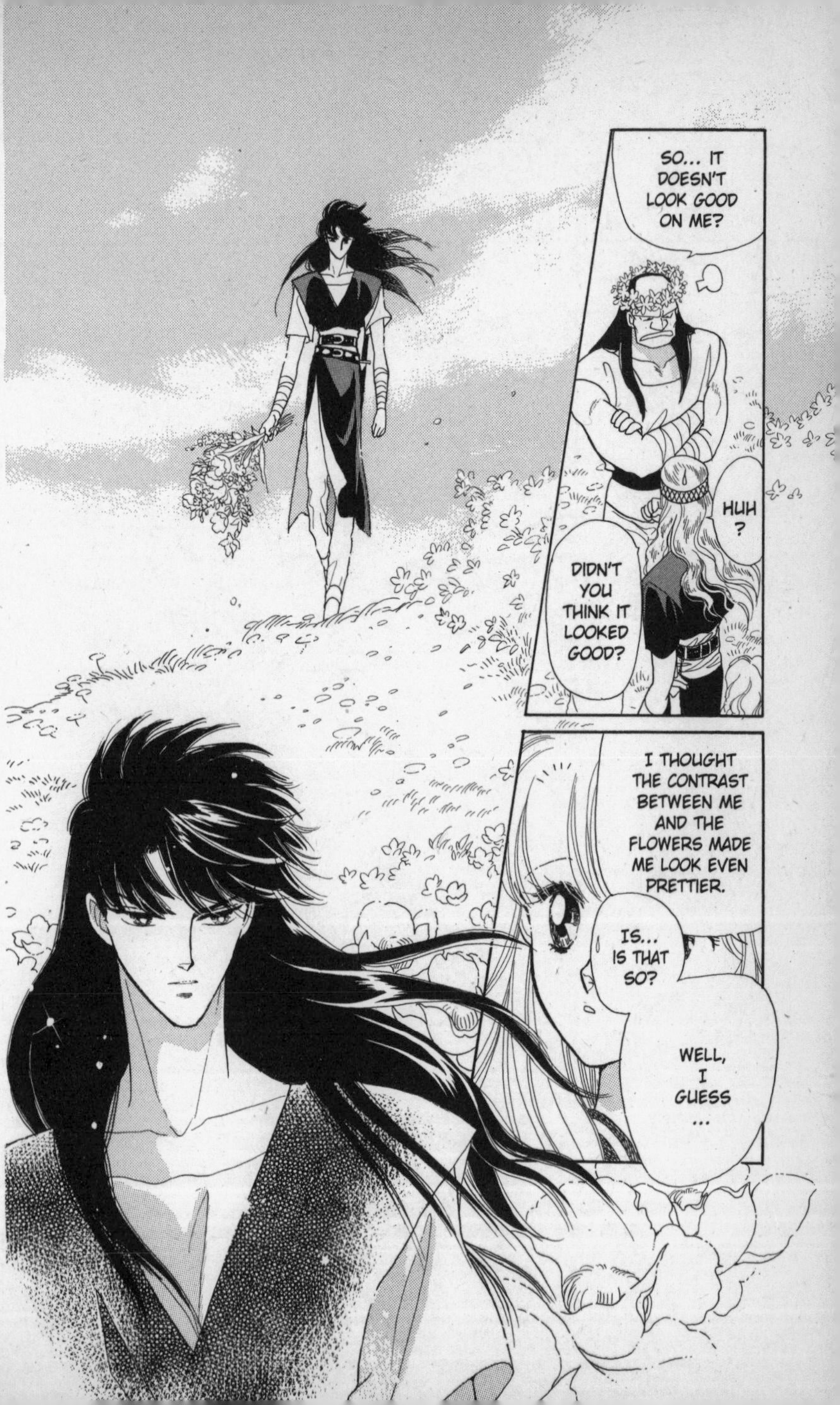
SO... IT DOESN'T LOOK GOOD ON ME?
HUH ?
DIDN'T YOU THINK IT LOOKED GOOD?
I THOUGHT THE CONTRAST BETWEEN ME AND THE FLOWERS MADE ME LOOK EVEN PRETTIER.
IS... IS THAT SO?
WELL, I GUESS ...

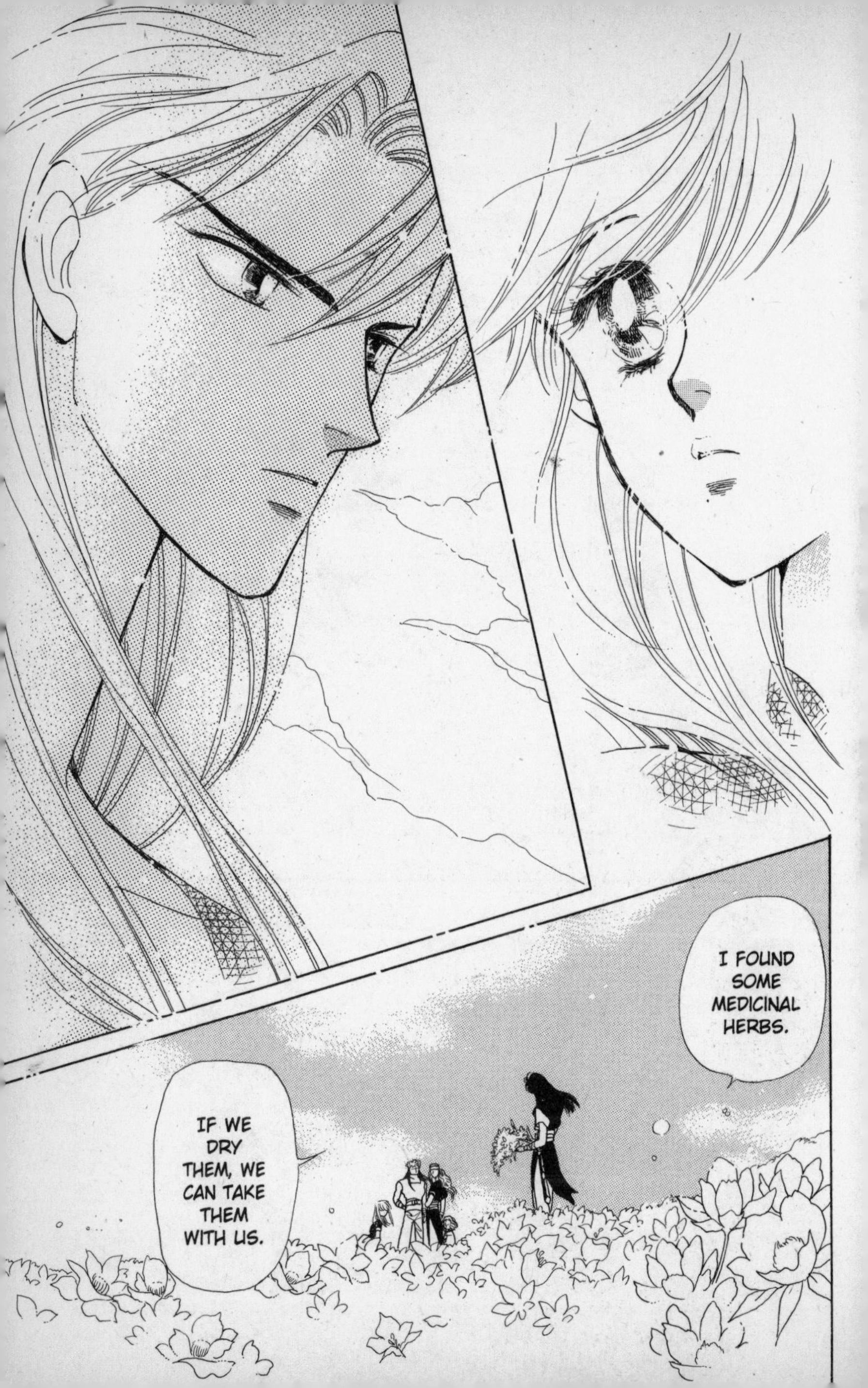
I FOUND SOME MEDICINAL HERBS.
IF WE DRY THEM, WE CAN TAKE THEM WITH US.

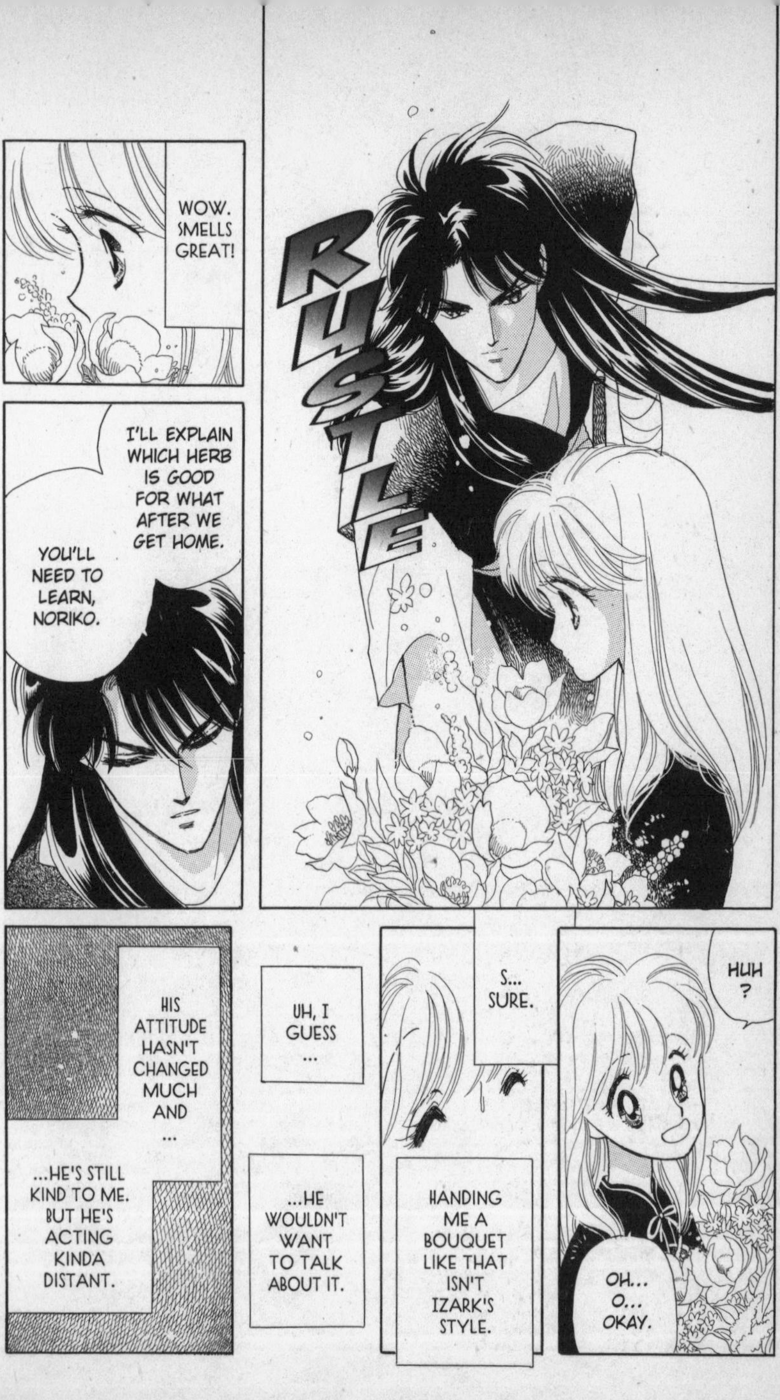
RUSTLE
WOW. SMELLS GREAT!
I'LL EXPLAIN WHICH HERB IS GOOD FOR WHAT AFTER WE GET HOME.
YOU'LL NEED TO LEARN, NORIKO.
HUH?
OH... O... OKAY.
S... SURE.
HANDING ME A BOUQUET LIKE THAT ISN'T IZARK'S STYLE.
UH, I GUESS...
...HE WOULDN'T WANT TO TALK ABOUT IT.
HIS ATTITUDE HASN'T CHANGED MUCH AND...
...HE'S STILL KIND TO ME. BUT HE'S ACTING KINDA DISTANT.

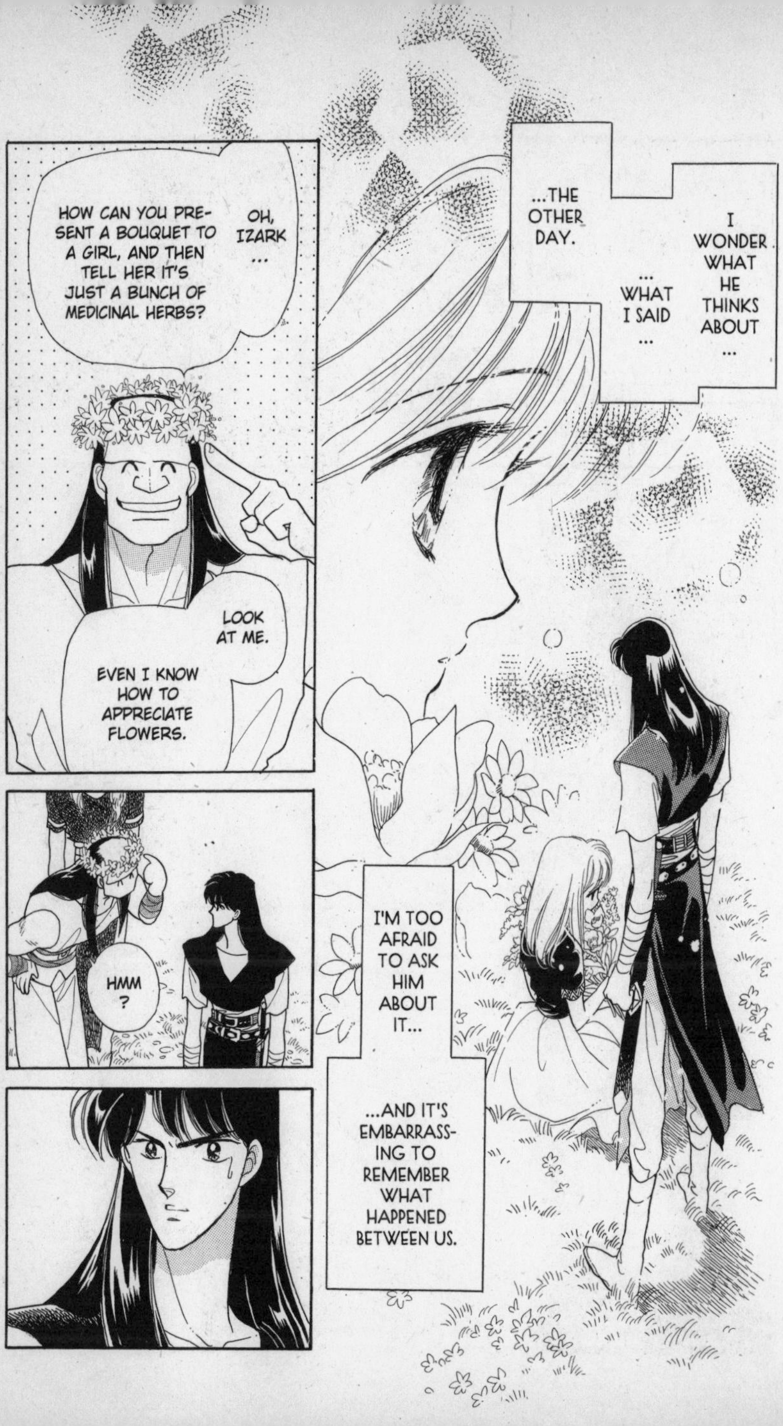
I WONDER WHAT HE THINKS ABOUT ...
... WHAT I SAID ...
...THE OTHER DAY.
I'M TOO AFRAID TO ASK HIM ABOUT IT...
...AND IT'S EMBARRASS-ING TO REMEMBER WHAT HAPPENED BETWEEN US.
OH, IZARK ...
HOW CAN YOU PRE-SENT A BOUQUET TO A GIRL, AND THEN TELL HER IT'S JUST A BUNCH OF MEDICINAL HERBS?
LOOK AT ME.
EVEN I KNOW HOW TO APPRECIATE FLOWERS.
HMM ?

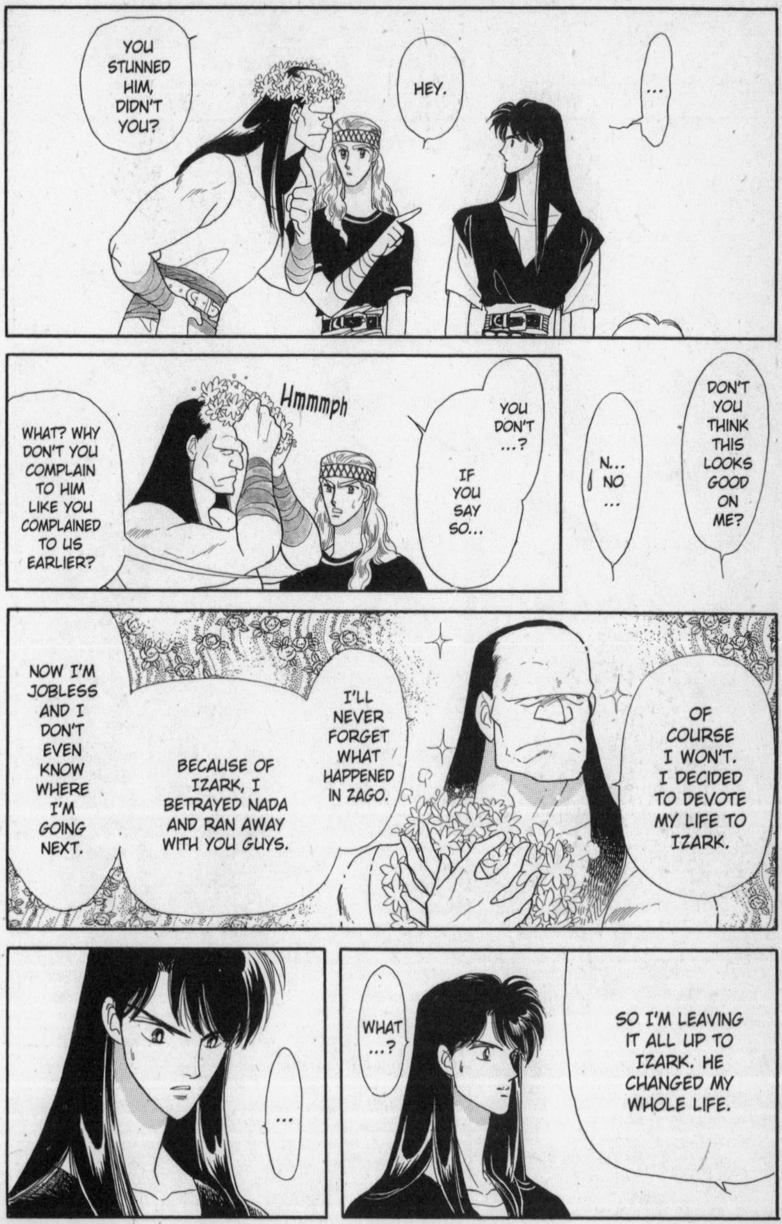
...
HEY.
YOU STUNNED HIM, DIDN'T YOU?
DON'T YOU THINK THIS LOOKS GOOD ON ME?
N... NO...
YOU DON'T...?
IF YOU SAY SO...
Hmmmph
WHAT? WHY DON'T YOU COMPLAIN TO HIM LIKE YOU COMPLAINED TO US EARLIER?
OF COURSE I WON'T. I DECIDED TO DEVOTE MY LIFE TO IZARK.
I'LL NEVER FORGET WHAT HAPPENED IN ZAGO.
BECAUSE OF IZARK, I BETRAYED NADA AND RAN AWAY WITH YOU GUYS.
NOW I'M JOBLESS AND I DON'T EVEN KNOW WHERE I'M GOING NEXT.
SO I'M LEAVING IT ALL UP TO IZARK. HE CHANGED MY WHOLE LIFE.
WHAT...?
...

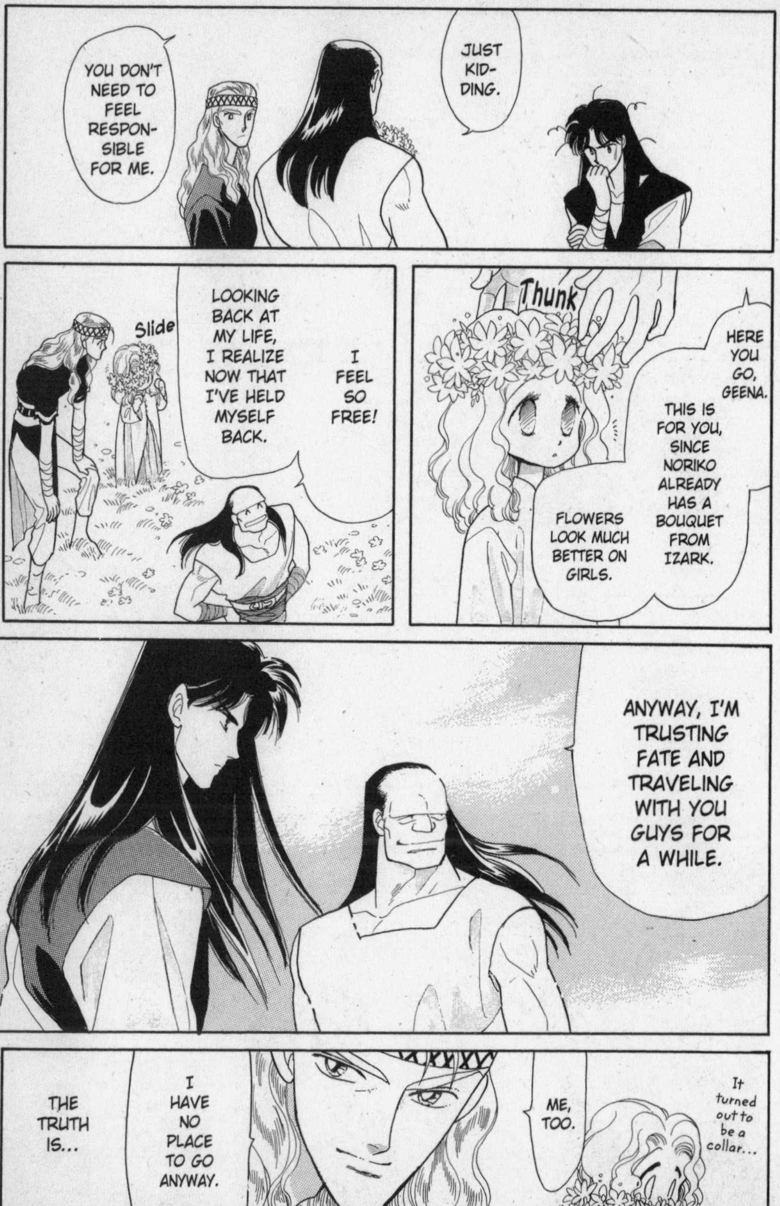
JUST KID-DING.
YOU DON'T NEED TO FEEL RESPON-SIBLE FOR ME.
Thunk
HERE YOU GO, GEENA.
THIS IS FOR YOU, SINCE NORIKO ALREADY HAS A BOUQUET FROM IZARK.
FLOWERS LOOK MUCH BETTER ON GIRLS.
I FEEL SO FREE!
LOOKING BACK AT MY LIFE, I REALIZE NOW THAT I'VE HELD MYSELF BACK.
Slide
ANYWAY, I'M TRUSTING FATE AND TRAVELING WITH YOU GUYS FOR A WHILE.
It turned out to be a collar...
ME, TOO.
I HAVE NO PLACE TO GO ANYWAY.
THE TRUTH IS...

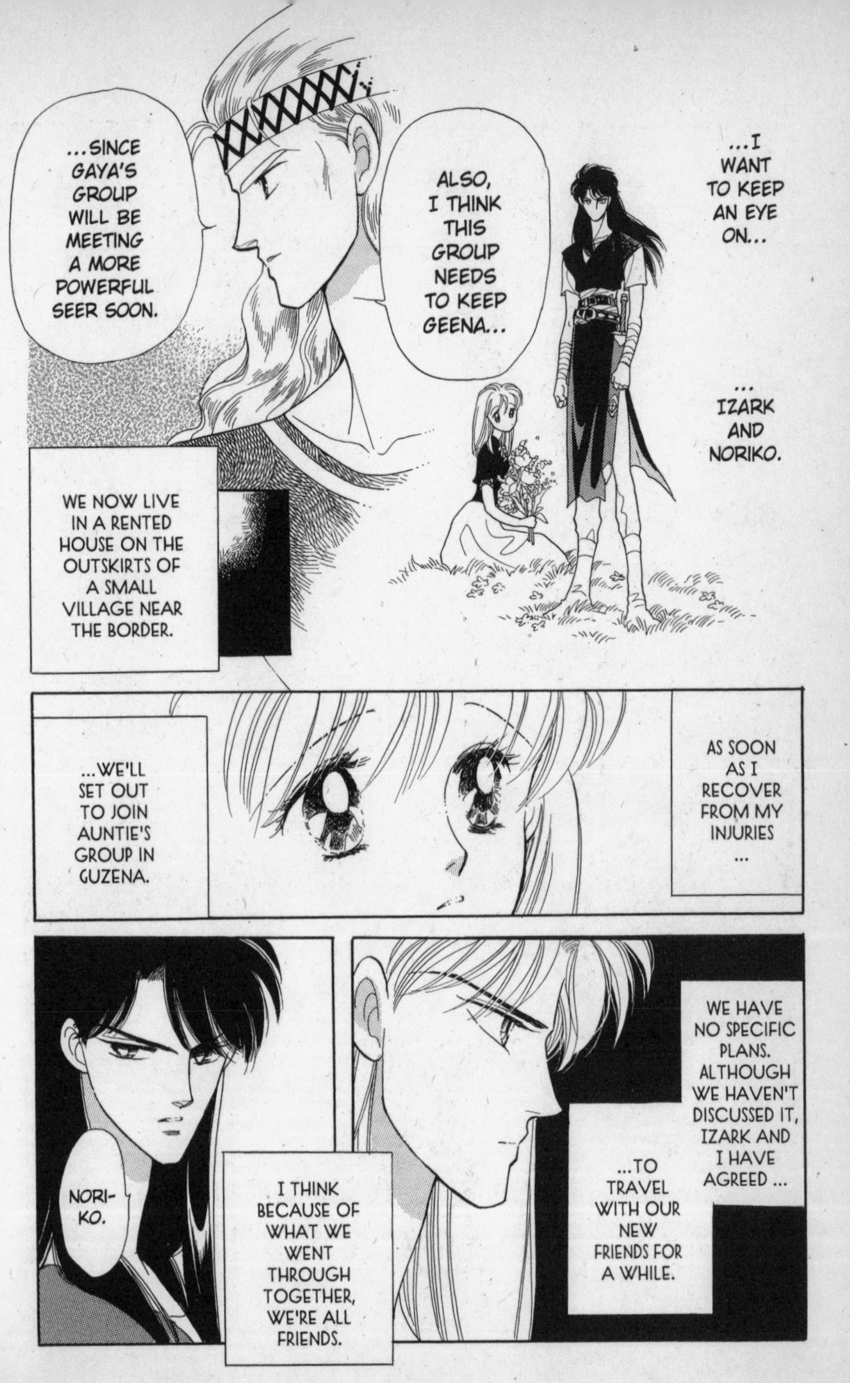
...I WANT TO KEEP AN EYE ON...
...IZARK AND NORIKO.
ALSO, I THINK THIS GROUP NEEDS TO KEEP GEENA...
...SINCE GAYA'S GROUP WILL BE MEETING A MORE POWERFUL SEER SOON.
WE NOW LIVE IN A RENTED HOUSE ON THE OUTSKIRTS OF A SMALL VILLAGE NEAR THE BORDER.
AS SOON AS I RECOVER FROM MY INJURIES ...
...WE'LL SET OUT TO JOIN AUNTIE'S GROUP IN GUZENA.
WE HAVE NO SPECIFIC PLANS. ALTHOUGH WE HAVEN'T DISCUSSED IT, IZARK AND I HAVE AGREED ...
...TO TRAVEL WITH OUR NEW FRIENDS FOR A WHILE.
I THINK BECAUSE OF WHAT WE WENT THROUGH TOGETHER, WE'RE ALL FRIENDS.
NORI-KO.

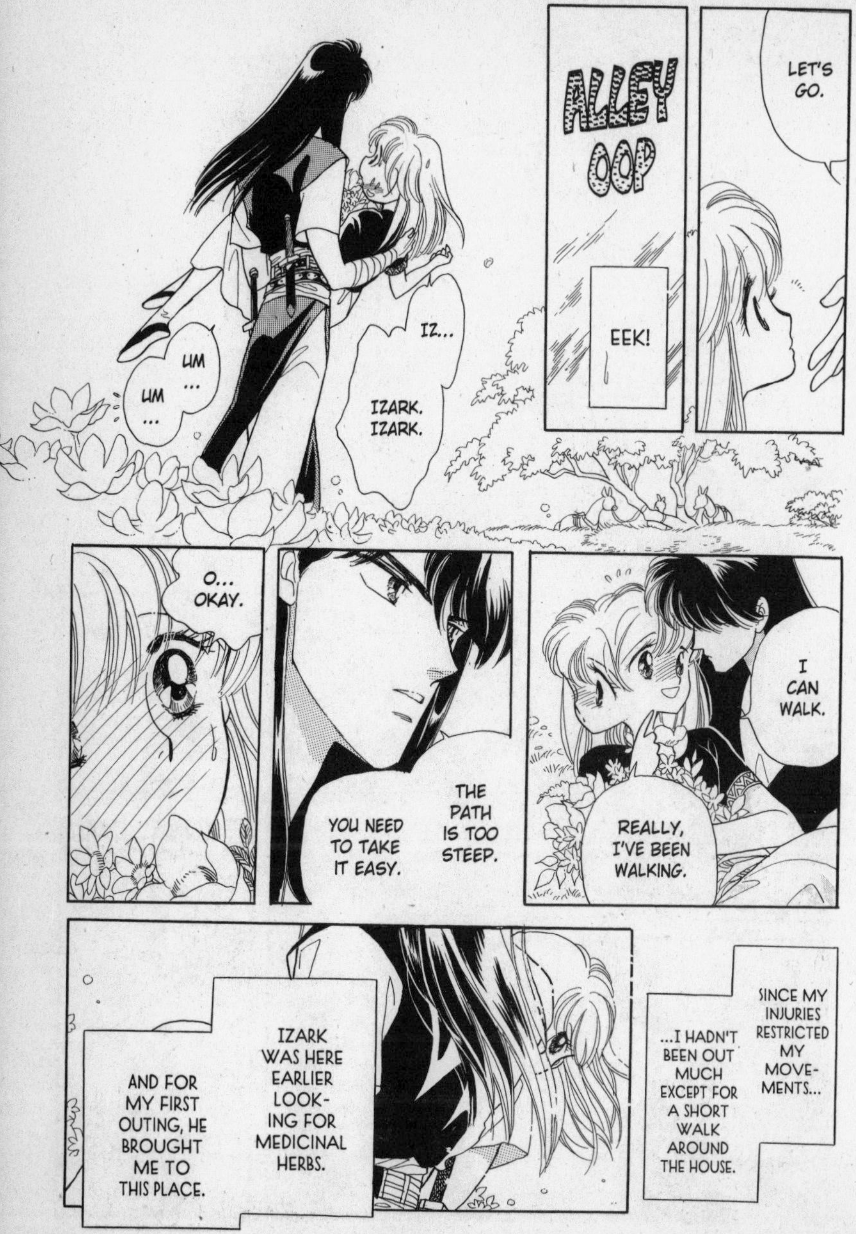
LET'S GO.
ALLEY OOP
EEK!
IZ...
IZARK. IZARK.
UM ...
UM ...
I CAN WALK.
REALLY, I'VE BEEN WALKING.
THE PATH IS TOO STEEP.
YOU NEED TO TAKE IT EASY.
O... OKAY.
SINCE MY INJURIES RESTRICTED MY MOVE-MENTS...
...I HADN'T BEEN OUT MUCH EXCEPT FOR A SHORT WALK AROUND THE HOUSE.
IZARK WAS HERE EARLIER LOOK-ING FOR MEDICINAL HERBS.
AND FOR MY FIRST OUTING, HE BROUGHT ME TO THIS PLACE.

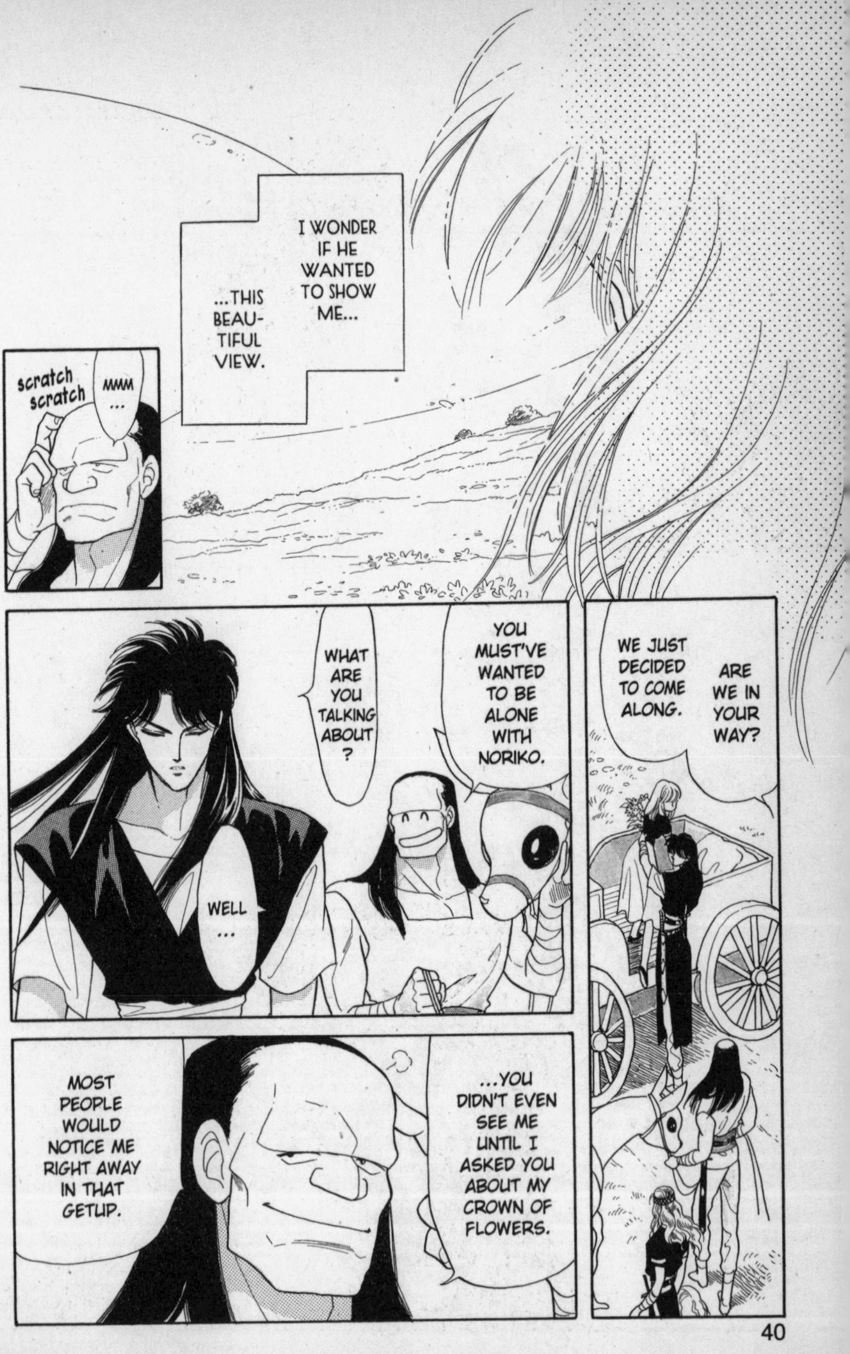
I WONDER IF HE WANTED TO SHOW ME...
...THIS BEAUTIFUL VIEW.
MMM ...
scratch scratch
WE JUST DECIDED TO COME ALONG.
ARE WE IN YOUR WAY?
YOU MUST'VE WANTED TO BE ALONE WITH NORIKO.
WHAT ARE YOU TALKING ABOUT?
WELL ...
...YOU DIDN'T EVEN SEE ME UNTIL I ASKED YOU ABOUT MY CROWN OF FLOWERS.
MOST PEOPLE WOULD NOTICE ME RIGHT AWAY IN THAT GETUP.

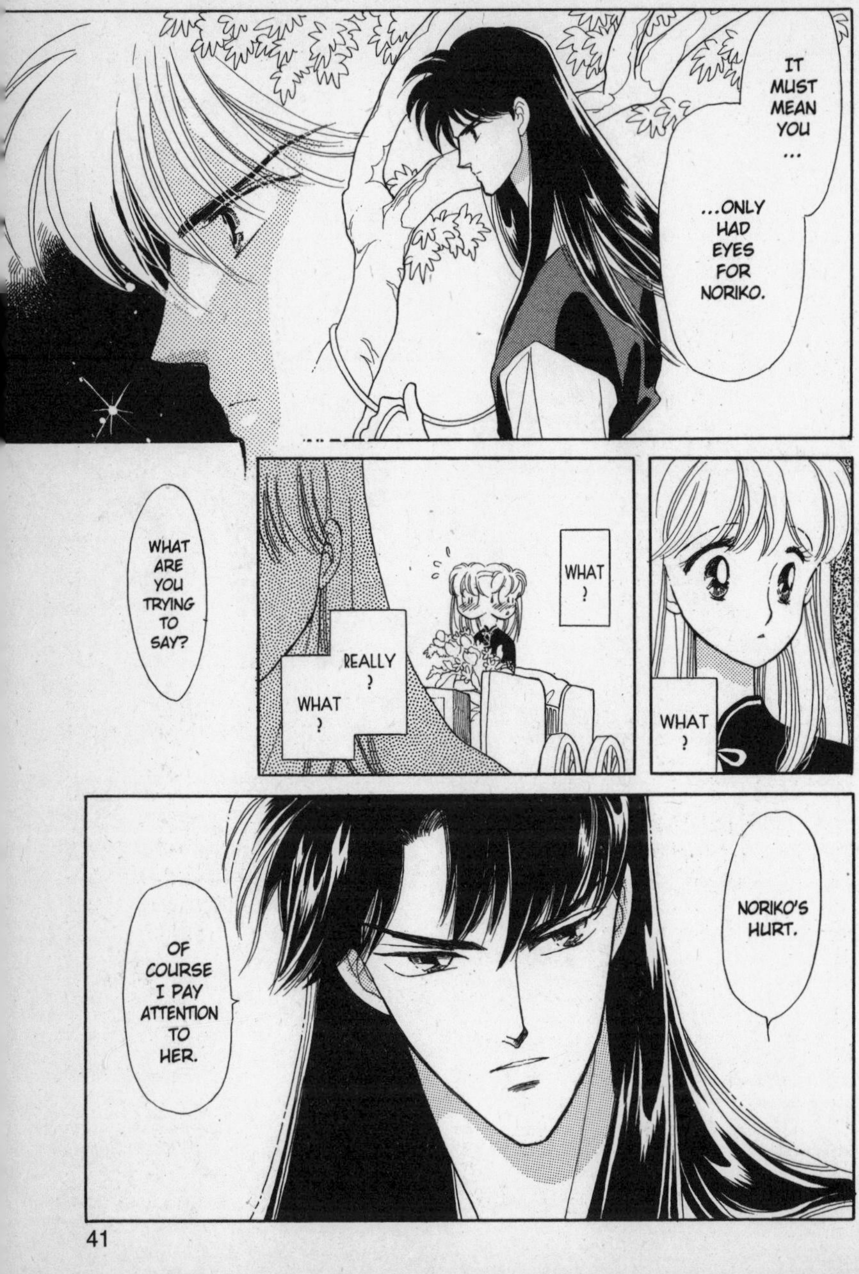
IT MUST MEAN YOU ...
...ONLY HAD EYES FOR NORIKO.
WHAT?
WHAT?
REALLY?
WHAT?
WHAT ARE YOU TRYING TO SAY?
NORIKO'S HURT.
OF COURSE I PAY ATTENTION TO HER.

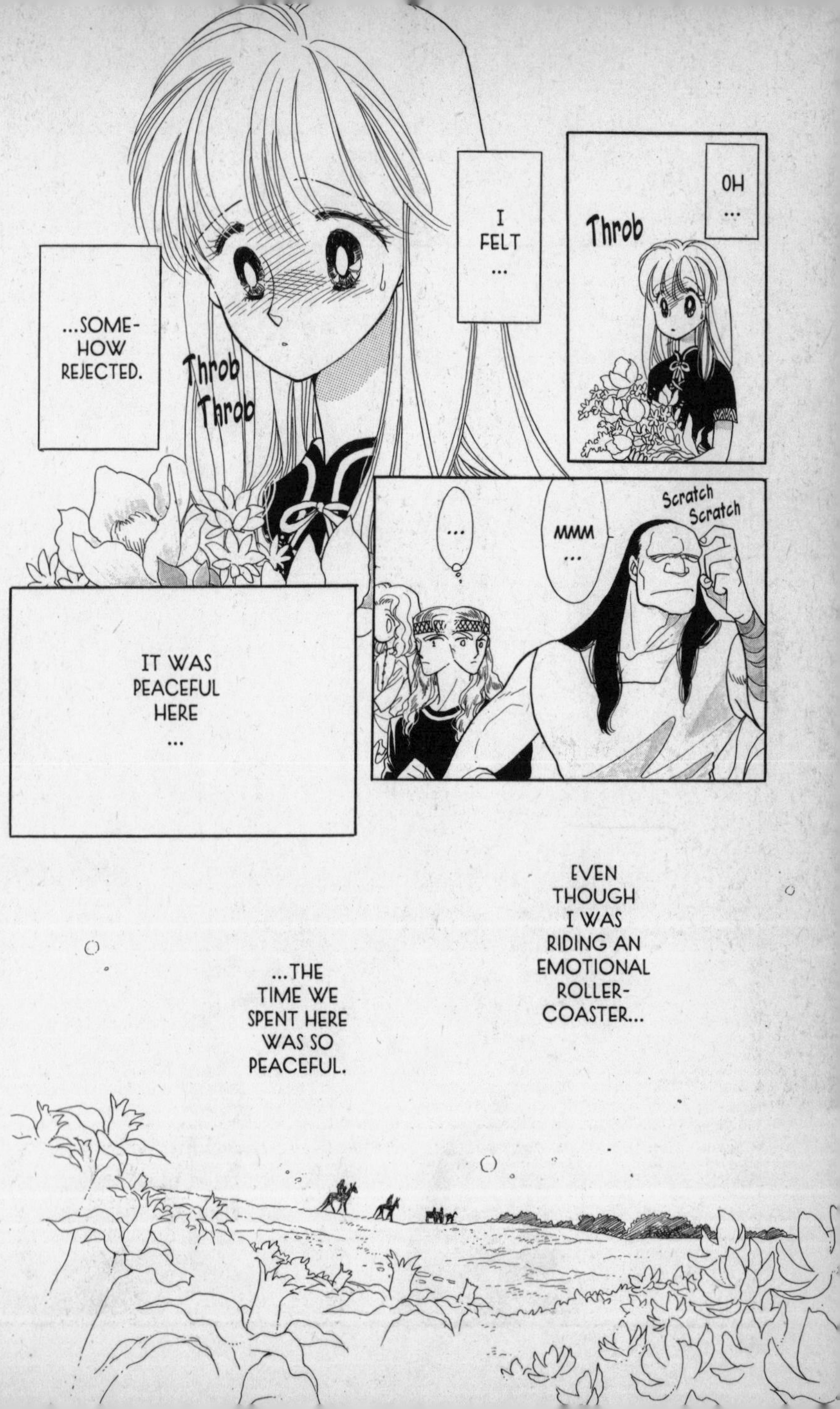
OH ...
Throb
I FELT ...
...SOME-HOW REJECTED.
Throb Throb
Scratch Scratch
MMM ...
...
IT WAS PEACEFUL HERE ...
EVEN THOUGH I WAS RIDING AN EMOTIONAL ROLLER-COASTER...
...THE TIME WE SPENT HERE WAS SO PEACEFUL.

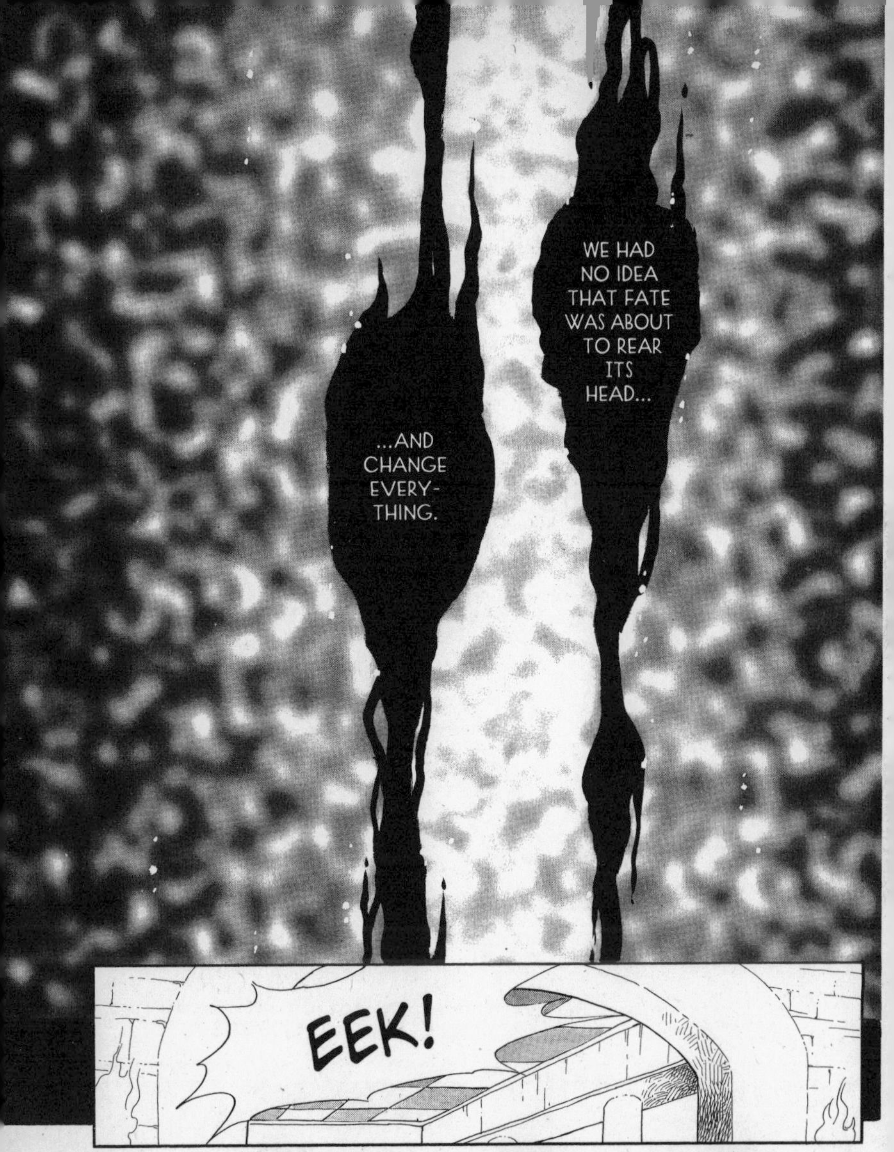
WE HAD NO IDEA THAT FATE WAS ABOUT TO REAR ITS HEAD...
...AND CHANGE EVERY-THING.
EEK!
HEE, HEE.

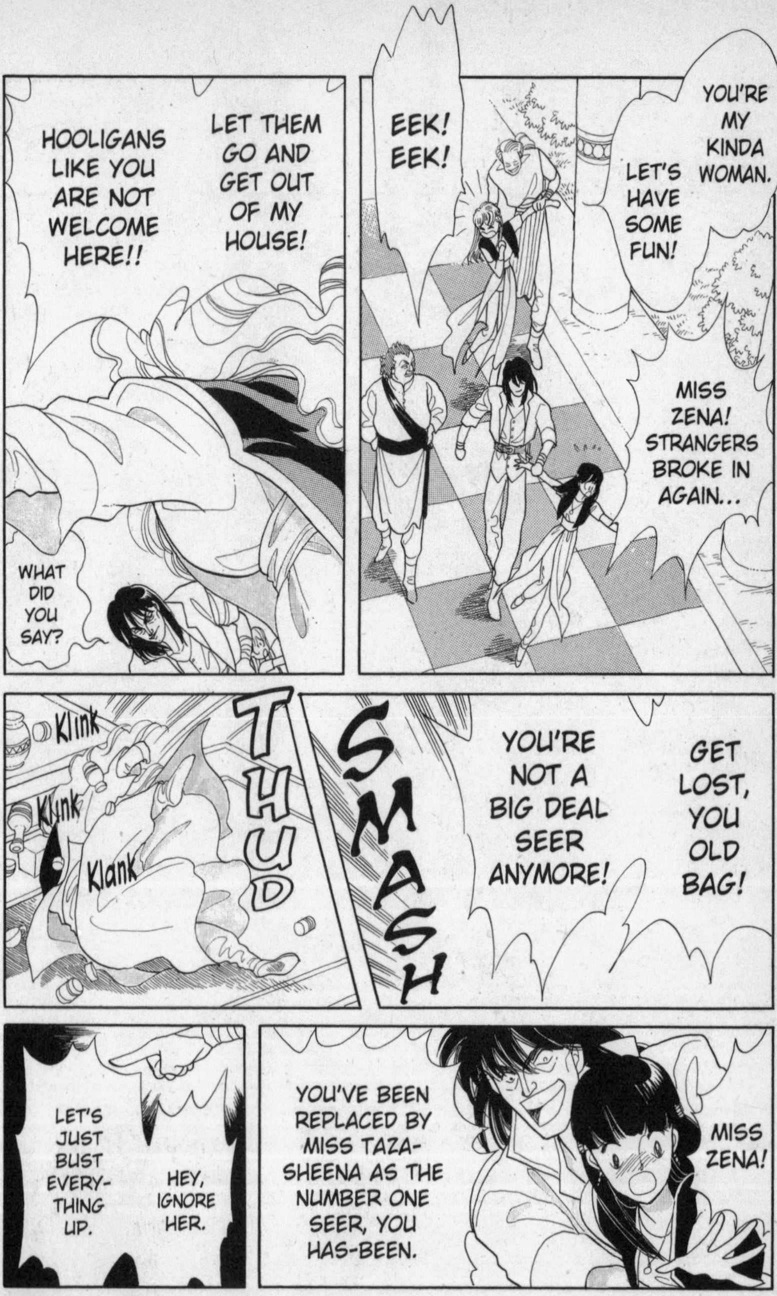
YOU'RE MY KINDA WOMAN.
LET'S HAVE SOME FUN!
EEK! EEK!
MISS ZENA! STRANGERS BROKE IN AGAIN...
LET THEM GO AND GET OUT OF MY HOUSE!
HOOLIGANS LIKE YOU ARE NOT WELCOME HERE!!
WHAT DID YOU SAY?
GET LOST, YOU OLD BAG!
YOU'RE NOT A BIG DEAL SEER ANYMORE!
SMASH
THUD
Klink
Klink
Klank
MISS ZENA!
YOU'VE BEEN REPLACED BY MISS TAZA-SHEENA AS THE NUMBER ONE SEER, YOU HAS-BEEN.
HEY, IGNORE HER.
LET'S JUST BUST EVERY-THING UP.

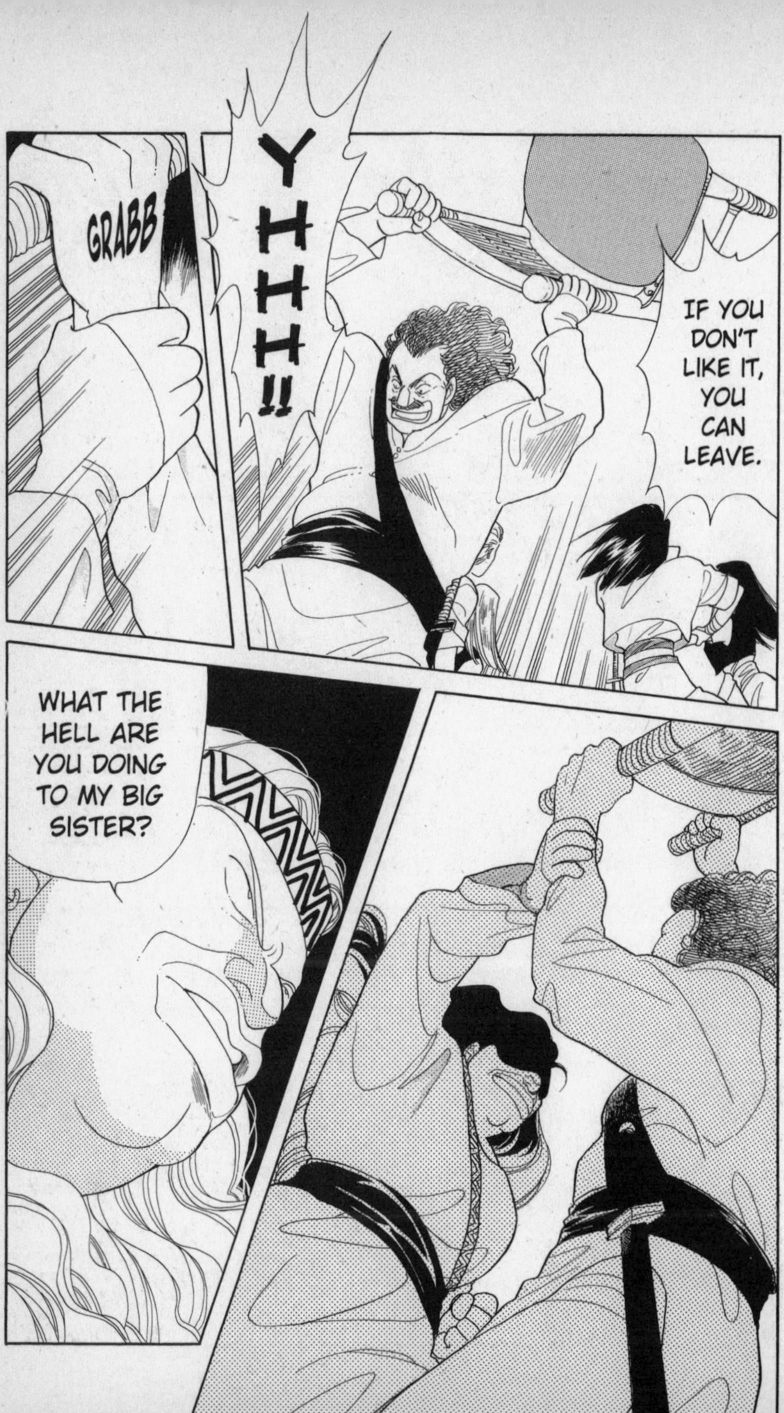
IF YOU DON'T LIKE IT, YOU CAN LEAVE.
YHHHH!!
GRABB
WHAT THE HELL ARE YOU DOING TO MY BIG SISTER?

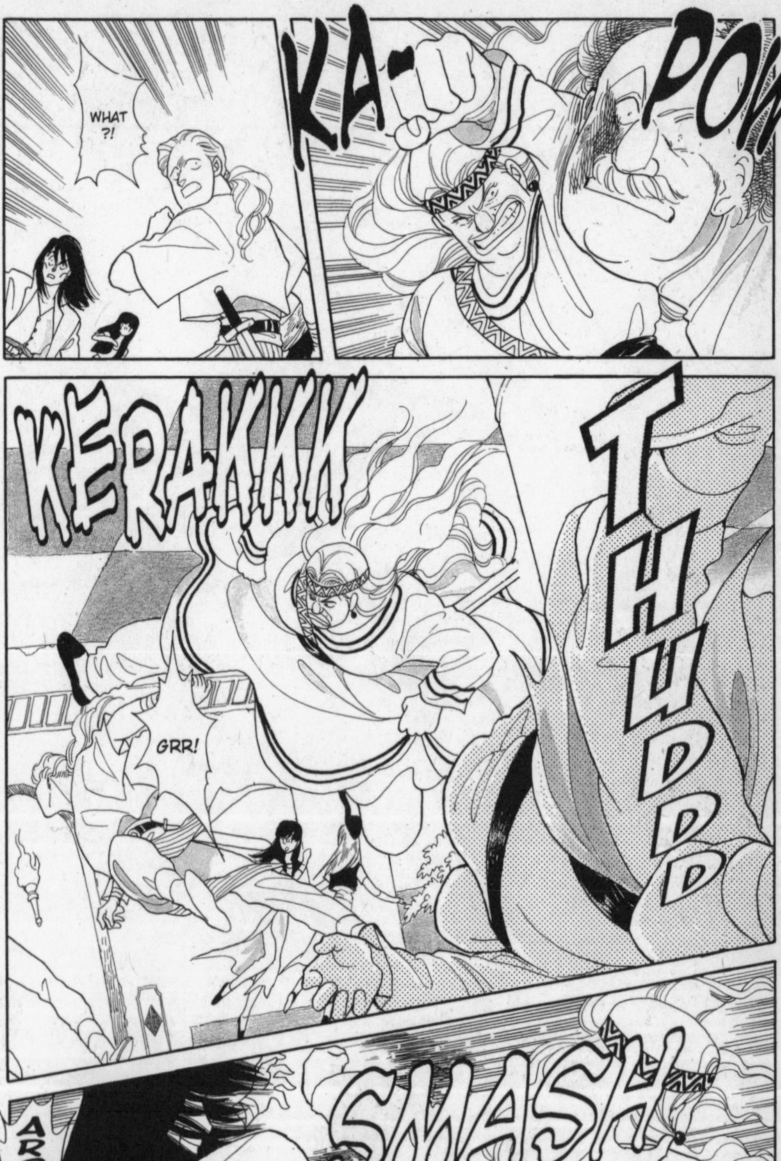
KA-POW
WHAT ?!
THUDDD
KERAKKK
GRR!
SMASH
ARGHH!!

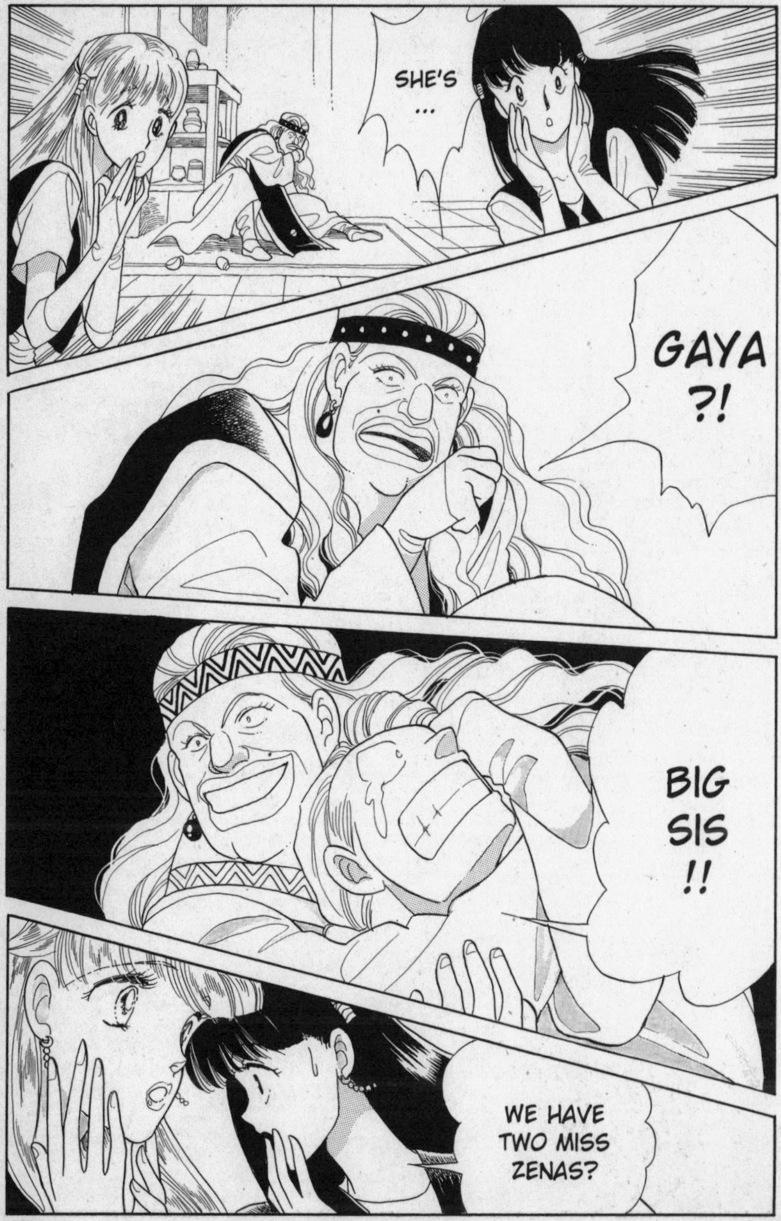
SHE'S ...
GAYA ?!
BIG SIS !!
WE HAVE TWO MISS ZENAS?

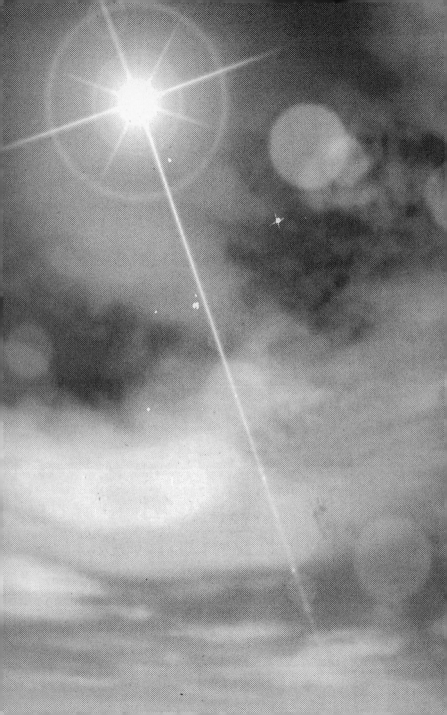

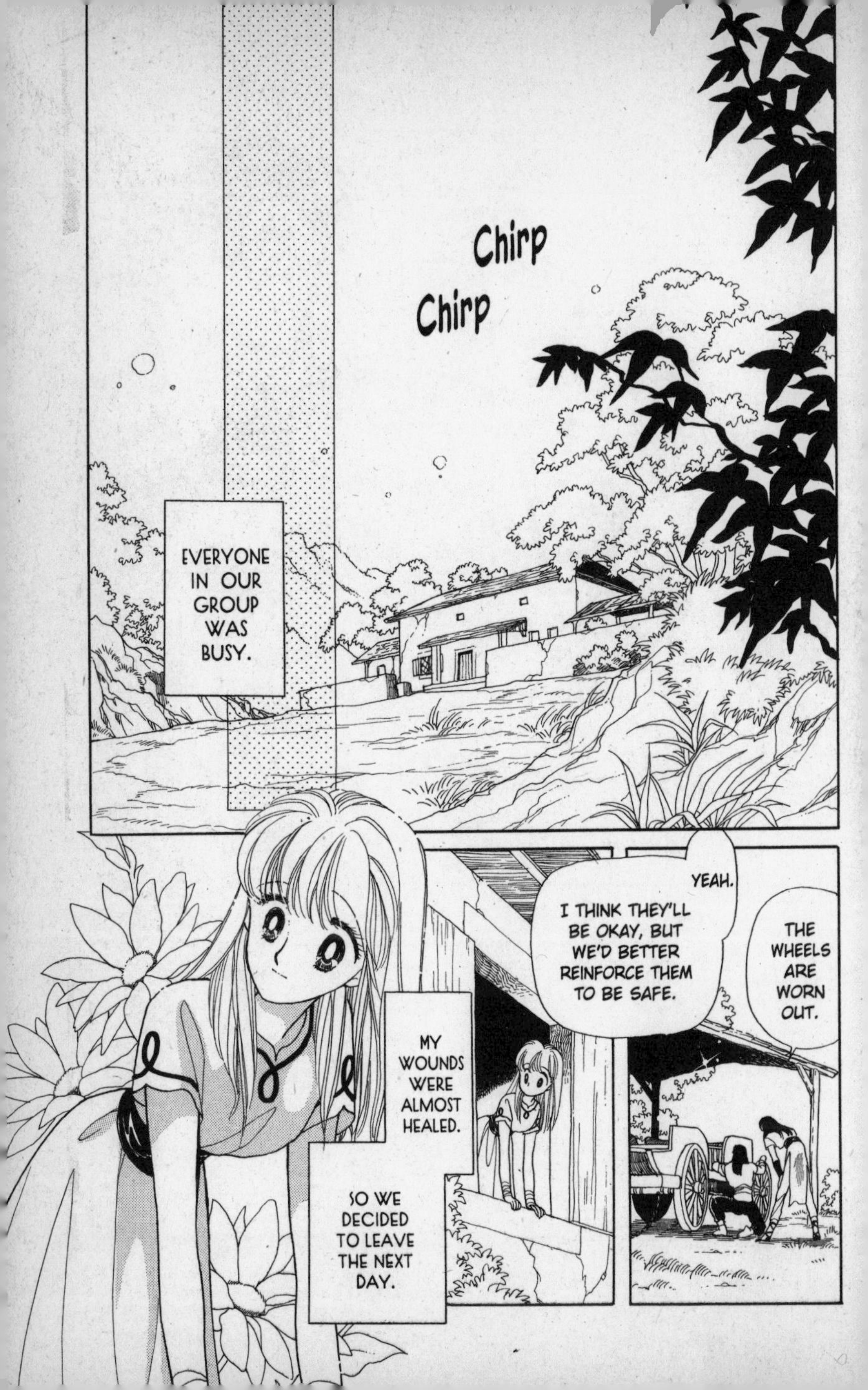
Chirp
Chirp
EVERYONE IN OUR GROUP WAS BUSY.
THE WHEELS ARE WORN OUT.
YEAH. I THINK THEY'LL BE OKAY, BUT WE'D BETTER REINFORCE THEM TO BE SAFE.
MY WOUNDS WERE ALMOST HEALED.
SO WE DECIDED TO LEAVE THE NEXT DAY.

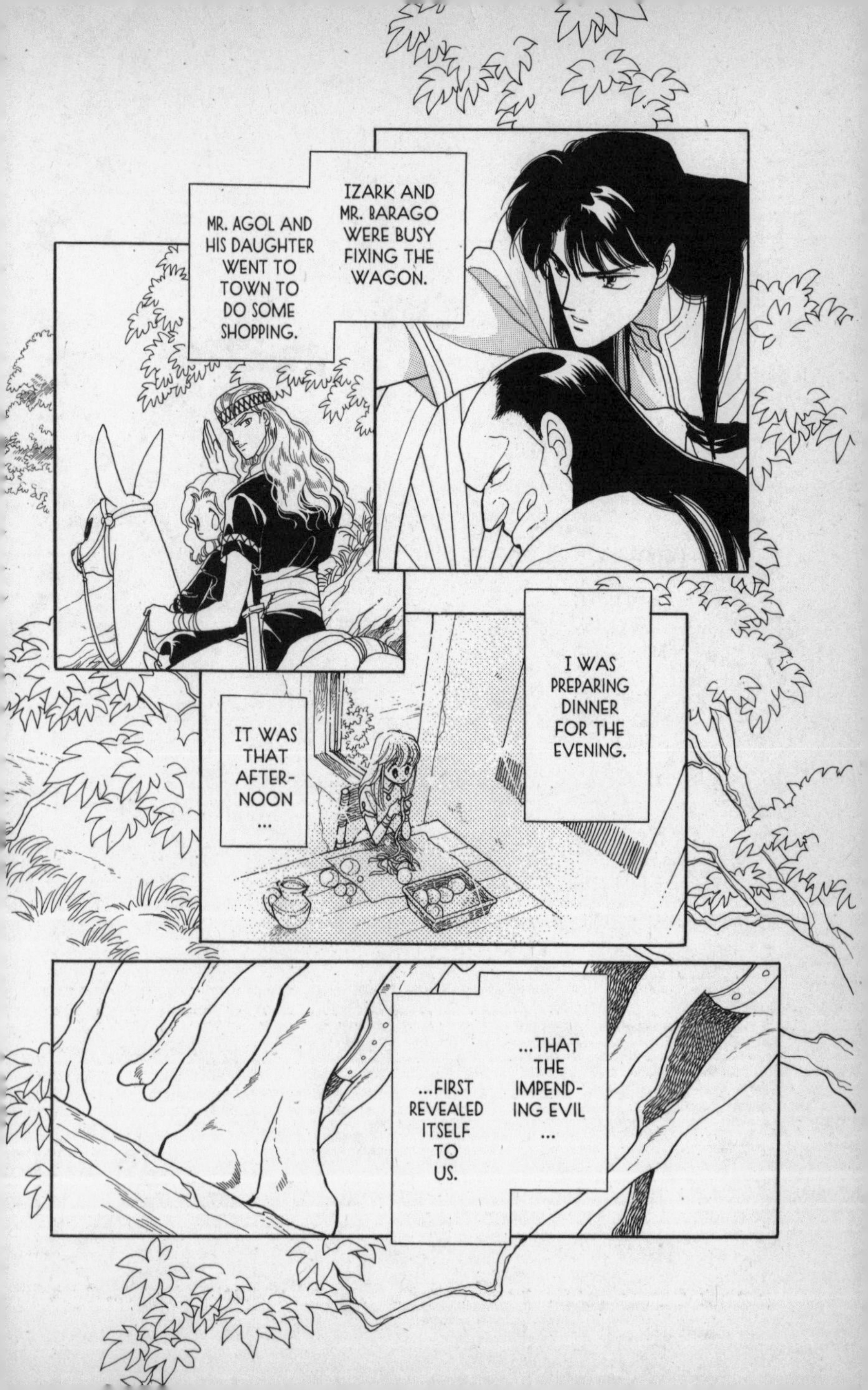
IZARK AND MR. BARAGO WERE BUSY FIXING THE WAGON.
MR. AGOL AND HIS DAUGHTER WENT TO TOWN TO DO SOME SHOPPING.
I WAS PREPARING DINNER FOR THE EVENING.
IT WAS THAT AFTER-NOON ...
...THAT THE IMPEND-ING EVIL ...
...FIRST REVEALED ITSELF TO US.

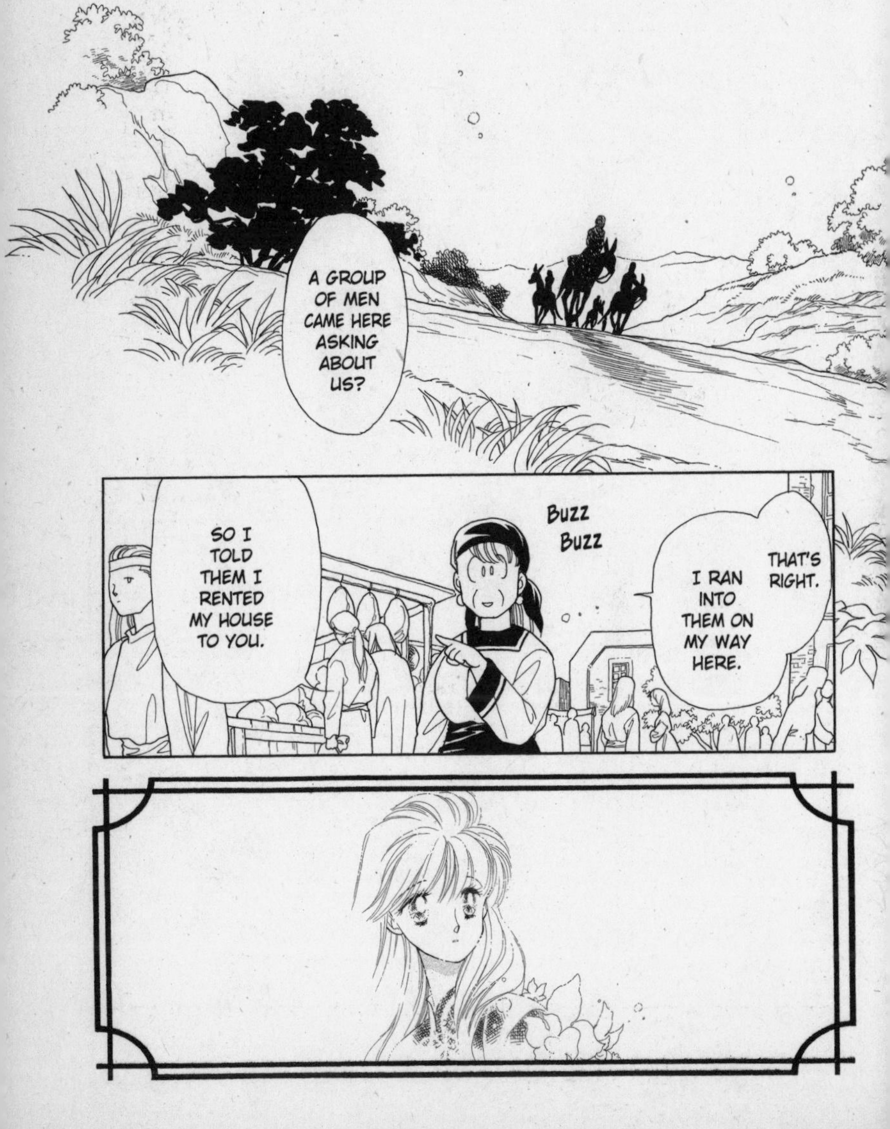
A GROUP OF MEN CAME HERE ASKING ABOUT US?
THAT'S RIGHT.
I RAN INTO THEM ON MY WAY HERE.
Buzz Buzz
SO I TOLD THEM I RENTED MY HOUSE TO YOU.

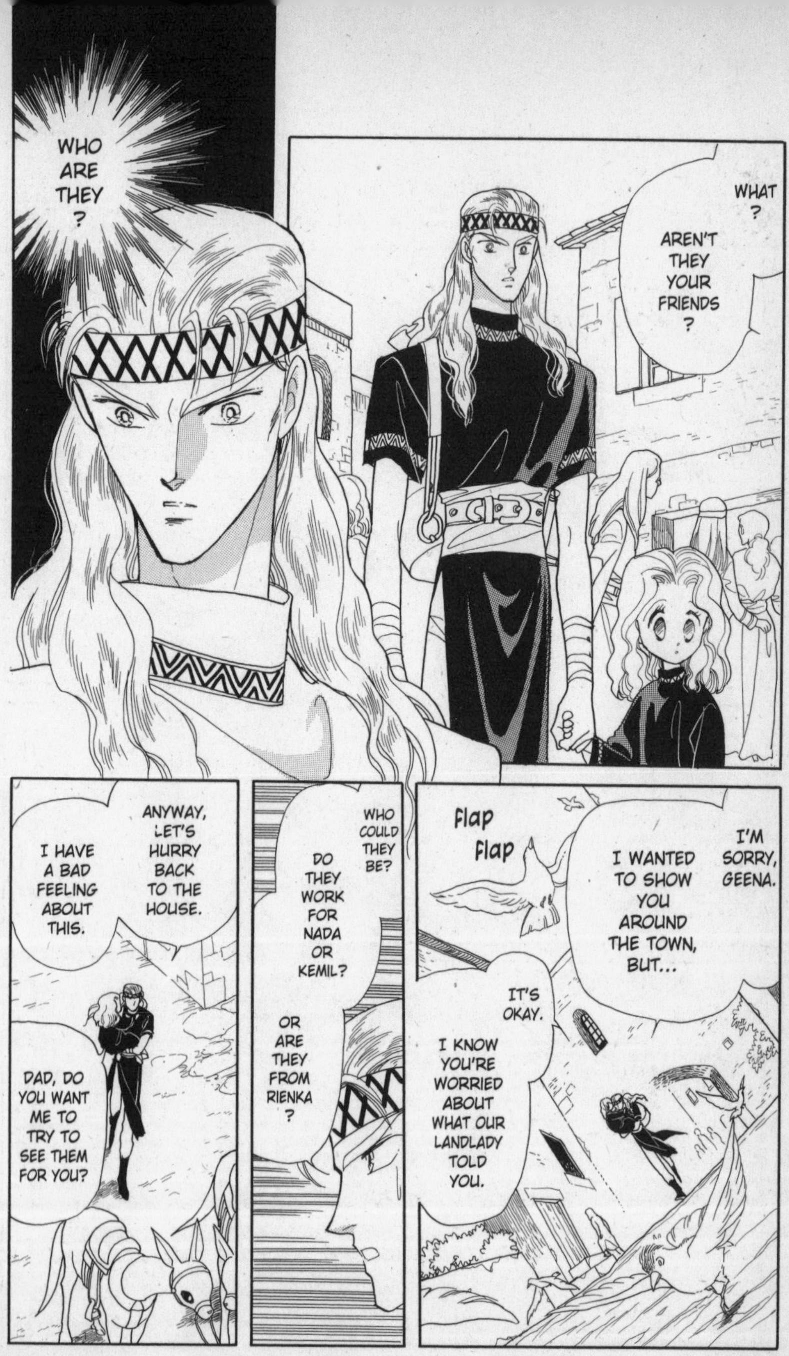
WHO ARE THEY?
WHAT?
AREN'T THEY YOUR FRIENDS?
I'M SORRY, GEENA.
I WANTED TO SHOW YOU AROUND THE TOWN, BUT...
Flap Flap
IT'S OKAY.
I KNOW YOU'RE WORRIED ABOUT WHAT OUR LANDLADY TOLD YOU.
WHO COULD THEY BE?
DO THEY WORK FOR NADA OR KEMIL?
OR ARE THEY FROM RIENKA?
ANYWAY, LET'S HURRY BACK TO THE HOUSE.
I HAVE A BAD FEELING ABOUT THIS.
DAD, DO YOU WANT ME TO TRY TO SEE THEM FOR YOU?

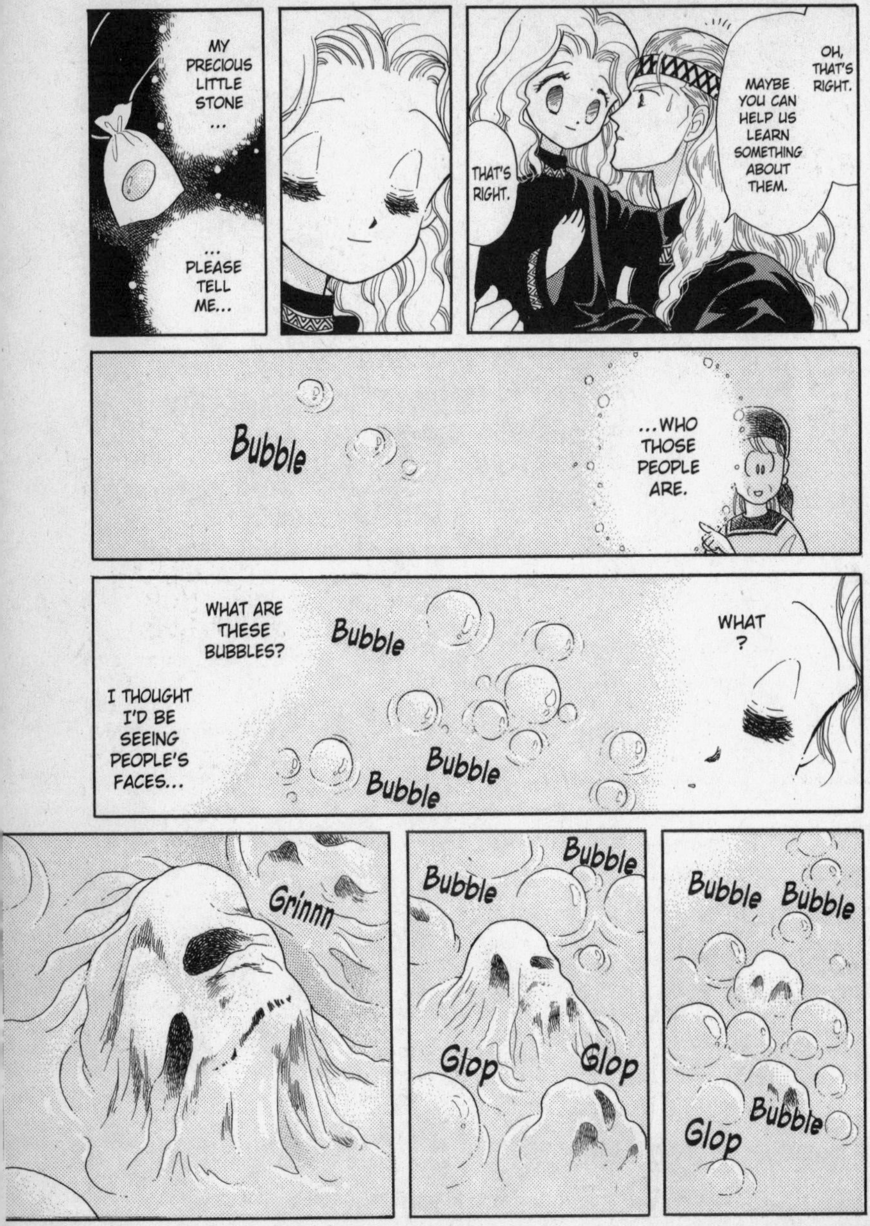
OH, THAT'S RIGHT.
MAYBE YOU CAN HELP US LEARN SOMETHING ABOUT THEM.
THAT'S RIGHT.
MY PRECIOUS LITTLE STONE ...
... PLEASE TELL ME...
...WHO THOSE PEOPLE ARE.
Bubble
WHAT ?
Bubble
Bubble
Bubble
WHAT ARE THESE BUBBLES?
I THOUGHT I'D BE SEEING PEOPLE'S FACES...
Bubble
Bubble
Bubble
Glop
Bubble
Bubble
Glop
Glop
Grinnn

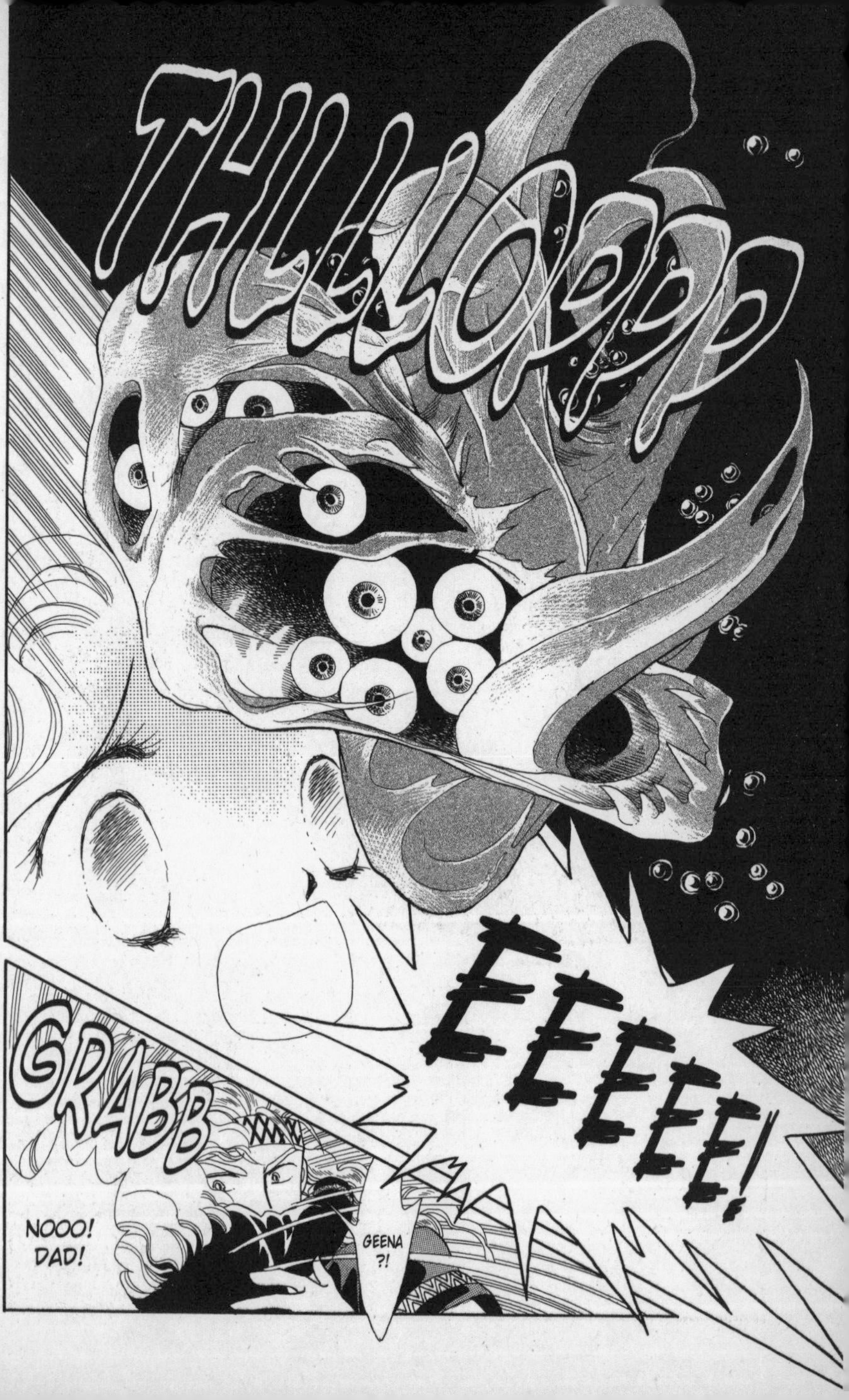
THLLOPPP
EEEEEE!
GRABB
GEENA ?!
NOOO! DAD!

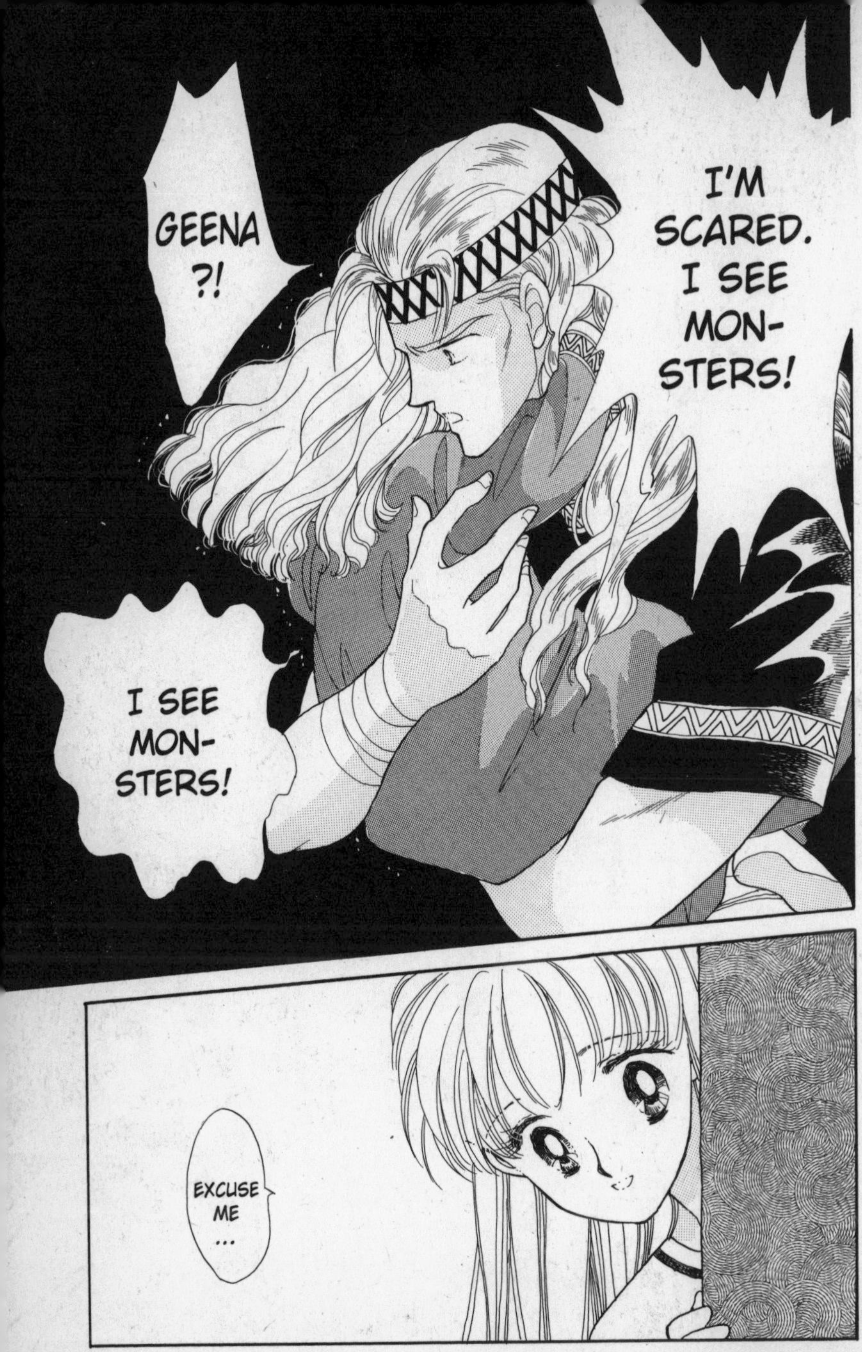
I'M SCARED. I SEE MONSTERS!
GEENA ?!
I SEE MONSTERS!
EXCUSE ME ...

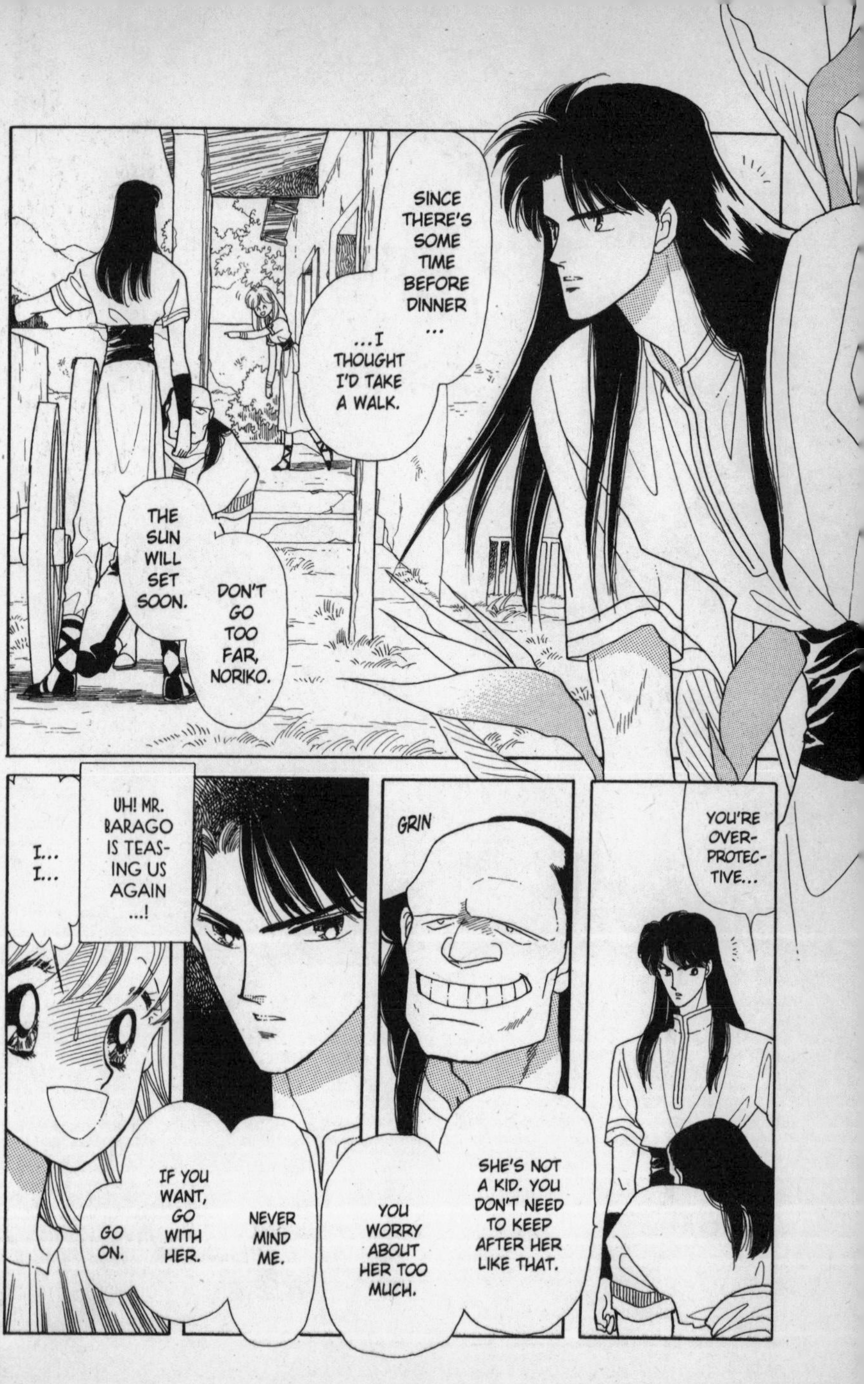
SINCE THERE'S SOME TIME BEFORE DINNER ...
...I THOUGHT I'D TAKE A WALK.
THE SUN WILL SET SOON.
DON'T GO TOO FAR, NORIKO.
YOU'RE OVER-PROTECTIVE...
GRIN
SHE'S NOT A KID. YOU DON'T NEED TO KEEP AFTER HER LIKE THAT.
YOU WORRY ABOUT HER TOO MUCH.
NEVER MIND ME.
IF YOU WANT, GO WITH HER.
GO ON.
UH! MR. BARAGO IS TEAS-ING US AGAIN ...!
I... I...

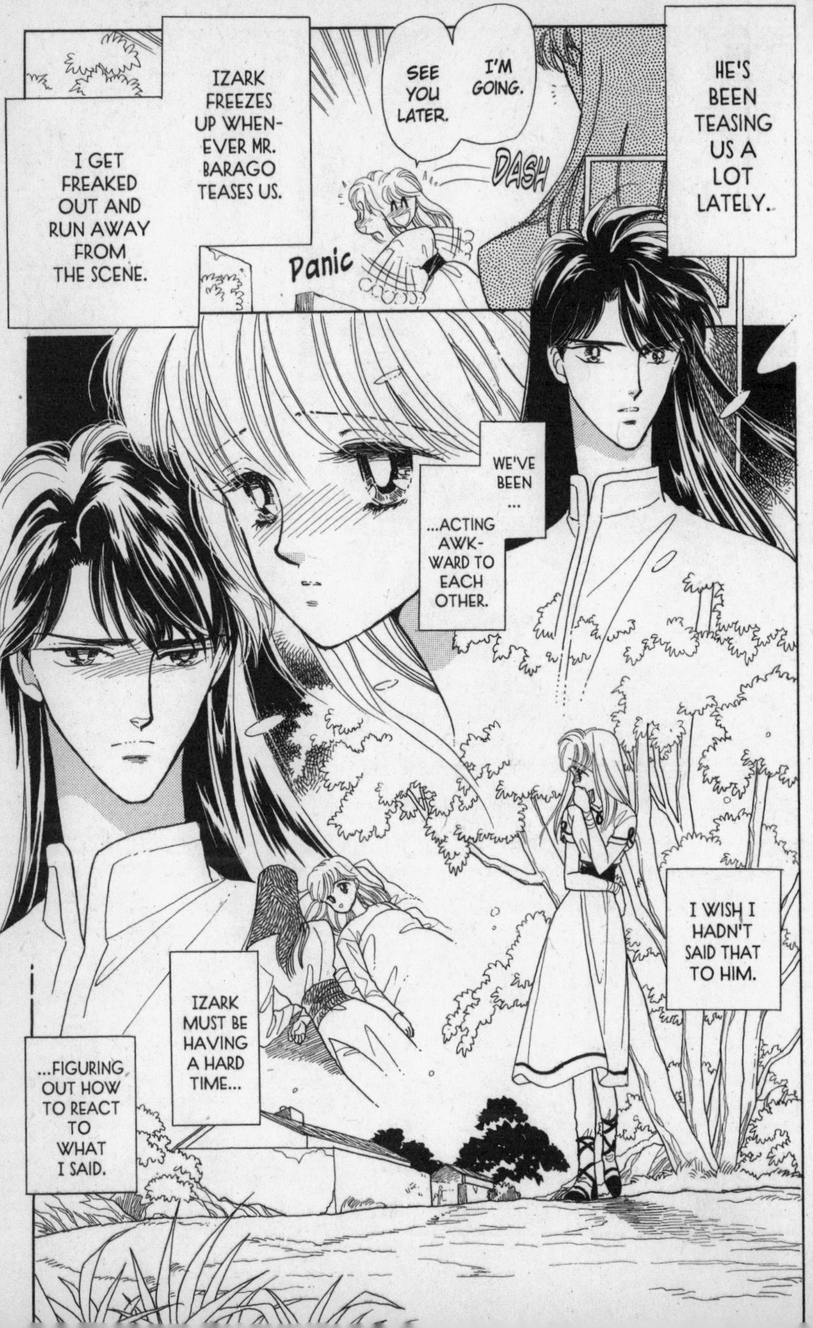
HE'S BEEN TEASING US A LOT LATELY.
I'M GOING. SEE YOU LATER.
DASH
Panic
IZARK FREEZES UP WHENEVER MR. BARAGO TEASES US.
I GET FREAKED OUT AND RUN AWAY FROM THE SCENE.
WE'VE BEEN ...
...ACTING AWKWARD TO EACH OTHER.
I WISH I HADN'T SAID THAT TO HIM.
IZARK MUST BE HAVING A HARD TIME...
...FIGURING OUT HOW TO REACT TO WHAT I SAID.

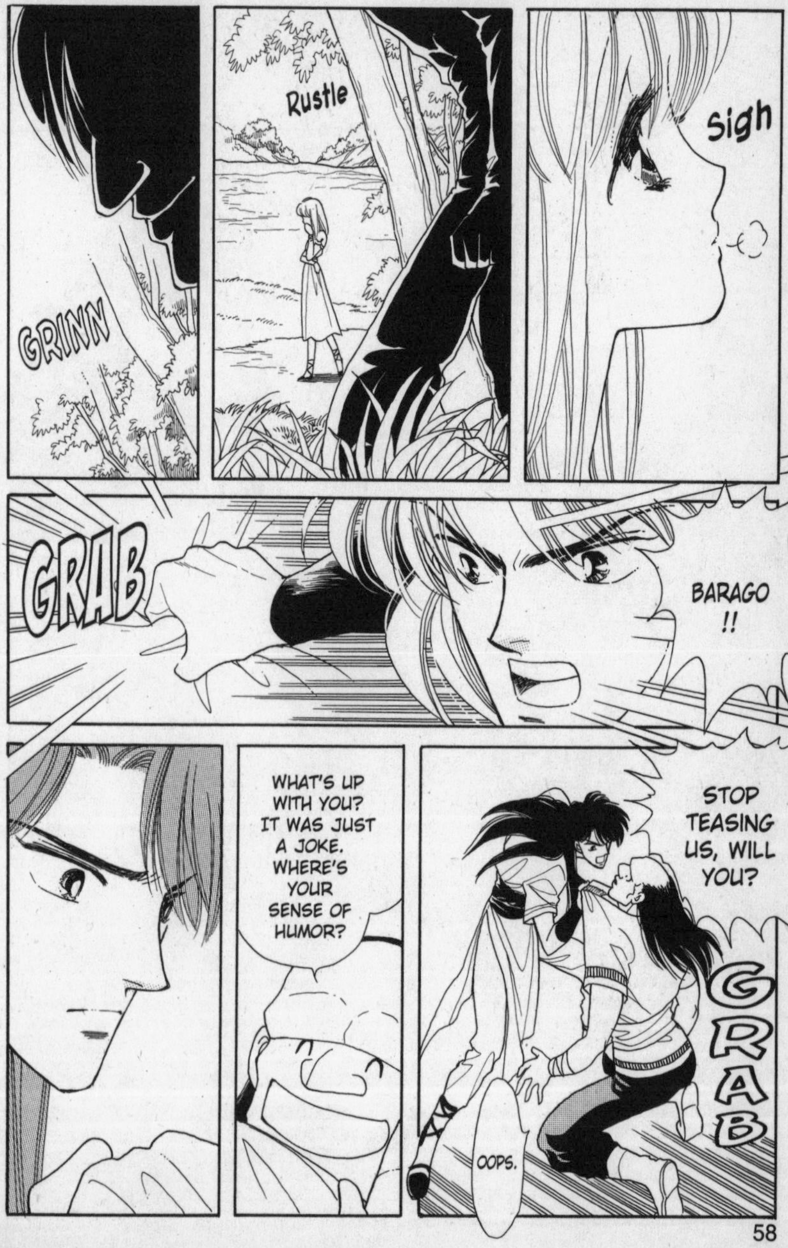
Sigh
Rustle
GRINN
BARAGO !!
GRAB
STOP TEASING US, WILL YOU?
GRAB
OOPS.
WHAT'S UP WITH YOU? IT WAS JUST A JOKE. WHERE'S YOUR SENSE OF HUMOR?

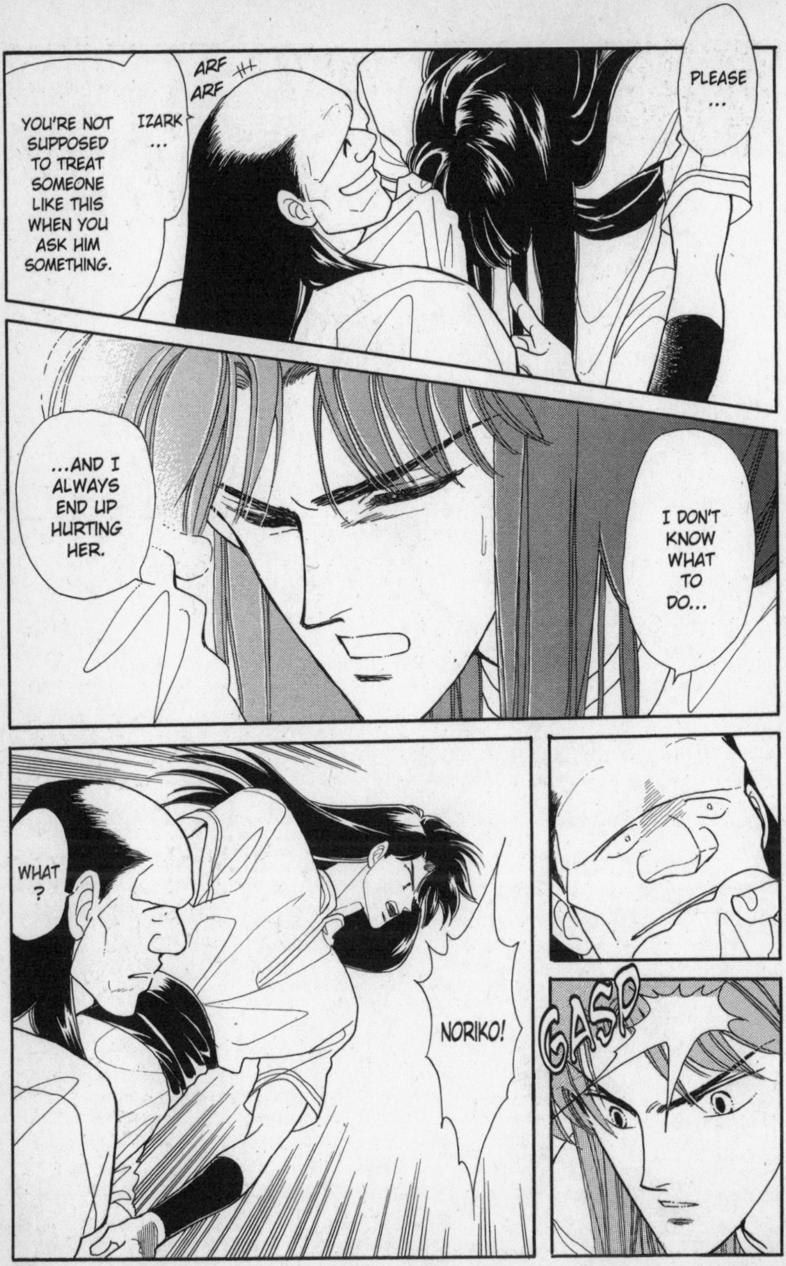
PLEASE ...
ARF ARF
IZARK ...
YOU'RE NOT SUPPOSED TO TREAT SOMEONE LIKE THIS WHEN YOU ASK HIM SOMETHING.
I DON'T KNOW WHAT TO DO...
...AND I ALWAYS END UP HURTING HER.
GASP
NORIKO!
WHAT ?

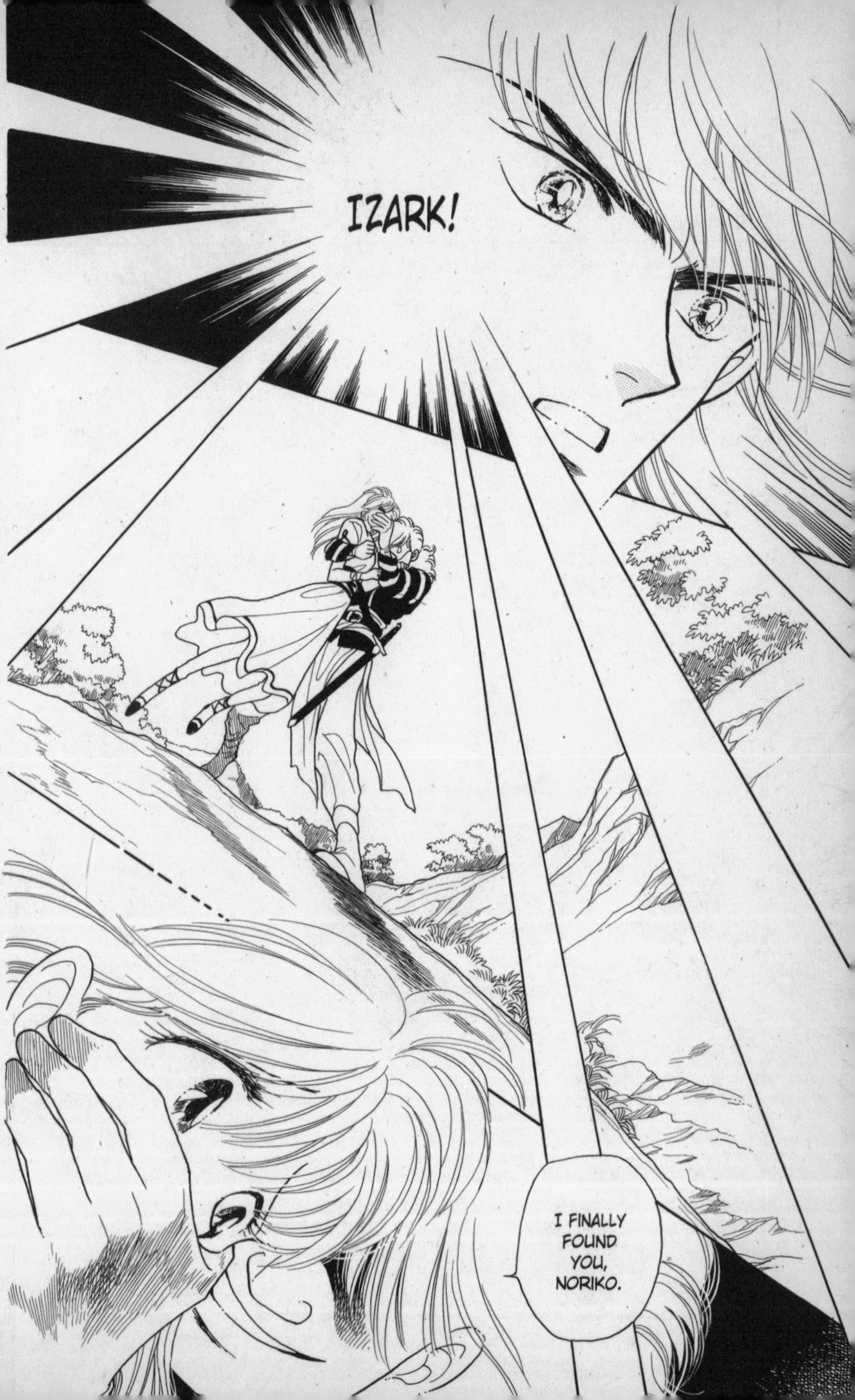
IZARK!
I FINALLY FOUND YOU, NORIKO.

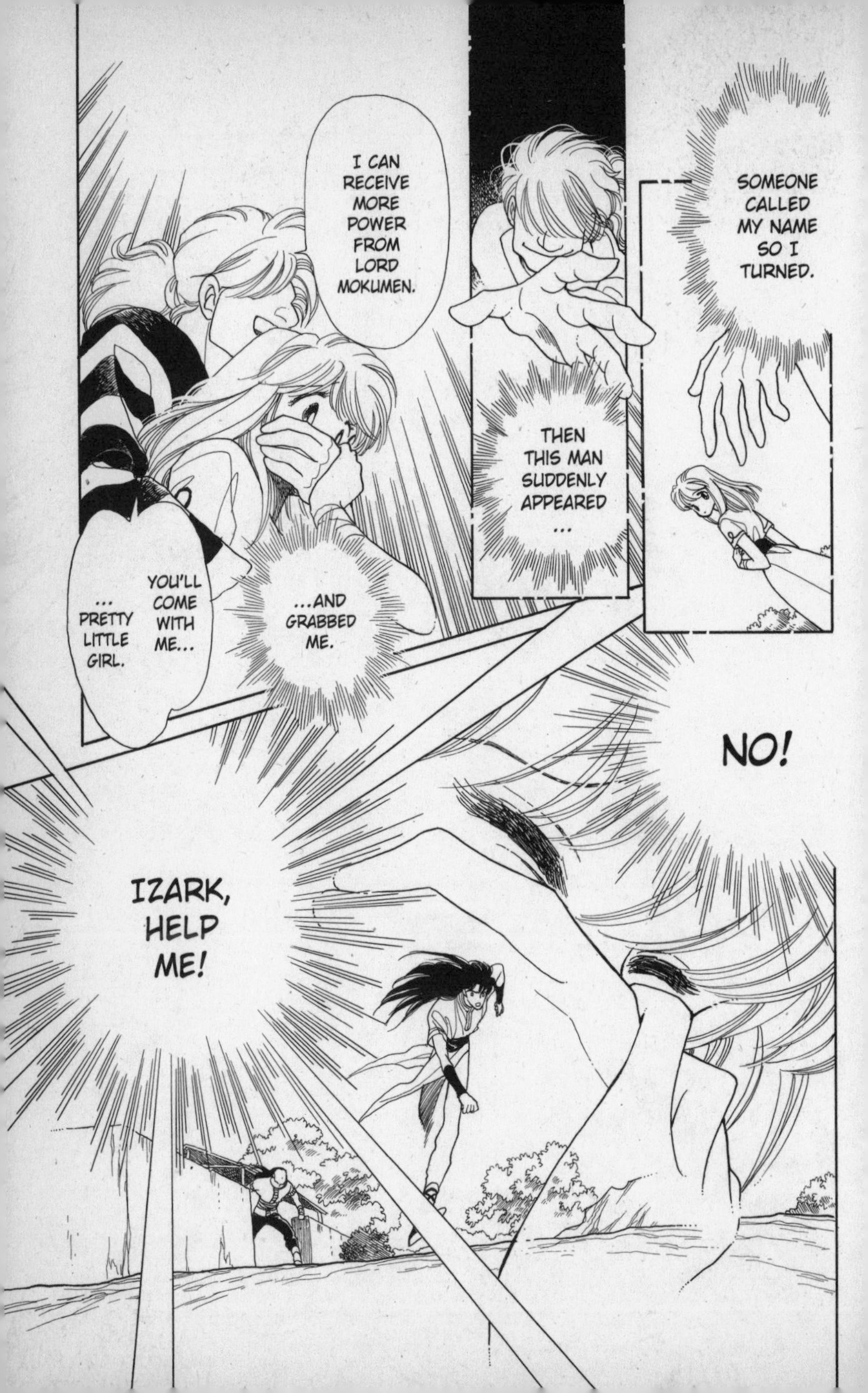
SOMEONE CALLED MY NAME SO I TURNED.
THEN THIS MAN SUDDENLY APPEARED ...
I CAN RECEIVE MORE POWER FROM LORD MOKUMEN.
...AND GRABBED ME.
YOU'LL COME WITH ME...
... PRETTY LITTLE GIRL.
NO!
IZARK, HELP ME!

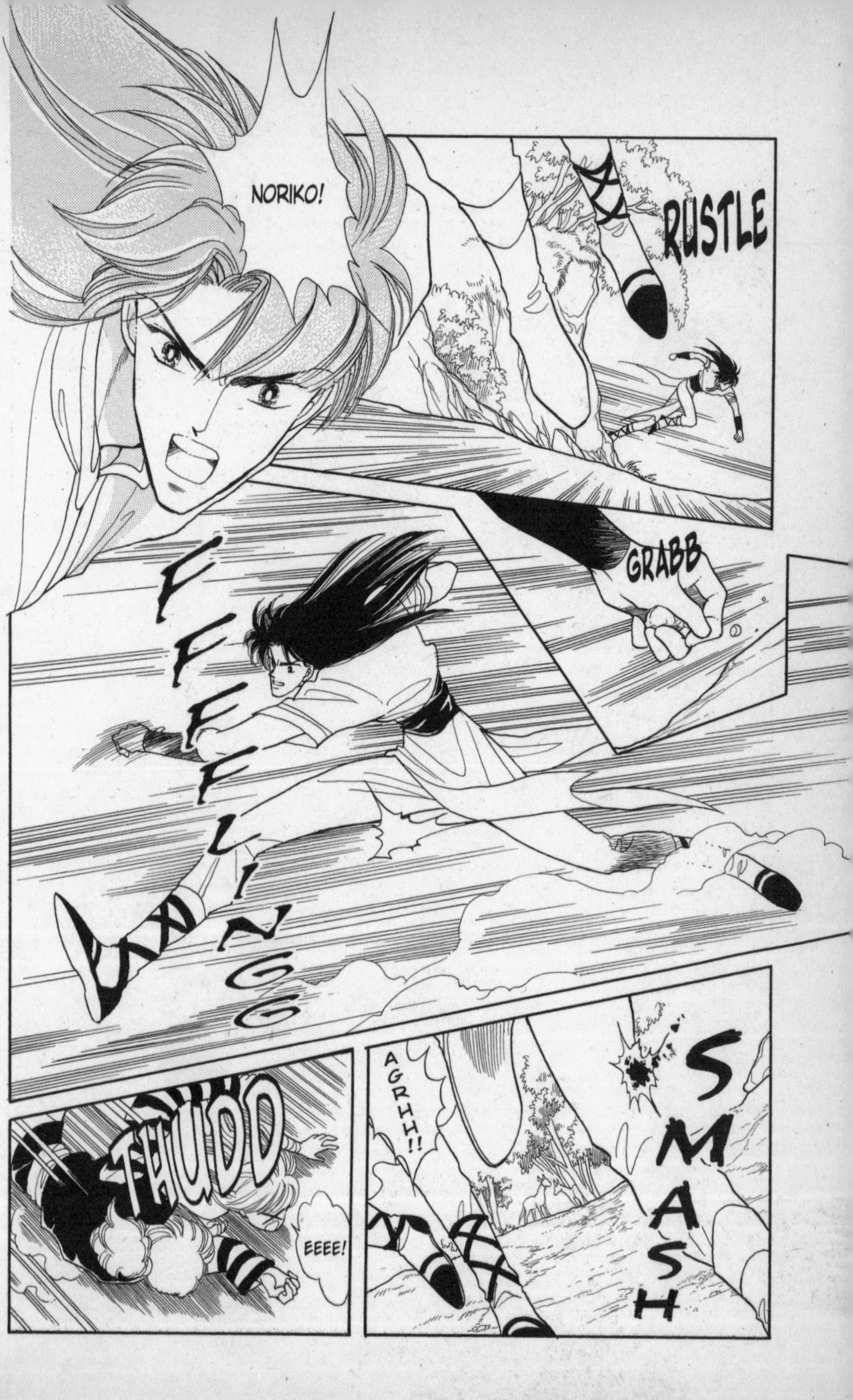
RUSTLE
NORIKO!
GRABB
FFFFLINGG
SMASH
AGRHH!!
THUDD
EEEE!

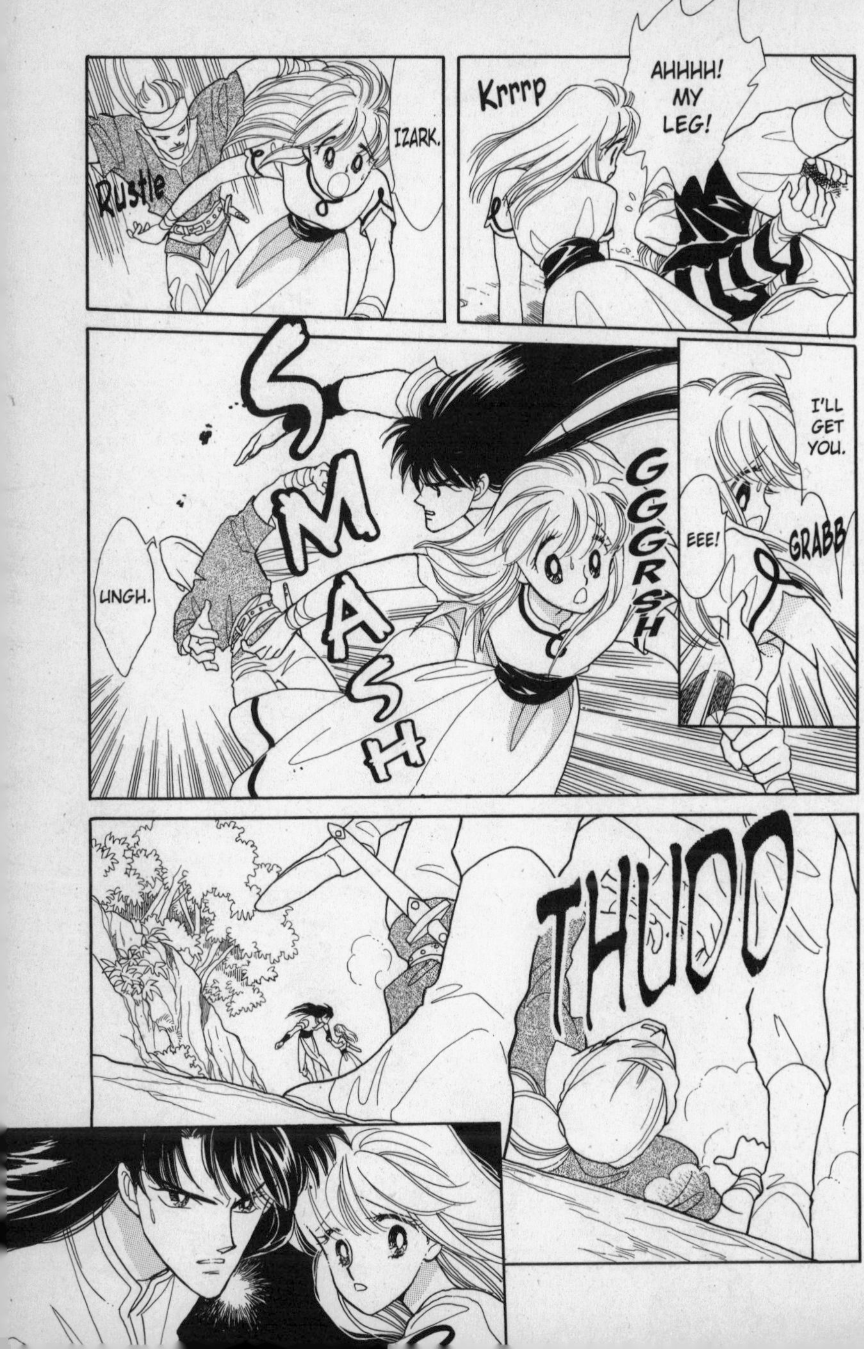
AHHHH! MY LEG!
Krrrp
IZARK.
Rustle
I'LL GET YOU.
GRABB
EEE!
GGGRSH
SMASH
UNGH.
THUDD

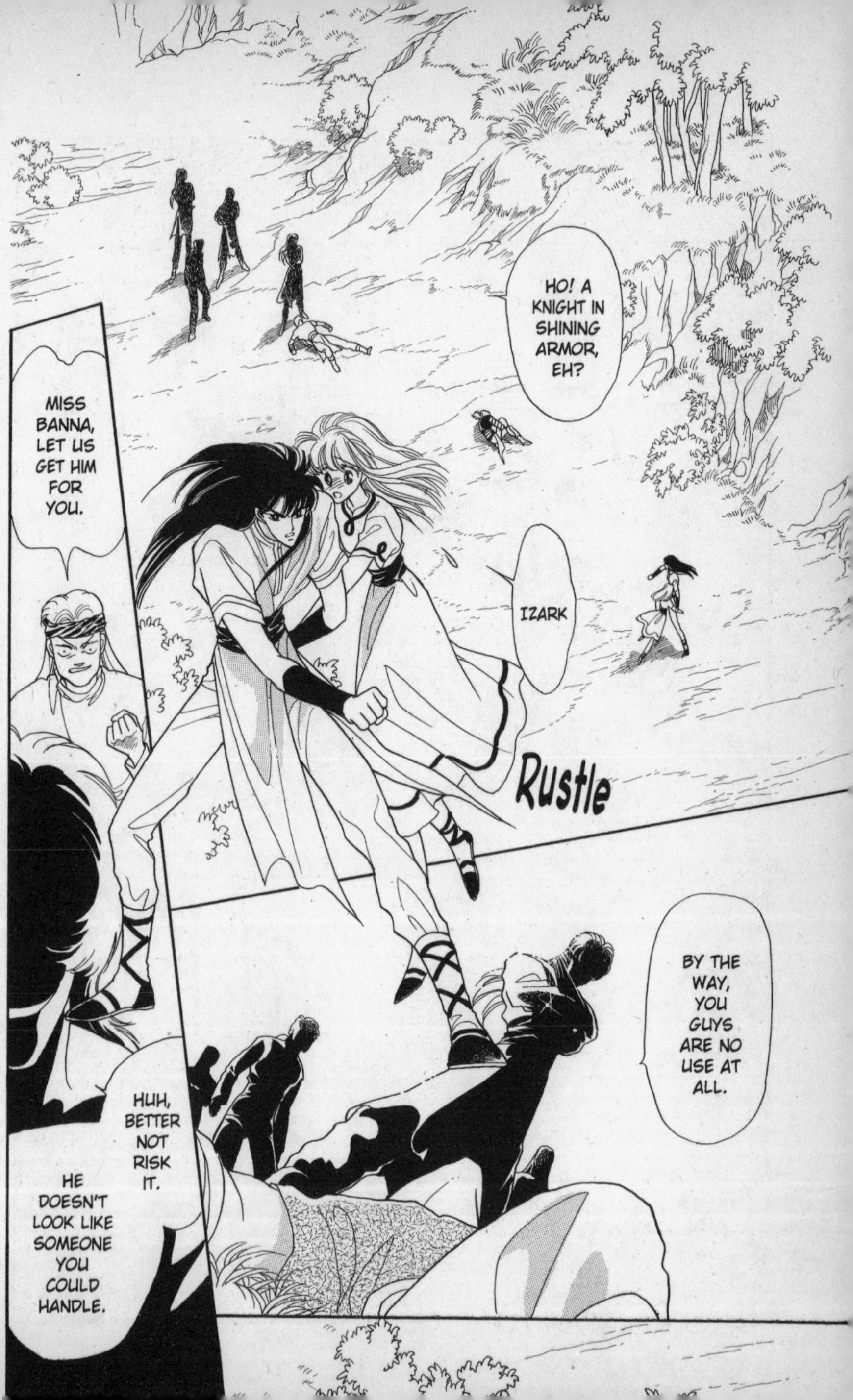
HO! A KNIGHT IN SHINING ARMOR, EH?
IZARK
Rustle
MISS BANNA, LET US GET HIM FOR YOU.
BY THE WAY, YOU GUYS ARE NO USE AT ALL.
HUH, BETTER NOT RISK IT.
HE DOESN'T LOOK LIKE SOMEONE YOU COULD HANDLE.

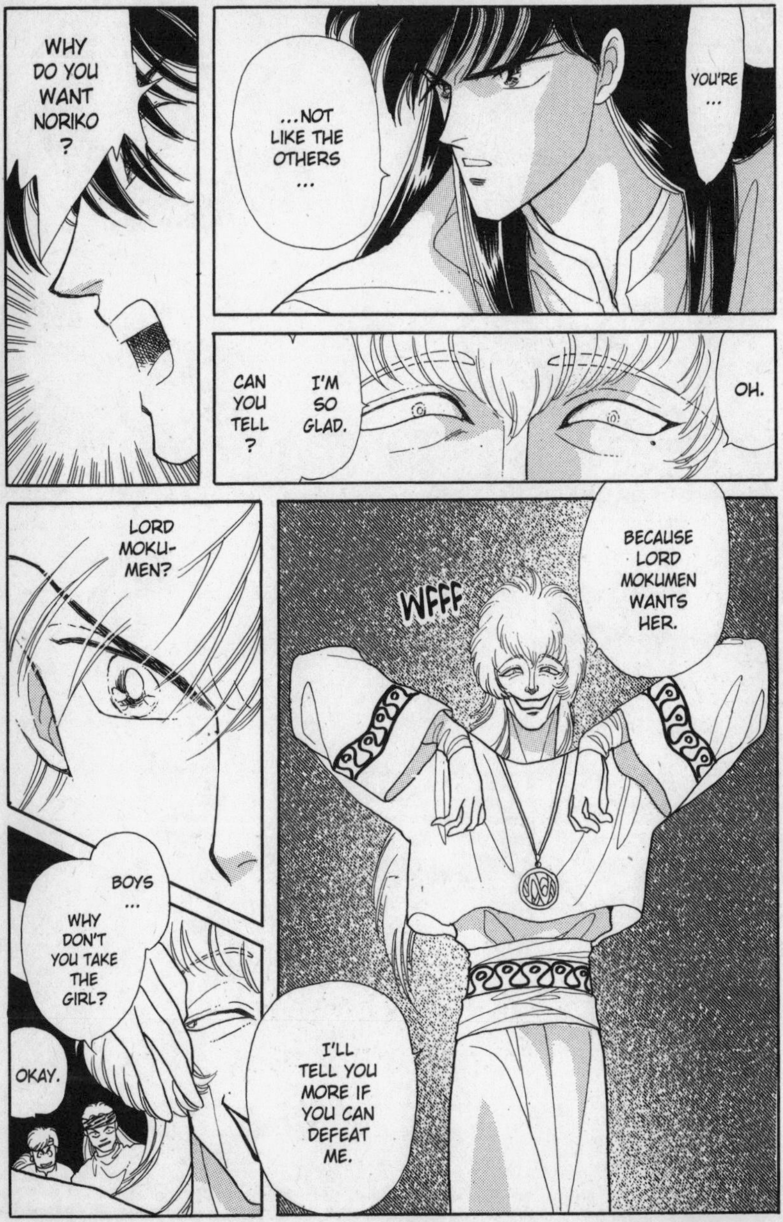
YOU'RE ...
...NOT LIKE THE OTHERS ...
OH.
I'M SO GLAD.
CAN YOU TELL ?
WHY DO YOU WANT NORIKO ?
BECAUSE LORD MOKUMEN WANTS HER.
WFFF
I'LL TELL YOU MORE IF YOU CAN DEFEAT ME.
LORD MOKU-MEN?
BOYS ...
WHY DON'T YOU TAKE THE GIRL?
OKAY.

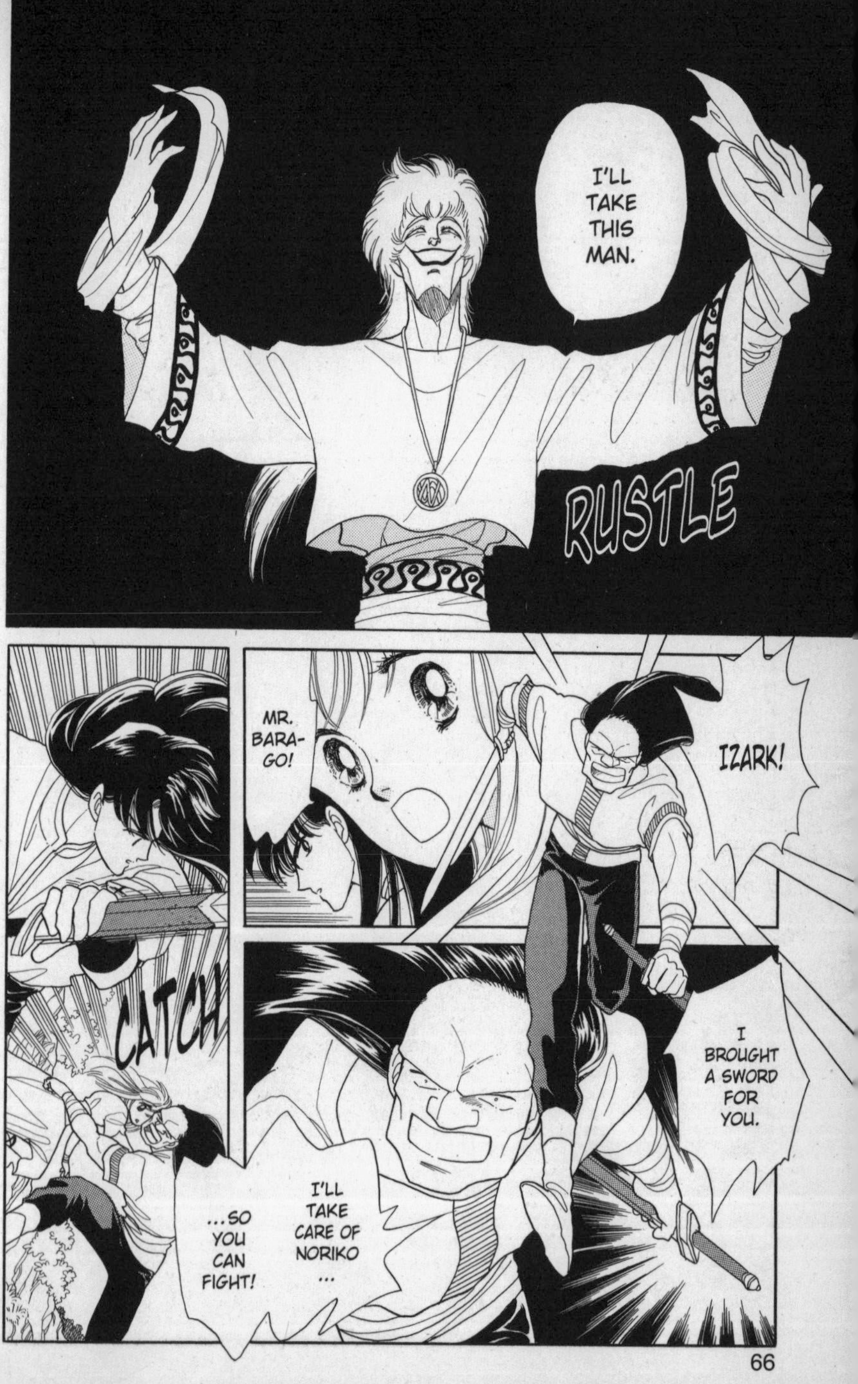
I'LL TAKE THIS MAN.
RUSTLE
IZARK!
MR. BARAGO!
CATCH
I BROUGHT A SWORD FOR YOU.
I'LL TAKE CARE OF NORIKO ...
...SO YOU CAN FIGHT!

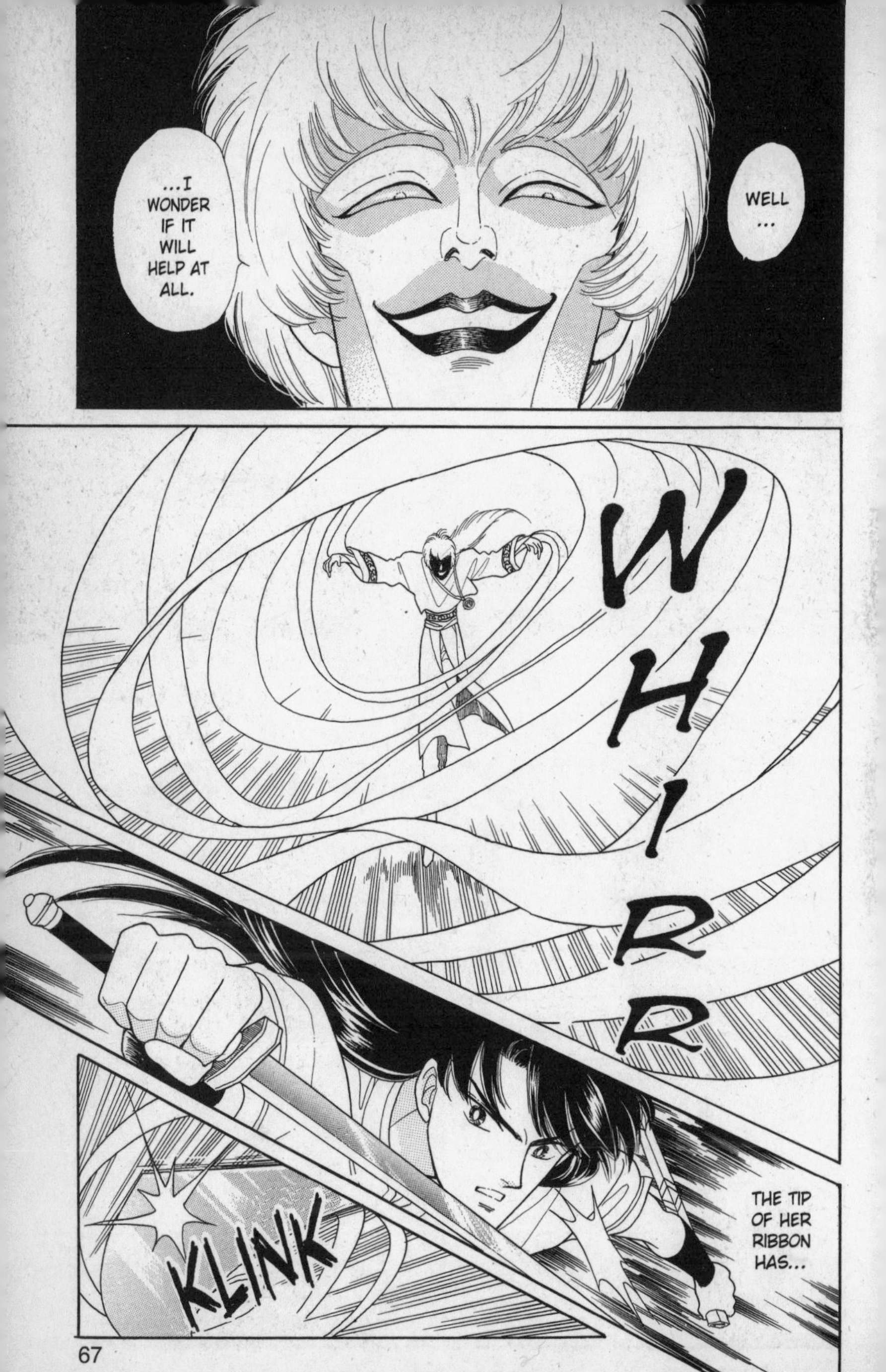
WELL ...
...I WONDER IF IT WILL HELP AT ALL.
WHIRRR
THE TIP OF HER RIBBON HAS...
KLINK

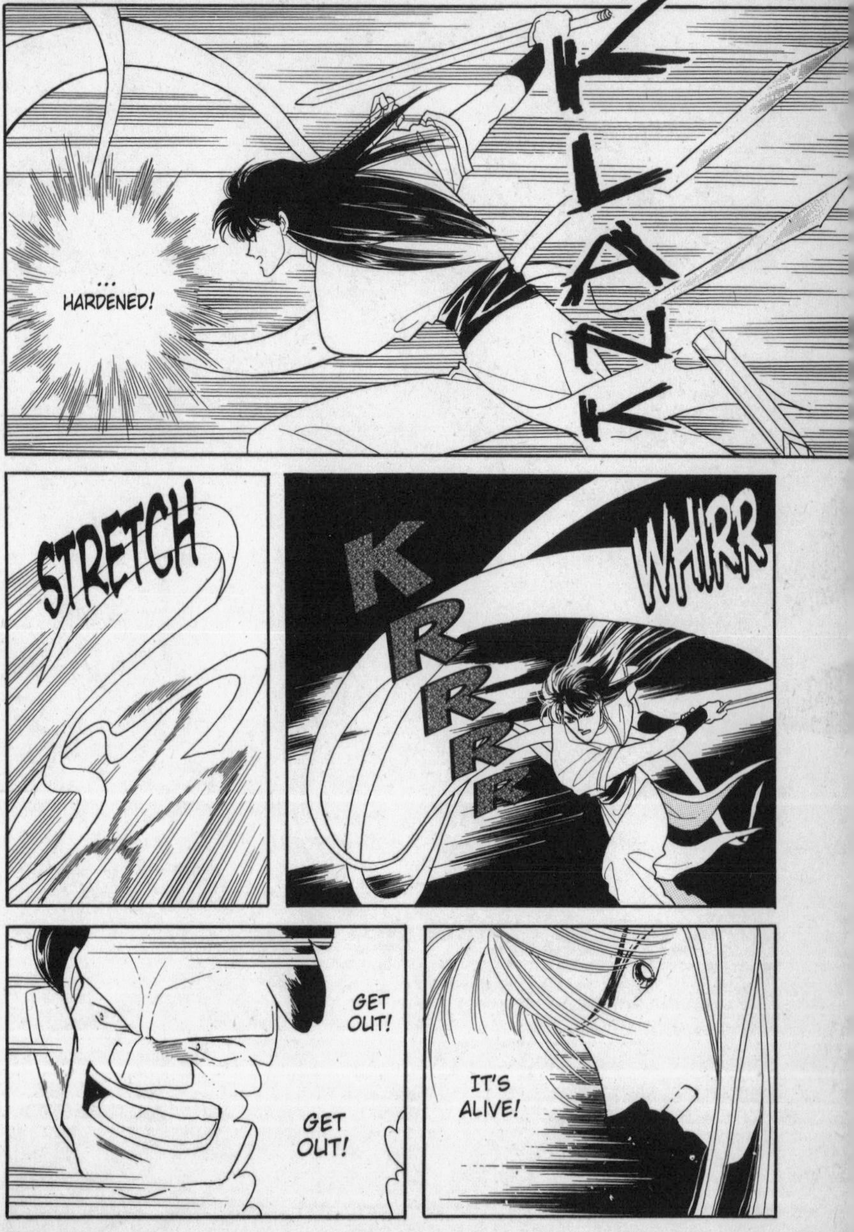
KLANK
... HARDENED!
WHIRR
KRRRR
STRETCH
IT'S ALIVE!
GET OUT!
GET OUT!

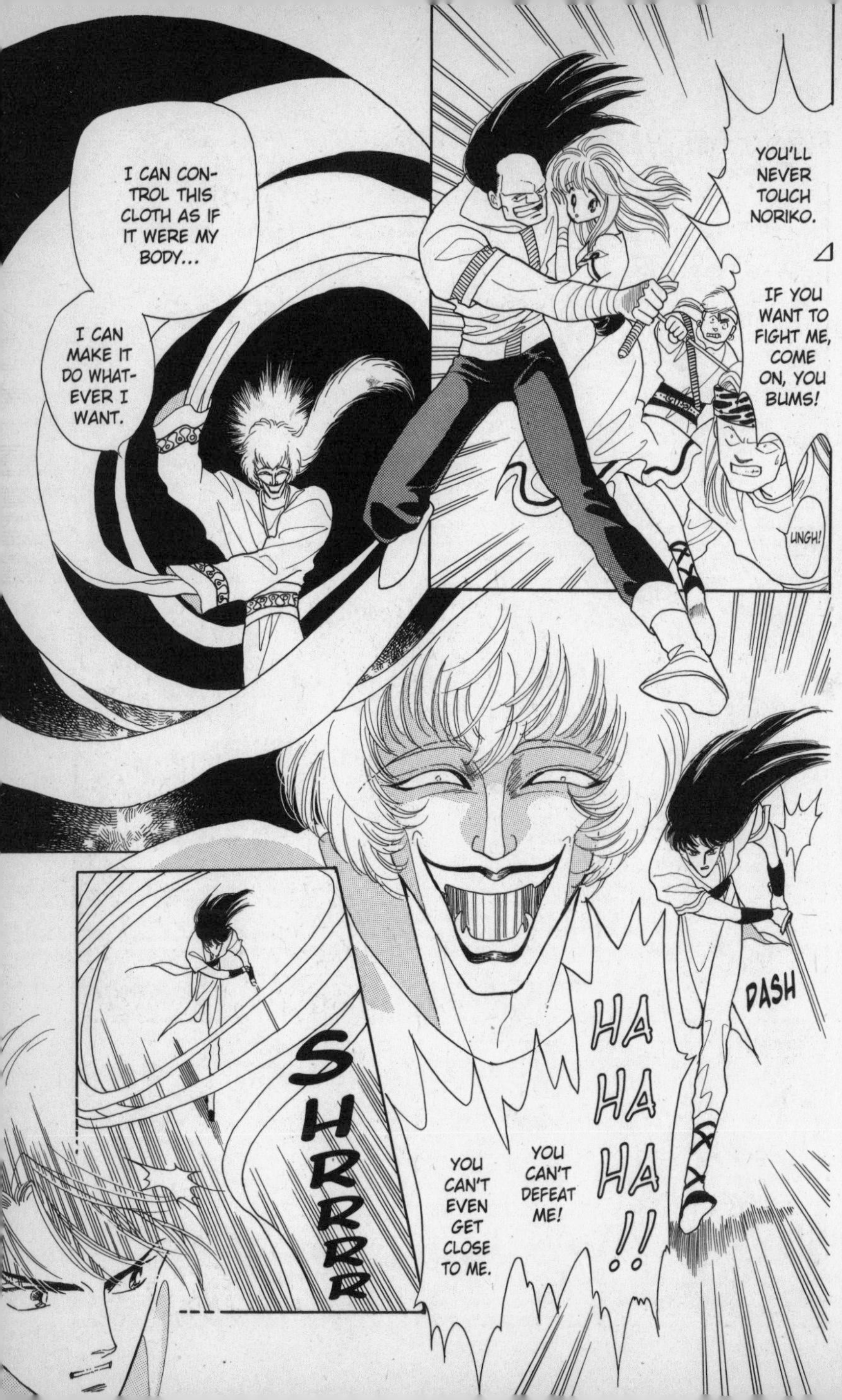
YOU'LL NEVER TOUCH NORIKO.
IF YOU WANT TO FIGHT ME, COME ON, YOU BUMS!
UNGH!
I CAN CONTROL THIS CLOTH AS IF IT WERE MY BODY...
I CAN MAKE IT DO WHATEVER I WANT.
DASH
HA HA HA HA!!
YOU CAN'T DEFEAT ME!
YOU CAN'T EVEN GET CLOSE TO ME.
SHRRRR

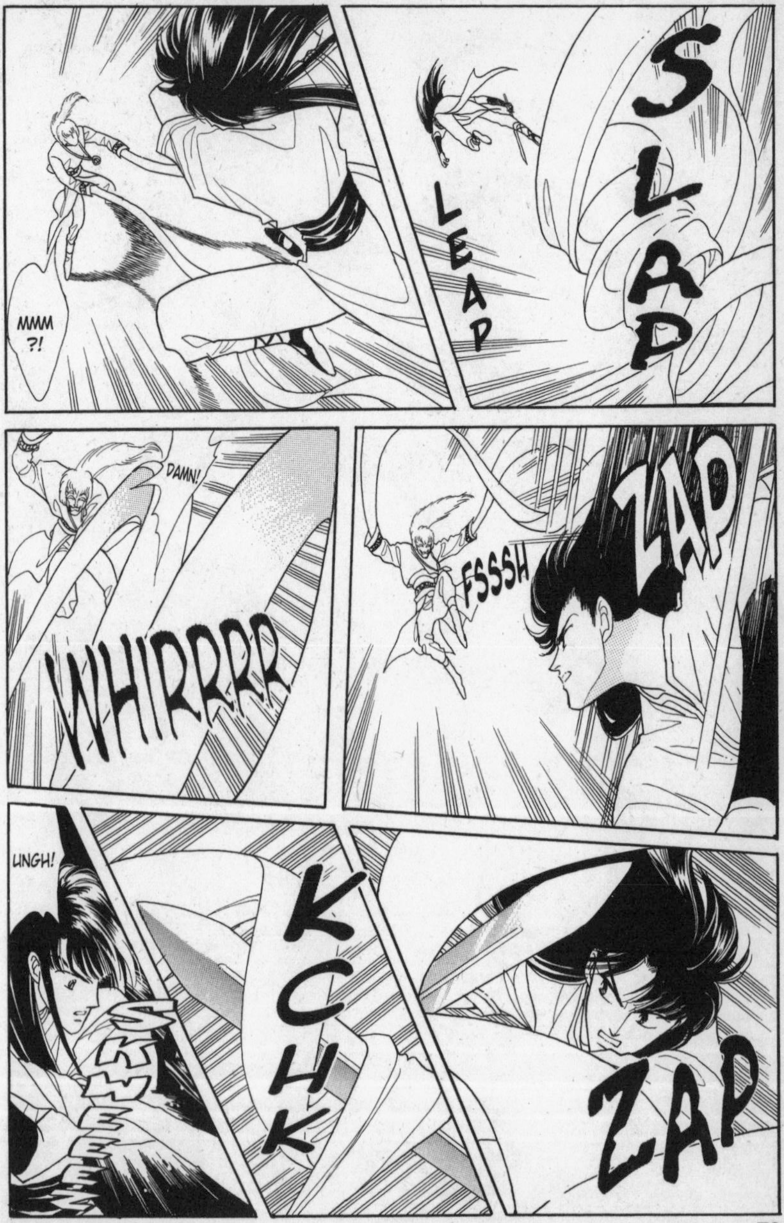
SLAP
LEAP
MMM ?!
ZAP
FSSSH
DAMN!
WHIRRRR
ZAP
KCHK
UNGH!
SKWEEEZ

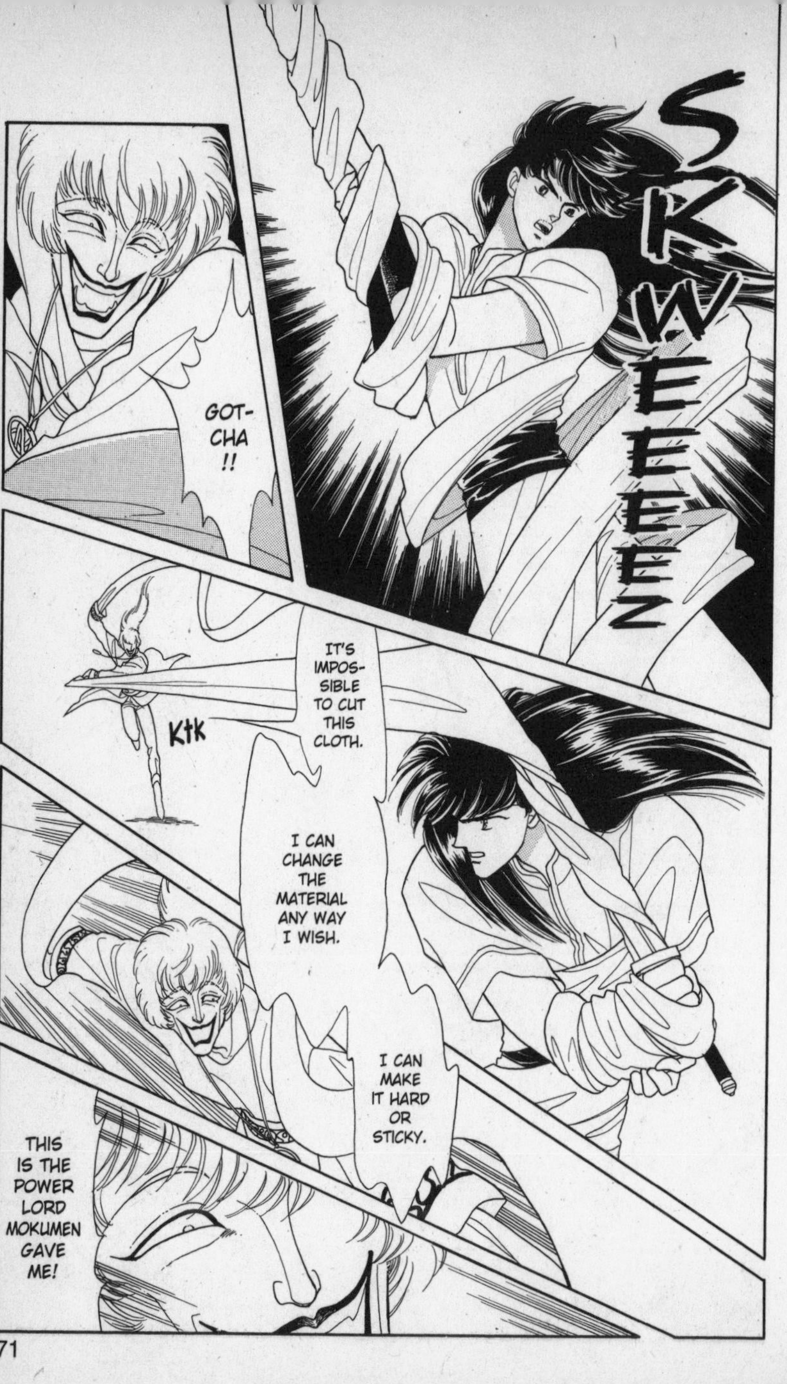
SKWEEEEZ
GOT-CHA!!
Ktk
IT'S IMPOS-SIBLE TO CUT THIS CLOTH.
I CAN CHANGE THE MATERIAL ANY WAY I WISH.
I CAN MAKE IT HARD OR STICKY.
THIS IS THE POWER LORD MOKUMEN GAVE ME!

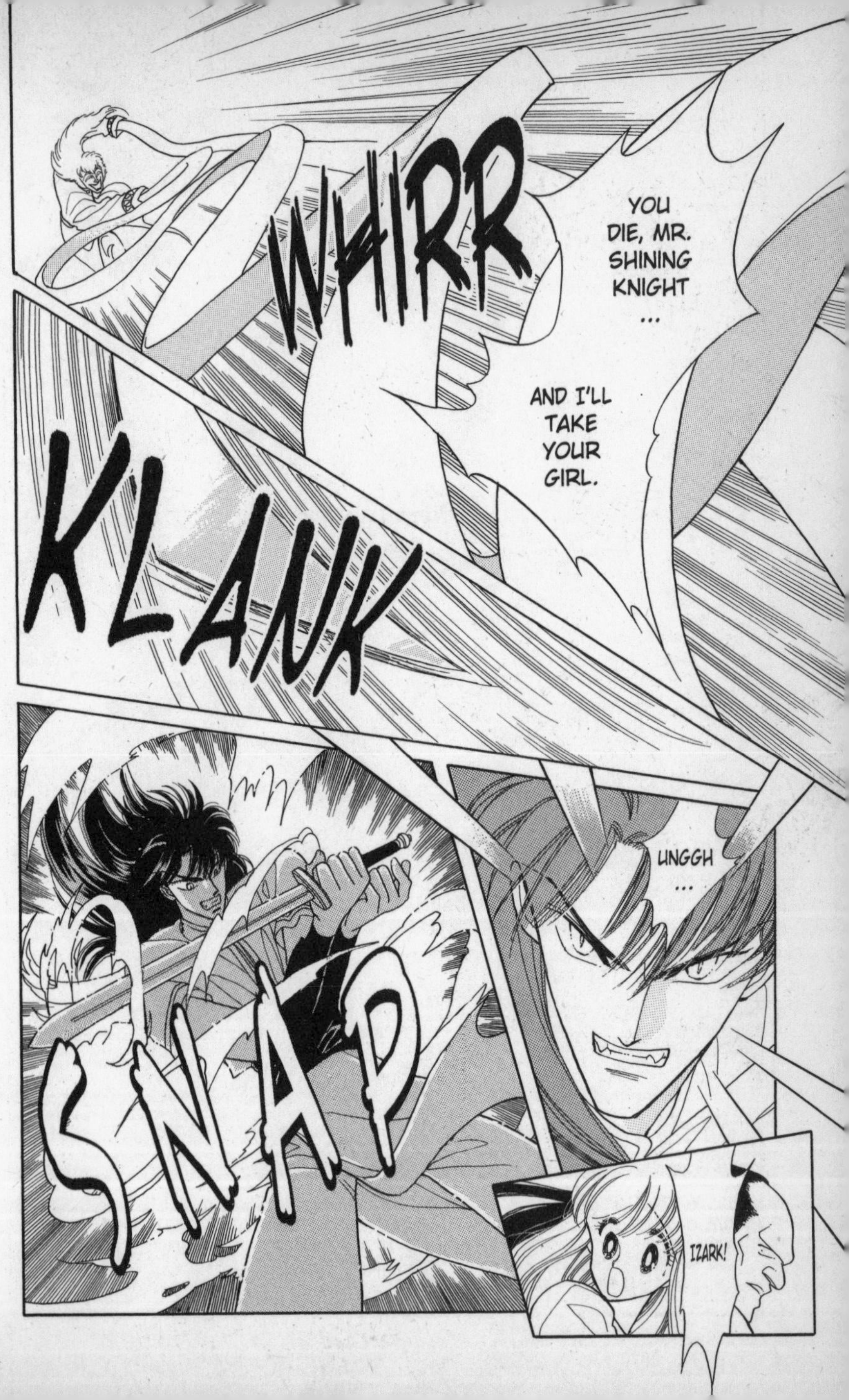

YOU DIE, MR. SHINING KNIGHT ...
AND I'LL TAKE YOUR GIRL.
WHIRR
KLANK
UNGGH ...
IZARK!
SNAP

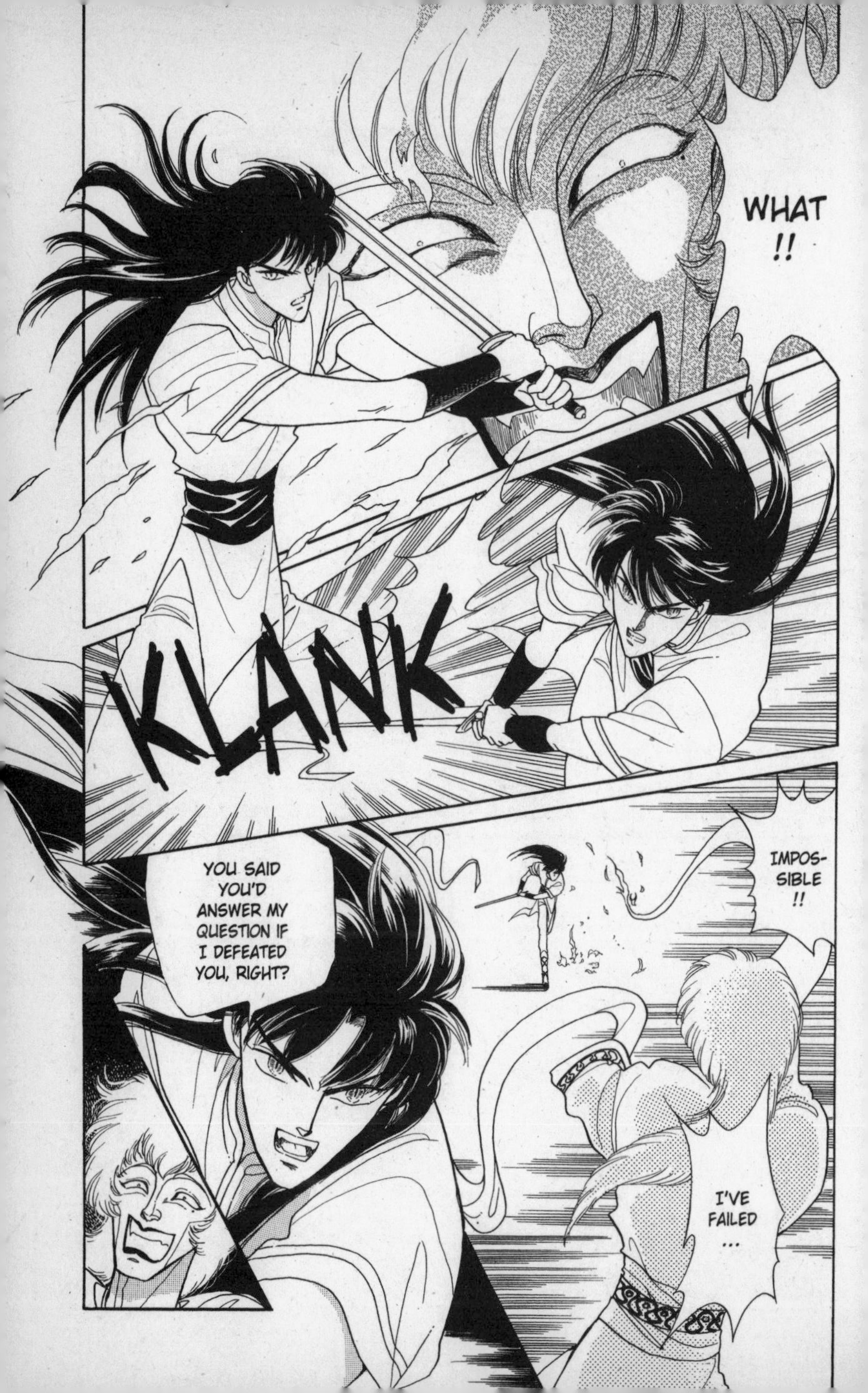
WHAT !!
KLANK
IMPOSSIBLE !!
YOU SAID YOU'D ANSWER MY QUESTION IF I DEFEATED YOU, RIGHT?
I'VE FAILED ...

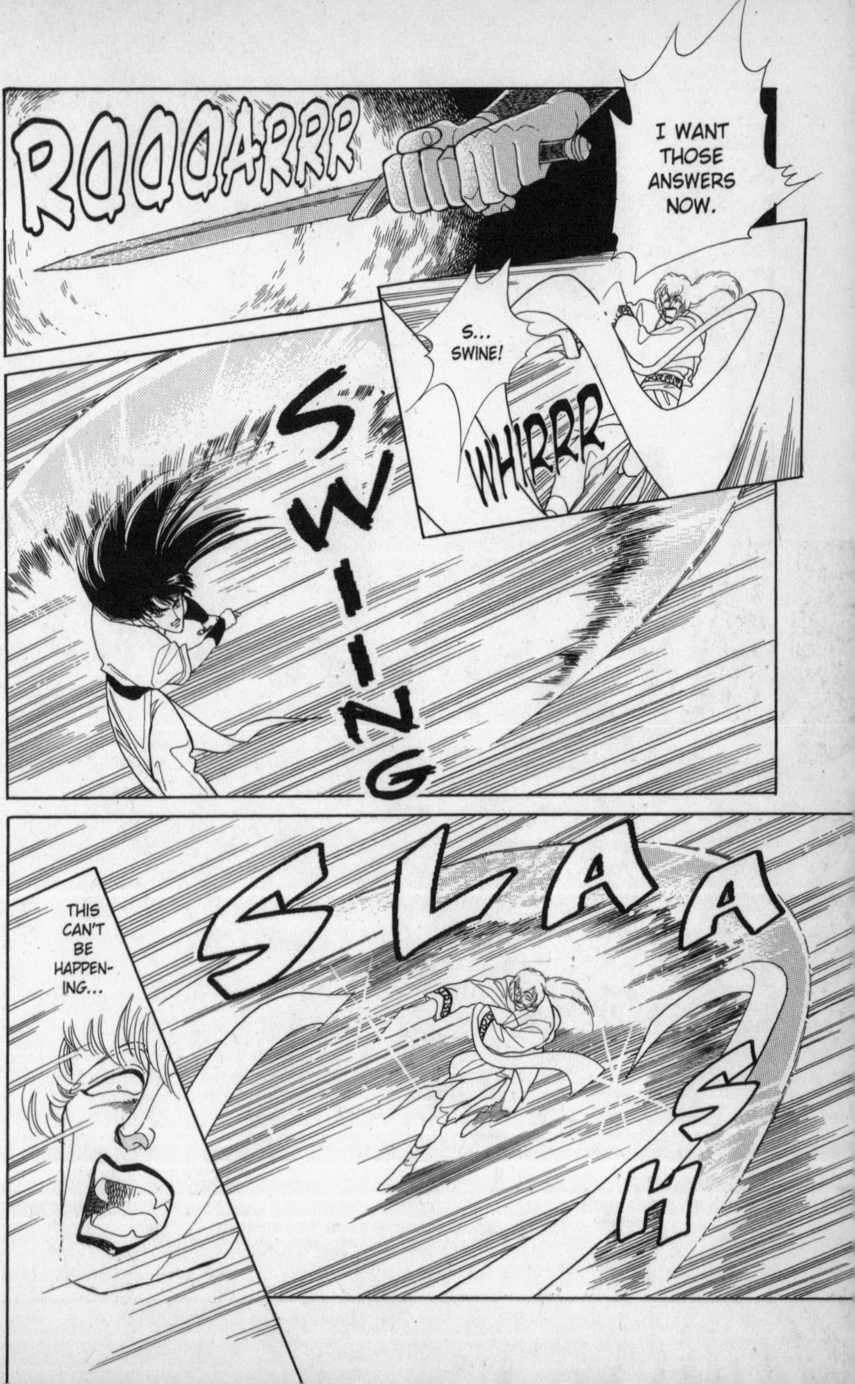
I WANT THOSE ANSWERS NOW.
ROOOARRR
S... SWINE!
WHIRRR
SWING
SLAASH
THIS CAN'T BE HAPPEN-ING...

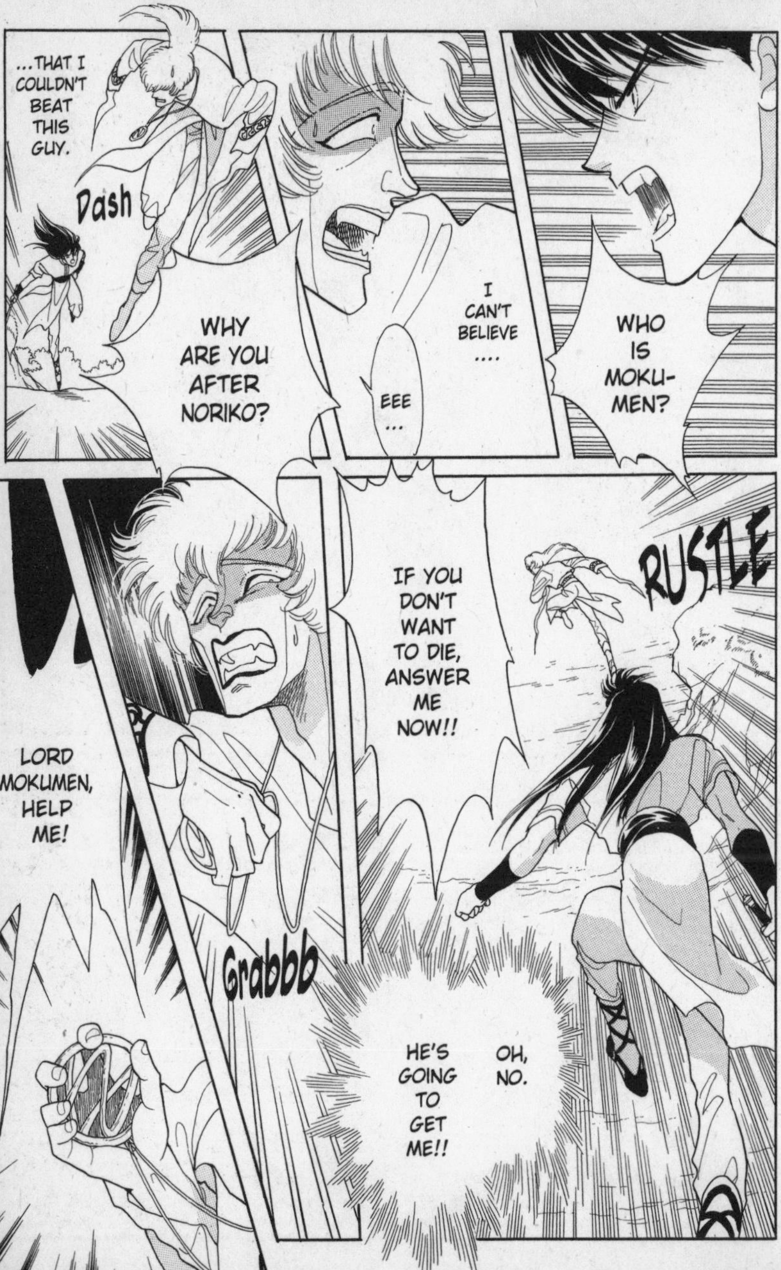
WHO IS MOKU-MEN?
I CAN'T BELIEVE ....
EEE ...
...THAT I COULDN'T BEAT THIS GUY.
Dash
WHY ARE YOU AFTER NORIKO?
RUSTLE
IF YOU DON'T WANT TO DIE, ANSWER ME NOW!!
OH, NO.
HE'S GOING TO GET ME!!
LORD MOKUMEN, HELP ME!
Grabbb

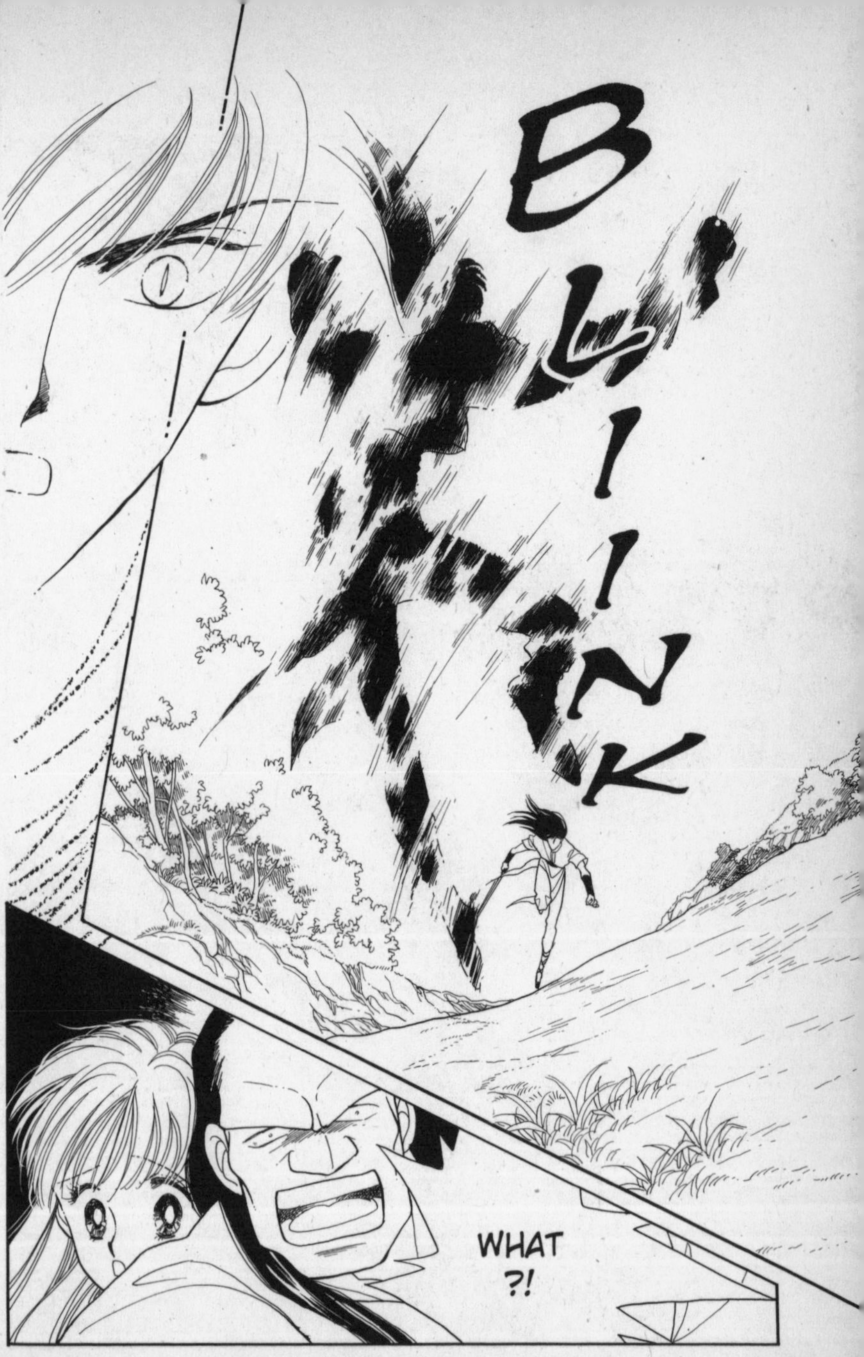
BLIIINK
WHAT?!

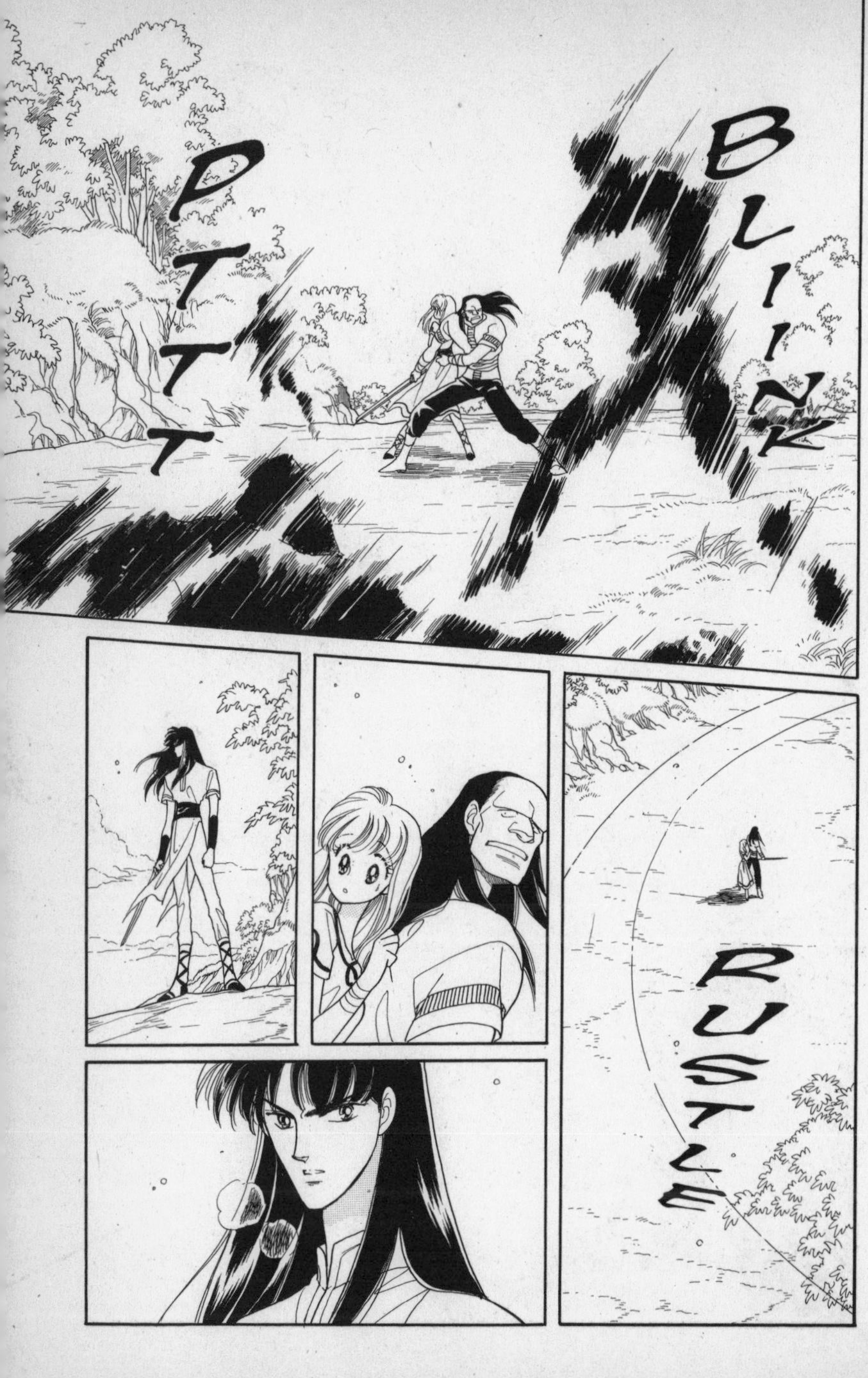
BLINK
PTTT
RUSTLE

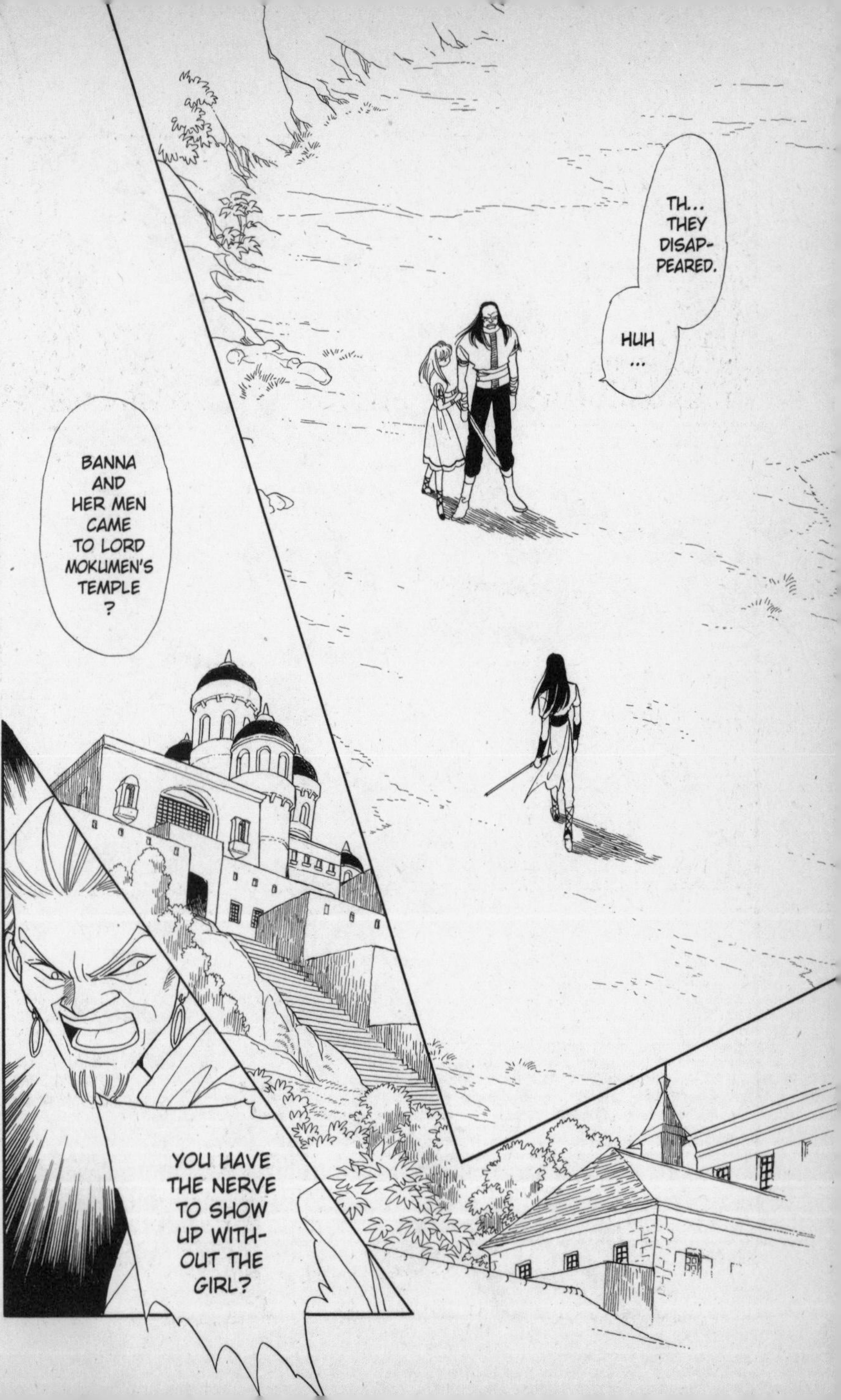
TH... THEY DISAP-PEARED.
HUH ...
BANNA AND HER MEN CAME TO LORD MOKUMEN'S TEMPLE ?
YOU HAVE THE NERVE TO SHOW UP WITH-OUT THE GIRL?

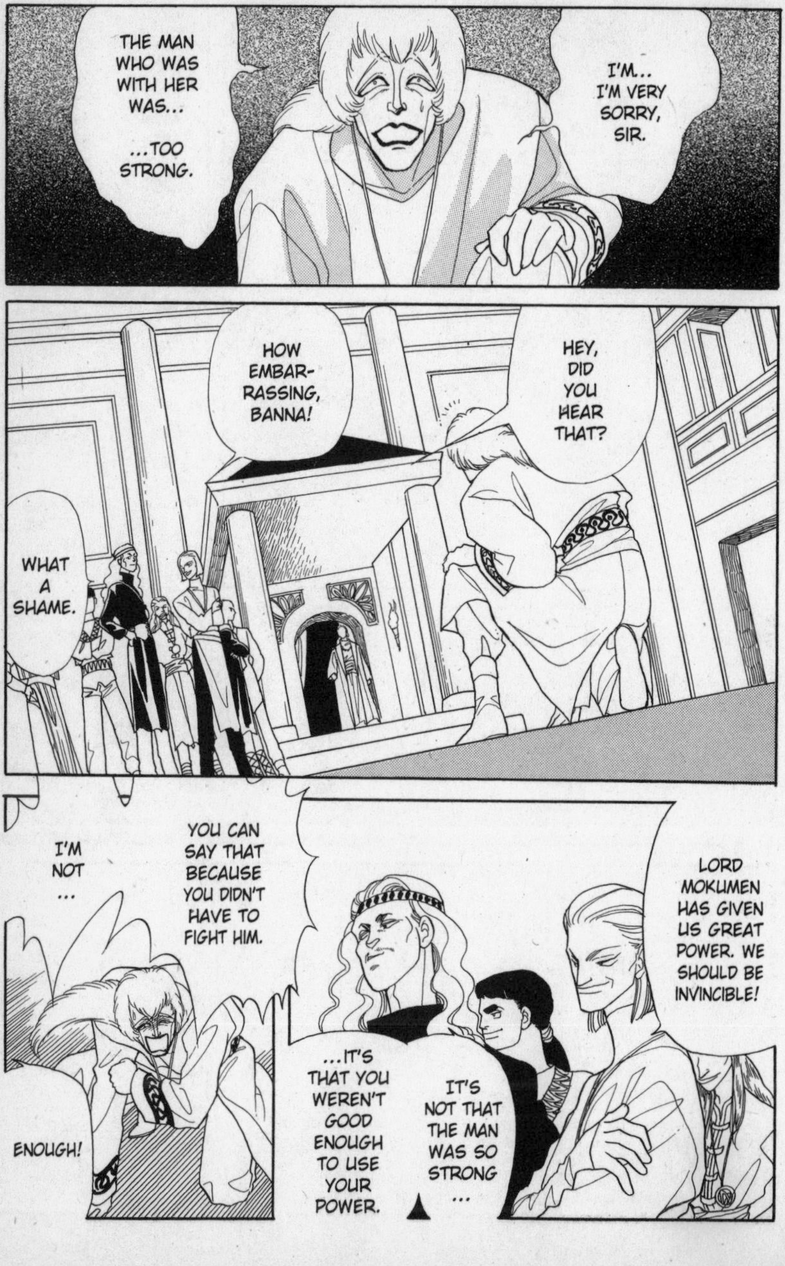
I'M... I'M VERY SORRY, SIR.
THE MAN WHO WAS WITH HER WAS... ...TOO STRONG.
HEY, DID YOU HEAR THAT?
HOW EMBAR-RASSING, BANNA!
WHAT A SHAME.
LORD MOKUMEN HAS GIVEN US GREAT POWER. WE SHOULD BE INVINCIBLE!
IT'S NOT THAT THE MAN WAS SO STRONG...
...IT'S THAT YOU WEREN'T GOOD ENOUGH TO USE YOUR POWER.
YOU CAN SAY THAT BECAUSE YOU DIDN'T HAVE TO FIGHT HIM.
I'M NOT...
ENOUGH!

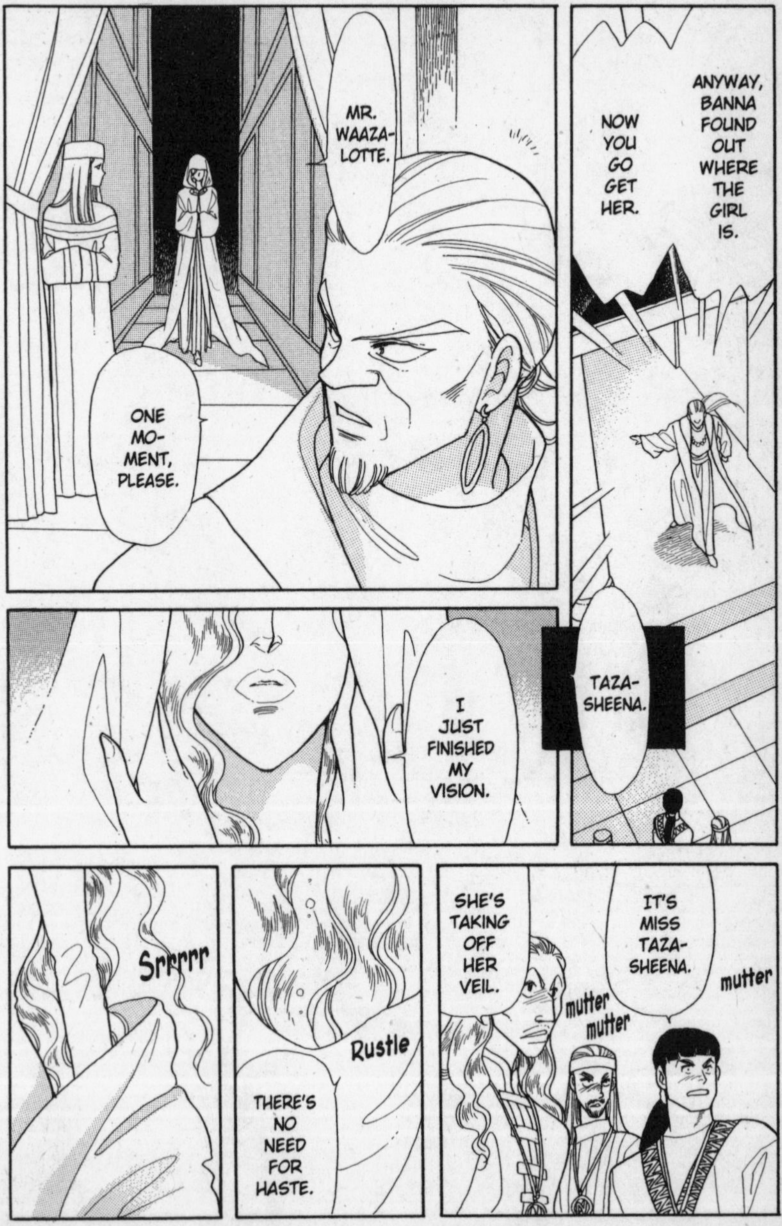
ANYWAY, BANNA FOUND OUT WHERE THE GIRL IS.
NOW YOU GO GET HER.
TAZA-SHEENA.
MR. WAAZA-LOTTE.
ONE MO-MENT, PLEASE.
I JUST FINISHED MY VISION.
IT'S MISS TAZA-SHEENA.
mutter
SHE'S TAKING OFF HER VEIL.
mutter mutter
Rustle
THERE'S NO NEED FOR HASTE.
Srrrrr

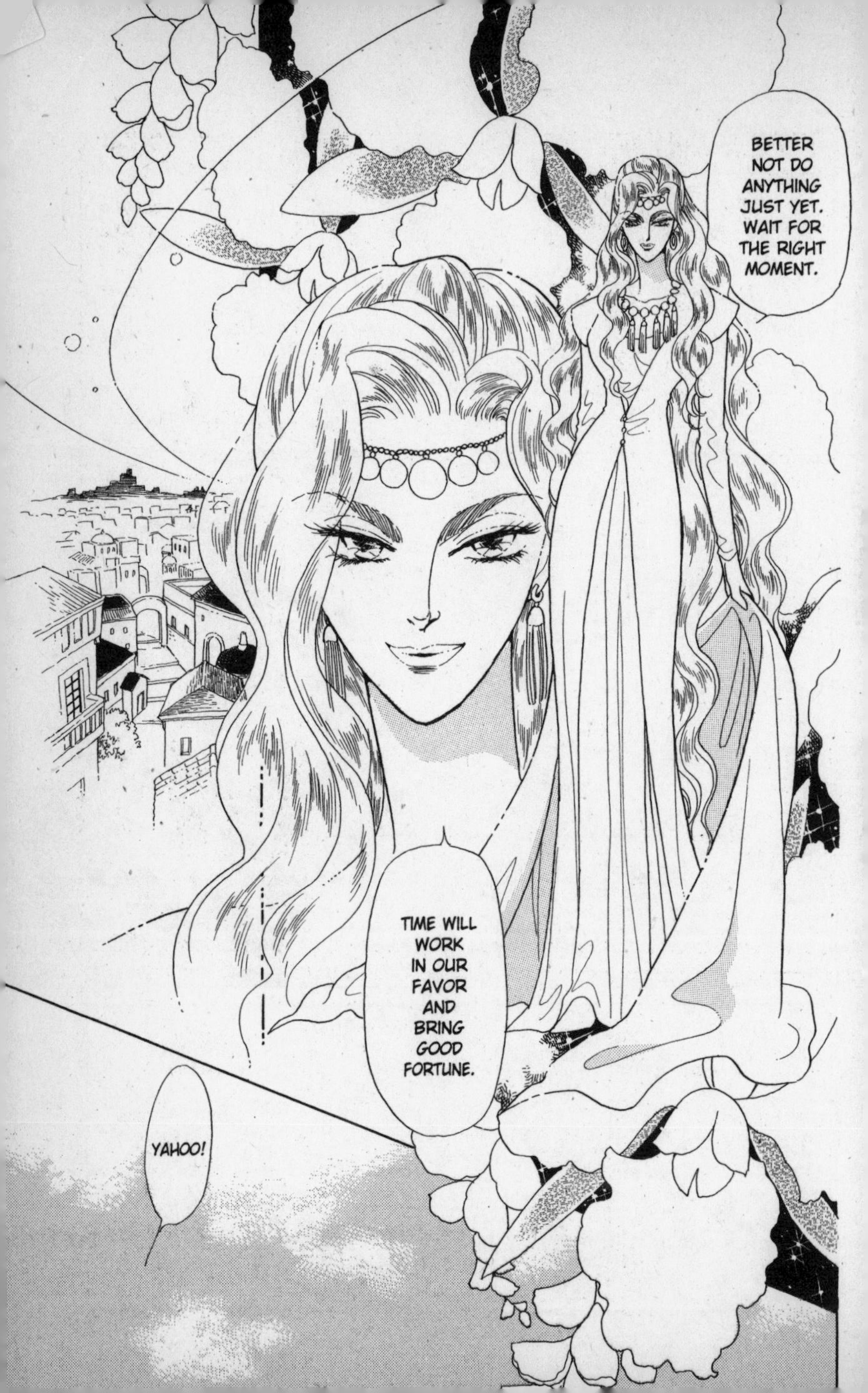
BETTER NOT DO ANYTHING JUST YET. WAIT FOR THE RIGHT MOMENT.
TIME WILL WORK IN OUR FAVOR AND BRING GOOD FORTUNE.
YAHOO!

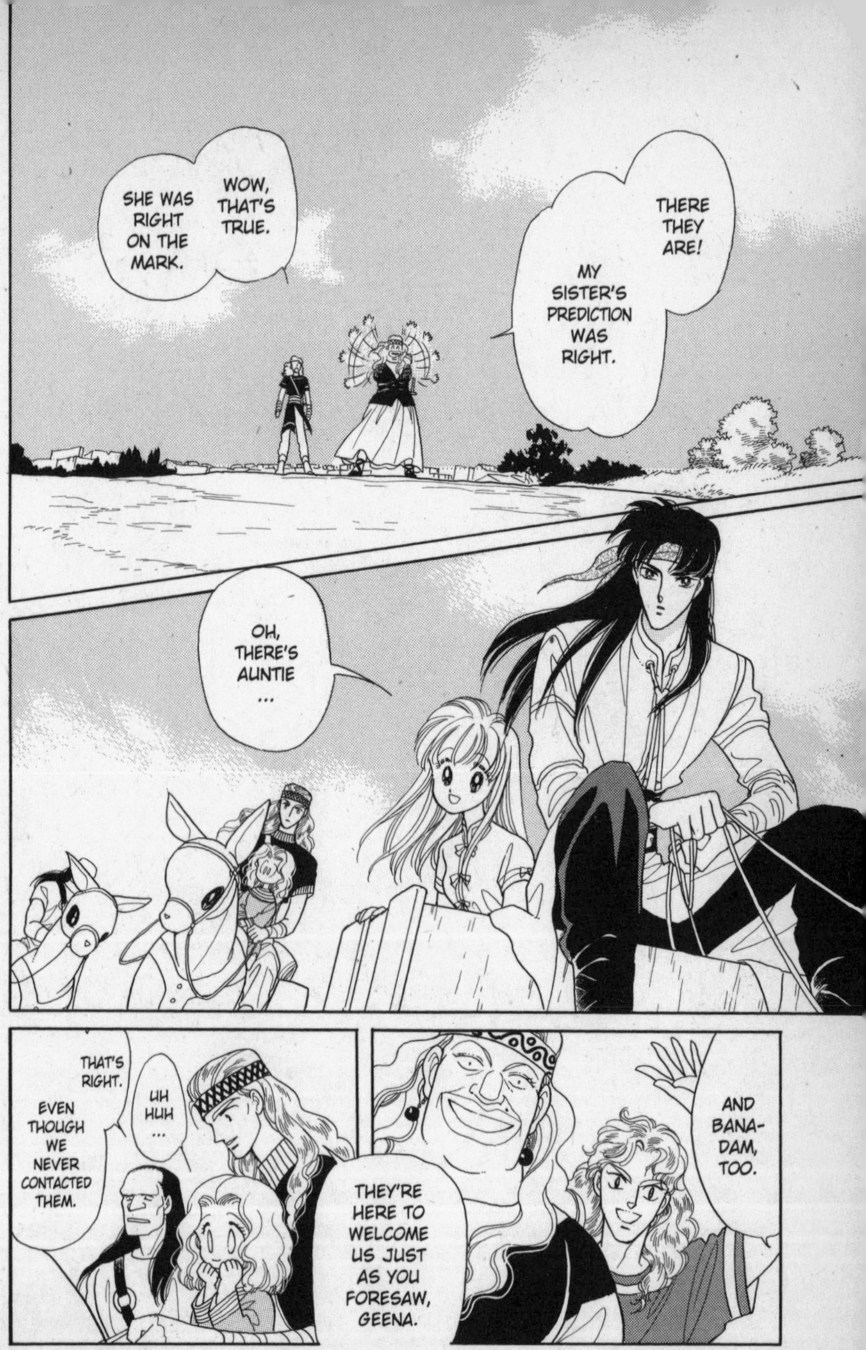
THERE THEY ARE!
MY SISTER'S PREDICTION WAS RIGHT.
WOW, THAT'S TRUE.
SHE WAS RIGHT ON THE MARK.
OH, THERE'S AUNTIE ...
AND BANA-DAM, TOO.
THEY'RE HERE TO WELCOME US JUST AS YOU FORESAW, GEENA.
UH HUH ...
THAT'S RIGHT.
EVEN THOUGH WE NEVER CONTACTED THEM.

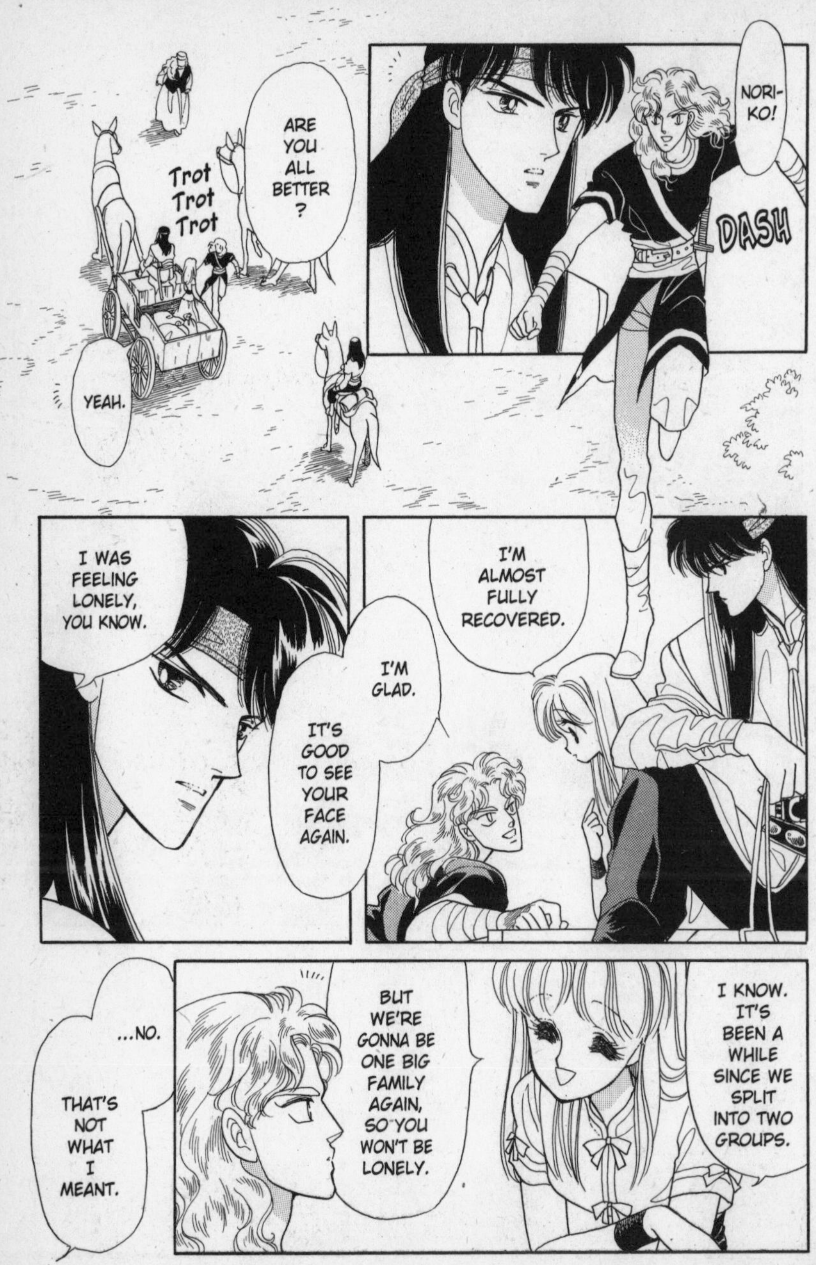
NORI-KO!
DASH
ARE YOU ALL BETTER?
Trot Trot Trot
YEAH.
I'M ALMOST FULLY RECOVERED.
I'M GLAD.
IT'S GOOD TO SEE YOUR FACE AGAIN.
I WAS FEELING LONELY, YOU KNOW.
I KNOW. IT'S BEEN A WHILE SINCE WE SPLIT INTO TWO GROUPS.
BUT WE'RE GONNA BE ONE BIG FAMILY AGAIN, SO YOU WON'T BE LONELY.
...NO.
THAT'S NOT WHAT I MEANT.

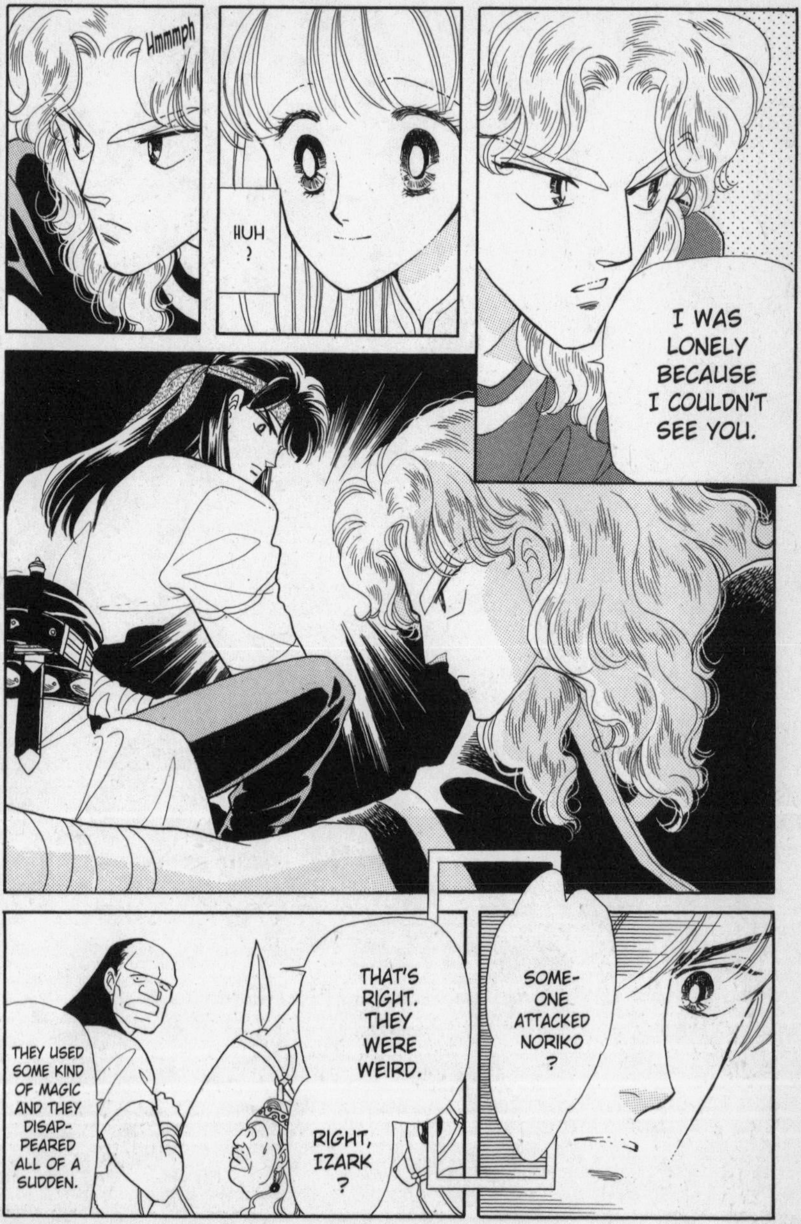
I WAS LONELY BECAUSE I COULDN'T SEE YOU.
HUH ?
Hmmmph
SOME-ONE ATTACKED NORIKO ?
THAT'S RIGHT. THEY WERE WEIRD.
THEY USED SOME KIND OF MAGIC AND THEY DISAP-PEARED ALL OF A SUDDEN.
RIGHT, IZARK ?

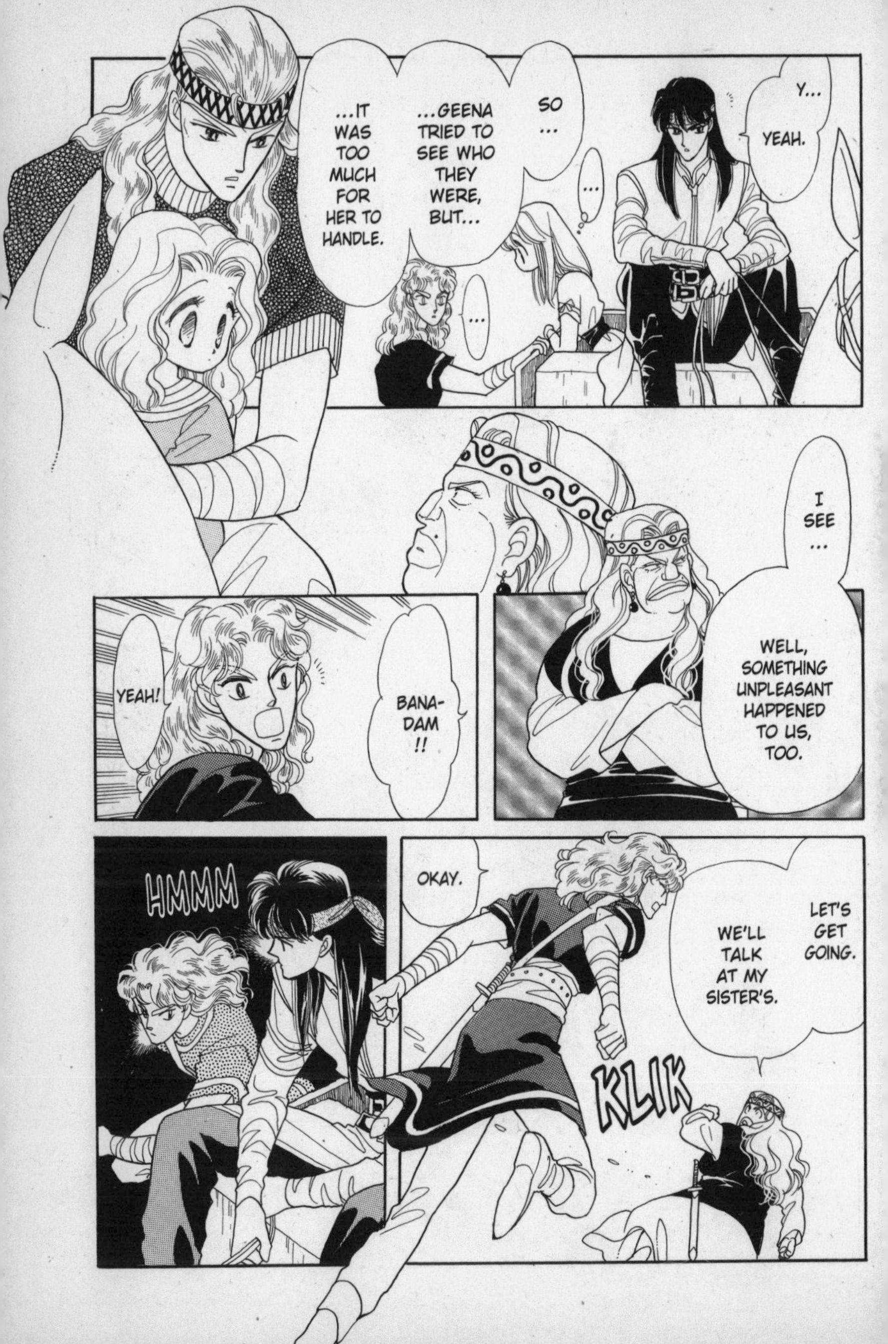
Y...
YEAH.
SO ...
...
...GEENA TRIED TO SEE WHO THEY WERE, BUT...
...IT WAS TOO MUCH FOR HER TO HANDLE.
...
I SEE ...
WELL, SOMETHING UNPLEASANT HAPPENED TO US, TOO.
BANA-DAM !!
YEAH!
LET'S GET GOING.
WE'LL TALK AT MY SISTER'S.
OKAY.
KLIK
HMMM

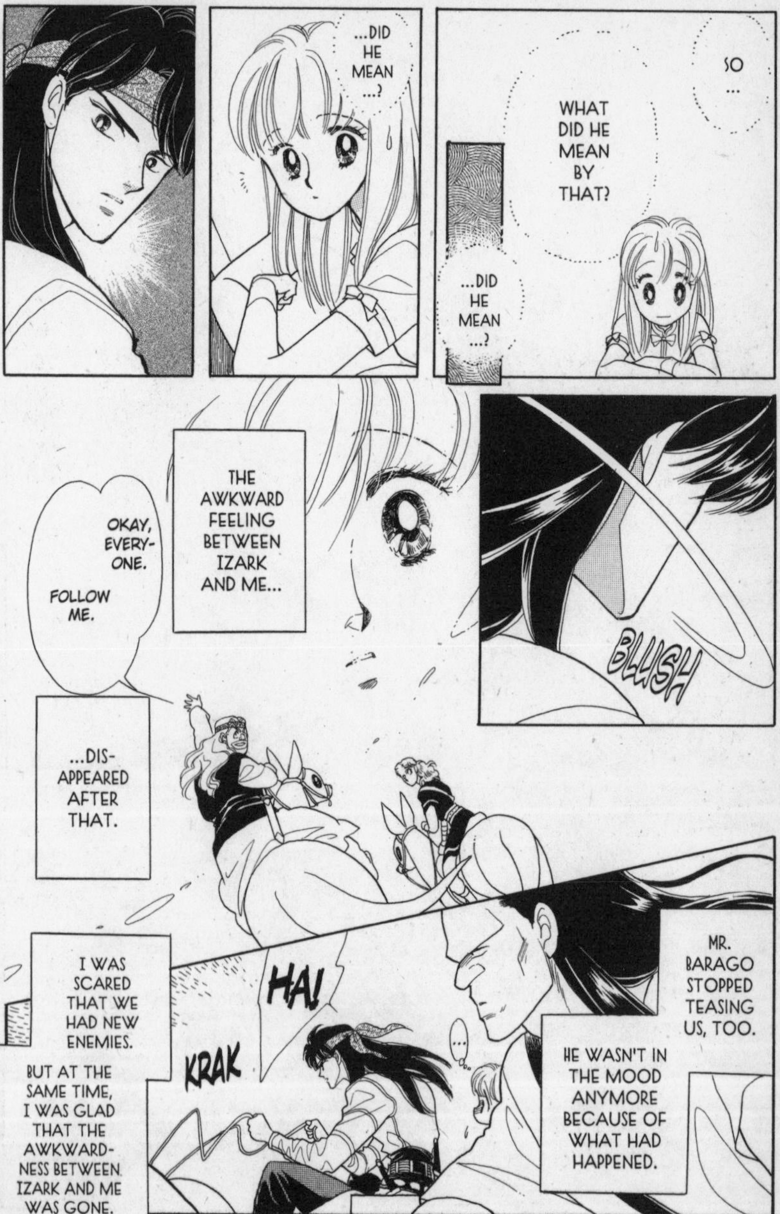
SO ...
WHAT DID HE MEAN BY THAT?
...DID HE MEAN ...?
...DID HE MEAN ...?
BLUSH
THE AWKWARD FEELING BETWEEN IZARK AND ME...
OKAY, EVERYONE.
FOLLOW ME.
...DISAPPEARED AFTER THAT.
MR. BARAGO STOPPED TEASING US, TOO.
HE WASN'T IN THE MOOD ANYMORE BECAUSE OF WHAT HAD HAPPENED.
...
HA!
KRAK
I WAS SCARED THAT WE HAD NEW ENEMIES.
BUT AT THE SAME TIME, I WAS GLAD THAT THE AWKWARDNESS BETWEEN IZARK AND ME WAS GONE.

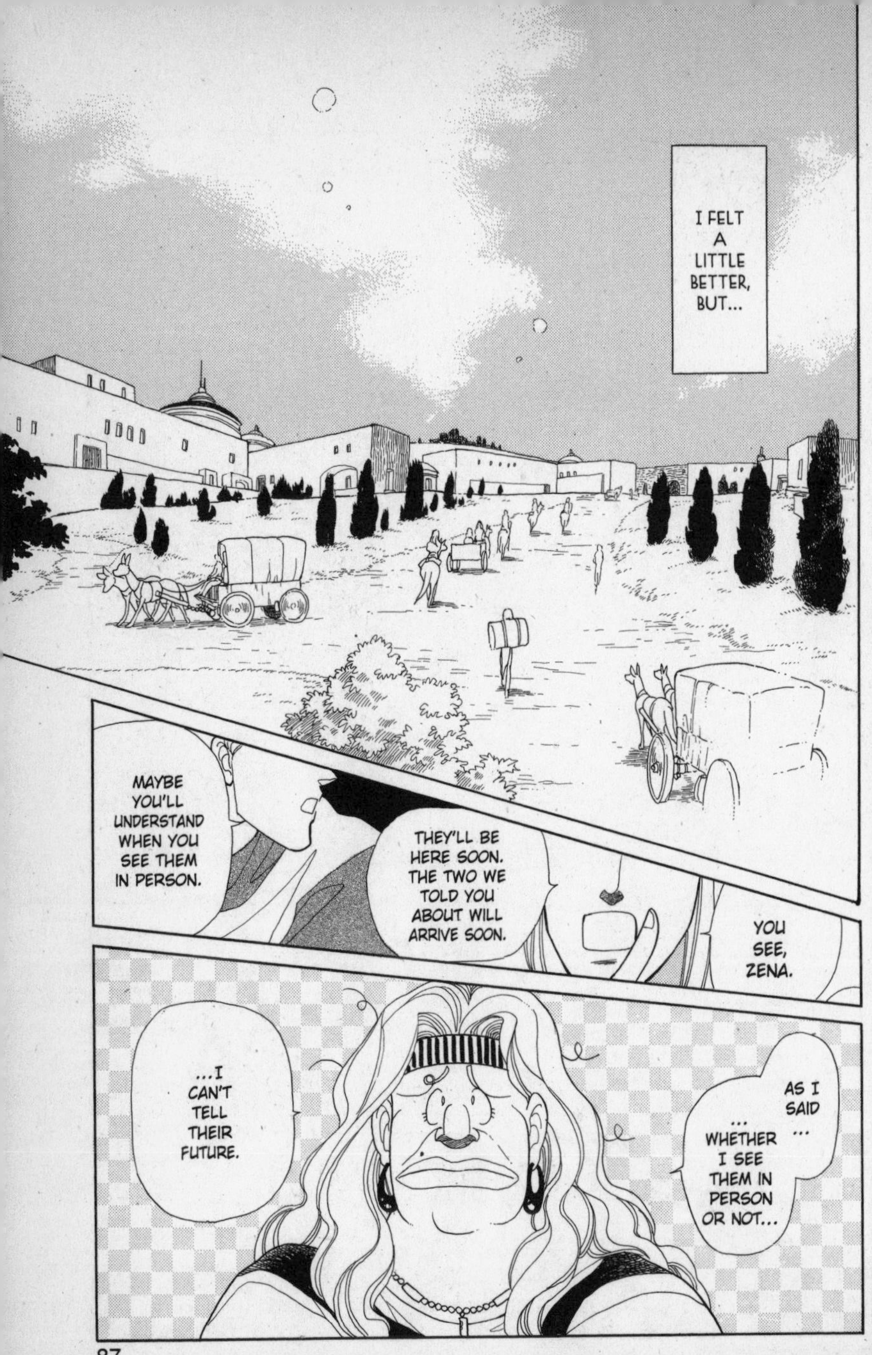
I FELT A LITTLE BETTER, BUT...
YOU SEE, ZENA.
THEY'LL BE HERE SOON. THE TWO WE TOLD YOU ABOUT WILL ARRIVE SOON.
MAYBE YOU'LL UNDERSTAND WHEN YOU SEE THEM IN PERSON.
AS I SAID ... WHETHER I SEE THEM IN PERSON OR NOT...
...I CAN'T TELL THEIR FUTURE.

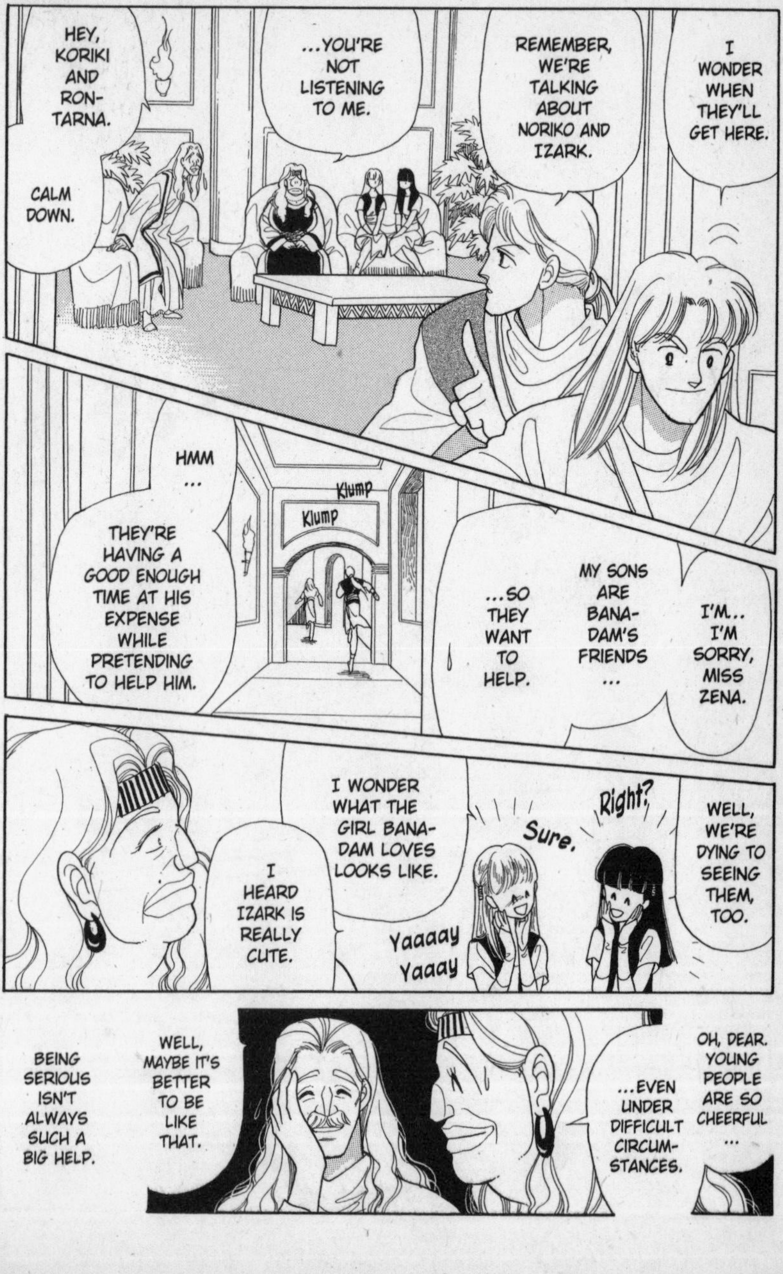
I WONDER WHEN THEY'LL GET HERE.
REMEMBER, WE'RE TALKING ABOUT NORIKO AND IZARK.
...YOU'RE NOT LISTENING TO ME.
HEY, KORIKI AND RON-TARNA.
CALM DOWN.
I'M... I'M SORRY, MISS ZENA.
MY SONS ARE BANA-DAM'S FRIENDS...
...SO THEY WANT TO HELP.
Klump
Klump
HMM...
THEY'RE HAVING A GOOD ENOUGH TIME AT HIS EXPENSE WHILE PRETENDING TO HELP HIM.
WELL, WE'RE DYING TO SEEING THEM, TOO.
Right?
Sure.
I WONDER WHAT THE GIRL BANA-DAM LOVES LOOKS LIKE.
I HEARD IZARK IS REALLY CUTE.
Yaaaay Yaaay
OH, DEAR. YOUNG PEOPLE ARE SO CHEERFUL...
...EVEN UNDER DIFFICULT CIRCUM-STANCES.
WELL, MAYBE IT'S BETTER TO BE LIKE THAT.
BEING SERIOUS ISN'T ALWAYS SUCH A BIG HELP.

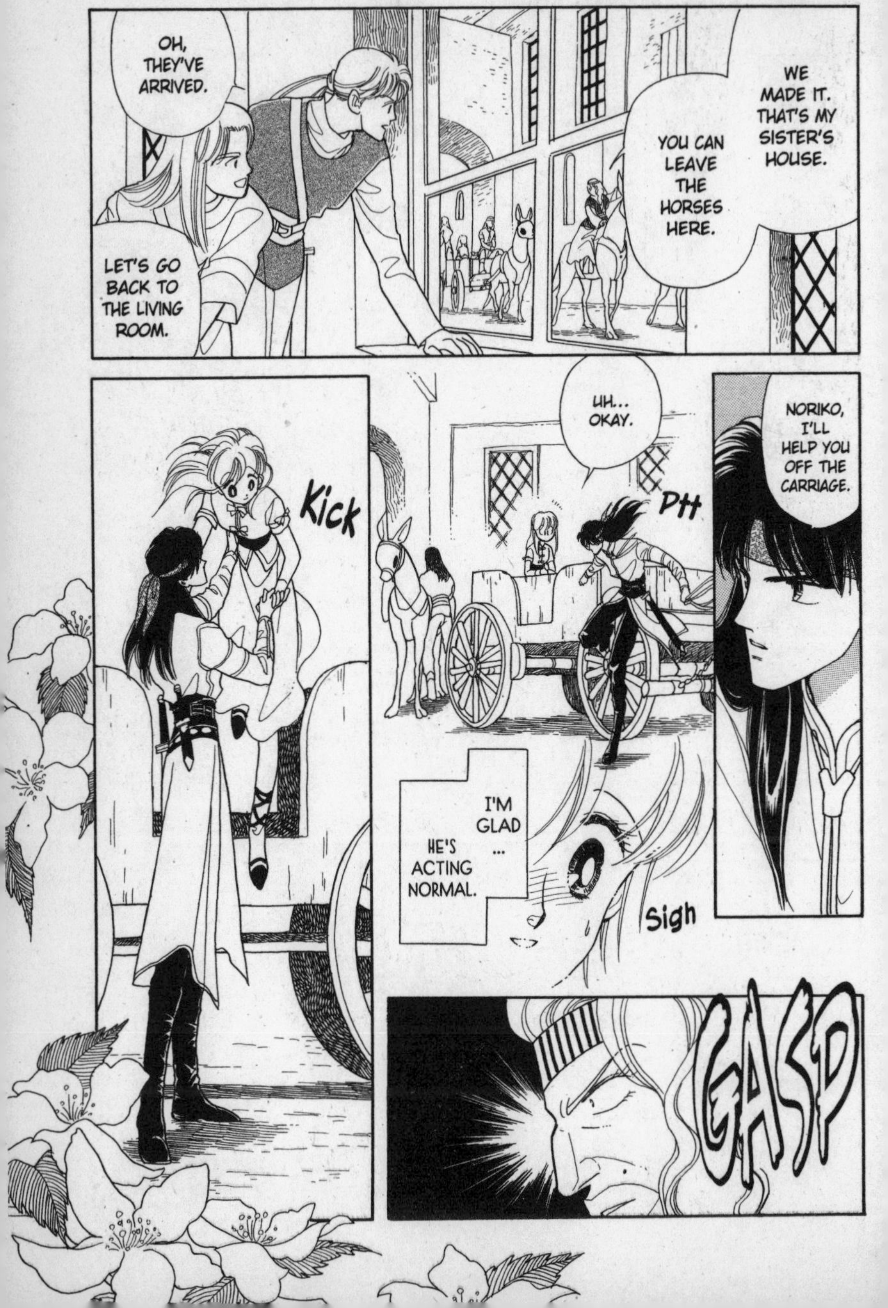
WE MADE IT. THAT'S MY SISTER'S HOUSE.
YOU CAN LEAVE THE HORSES HERE.
OH, THEY'VE ARRIVED.
LET'S GO BACK TO THE LIVING ROOM.
NORIKO, I'LL HELP YOU OFF THE CARRIAGE.
UH... OKAY.
Ptt
I'M GLAD ... HE'S ACTING NORMAL.
Sigh
GASP
Kick

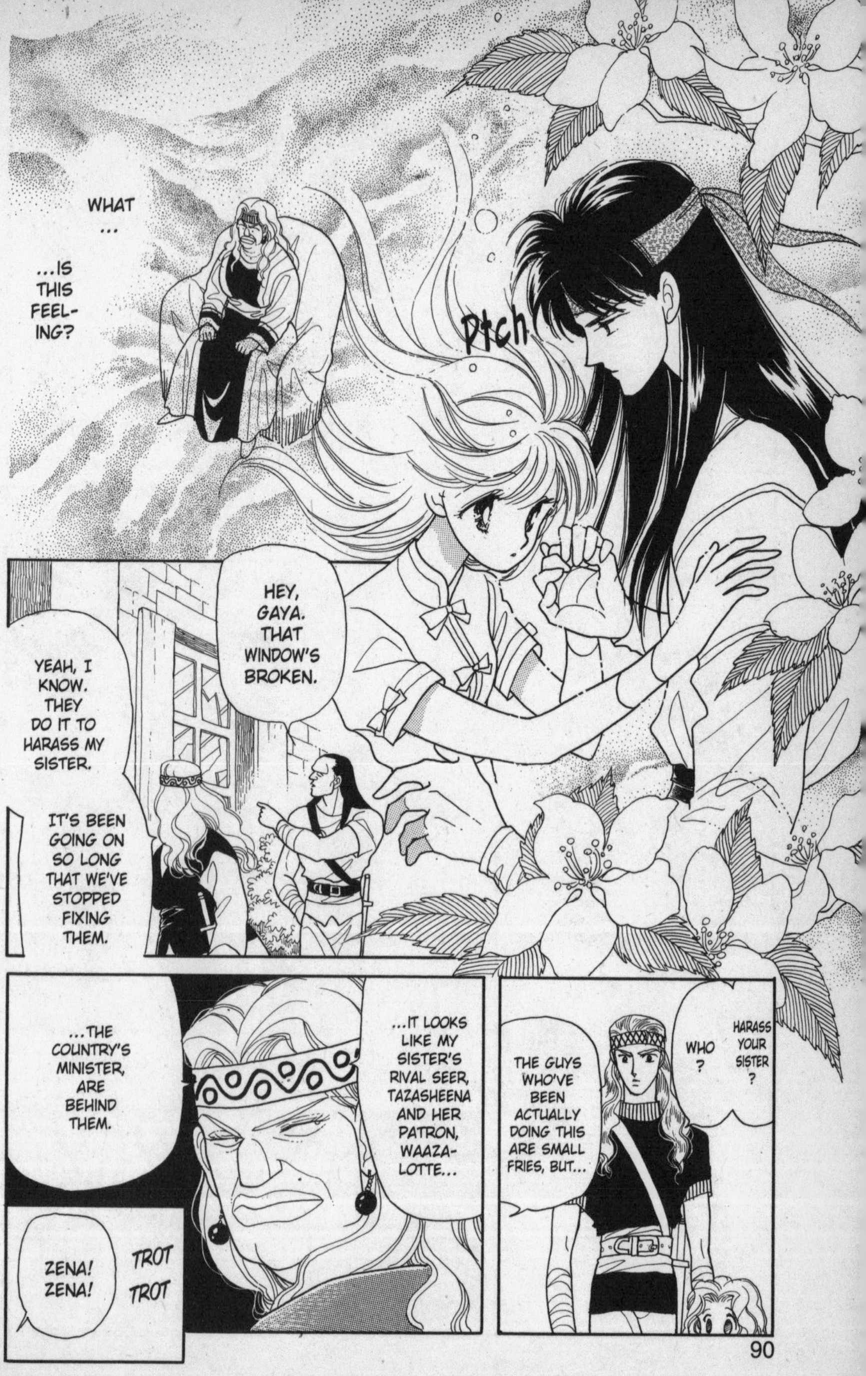
Ptch
WHAT ...
...IS THIS FEEL-ING?
HEY, GAYA. THAT WINDOW'S BROKEN.
YEAH, I KNOW. THEY DO IT TO HARASS MY SISTER.
IT'S BEEN GOING ON SO LONG THAT WE'VE STOPPED FIXING THEM.
HARASS YOUR SISTER?
WHO?
THE GUYS WHO'VE BEEN ACTUALLY DOING THIS ARE SMALL FRIES, BUT...
...IT LOOKS LIKE MY SISTER'S RIVAL SEER, TAZASHEENA AND HER PATRON, WAAZA-LOTTE...
...THE COUNTRY'S MINISTER, ARE BEHIND THEM.
ZENA! ZENA!
TROT
TROT

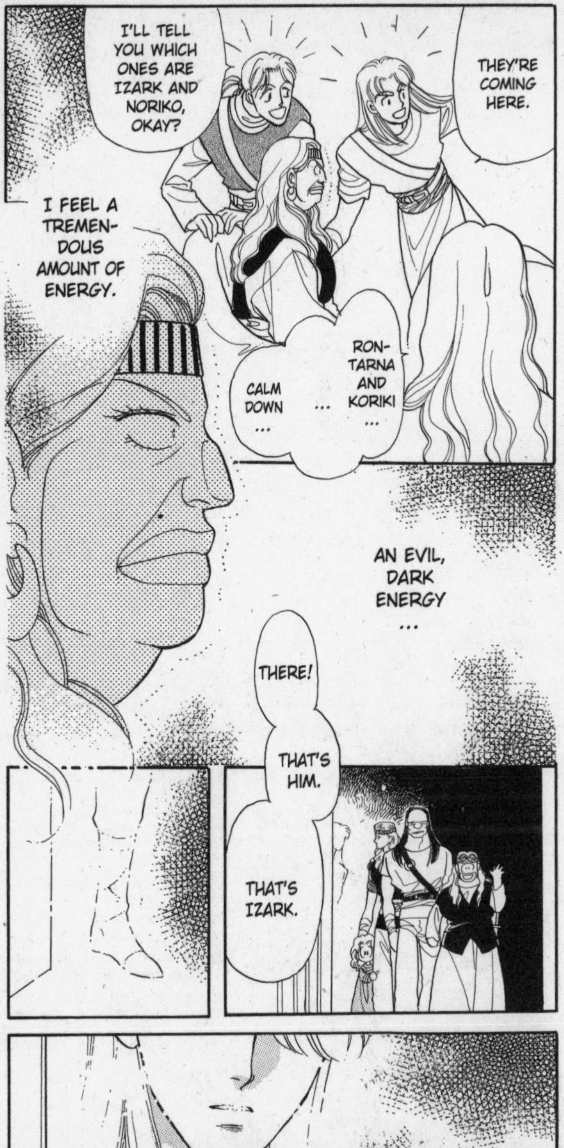
THEY'RE COMING HERE.
I'LL TELL YOU WHICH ONES ARE IZARK AND NORIKO, OKAY?
RON-TARNA AND KORIKI ...
...
CALM DOWN ...
I FEEL A TREMENDOUS AMOUNT OF ENERGY.
AN EVIL, DARK ENERGY ...
THERE!
THAT'S HIM.
THAT'S IZARK.

Last time, I wrote about my reader's age groups. Later, a lady in her fifties wrote to tell me that she, too, was a fan.

Thank you so much for letting me know.

Another reader asked me about the ratio between the male and female readers. The answer is: female 99% vs. male 1%.

Fascinating statistics!

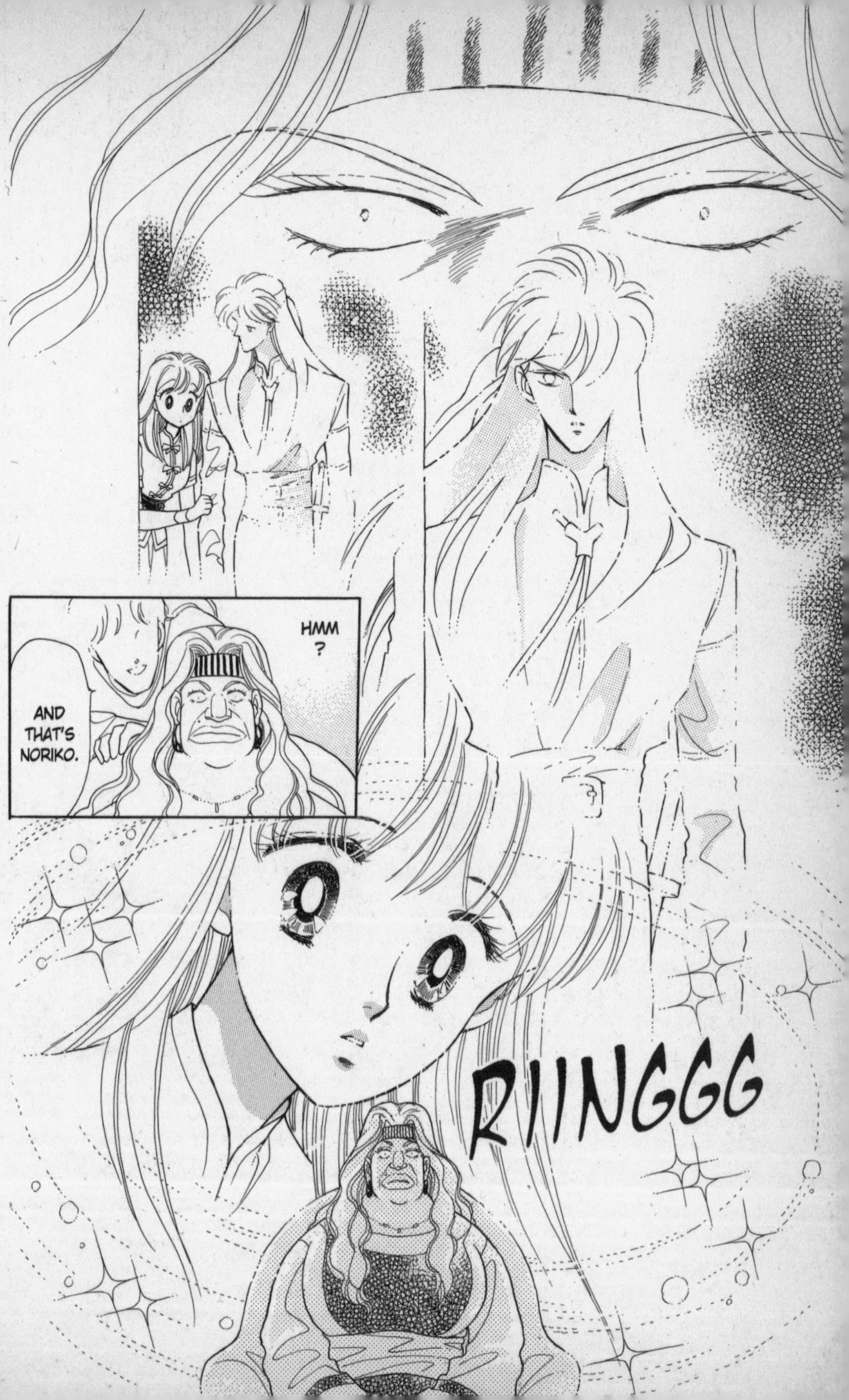
HMM ?
AND THAT'S NORIKO.
RIINGGG

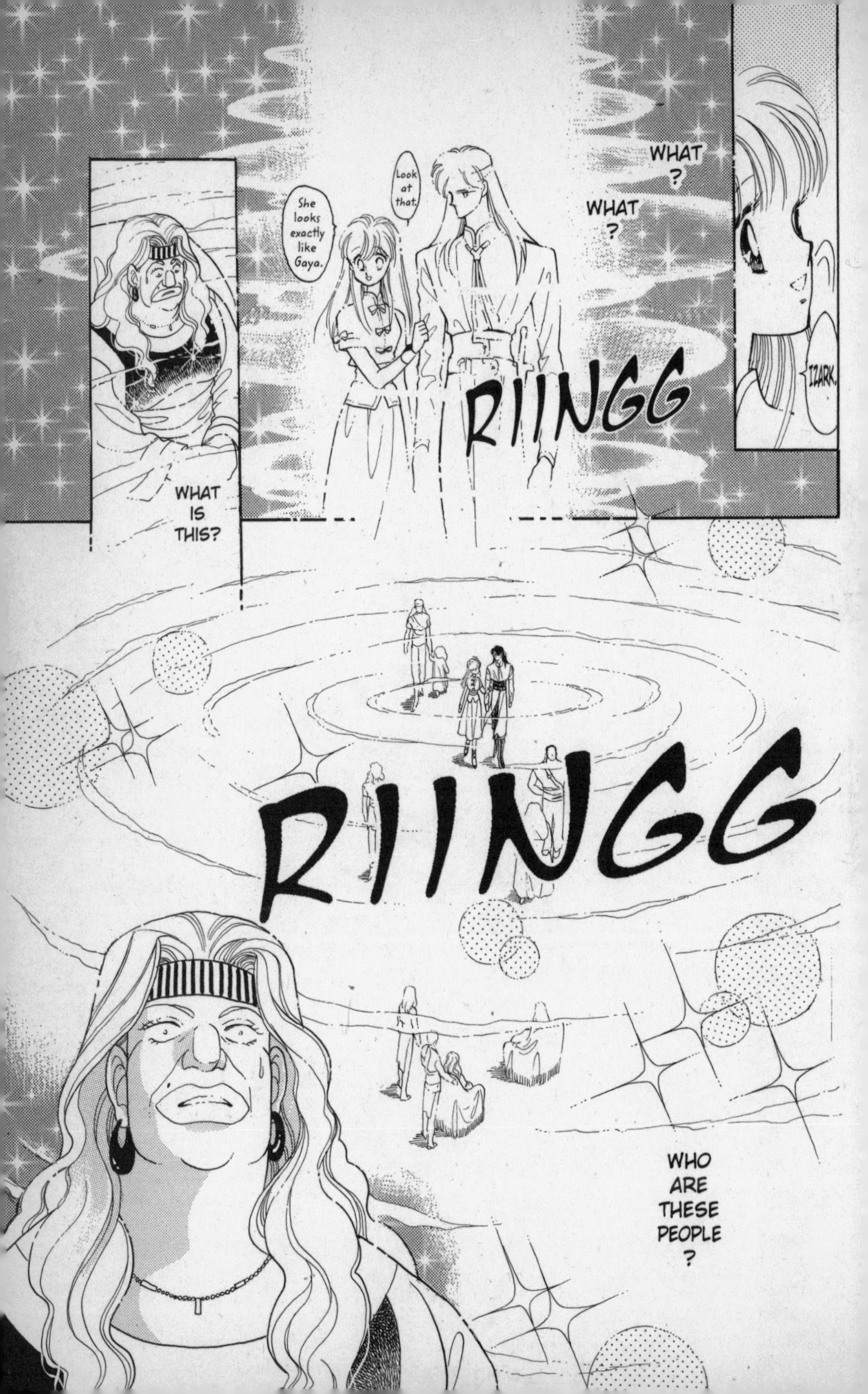
WHAT?
WHAT?
IZARK.
Look at that.
She looks exactly like Gaya.
RIINGG
WHAT IS THIS?
RIINGG
WHO ARE THESE PEOPLE?

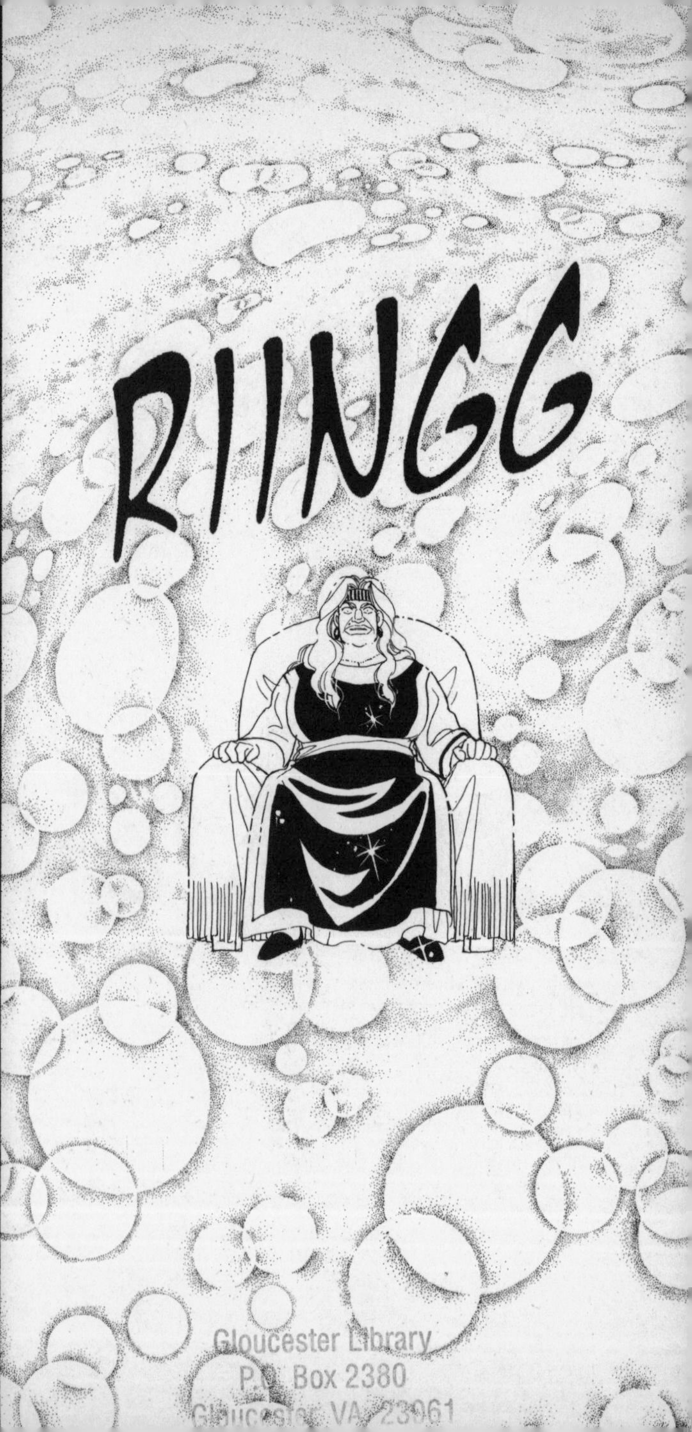
RIINGG

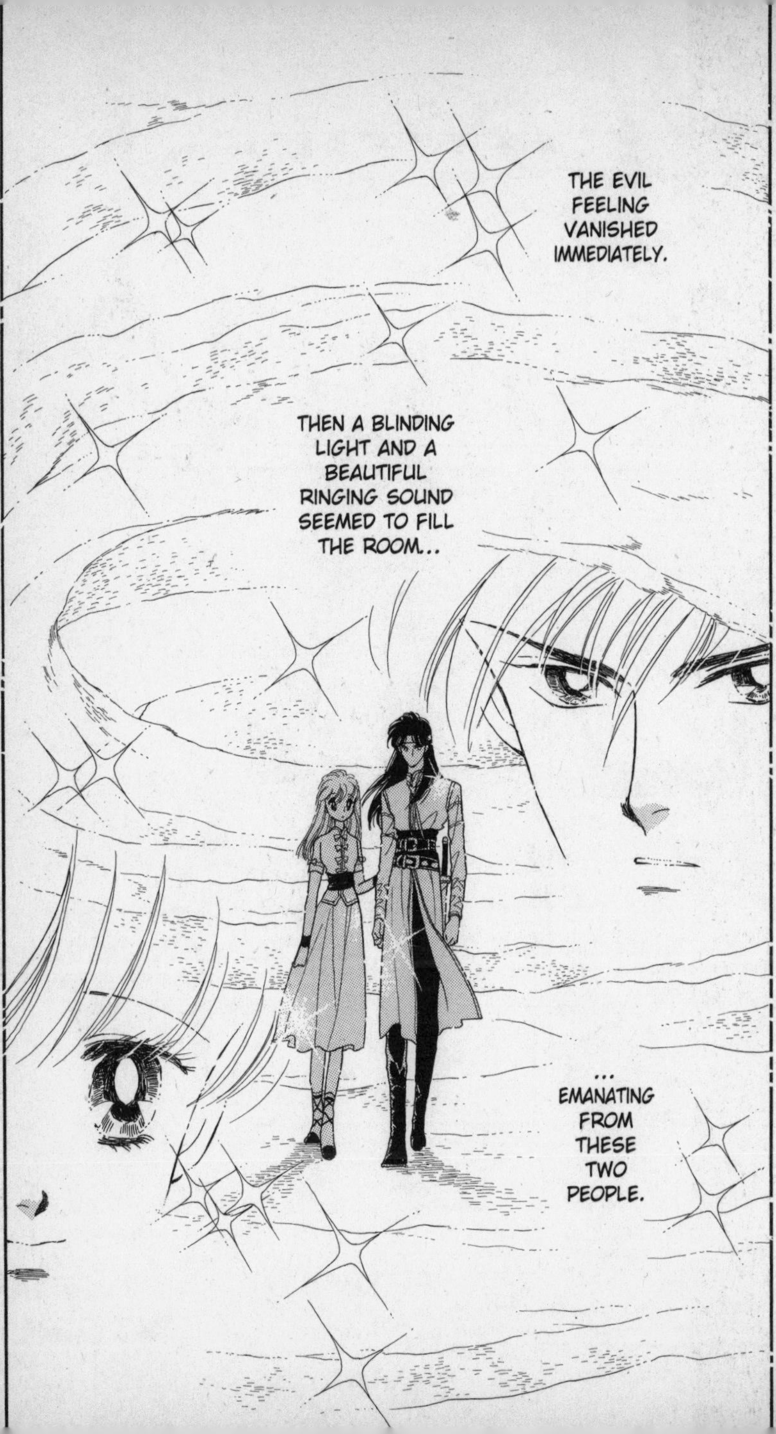
THE EVIL FEELING VANISHED IMMEDIATELY.
THEN A BLINDING LIGHT AND A BEAUTIFUL RINGING SOUND SEEMED TO FILL THE ROOM...
... EMANATING FROM THESE TWO PEOPLE.

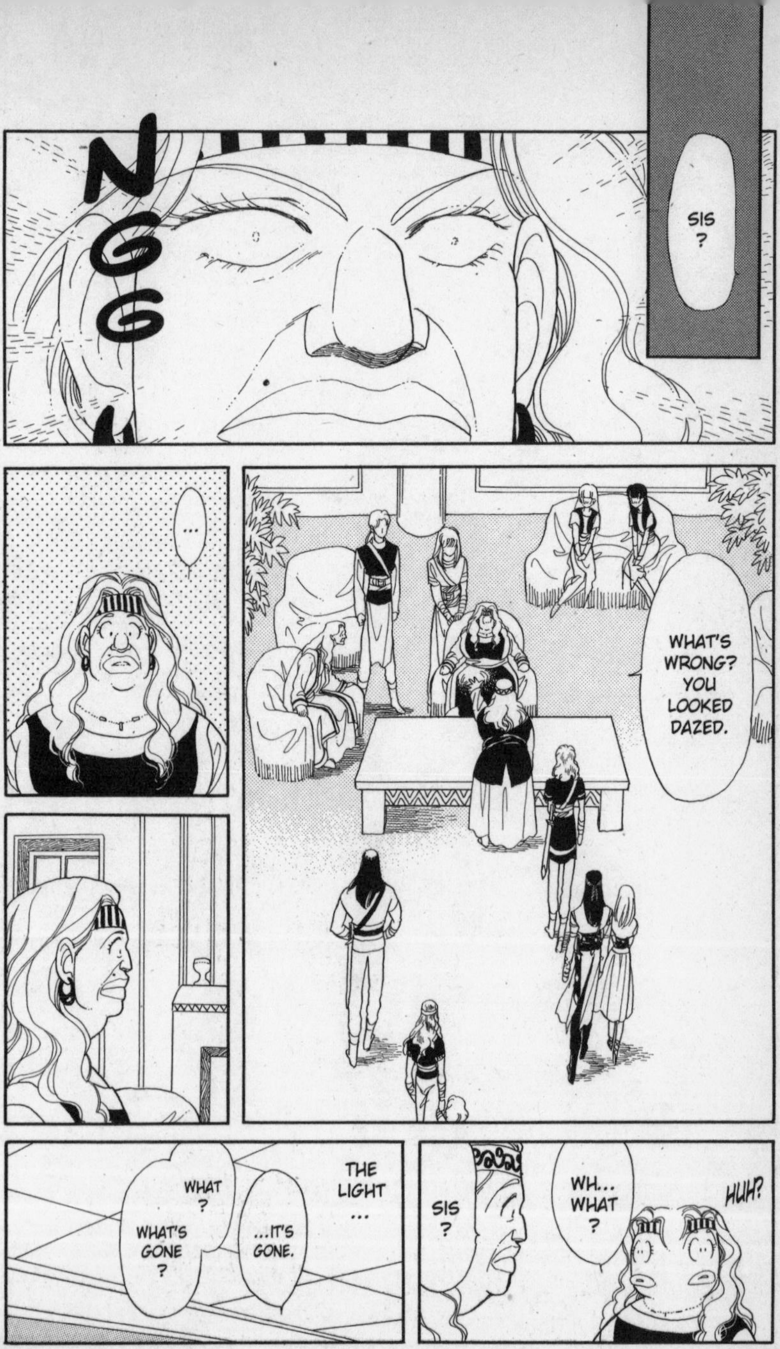
SIS ?
NGG
WHAT'S WRONG? YOU LOOKED DAZED.
...
HUH?
WH... WHAT ?
SIS ?
THE LIGHT ...
...IT'S GONE.
WHAT ? WHAT'S GONE ?

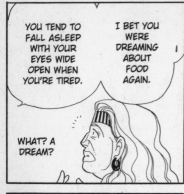

IT VANISHED.
WHY ...?
THE ROOM WAS FILLED WITH LIGHT.
SIS, WHAT ARE YOU TALKING ABOUT?
I BET YOU WERE DREAMING ABOUT FOOD AGAIN.
YOU TEND TO FALL ASLEEP WITH YOUR EYES WIDE OPEN WHEN YOU'RE TIRED.
WHAT? A DREAM?
THAT WAS A DREAM ?

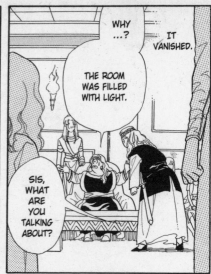

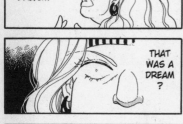

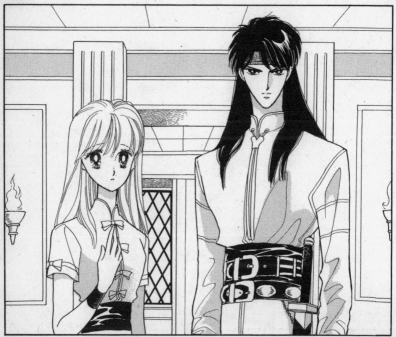

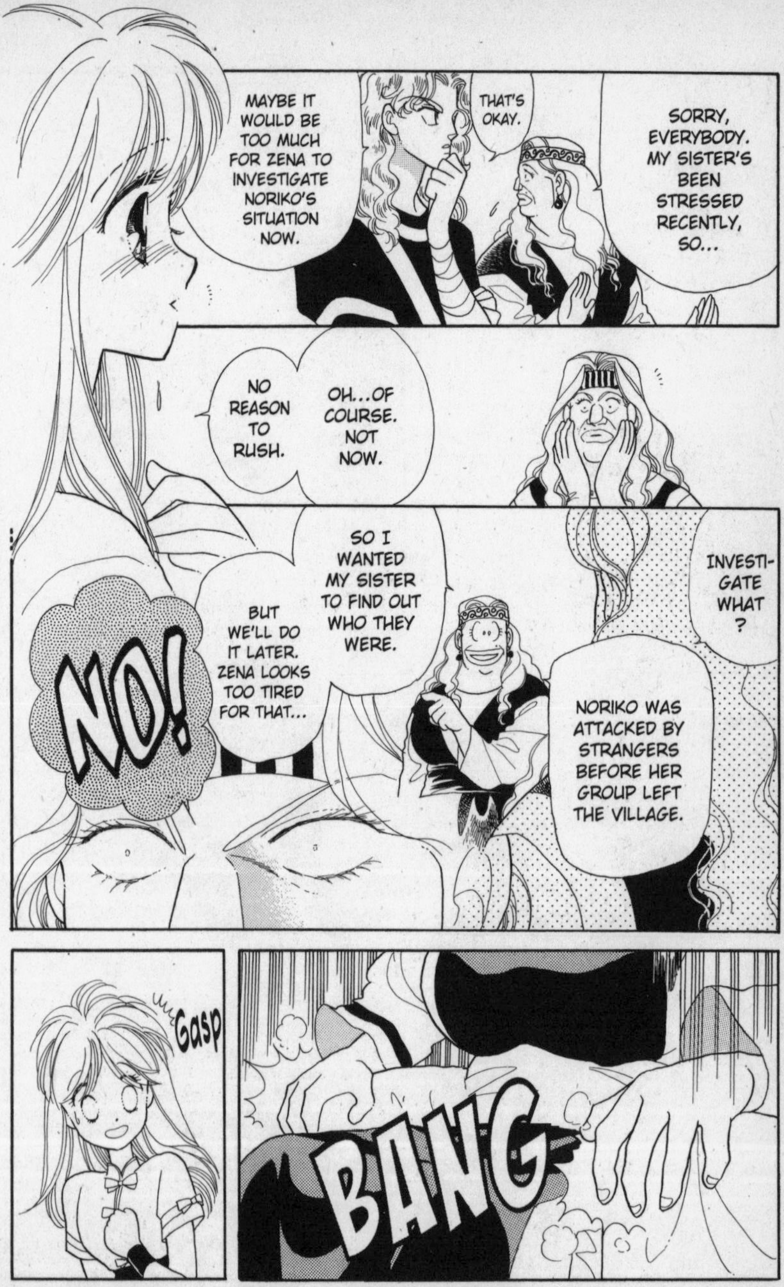
SORRY, EVERYBODY. MY SISTER'S BEEN STRESSED RECENTLY, SO...
THAT'S OKAY.
MAYBE IT WOULD BE TOO MUCH FOR ZENA TO INVESTIGATE NORIKO'S SITUATION NOW.
OH...OF COURSE. NOT NOW.
NO REASON TO RUSH.
INVESTI-GATE WHAT?
NORIKO WAS ATTACKED BY STRANGERS BEFORE HER GROUP LEFT THE VILLAGE.
SO I WANTED MY SISTER TO FIND OUT WHO THEY WERE.
BUT WE'LL DO IT LATER. ZENA LOOKS TOO TIRED FOR THAT...
NO!
BANG
Gasp

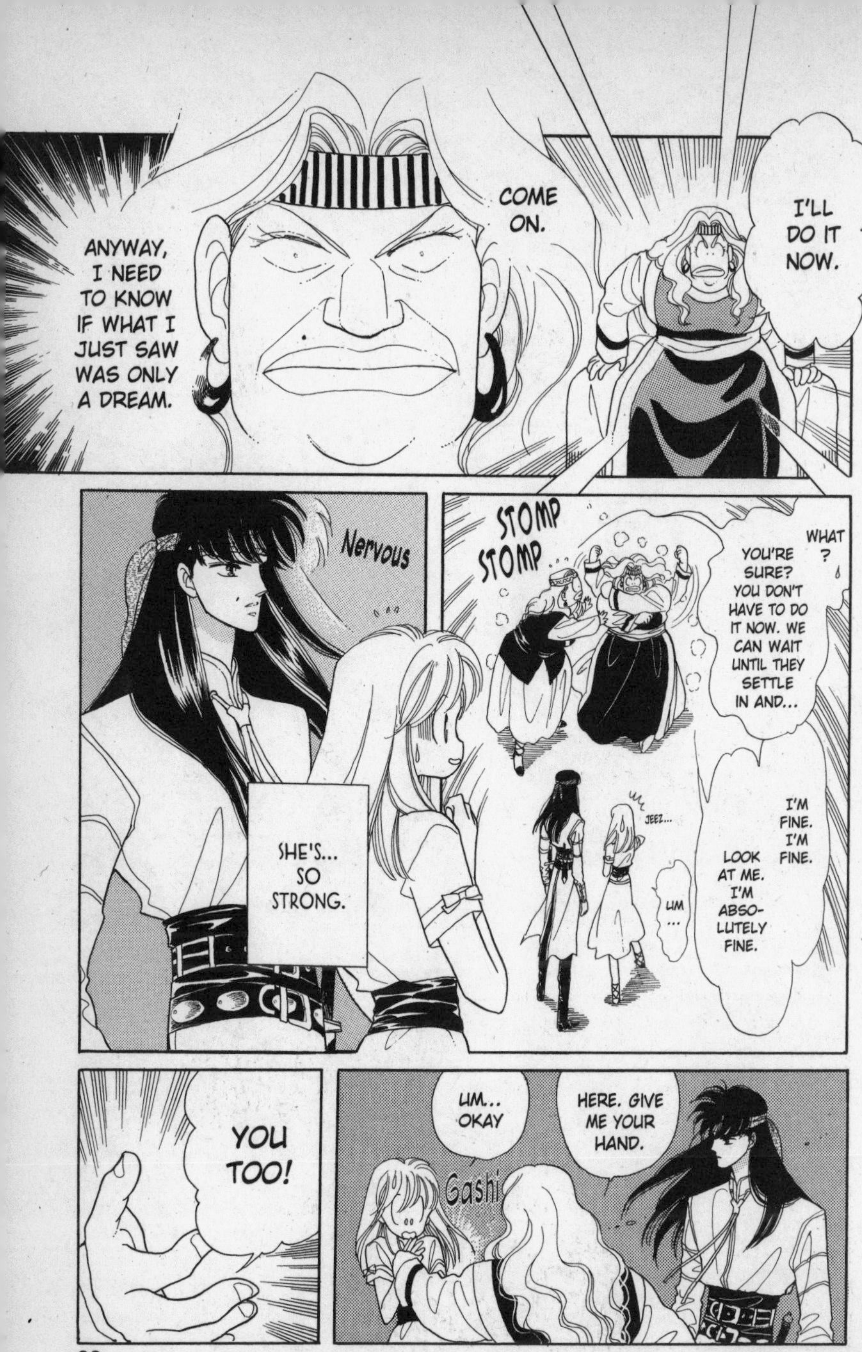
I'LL DO IT NOW.
COME ON.
ANYWAY, I NEED TO KNOW IF WHAT I JUST SAW WAS ONLY A DREAM.
WHAT?
STOMP STOMP
YOU'RE SURE? YOU DON'T HAVE TO DO IT NOW. WE CAN WAIT UNTIL THEY SETTLE IN AND...
I'M FINE. I'M FINE.
LOOK AT ME. I'M ABSO-LUTELY FINE.
JEEZ...
UM...
Nervous
SHE'S... SO STRONG.
HERE. GIVE ME YOUR HAND.
UM... OKAY
Gashi
YOU TOO!

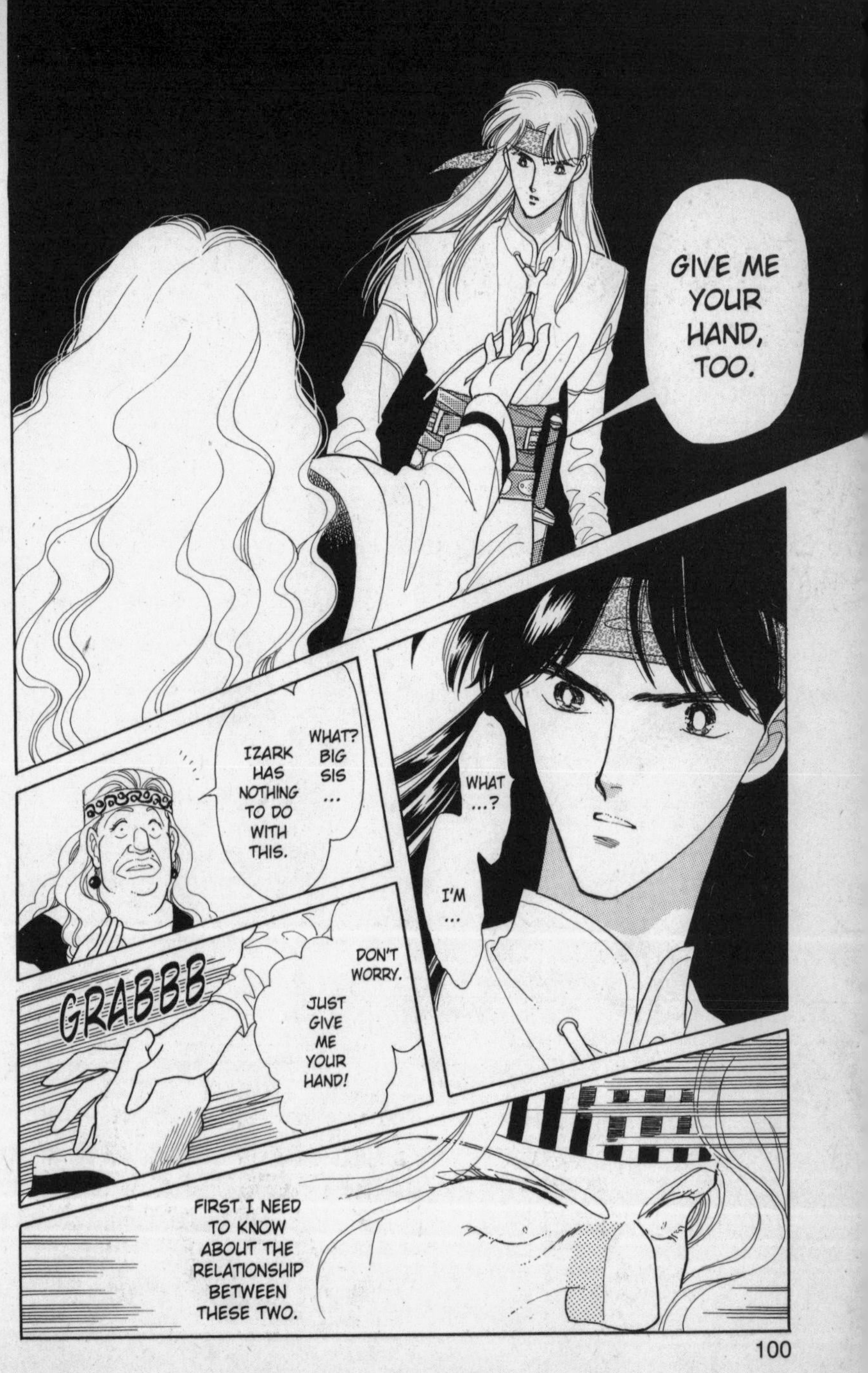
GIVE ME YOUR HAND, TOO.
WHAT ...?
I'M ...
WHAT? BIG SIS ...
IZARK HAS NOTHING TO DO WITH THIS.
DON'T WORRY.
JUST GIVE ME YOUR HAND!
GRABBB
FIRST I NEED TO KNOW ABOUT THE RELATIONSHIP BETWEEN THESE TWO.

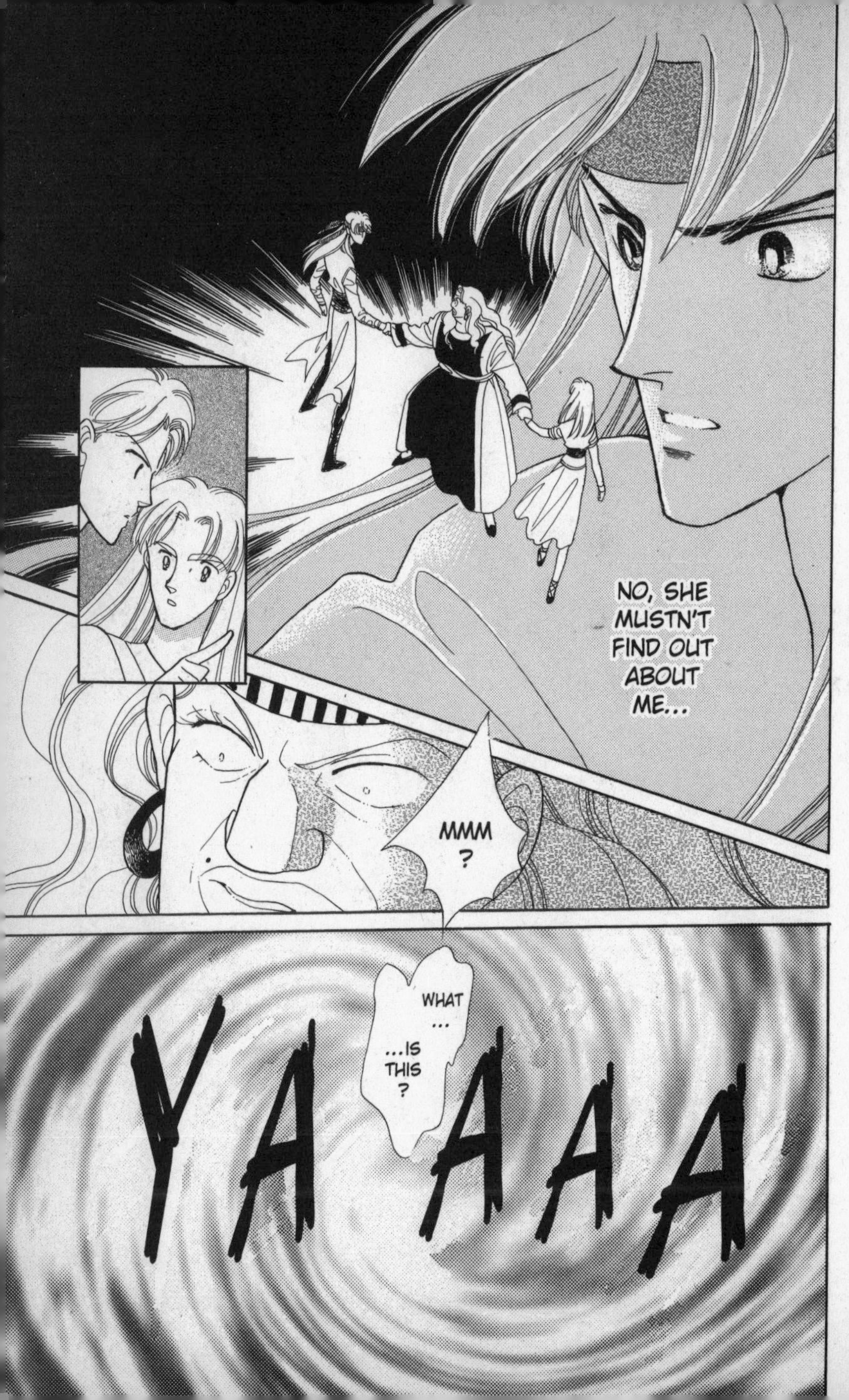
NO, SHE MUSTN'T FIND OUT ABOUT ME...
MMM ?
WHAT ... ...IS THIS ?
YA AAA

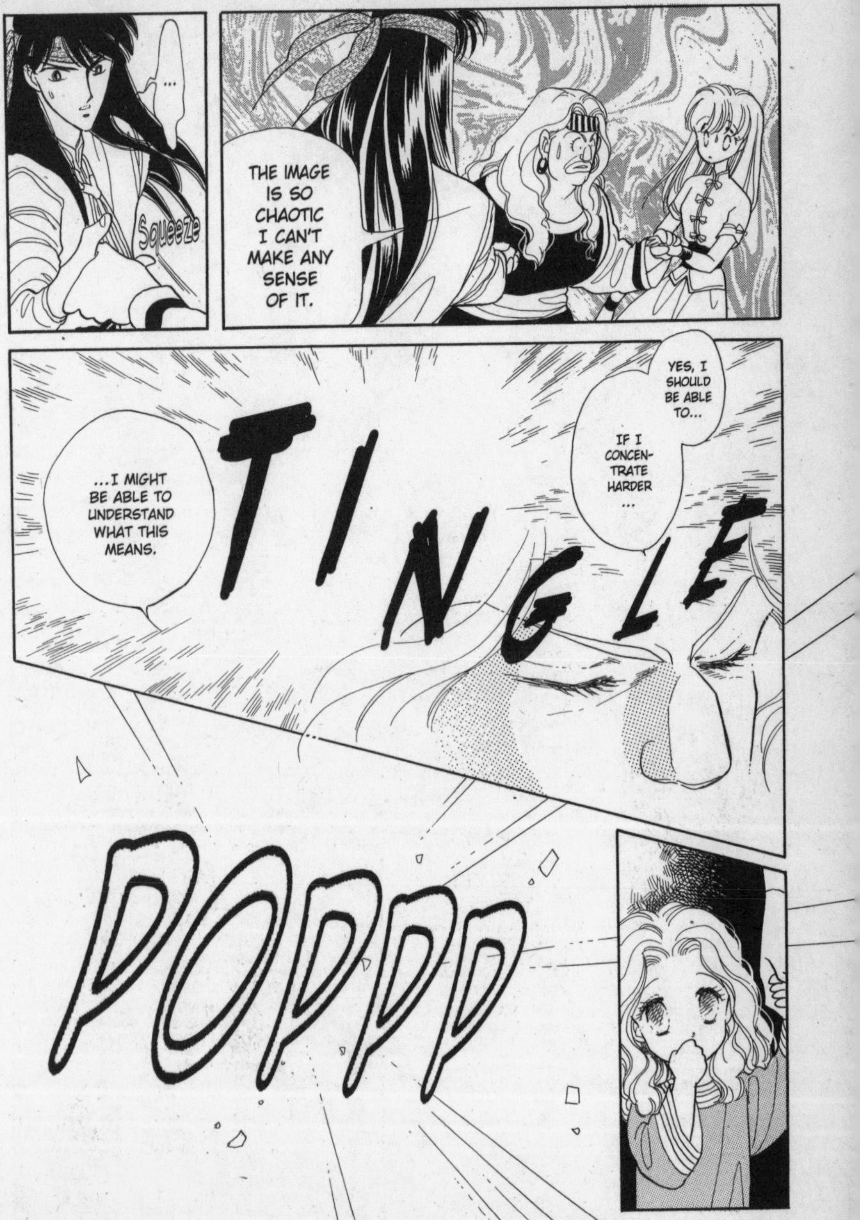
THE IMAGE IS SO CHAOTIC I CAN'T MAKE ANY SENSE OF IT.
...
Squeeze
YES, I SHOULD BE ABLE TO...
IF I CONCENTRATE HARDER ...
TINGLE
...I MIGHT BE ABLE TO UNDERSTAND WHAT THIS MEANS.
POPPP

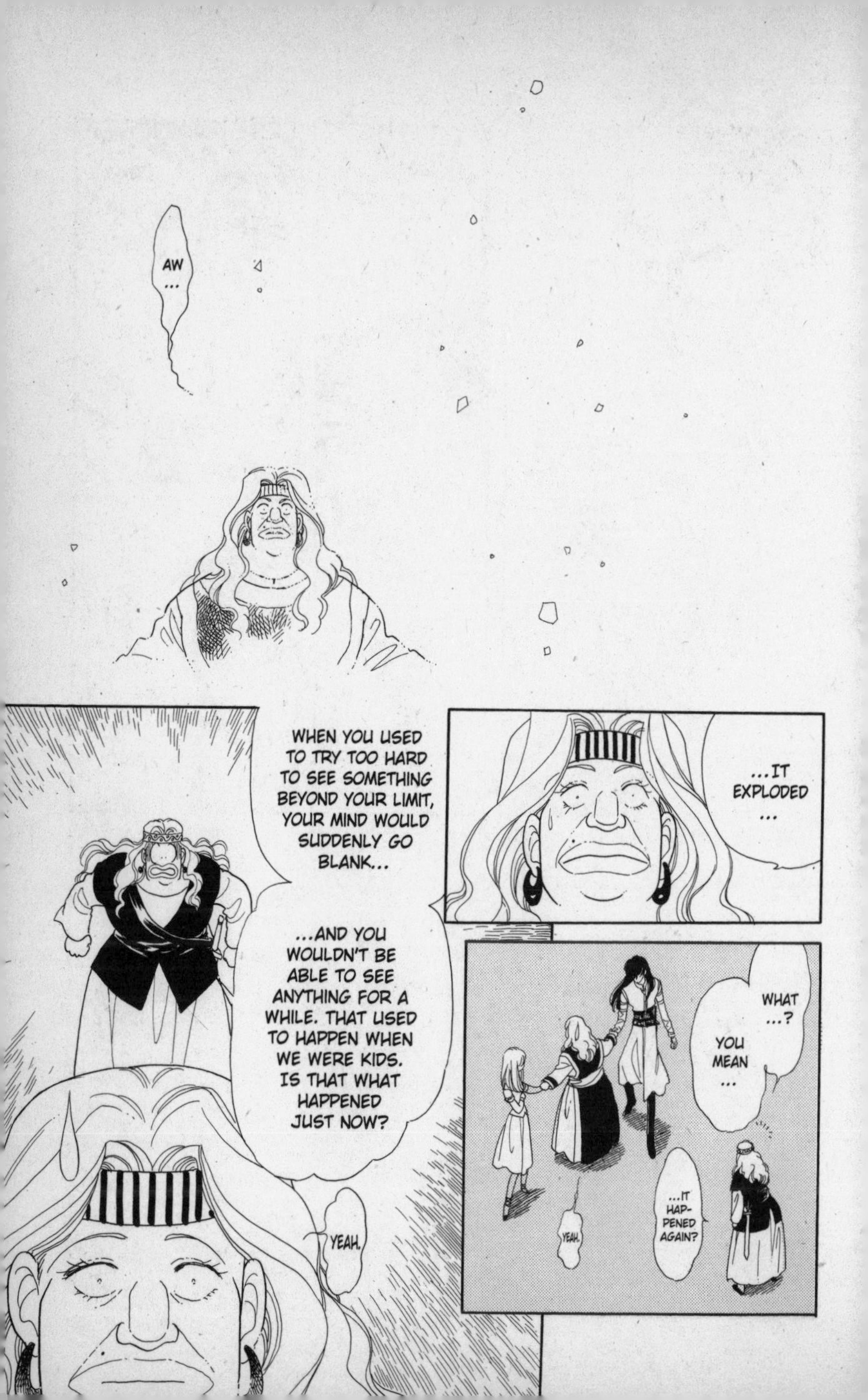
AW ...
...IT EXPLODED ...
WHAT ...?
YOU MEAN ...
...IT HAPPENED AGAIN?
YEAH.
WHEN YOU USED TO TRY TOO HARD TO SEE SOMETHING BEYOND YOUR LIMIT, YOUR MIND WOULD SUDDENLY GO BLANK...
...AND YOU WOULDN'T BE ABLE TO SEE ANYTHING FOR A WHILE. THAT USED TO HAPPEN WHEN WE WERE KIDS. IS THAT WHAT HAPPENED JUST NOW?
YEAH.

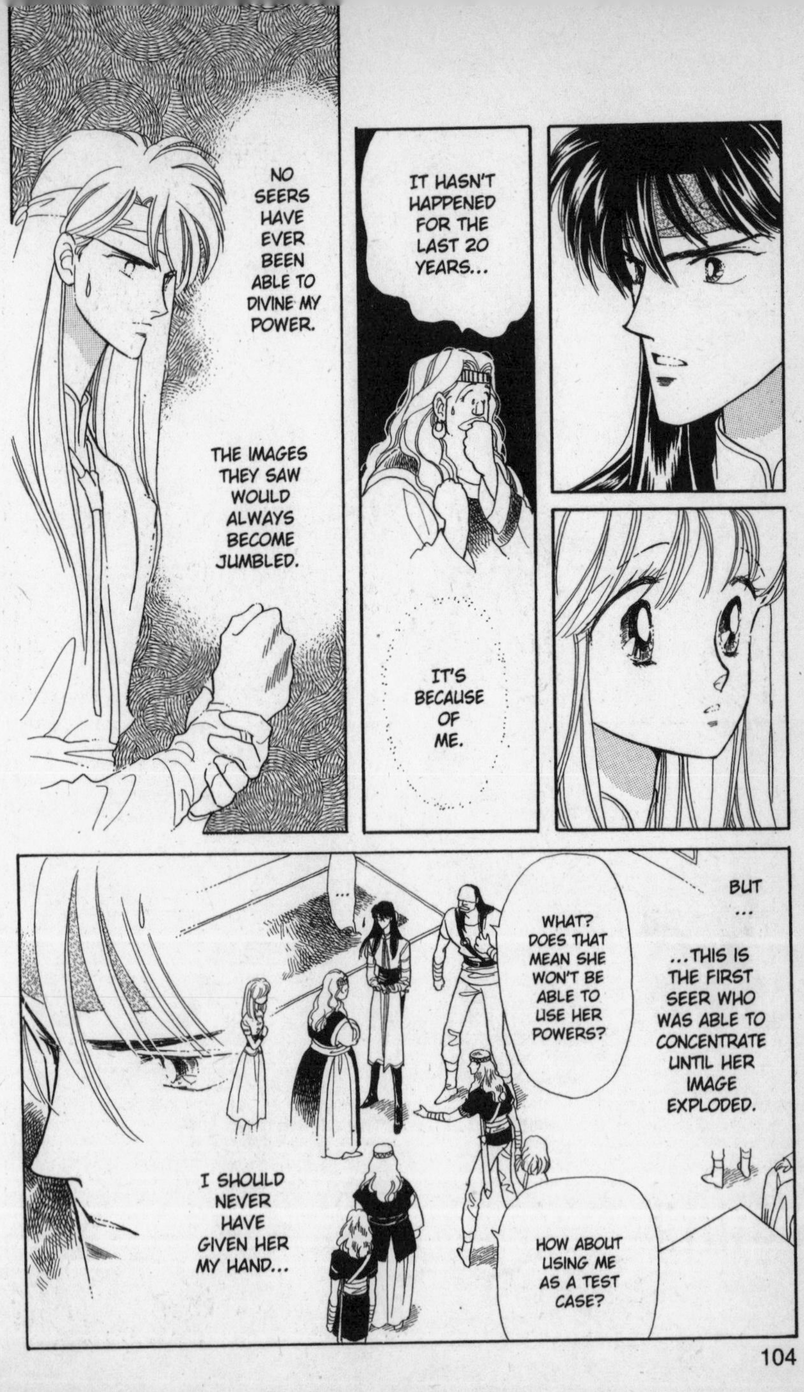
IT HASN'T HAPPENED FOR THE LAST 20 YEARS...
IT'S BECAUSE OF ME.
NO SEERS HAVE EVER BEEN ABLE TO DIVINE MY POWER.
THE IMAGES THEY SAW WOULD ALWAYS BECOME JUMBLED.
BUT ...
...THIS IS THE FIRST SEER WHO WAS ABLE TO CONCENTRATE UNTIL HER IMAGE EXPLODED.
WHAT? DOES THAT MEAN SHE WON'T BE ABLE TO USE HER POWERS?
...
HOW ABOUT USING ME AS A TEST CASE?
I SHOULD NEVER HAVE GIVEN HER MY HAND...

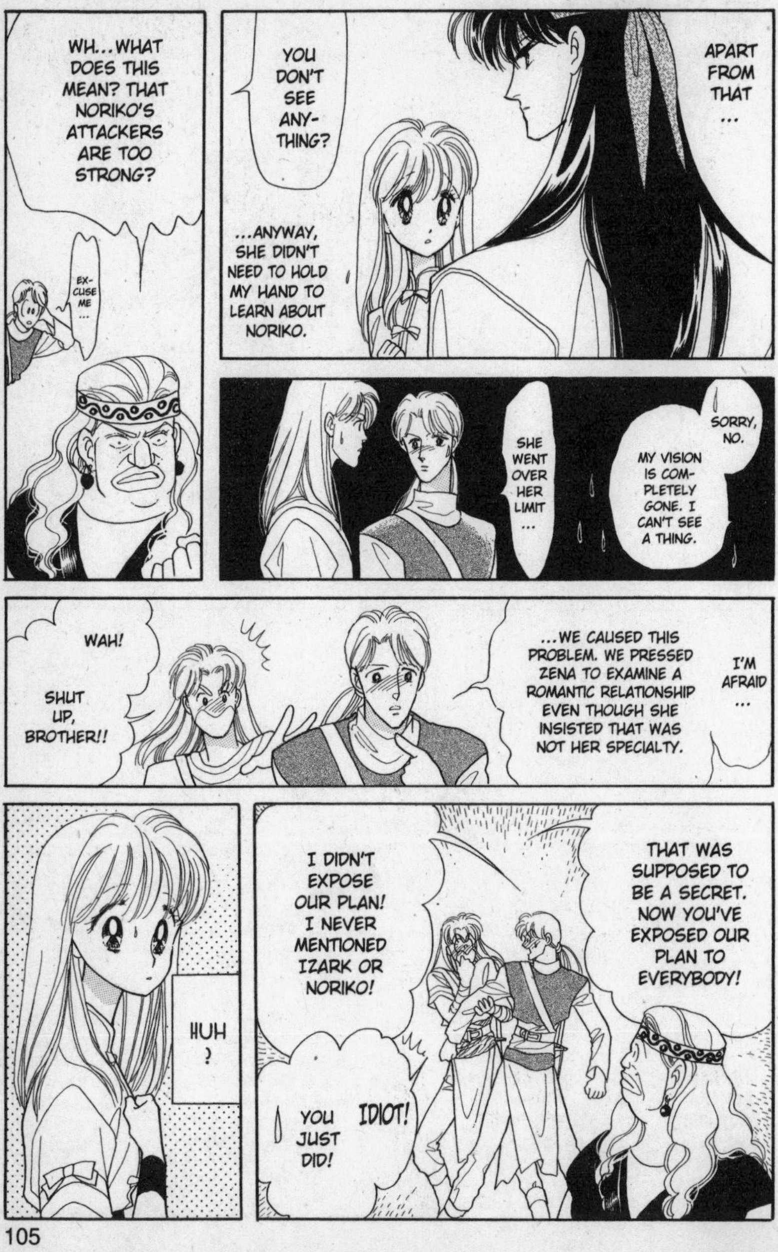
APART FROM THAT ...
YOU DON'T SEE ANY-THING?
...ANYWAY, SHE DIDN'T NEED TO HOLD MY HAND TO LEARN ABOUT NORIKO.
SORRY, NO.
MY VISION IS COM-PLETELY GONE. I CAN'T SEE A THING.
SHE WENT OVER HER LIMIT ...
WH...WHAT DOES THIS MEAN? THAT NORIKO'S ATTACKERS ARE TOO STRONG?
EX-CUSE ME ...
I'M AFRAID ...
...WE CAUSED THIS PROBLEM. WE PRESSED ZENA TO EXAMINE A ROMANTIC RELATIONSHIP EVEN THOUGH SHE INSISTED THAT WAS NOT HER SPECIALTY.
WAH!
SHUT UP, BROTHER!!
THAT WAS SUPPOSED TO BE A SECRET. NOW YOU'VE EXPOSED OUR PLAN TO EVERYBODY!
I DIDN'T EXPOSE OUR PLAN! I NEVER MENTIONED IZARK OR NORIKO!
IDIOT!
YOU JUST DID!
HUH?

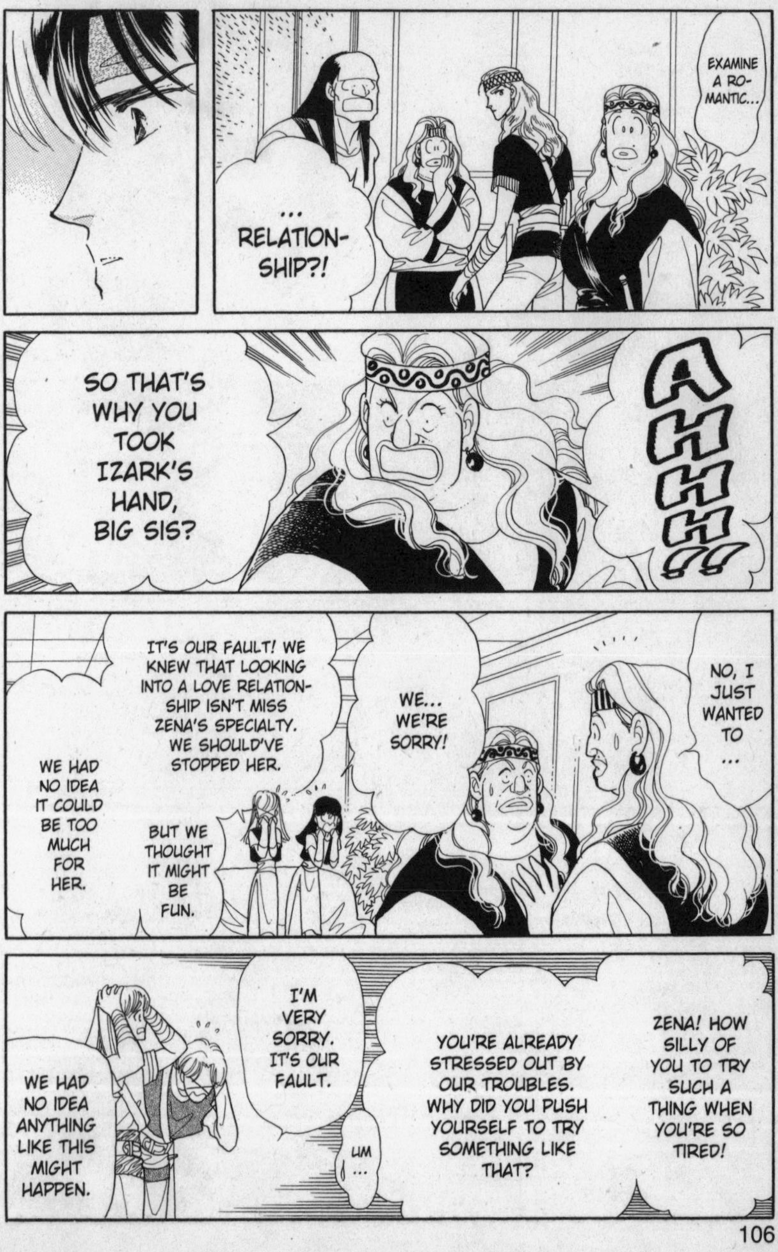
EXAMINE A RO-MANTIC...
... RELATIONSHIP?!
AHHHH!!
SO THAT'S WHY YOU TOOK IZARK'S HAND, BIG SIS?
NO, I JUST WANTED TO ...
WE... WE'RE SORRY!
IT'S OUR FAULT! WE KNEW THAT LOOKING INTO A LOVE RELATIONSHIP ISN'T MISS ZENA'S SPECIALTY. WE SHOULD'VE STOPPED HER.
BUT WE THOUGHT IT MIGHT BE FUN.
WE HAD NO IDEA IT COULD BE TOO MUCH FOR HER.
ZENA! HOW SILLY OF YOU TO TRY SUCH A THING WHEN YOU'RE SO TIRED!
YOU'RE ALREADY STRESSED OUT BY OUR TROUBLES. WHY DID YOU PUSH YOURSELF TO TRY SOMETHING LIKE THAT?
UM ...
I'M VERY SORRY. IT'S OUR FAULT.
WE HAD NO IDEA ANYTHING LIKE THIS MIGHT HAPPEN.

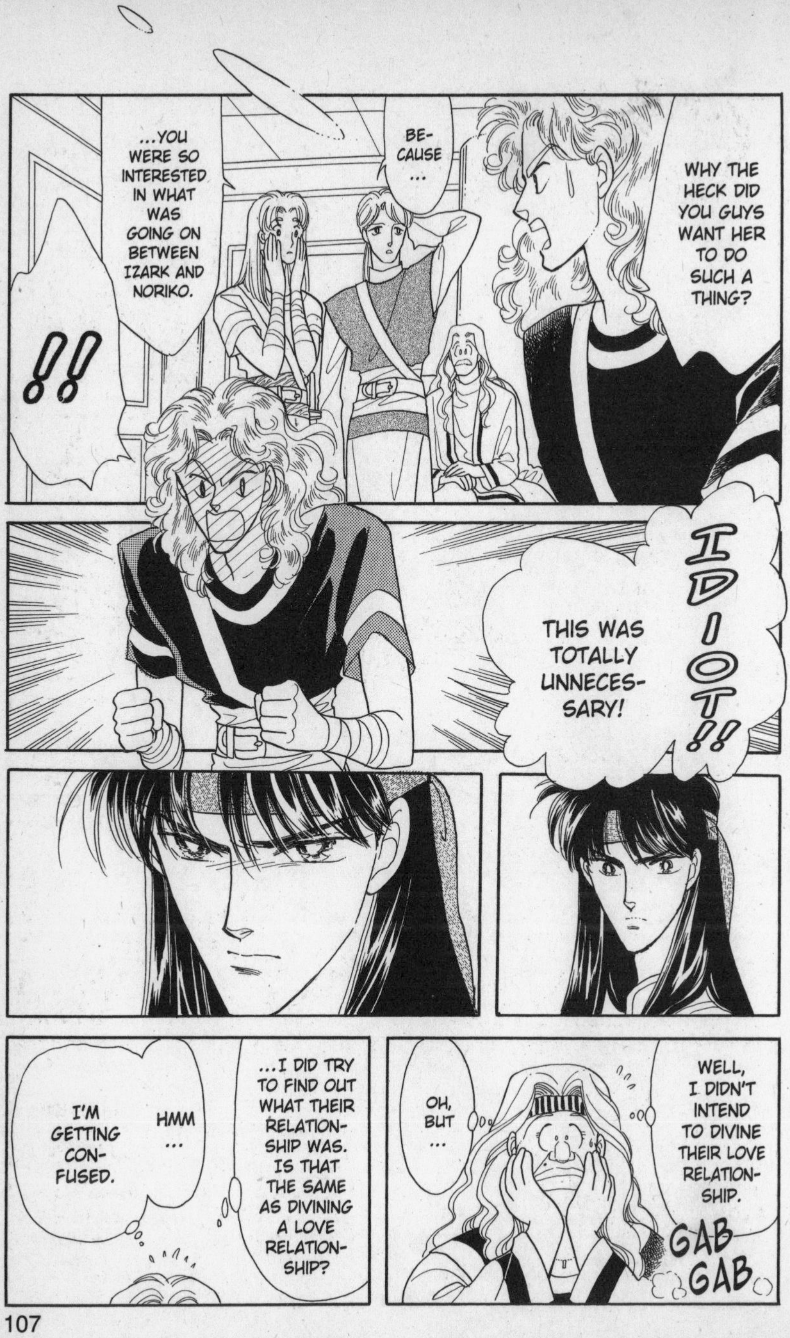
WHY THE HECK DID YOU GUYS WANT HER TO DO SUCH A THING?
BE-CAUSE ...
...YOU WERE SO INTERESTED IN WHAT WAS GOING ON BETWEEN IZARK AND NORIKO.
!!
IDIOT!!
THIS WAS TOTALLY UNNECES-SARY!
WELL, I DIDN'T INTEND TO DIVINE THEIR LOVE RELATION-SHIP.
GAB GAB
OH, BUT ...
...I DID TRY TO FIND OUT WHAT THEIR RELATION-SHIP WAS. IS THAT THE SAME AS DIVINING A LOVE RELATION-SHIP?
HMM ...
I'M GETTING CON-FUSED.

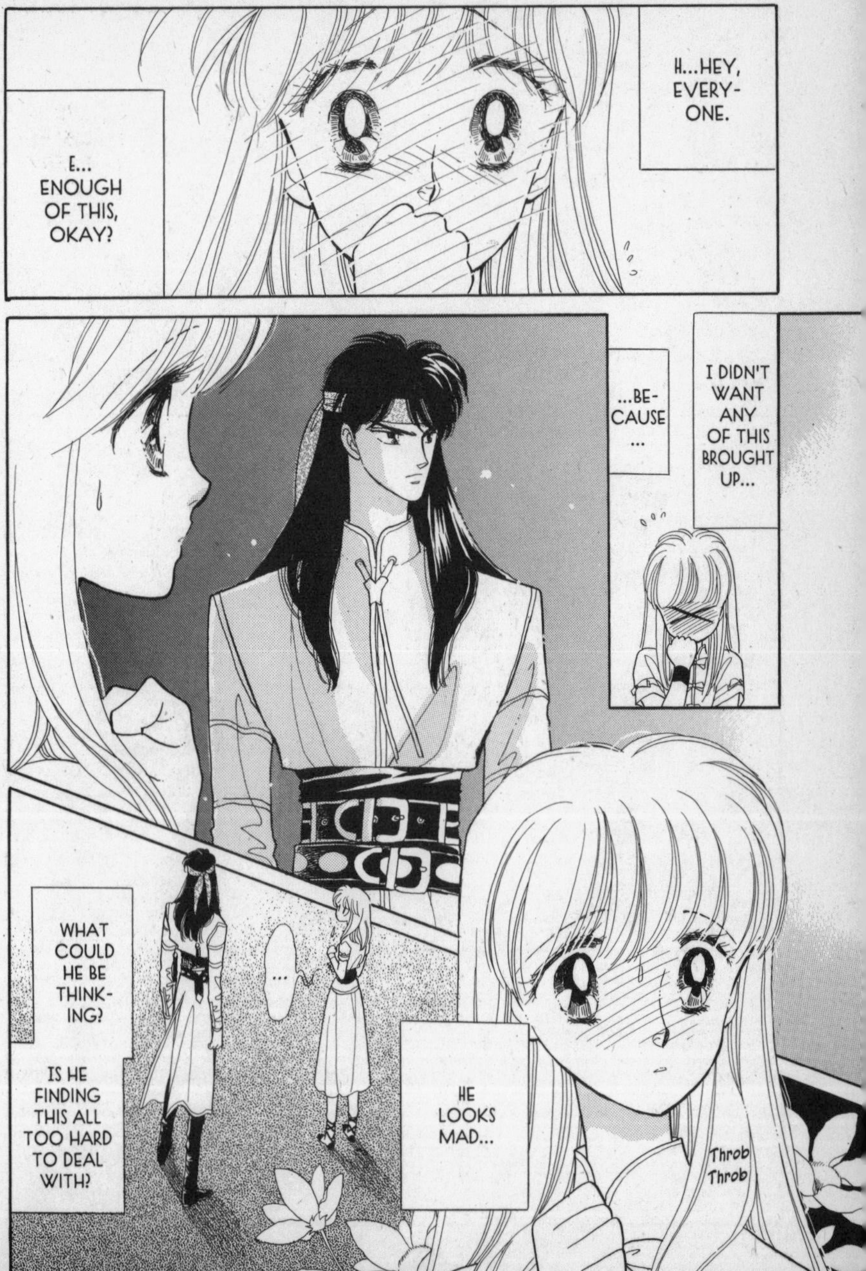
H...HEY, EVERY-ONE.
E... ENOUGH OF THIS, OKAY?
I DIDN'T WANT ANY OF THIS BROUGHT UP...
...BE-CAUSE ...
HE LOOKS MAD...
Throb Throb
...
WHAT COULD HE BE THINKING?
IS HE FINDING THIS ALL TOO HARD TO DEAL WITH?

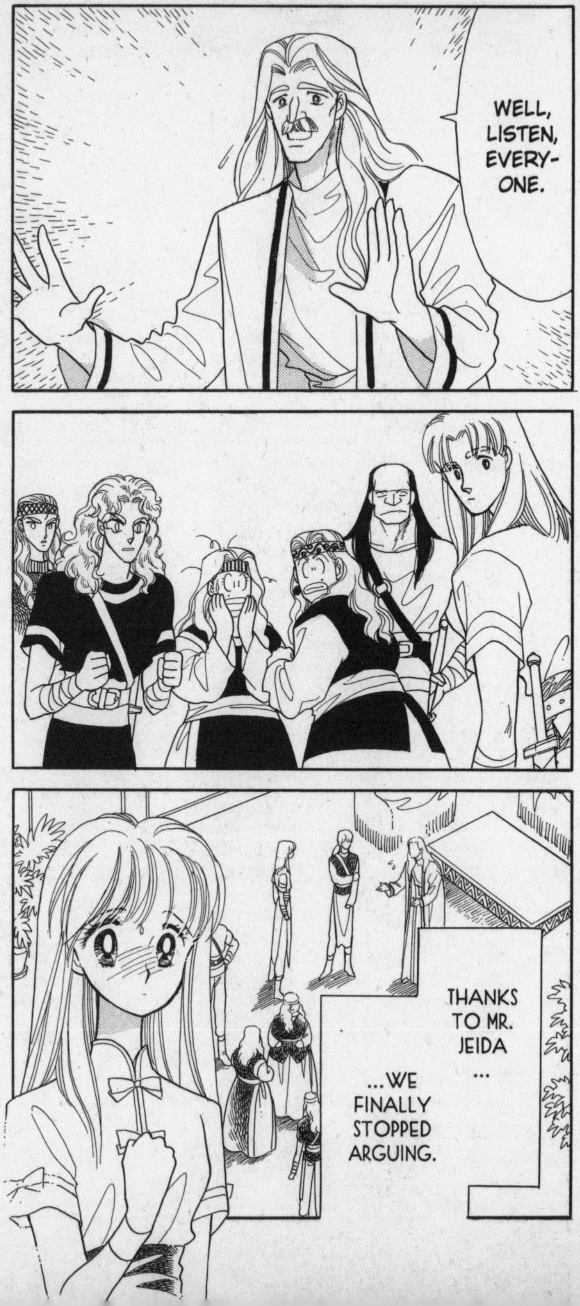
WELL, LISTEN, EVERY-ONE.
THANKS TO MR. JEIDA ...
...WE FINALLY STOPPED ARGUING.

Sometimes I get letters, along with drawings, suggesting ideas for the characters' costumes. They are quite pretty and I'm tempted to use them. However, the designs are often too complicated or require some fancy coloring so I end up not using them.

I try to keep my characters' costumes as simple as possible so they'll be easy to draw.

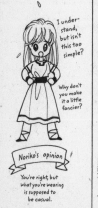

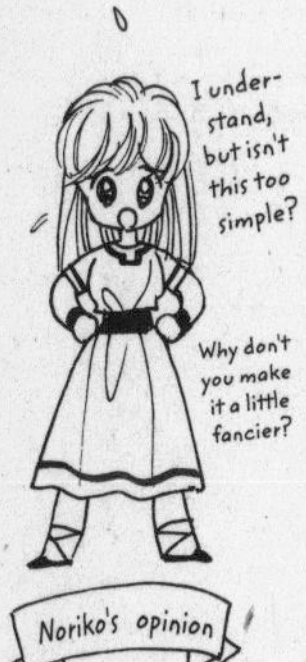
I under-stand, but isn't this too simple?
Why don't you make it a little fancier?
Noriko's opinion

You're right, but what you're wearing is supposed to be casual.

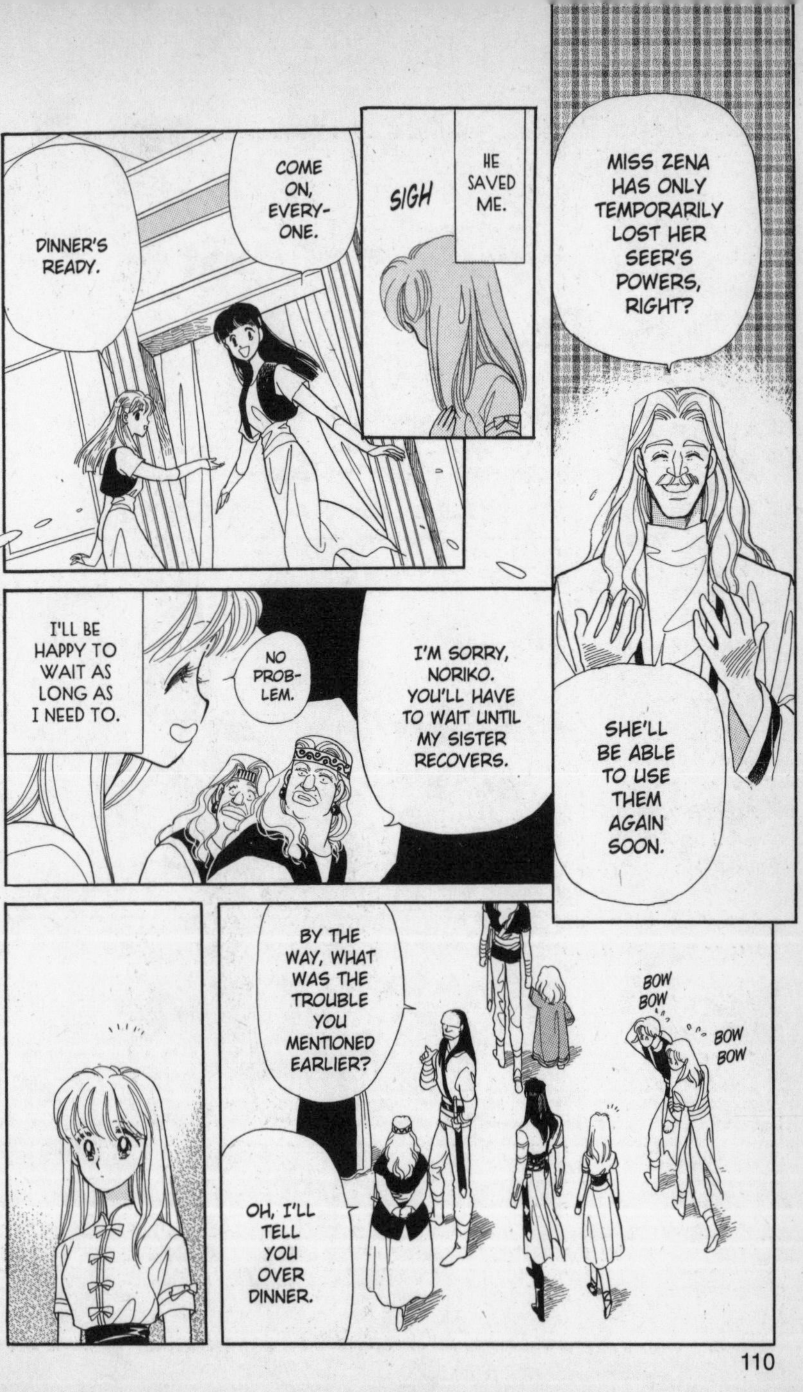
MISS ZENA HAS ONLY TEMPORARILY LOST HER SEER'S POWERS, RIGHT?
SHE'LL BE ABLE TO USE THEM AGAIN SOON.
HE SAVED ME.
SIGH
COME ON, EVERY-ONE.
DINNER'S READY.
I'M SORRY, NORIKO. YOU'LL HAVE TO WAIT UNTIL MY SISTER RECOVERS.
NO PROB-LEM.
I'LL BE HAPPY TO WAIT AS LONG AS I NEED TO.
BOW BOW
BOW BOW
BY THE WAY, WHAT WAS THE TROUBLE YOU MENTIONED EARLIER?
OH, I'LL TELL YOU OVER DINNER.

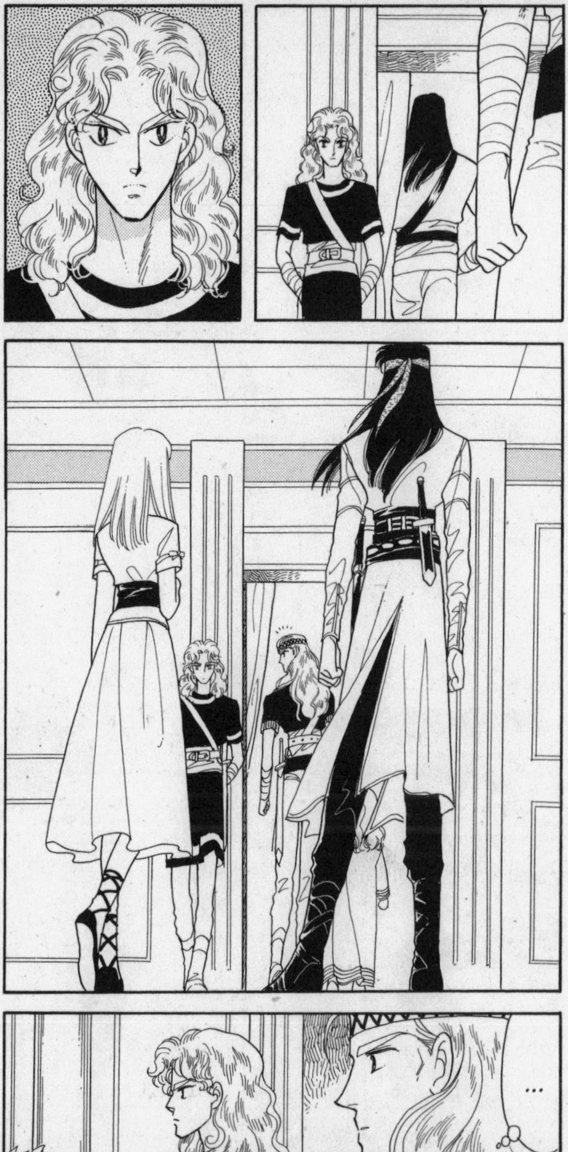
...

About the characters' ages: Izark was 19 years old when he met Noriko and he's turned 20 in this volume. Noriko's about 17 or 18.

Gaya is 53.
Agol is 31.
Geena is 7.
Barago is 25.
Jeida is 52.
Rontarna is 22.
Koriki is 19.
Banadam is 19.
Zena is 53

(After all, She's Gaya's twin sister).

Anita is 16.
Rottenina is 17.
Rachef is 33.
Keimos is 20.

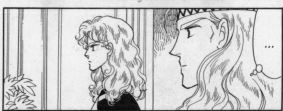

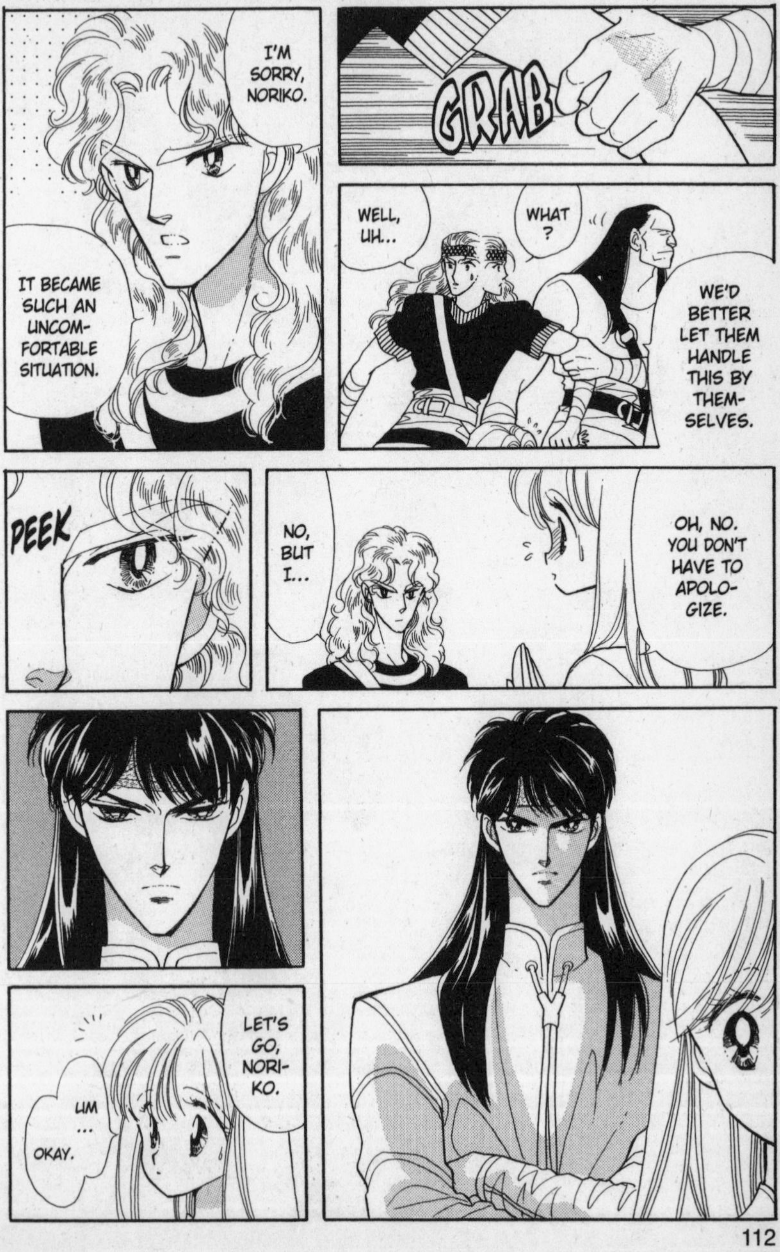
GRAB
WHAT ?
WELL, UH...
WE'D BETTER LET THEM HANDLE THIS BY THEM-SELVES.
I'M SORRY, NORIKO.
IT BECAME SUCH AN UNCOM-FORTABLE SITUATION.
OH, NO. YOU DON'T HAVE TO APOLO-GIZE.
NO, BUT I...
PEEK
LET'S GO, NORI-KO.
UM ... OKAY.

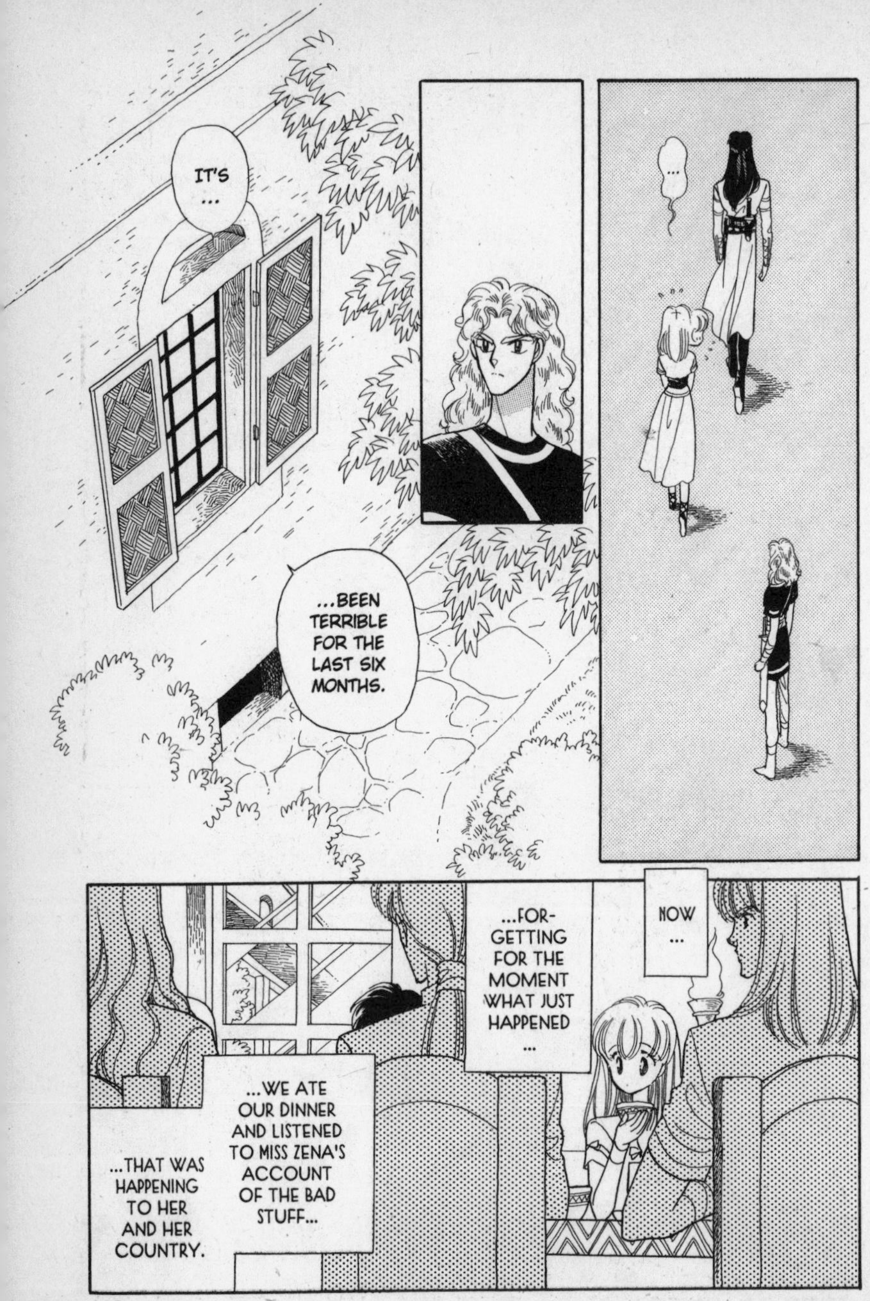
...
IT'S ...
...BEEN TERRIBLE FOR THE LAST SIX MONTHS.
NOW ...
...FOR-GETTING FOR THE MOMENT WHAT JUST HAPPENED ...
...WE ATE OUR DINNER AND LISTENED TO MISS ZENA'S ACCOUNT OF THE BAD STUFF...
...THAT WAS HAPPENING TO HER AND HER COUNTRY.

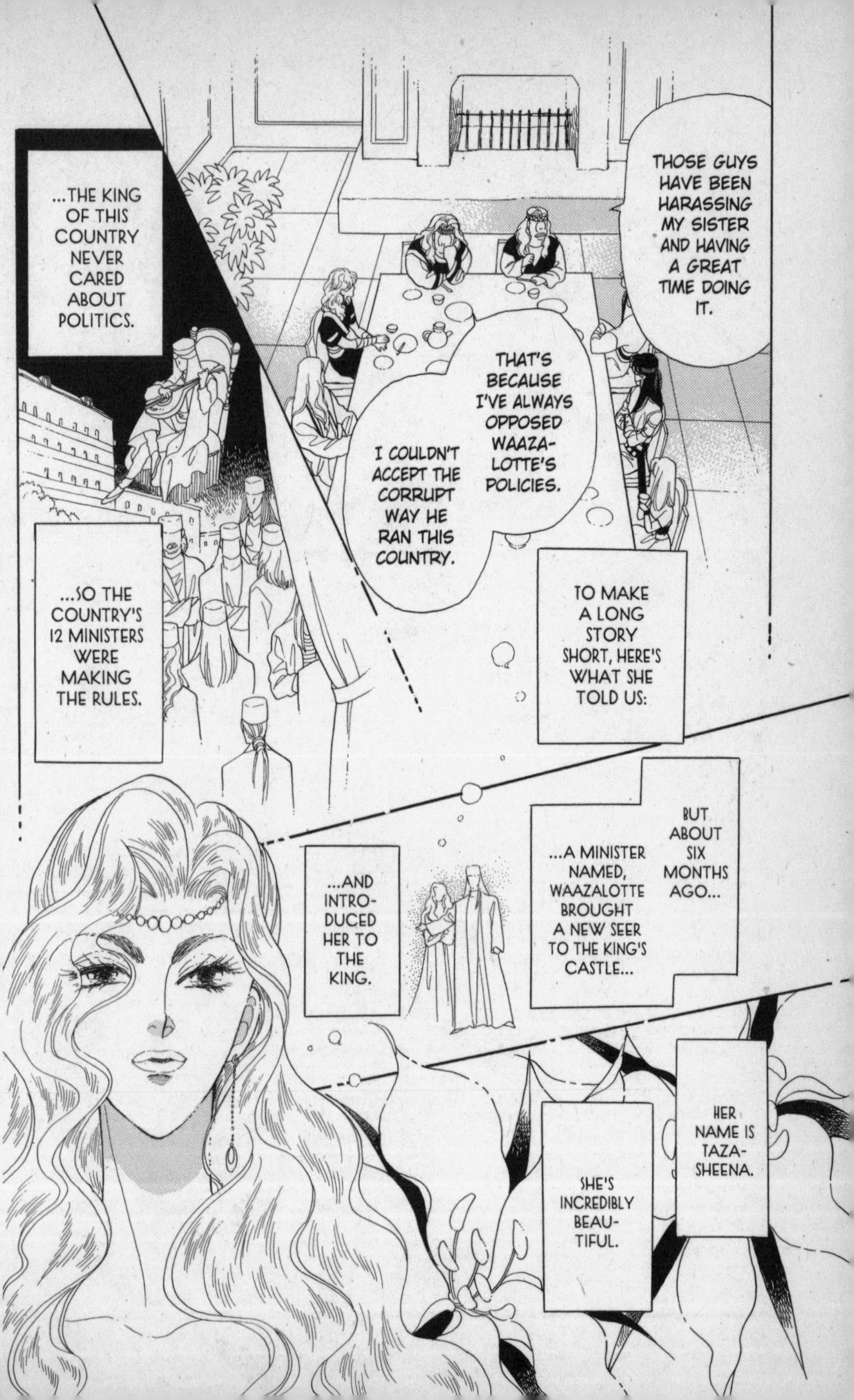
THOSE GUYS HAVE BEEN HARASSING MY SISTER AND HAVING A GREAT TIME DOING IT.
THAT'S BECAUSE I'VE ALWAYS OPPOSED WAAZA-LOTTE'S POLICIES.
I COULDN'T ACCEPT THE CORRUPT WAY HE RAN THIS COUNTRY.
TO MAKE A LONG STORY SHORT, HERE'S WHAT SHE TOLD US:
...THE KING OF THIS COUNTRY NEVER CARED ABOUT POLITICS.
...SO THE COUNTRY'S 12 MINISTERS WERE MAKING THE RULES.
BUT ABOUT SIX MONTHS AGO...
...A MINISTER NAMED, WAAZALOTTE BROUGHT A NEW SEER TO THE KING'S CASTLE...
...AND INTRO-DUCED HER TO THE KING.
HER NAME IS TAZA-SHEENA.
SHE'S INCREDIBLY BEAU-TIFUL.

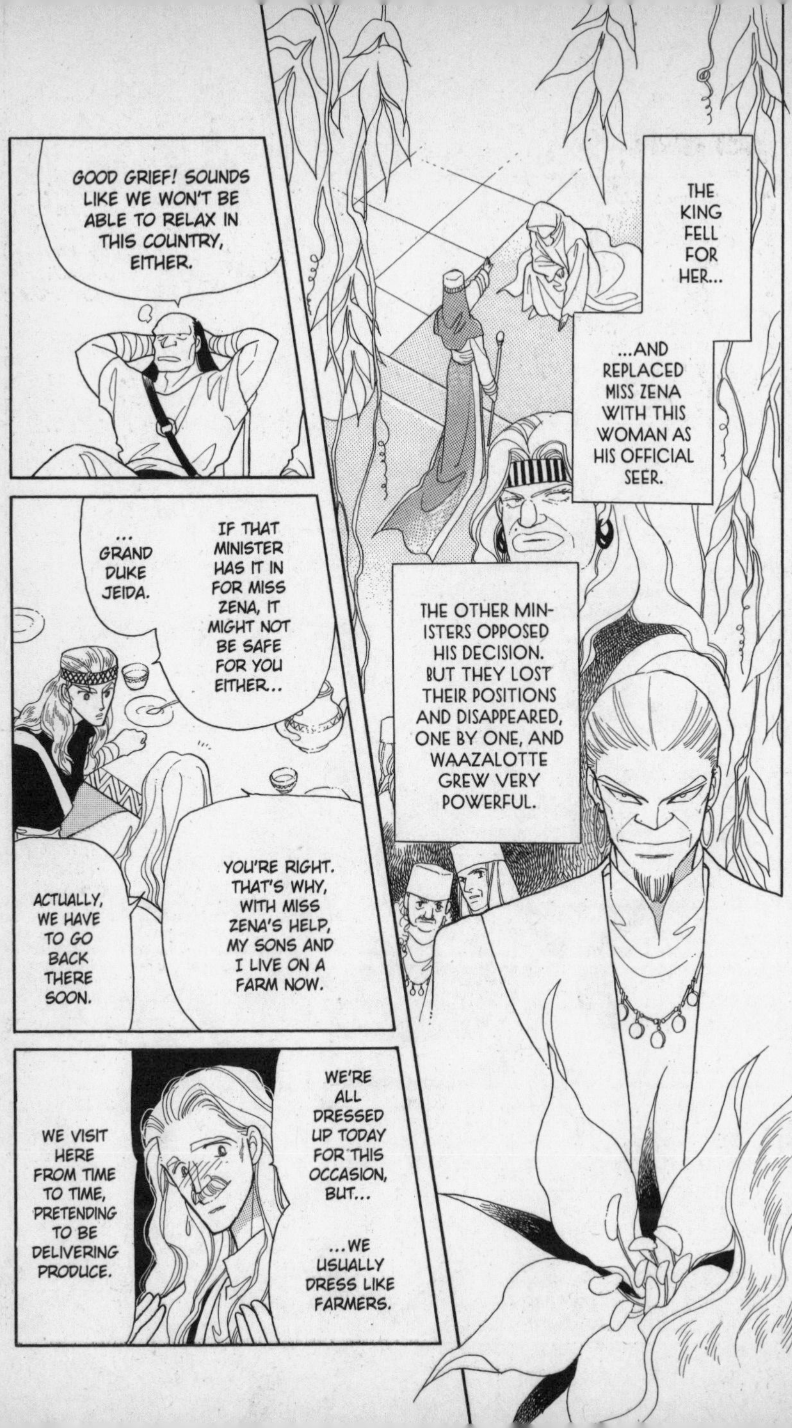
THE KING FELL FOR HER...
...AND REPLACED MISS ZENA WITH THIS WOMAN AS HIS OFFICIAL SEER.
THE OTHER MINISTERS OPPOSED HIS DECISION. BUT THEY LOST THEIR POSITIONS AND DISAPPEARED, ONE BY ONE, AND WAAZALOTTE GREW VERY POWERFUL.
GOOD GRIEF! SOUNDS LIKE WE WON'T BE ABLE TO RELAX IN THIS COUNTRY, EITHER.
IF THAT MINISTER HAS IT IN FOR MISS ZENA, IT MIGHT NOT BE SAFE FOR YOU EITHER..
... GRAND DUKE JEIDA.
YOU'RE RIGHT. THAT'S WHY, WITH MISS ZENA'S HELP, MY SONS AND I LIVE ON A FARM NOW.
ACTUALLY, WE HAVE TO GO BACK THERE SOON.
WE'RE ALL DRESSED UP TODAY FOR THIS OCCASION, BUT...
...WE USUALLY DRESS LIKE FARMERS.
WE VISIT HERE FROM TIME TO TIME, PRETENDING TO BE DELIVERING PRODUCE.

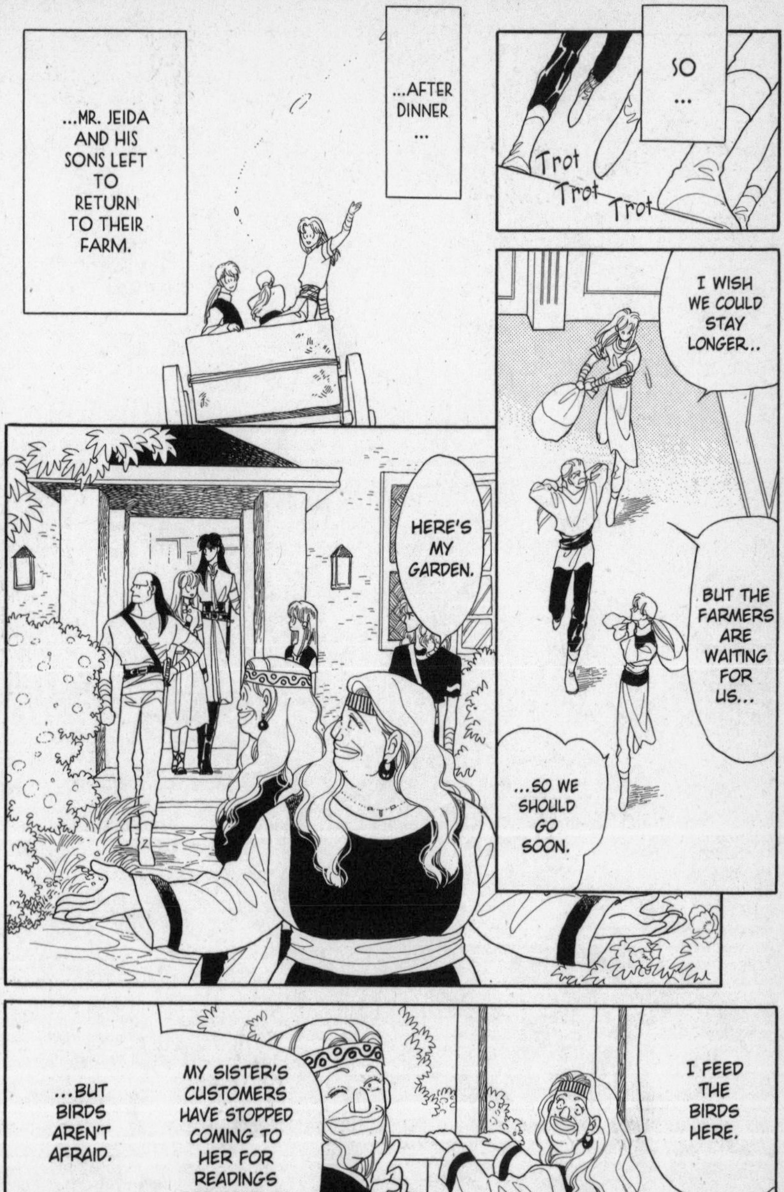
SO ...
Trot
Trot
Trot
...AFTER DINNER ...
...MR. JEIDA AND HIS SONS LEFT TO RETURN TO THEIR FARM.
I WISH WE COULD STAY LONGER..
BUT THE FARMERS ARE WAITING FOR US...
...SO WE SHOULD GO SOON.
HERE'S MY GARDEN.
I FEED THE BIRDS HERE.
MY SISTER'S CUSTOMERS HAVE STOPPED COMING TO HER FOR READINGS FOR FEAR OF WAAZALOTTE...
...BUT BIRDS AREN'T AFRAID.

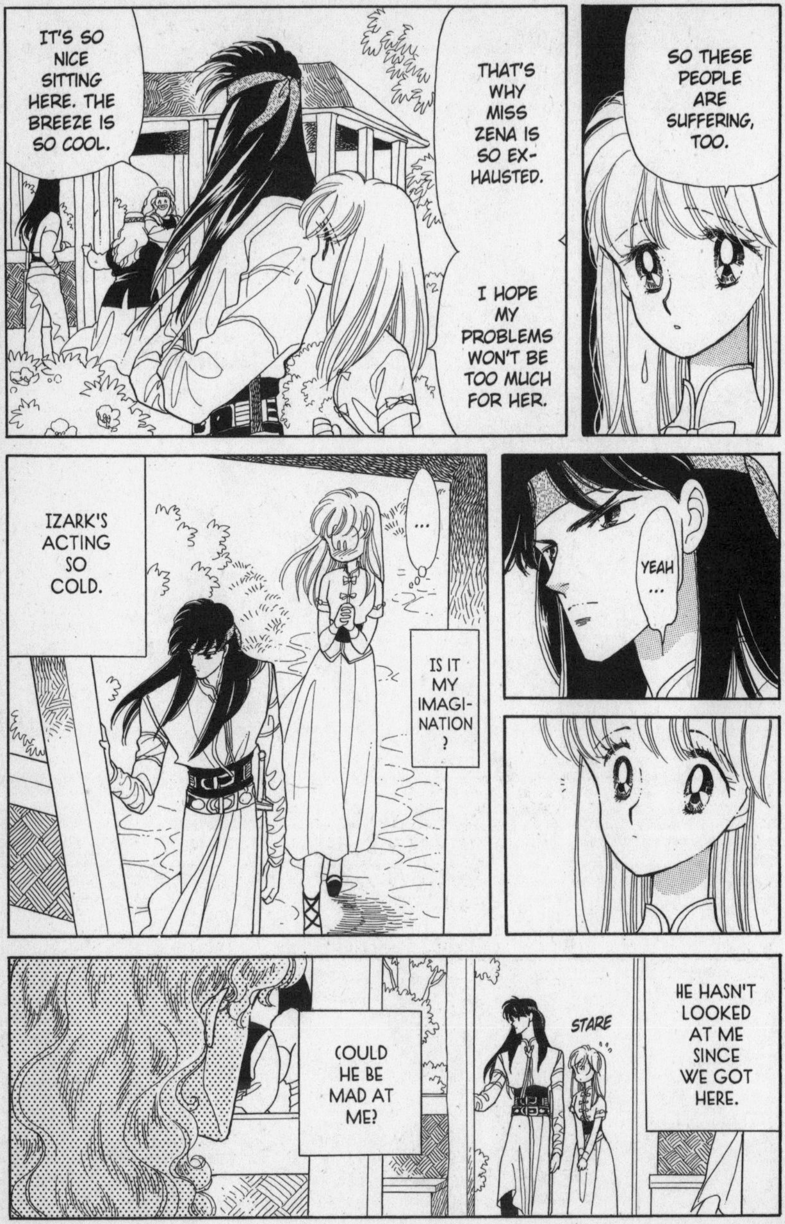
SO THESE PEOPLE ARE SUFFERING, TOO.
THAT'S WHY MISS ZENA IS SO EX-HAUSTED.
I HOPE MY PROBLEMS WON'T BE TOO MUCH FOR HER.
IT'S SO NICE SITTING HERE. THE BREEZE IS SO COOL.
YEAH ...
...
IZARK'S ACTING SO COLD.
IS IT MY IMAGINATION?
HE HASN'T LOOKED AT ME SINCE WE GOT HERE.
STARE
COULD HE BE MAD AT ME?

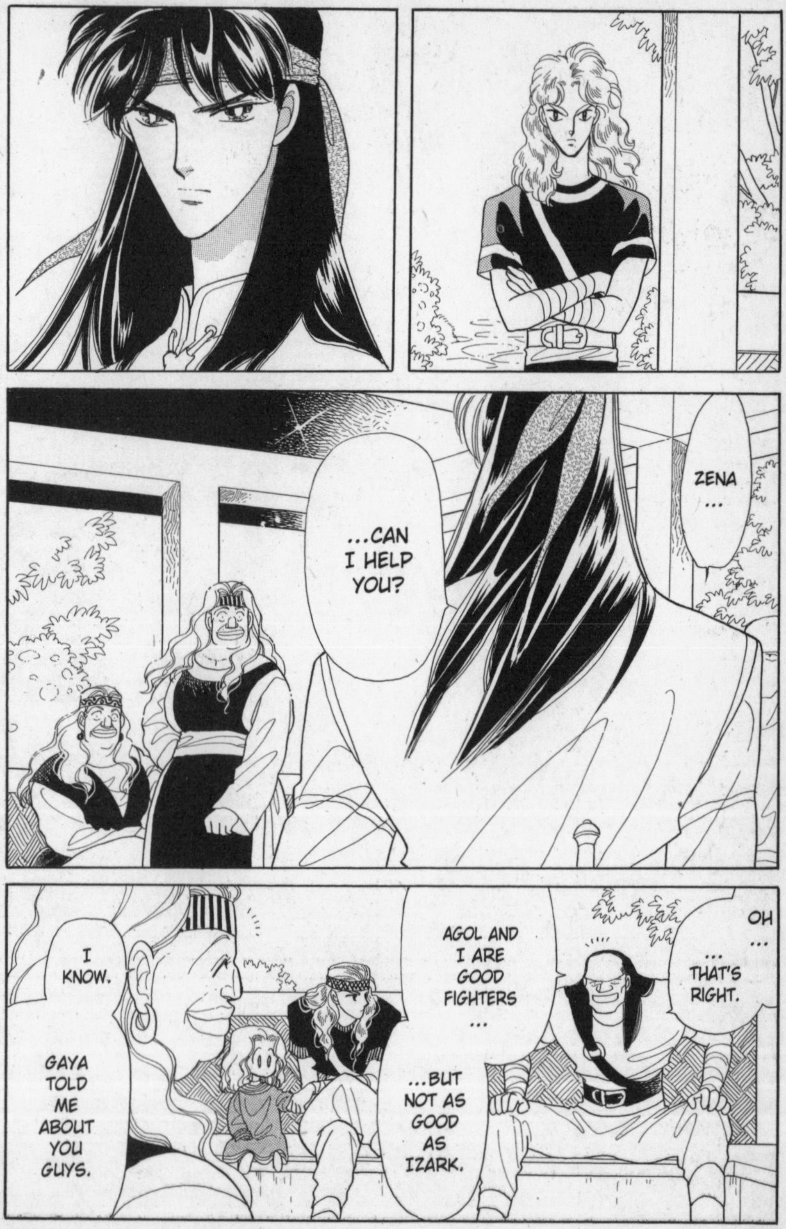
ZENA ...
...CAN I HELP YOU?
OH ...
... THAT'S RIGHT.
AGOL AND I ARE GOOD FIGHTERS ...
...BUT NOT AS GOOD AS IZARK.
I KNOW.
GAYA TOLD ME ABOUT YOU GUYS.

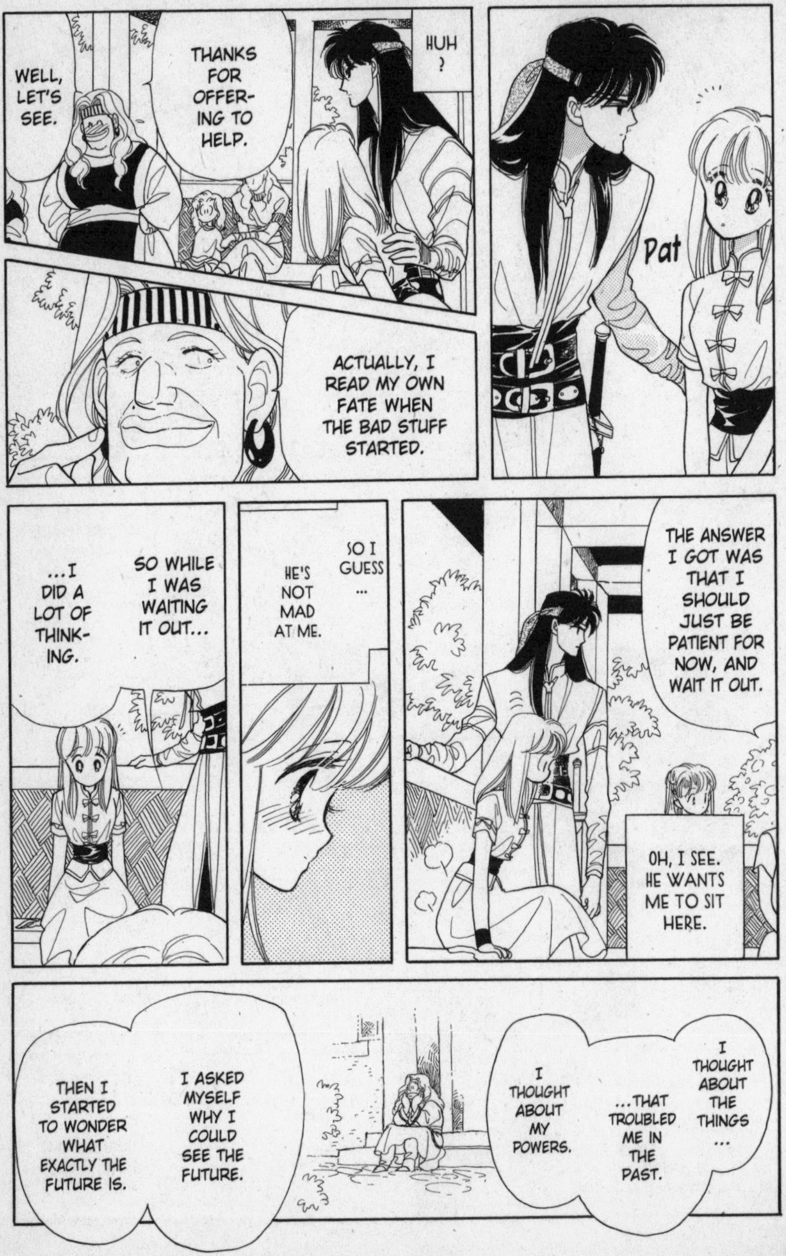
Pat
HUH ?
THANKS FOR OFFERING TO HELP.
WELL, LET'S SEE.
ACTUALLY, I READ MY OWN FATE WHEN THE BAD STUFF STARTED.
THE ANSWER I GOT WAS THAT I SHOULD JUST BE PATIENT FOR NOW, AND WAIT IT OUT.
OH, I SEE. HE WANTS ME TO SIT HERE.
SO I GUESS ...
HE'S NOT MAD AT ME.
SO WHILE I WAS WAITING IT OUT...
...I DID A LOT OF THINKING.
I THOUGHT ABOUT THE THINGS ...
...THAT TROUBLED ME IN THE PAST.
I THOUGHT ABOUT MY POWERS.
I ASKED MYSELF WHY I COULD SEE THE FUTURE.
THEN I STARTED TO WONDER WHAT EXACTLY THE FUTURE IS.

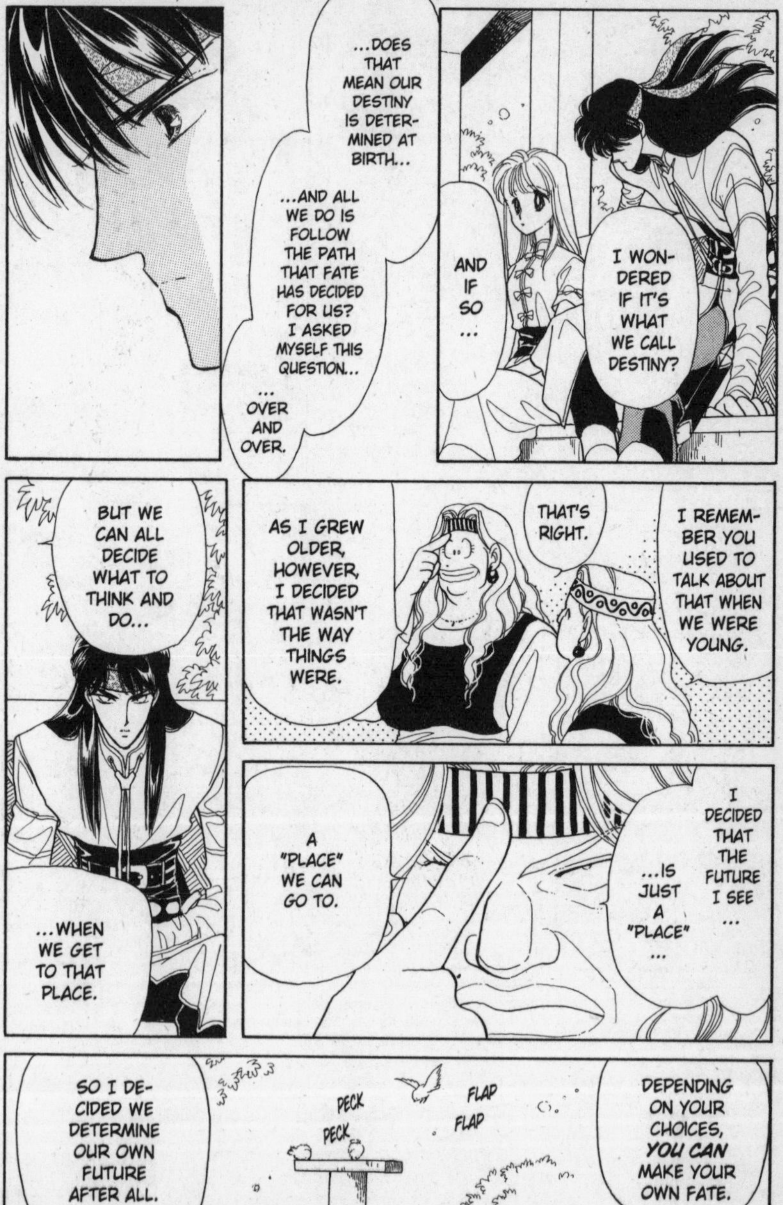
I WONDERED IF IT'S WHAT WE CALL DESTINY?
AND IF SO ...
...DOES THAT MEAN OUR DESTINY IS DETERMINED AT BIRTH...
...AND ALL WE DO IS FOLLOW THE PATH THAT FATE HAS DECIDED FOR US? I ASKED MYSELF THIS QUESTION...
... OVER AND OVER.
I REMEMBER YOU USED TO TALK ABOUT THAT WHEN WE WERE YOUNG.
THAT'S RIGHT.
AS I GREW OLDER, HOWEVER, I DECIDED THAT WASN'T THE WAY THINGS WERE.
I DECIDED THAT THE FUTURE I SEE ...
...IS JUST A "PLACE" ...
A "PLACE" WE CAN GO TO.
BUT WE CAN ALL DECIDE WHAT TO THINK AND DO...
...WHEN WE GET TO THAT PLACE.
DEPENDING ON YOUR CHOICES, ***YOU CAN*** MAKE YOUR OWN FATE.
FLAP
FLAP
PECK
PECK
SO I DECIDED WE DETERMINE OUR OWN FUTURE AFTER ALL.

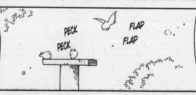

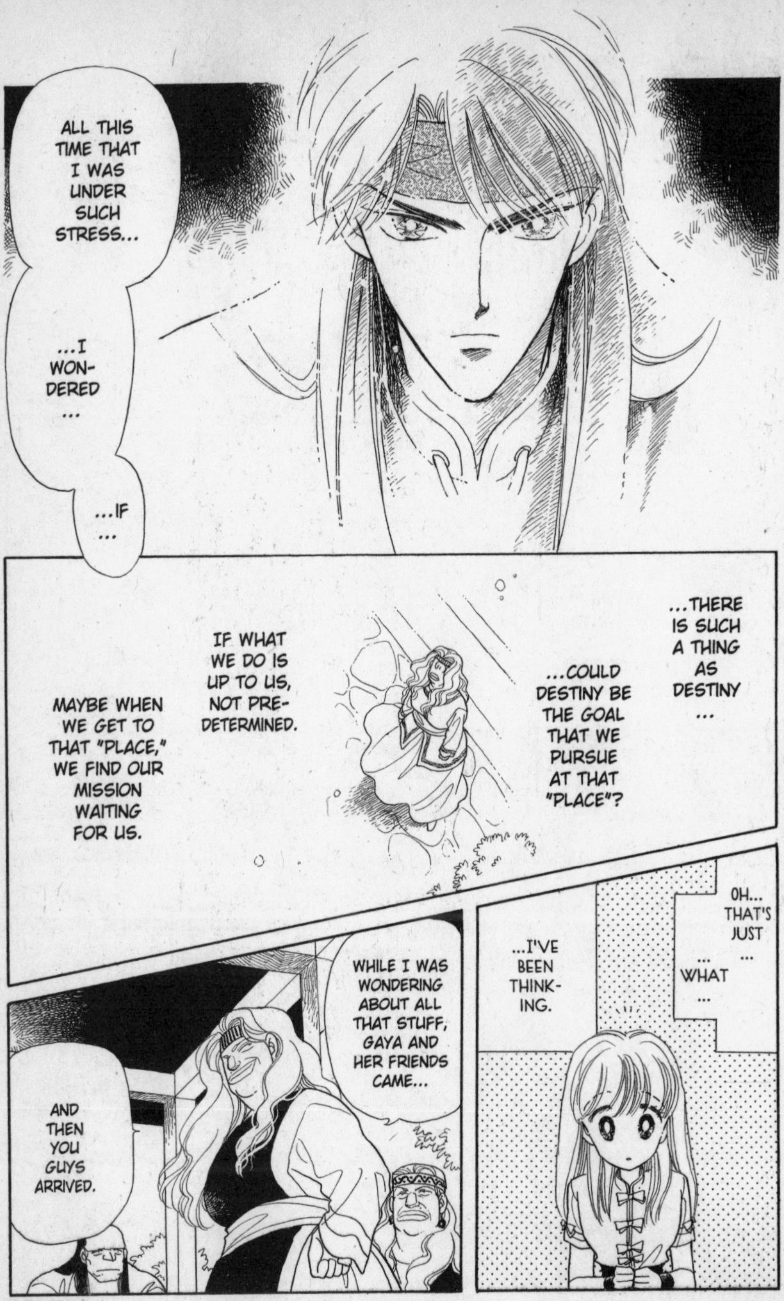
ALL THIS TIME THAT I WAS UNDER SUCH STRESS...
...I WONDERED...
...IF...
...THERE IS SUCH A THING AS DESTINY...
...COULD DESTINY BE THE GOAL THAT WE PURSUE AT THAT "PLACE"?
IF WHAT WE DO IS UP TO US, NOT PRE-DETERMINED.
MAYBE WHEN WE GET TO THAT "PLACE," WE FIND OUR MISSION WAITING FOR US.
OH... THAT'S JUST...
...WHAT...
...I'VE BEEN THINK-ING.
WHILE I WAS WONDERING ABOUT ALL THAT STUFF, GAYA AND HER FRIENDS CAME...
AND THEN YOU GUYS ARRIVED.

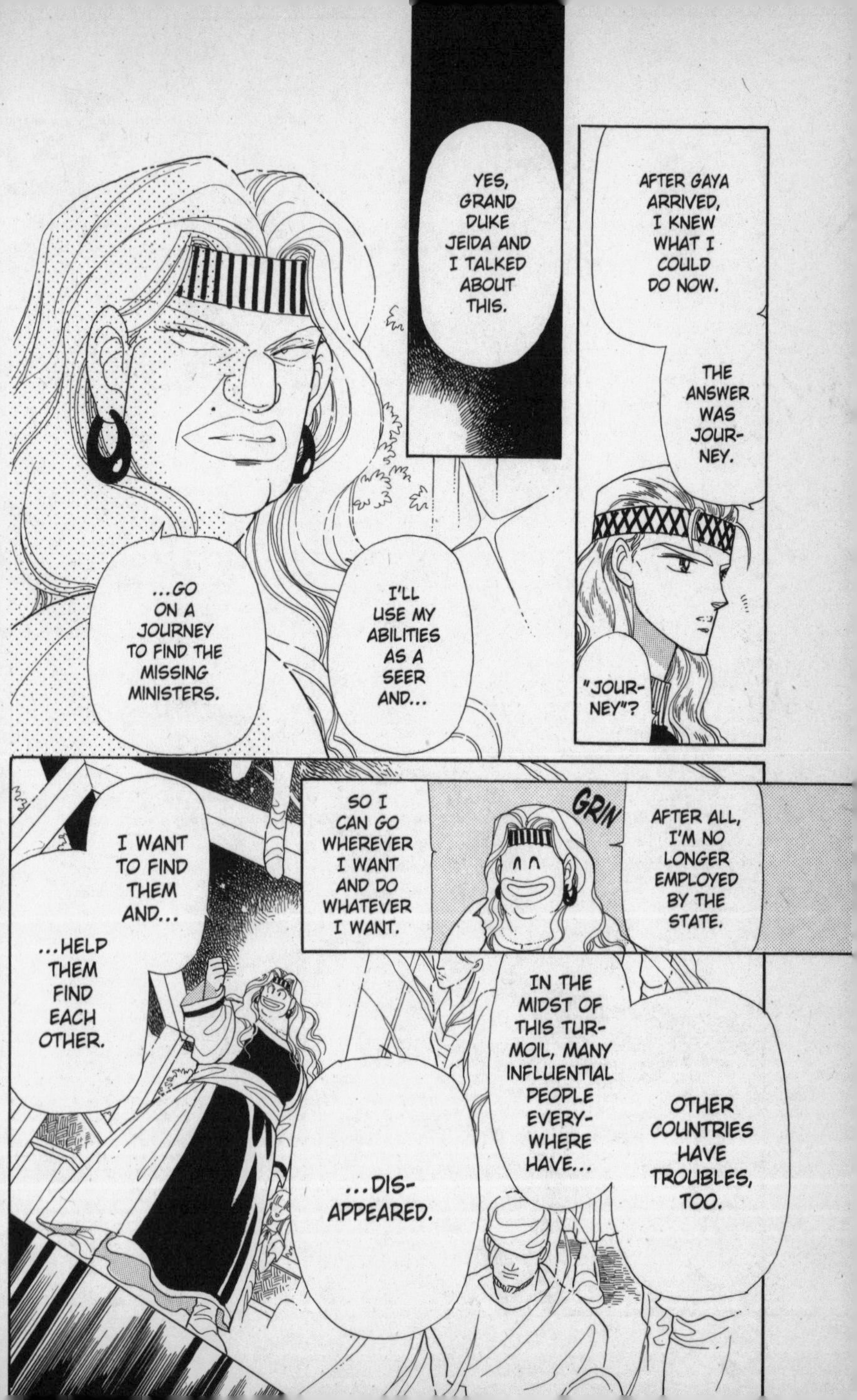
YES, GRAND DUKE JEIDA AND I TALKED ABOUT THIS.
AFTER GAYA ARRIVED, I KNEW WHAT I COULD DO NOW.
THE ANSWER WAS JOURNEY.
"JOURNEY"?
I'LL USE MY ABILITIES AS A SEER AND...
...GO ON A JOURNEY TO FIND THE MISSING MINISTERS.
AFTER ALL, I'M NO LONGER EMPLOYED BY THE STATE.
GRIN
SO I CAN GO WHEREVER I WANT AND DO WHATEVER I WANT.
OTHER COUNTRIES HAVE TROUBLES, TOO.
IN THE MIDST OF THIS TURMOIL, MANY INFLUENTIAL PEOPLE EVERYWHERE HAVE...
...DISAPPEARED.
I WANT TO FIND THEM AND...
...HELP THEM FIND EACH OTHER.

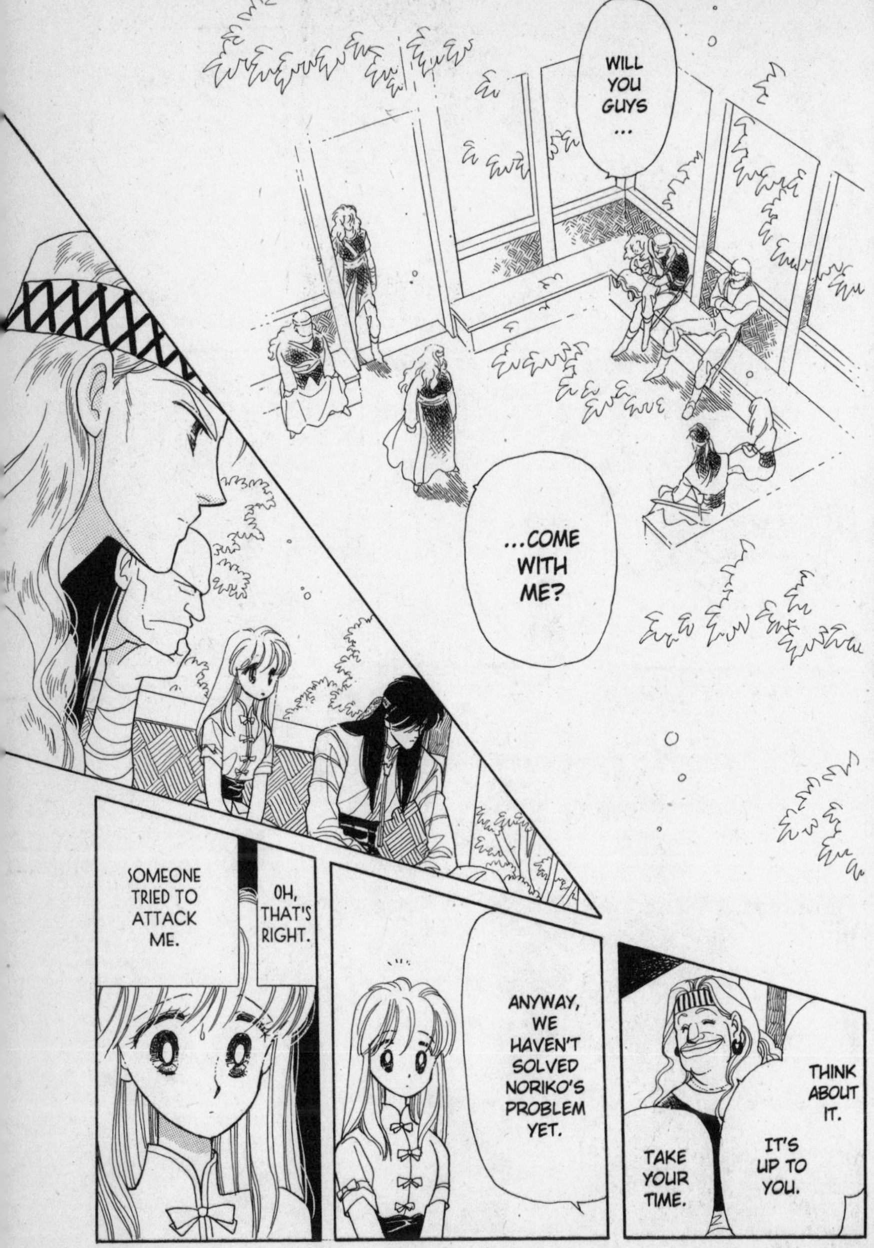
WILL YOU GUYS ...
...COME WITH ME?
THINK ABOUT IT.
IT'S UP TO YOU.
TAKE YOUR TIME.
ANYWAY, WE HAVEN'T SOLVED NORIKO'S PROBLEM YET.
OH, THAT'S RIGHT.
SOMEONE TRIED TO ATTACK ME.

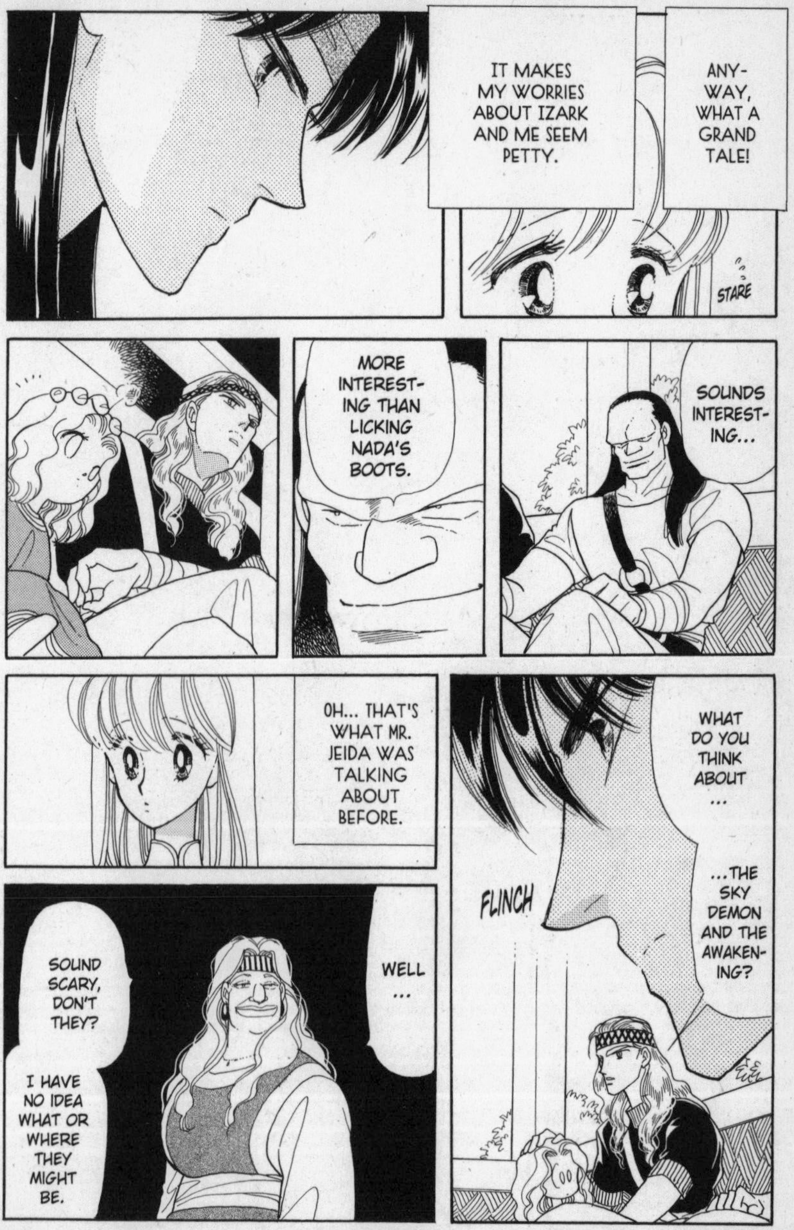
ANY-WAY, WHAT A GRAND TALE!
IT MAKES MY WORRIES ABOUT IZARK AND ME SEEM PETTY.
STARE
SOUNDS INTEREST-ING...
MORE INTEREST-ING THAN LICKING NADA'S BOOTS.
...
WHAT DO YOU THINK ABOUT ...
...THE SKY DEMON AND THE AWAKEN-ING?
FLINCH
OH... THAT'S WHAT MR. JEIDA WAS TALKING ABOUT BEFORE.
WELL ...
SOUND SCARY, DON'T THEY?
I HAVE NO IDEA WHAT OR WHERE THEY MIGHT BE.

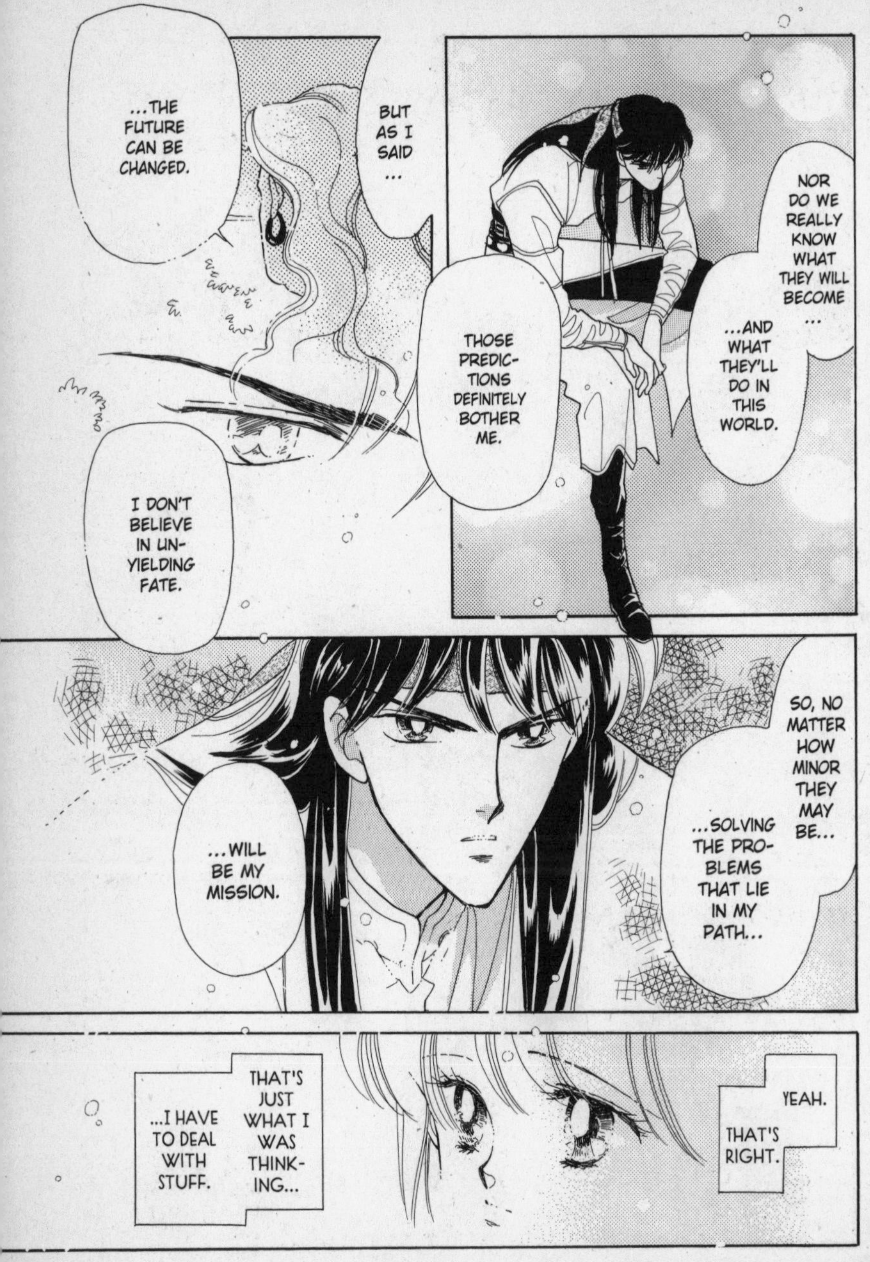
NOR DO WE REALLY KNOW WHAT THEY WILL BECOME...
...AND WHAT THEY'LL DO IN THIS WORLD.
THOSE PREDICTIONS DEFINITELY BOTHER ME.
BUT AS I SAID...
...THE FUTURE CAN BE CHANGED.
I DON'T BELIEVE IN UNYIELDING FATE.
SO, NO MATTER HOW MINOR THEY MAY BE...
...SOLVING THE PROBLEMS THAT LIE IN MY PATH...
...WILL BE MY MISSION.
YEAH.
THAT'S RIGHT.
THAT'S JUST WHAT I WAS THINKING...
...I HAVE TO DEAL WITH STUFF.

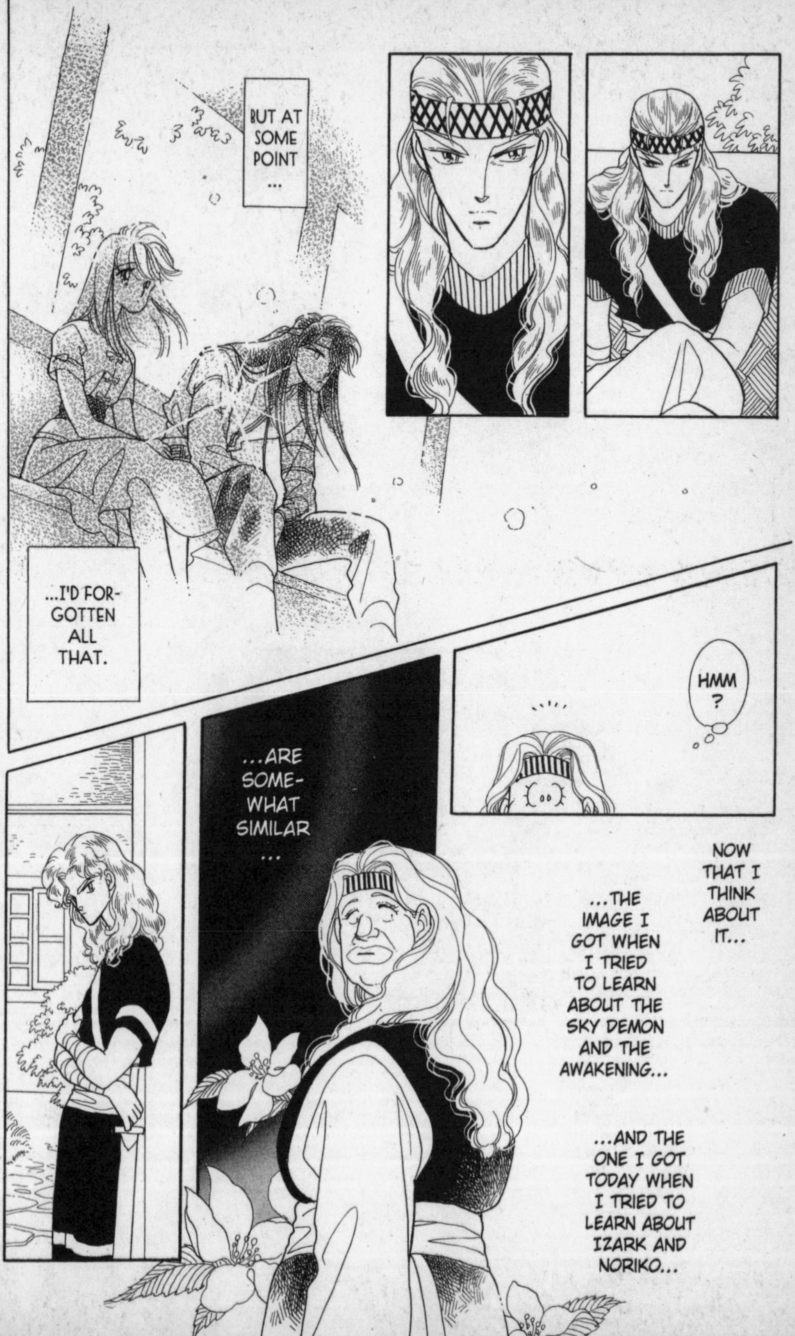
BUT AT SOME POINT...
...I'D FORGOTTEN ALL THAT.
HMM?
NOW THAT I THINK ABOUT IT...
...THE IMAGE I GOT WHEN I TRIED TO LEARN ABOUT THE SKY DEMON AND THE AWAKENING...
...AND THE ONE I GOT TODAY WHEN I TRIED TO LEARN ABOUT IZARK AND NORIKO...
...ARE SOMEWHAT SIMILAR...

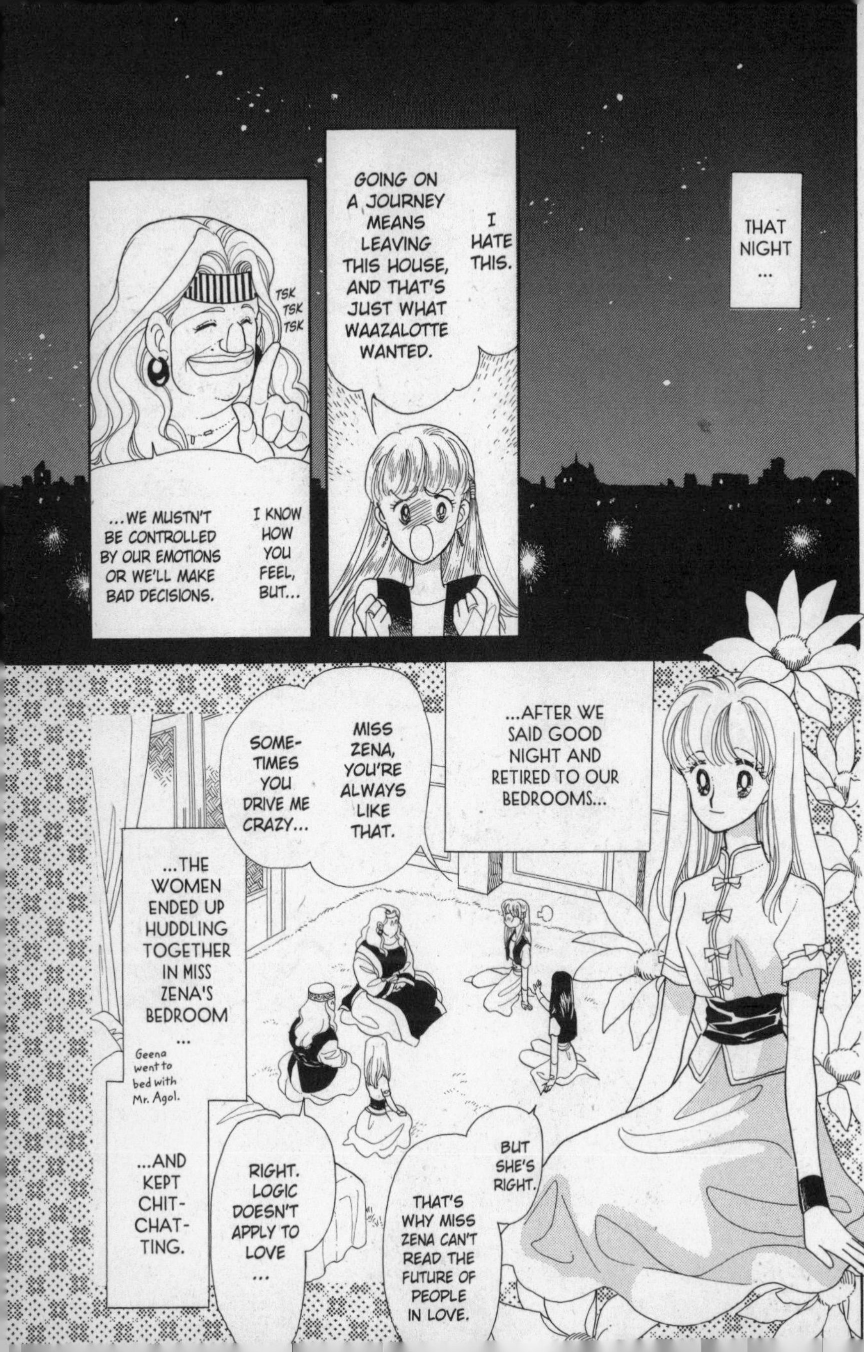
THAT NIGHT ...
I HATE THIS.
GOING ON A JOURNEY MEANS LEAVING THIS HOUSE, AND THAT'S JUST WHAT WAAZALOTTE WANTED.
TSK TSK TSK
I KNOW HOW YOU FEEL, BUT...
...WE MUSTN'T BE CONTROLLED BY OUR EMOTIONS OR WE'LL MAKE BAD DECISIONS.
...AFTER WE SAID GOOD NIGHT AND RETIRED TO OUR BEDROOMS...
MISS ZENA, YOU'RE ALWAYS LIKE THAT.
SOME-TIMES YOU DRIVE ME CRAZY...
...THE WOMEN ENDED UP HUDDLING TOGETHER IN MISS ZENA'S BEDROOM ...
Geena went to bed with Mr. Agol.
BUT SHE'S RIGHT.
THAT'S WHY MISS ZENA CAN'T READ THE FUTURE OF PEOPLE IN LOVE.
RIGHT. LOGIC DOESN'T APPLY TO LOVE ...
...AND KEPT CHIT-CHAT-TING.

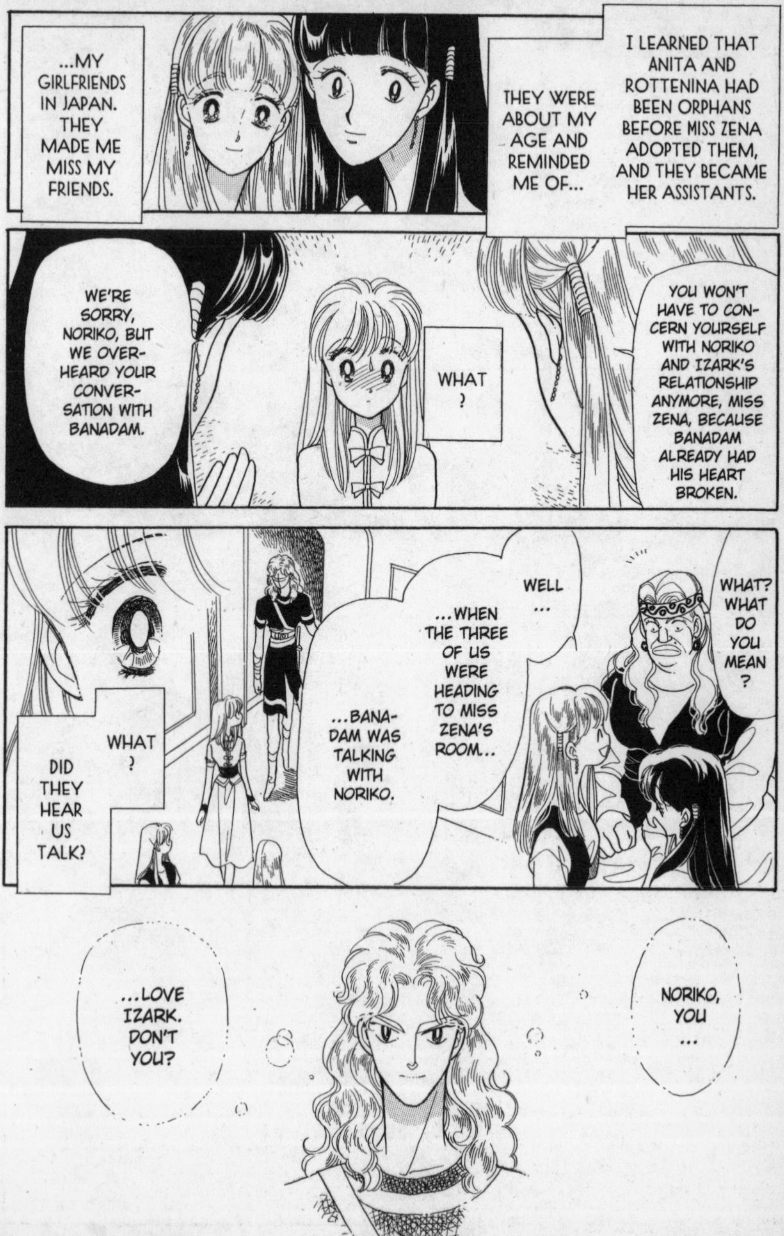
I LEARNED THAT ANITA AND ROTTENINA HAD BEEN ORPHANS BEFORE MISS ZENA ADOPTED THEM, AND THEY BECAME HER ASSISTANTS.
THEY WERE ABOUT MY AGE AND REMINDED ME OF...
...MY GIRLFRIENDS IN JAPAN. THEY MADE ME MISS MY FRIENDS.
YOU WON'T HAVE TO CONCERN YOURSELF WITH NORIKO AND IZARK'S RELATIONSHIP ANYMORE, MISS ZENA, BECAUSE BANADAM ALREADY HAD HIS HEART BROKEN.
WHAT ?
WE'RE SORRY, NORIKO, BUT WE OVERHEARD YOUR CONVERSATION WITH BANADAM.
WHAT? WHAT DO YOU MEAN ?
WELL ...
...WHEN THE THREE OF US WERE HEADING TO MISS ZENA'S ROOM...
...BANADAM WAS TALKING WITH NORIKO.
WHAT ?
DID THEY HEAR US TALK?
NORIKO, YOU ...
...LOVE IZARK. DON'T YOU?

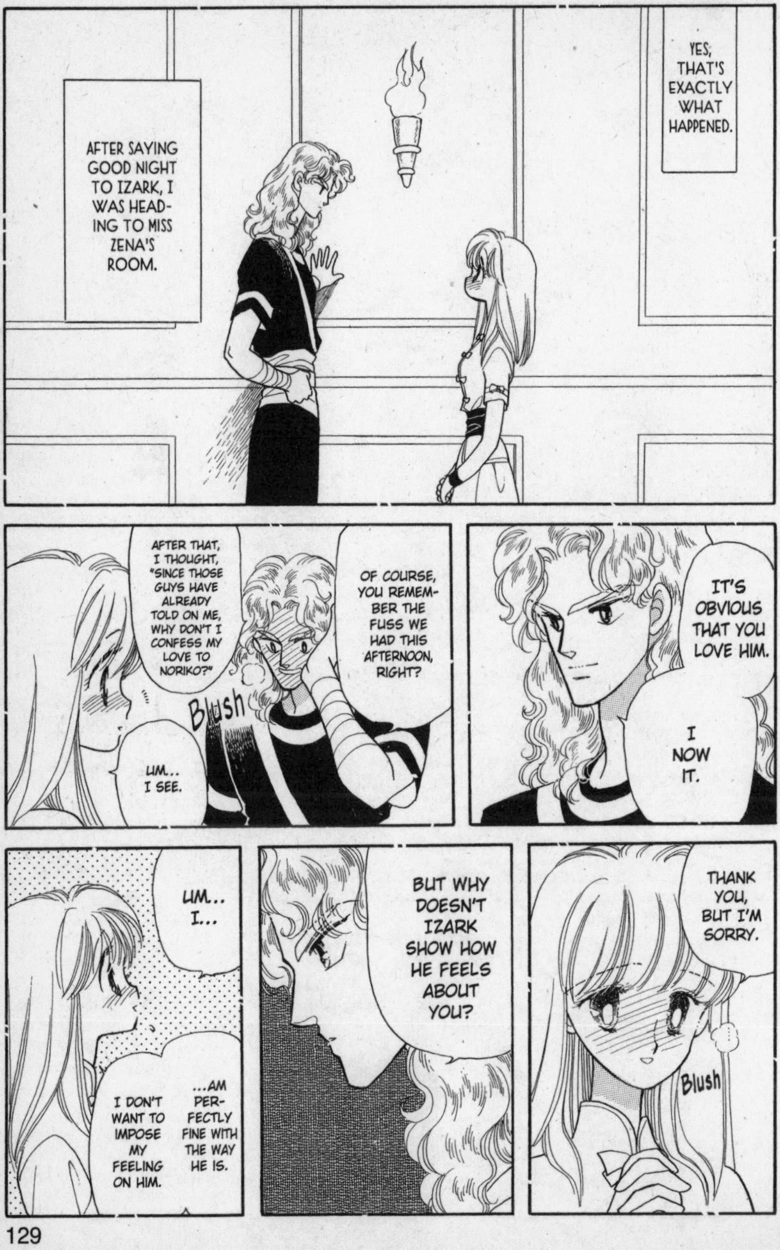
YES, THAT'S EXACTLY WHAT HAPPENED.
AFTER SAYING GOOD NIGHT TO IZARK, I WAS HEADING TO MISS ZENA'S ROOM.
IT'S OBVIOUS THAT YOU LOVE HIM.
I NOW IT.
OF COURSE, YOU REMEMBER THE FUSS WE HAD THIS AFTERNOON, RIGHT?
AFTER THAT, I THOUGHT, "SINCE THOSE GUYS HAVE ALREADY TOLD ON ME, WHY DON'T I CONFESS MY LOVE TO NORIKO?"
Blush
UM... I SEE.
THANK YOU, BUT I'M SORRY.
Blush
BUT WHY DOESN'T IZARK SHOW HOW HE FEELS ABOUT YOU?
UM... I...
...AM PERFECTLY FINE WITH THE WAY HE IS.
I DON'T WANT TO IMPOSE MY FEELING ON HIM.

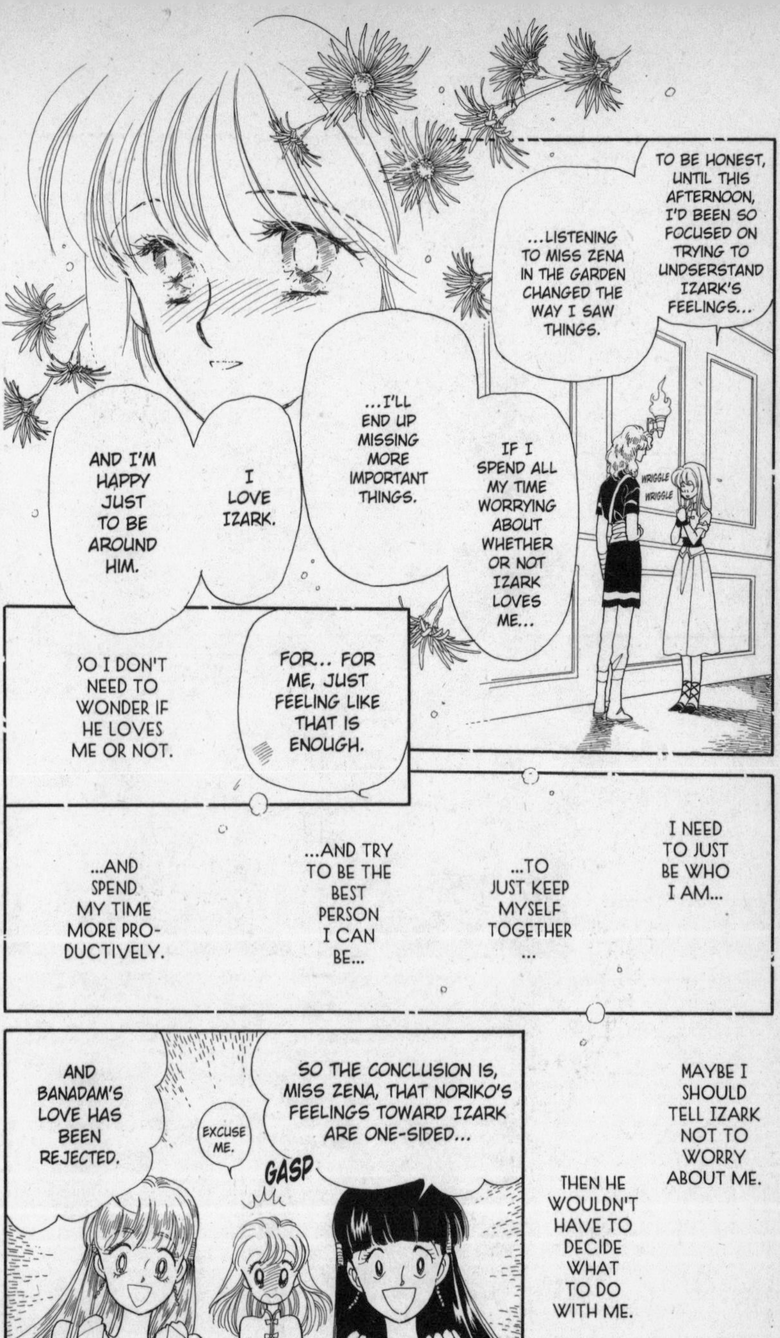
TO BE HONEST, UNTIL THIS AFTERNOON, I'D BEEN SO FOCUSED ON TRYING TO UNDSERSTAND IZARK'S FEELINGS...
...LISTENING TO MISS ZENA IN THE GARDEN CHANGED THE WAY I SAW THINGS.
WRIGGLE
WRIGGLE
IF I SPEND ALL MY TIME WORRYING ABOUT WHETHER OR NOT IZARK LOVES ME...
...I'LL END UP MISSING MORE IMPORTANT THINGS.
I LOVE IZARK.
AND I'M HAPPY JUST TO BE AROUND HIM.
FOR... FOR ME, JUST FEELING LIKE THAT IS ENOUGH.
SO I DON'T NEED TO WONDER IF HE LOVES ME OR NOT.
I NEED TO JUST BE WHO I AM...
...TO JUST KEEP MYSELF TOGETHER ...
...AND TRY TO BE THE BEST PERSON I CAN BE...
...AND SPEND MY TIME MORE PRO-DUCTIVELY.
MAYBE I SHOULD TELL IZARK NOT TO WORRY ABOUT ME.
THEN HE WOULDN'T HAVE TO DECIDE WHAT TO DO WITH ME.
SO THE CONCLUSION IS, MISS ZENA, THAT NORIKO'S FEELINGS TOWARD IZARK ARE ONE-SIDED...
GASP
EXCUSE ME.
AND BANADAM'S LOVE HAS BEEN REJECTED.

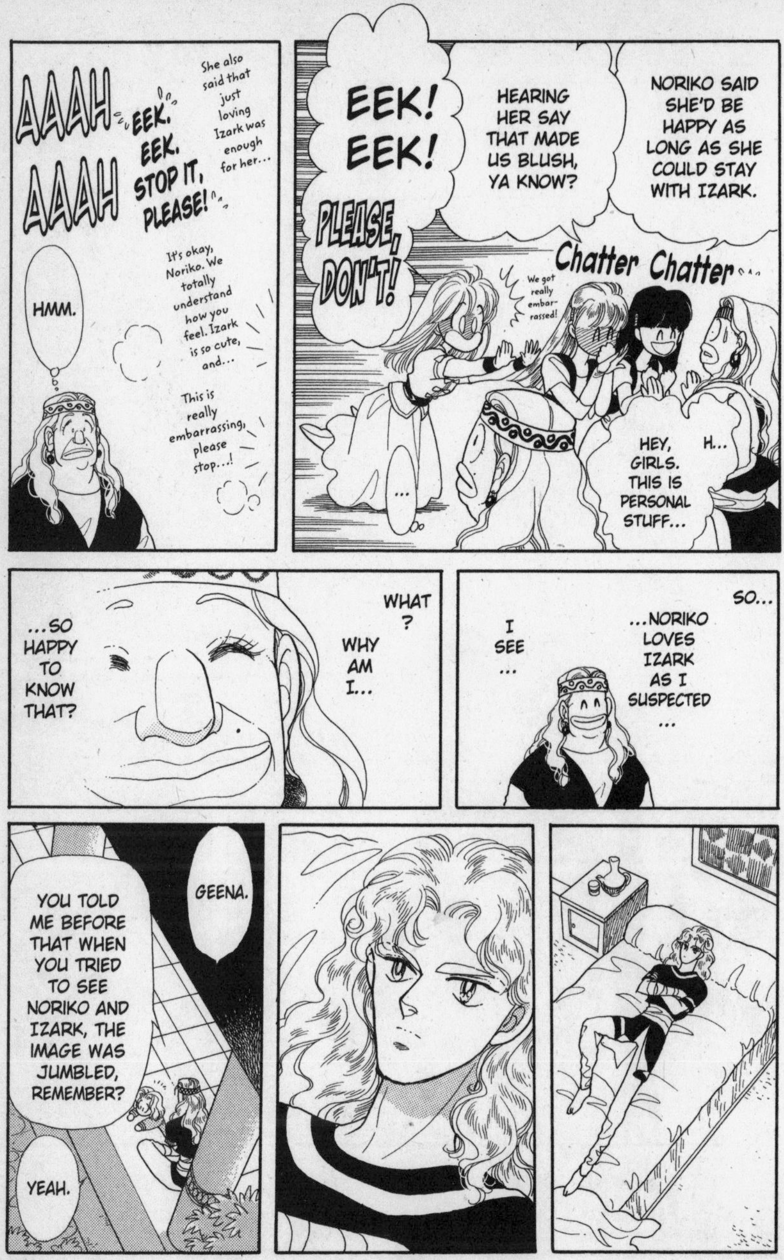
NORIKO SAID SHE'D BE HAPPY AS LONG AS SHE COULD STAY WITH IZARK.
HEARING HER SAY THAT MADE US BLUSH, YA KNOW?
EEK! EEK!
PLEASE, DON'T!
Chatter Chatter
We got really embar-rassed!
H...
HEY, GIRLS. THIS IS PERSONAL STUFF...
...
She also said that just loving Izark was enough for her...
EEK. EEK. STOP IT, PLEASE!
AAAH AAAH
It's okay, Noriko. We totally understand how you feel. Izark is so cute, and...
This is really embarrassing, please stop...!
HMM.
SO...
...NORIKO LOVES IZARK AS I SUSPECTED ...
I SEE ...
WHAT? WHY AM I...
...SO HAPPY TO KNOW THAT?
GEENA.
YOU TOLD ME BEFORE THAT WHEN YOU TRIED TO SEE NORIKO AND IZARK, THE IMAGE WAS JUMBLED, REMEMBER?
YEAH.

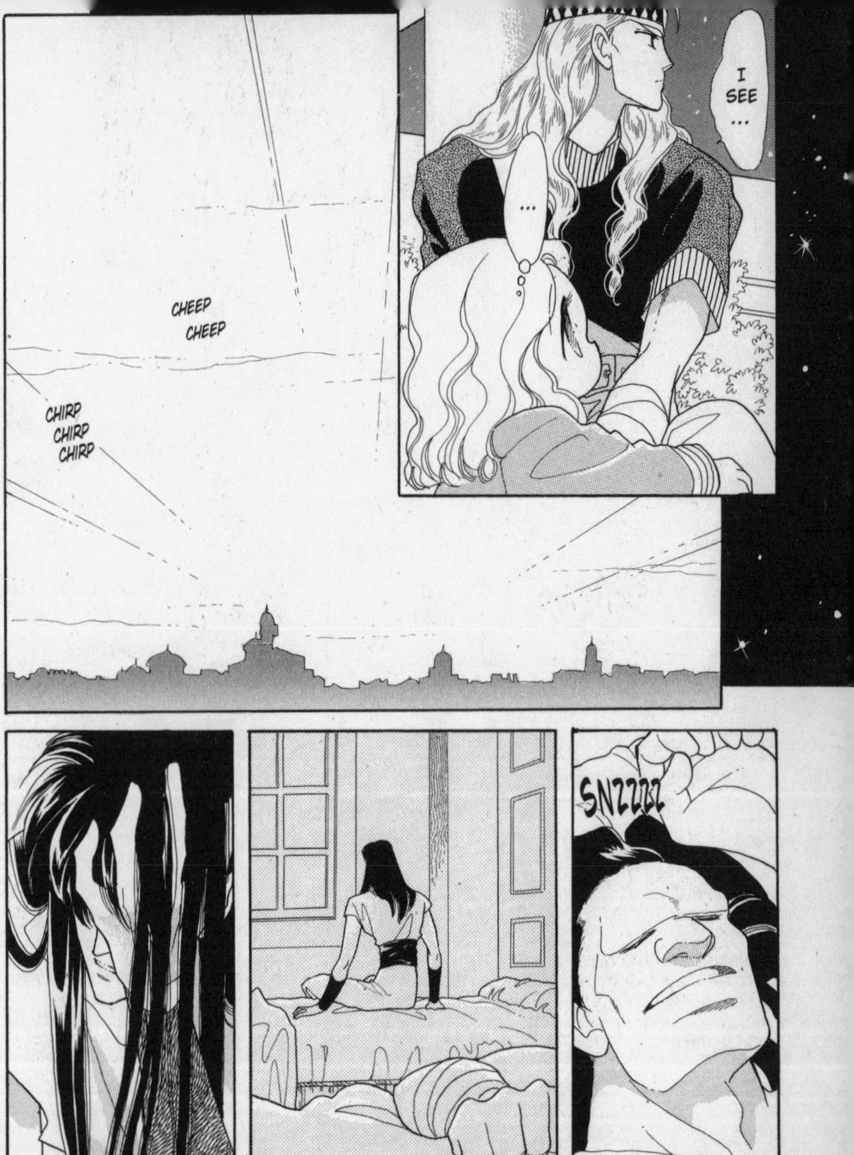
I SEE ...
...
CHEEP
CHEEP
CHIRP
CHIRP
CHIRP
SNZZZZZ

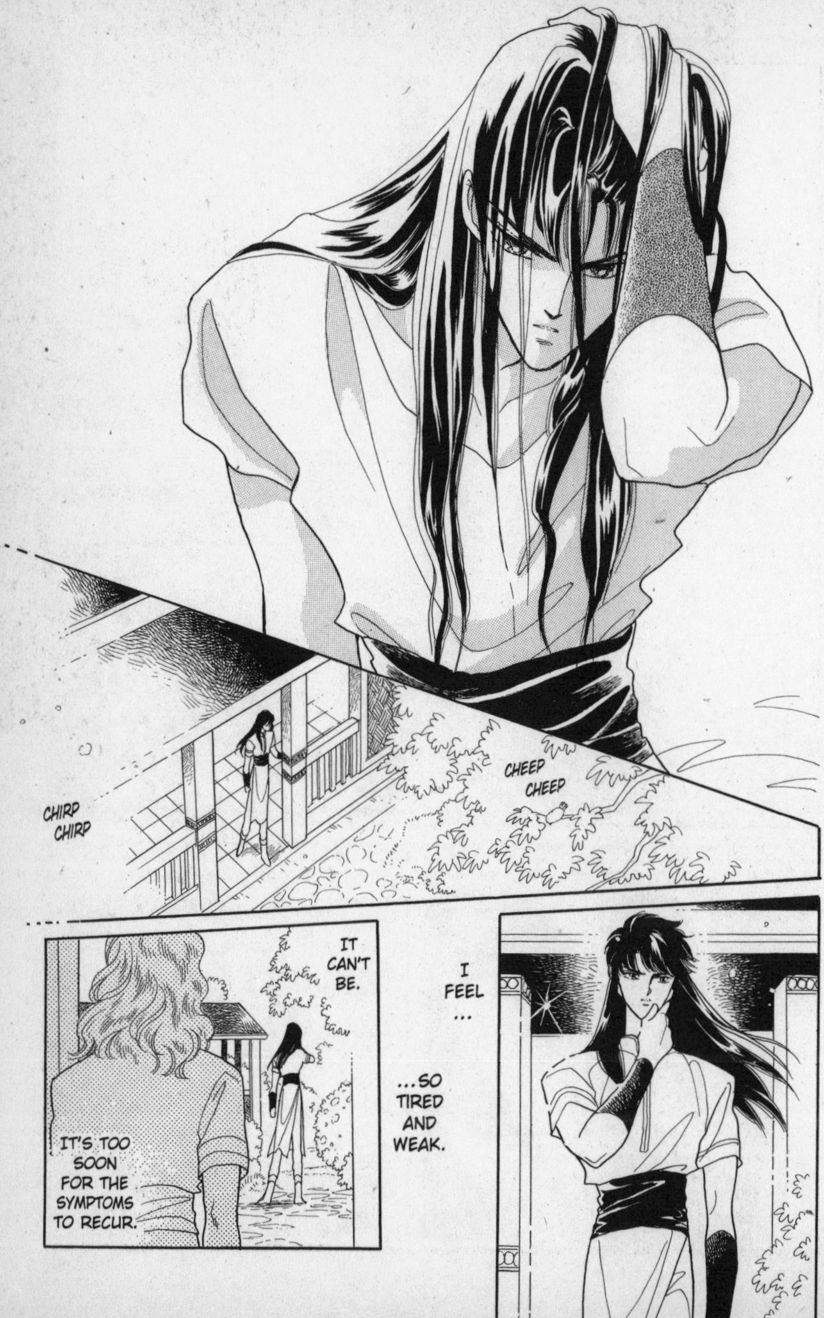
CHEEP CHEEP
CHIRP CHIRP
I FEEL ...
...SO TIRED AND WEAK.
IT CAN'T BE.
IT'S TOO SOON FOR THE SYMPTOMS TO RECUR.

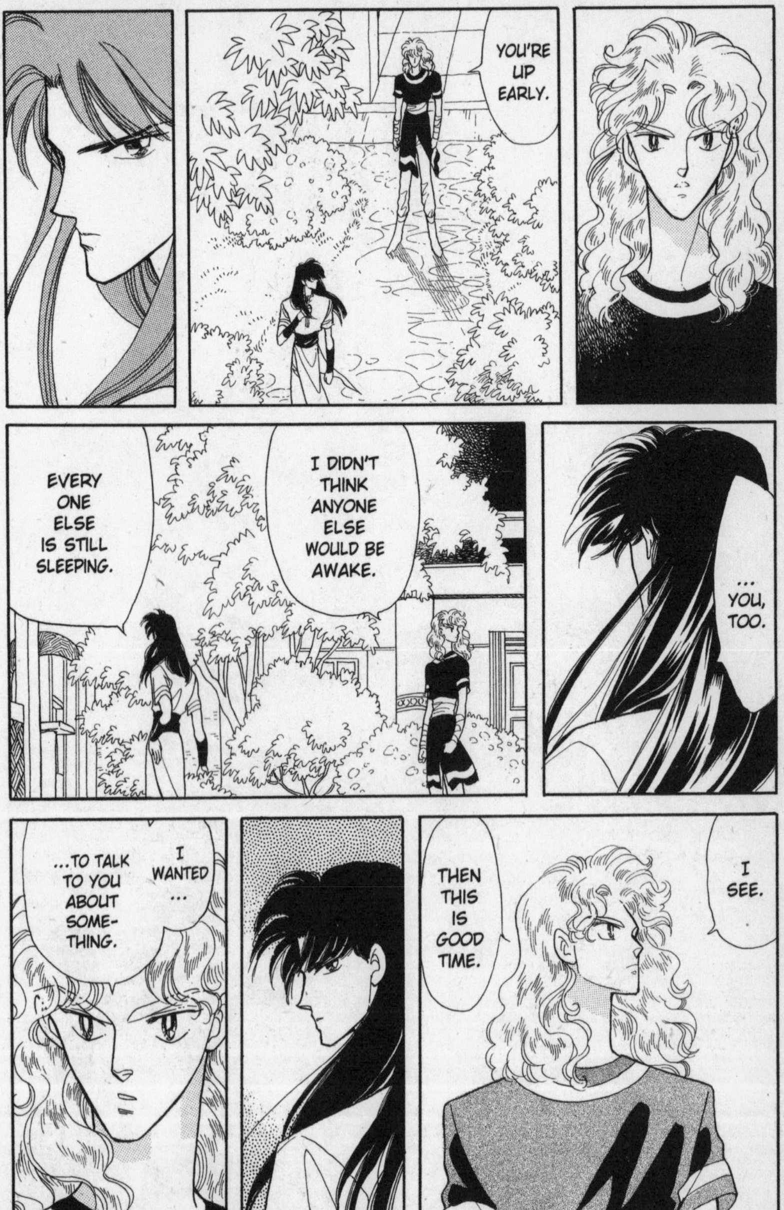
YOU'RE UP EARLY.
... YOU, TOO.
I DIDN'T THINK ANYONE ELSE WOULD BE AWAKE.
EVERY ONE ELSE IS STILL SLEEPING.
I SEE.
THEN THIS IS GOOD TIME.
I WANTED ...
...TO TALK TO YOU ABOUT SOME-THING.

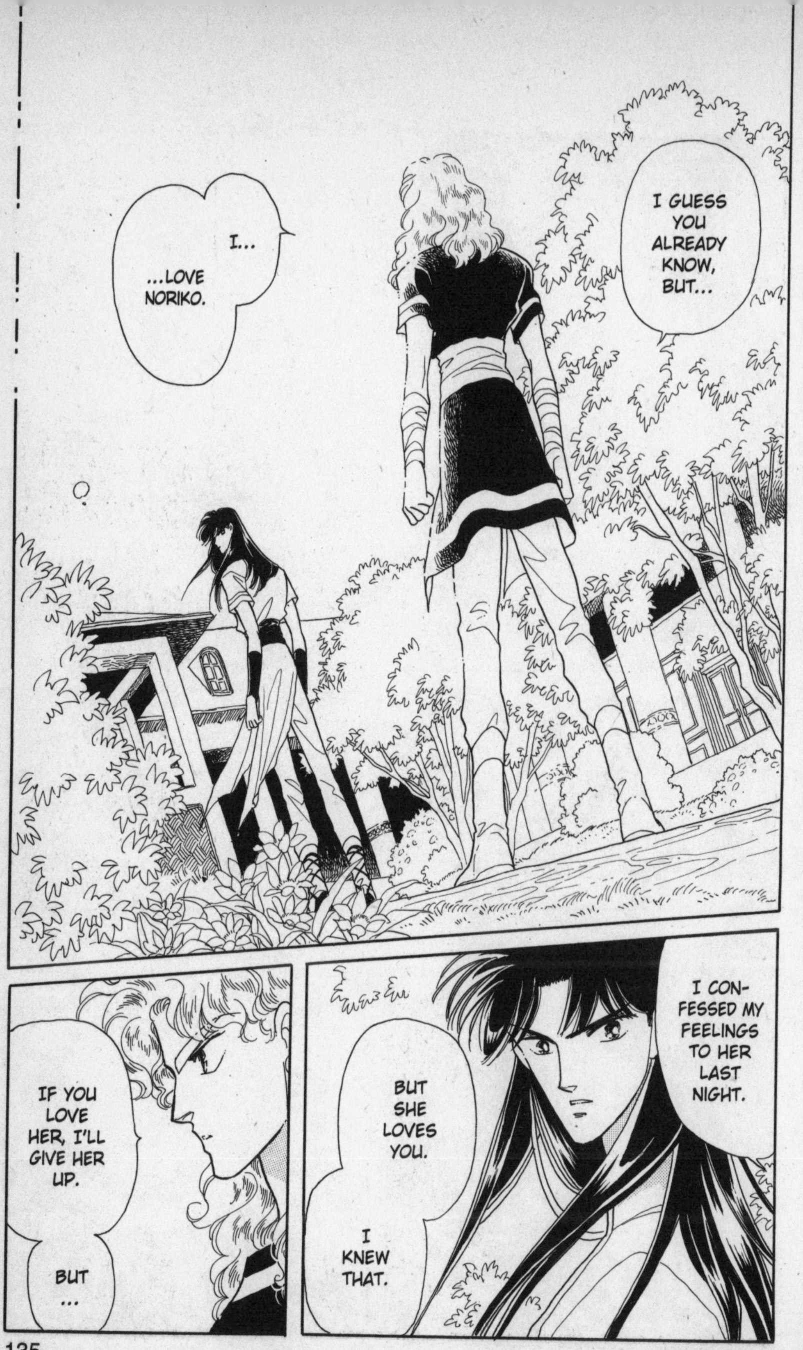
I GUESS YOU ALREADY KNOW, BUT...
I... ...LOVE NORIKO.
I CON-FESSED MY FEELINGS TO HER LAST NIGHT.
BUT SHE LOVES YOU.
I KNEW THAT.
IF YOU LOVE HER, I'LL GIVE HER UP.
BUT ...

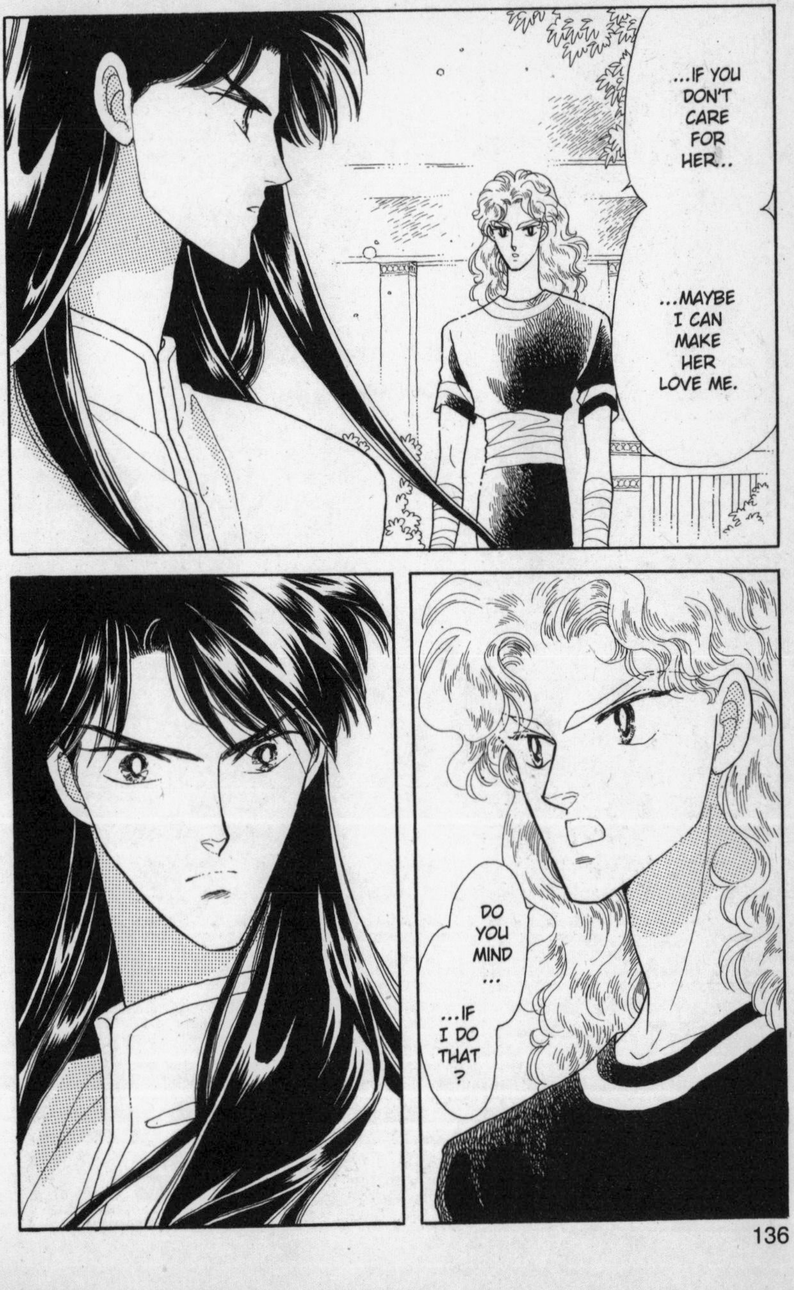
...IF YOU DON'T CARE FOR HER..
...MAYBE I CAN MAKE HER LOVE ME.
DO YOU MIND ...
...IF I DO THAT ?

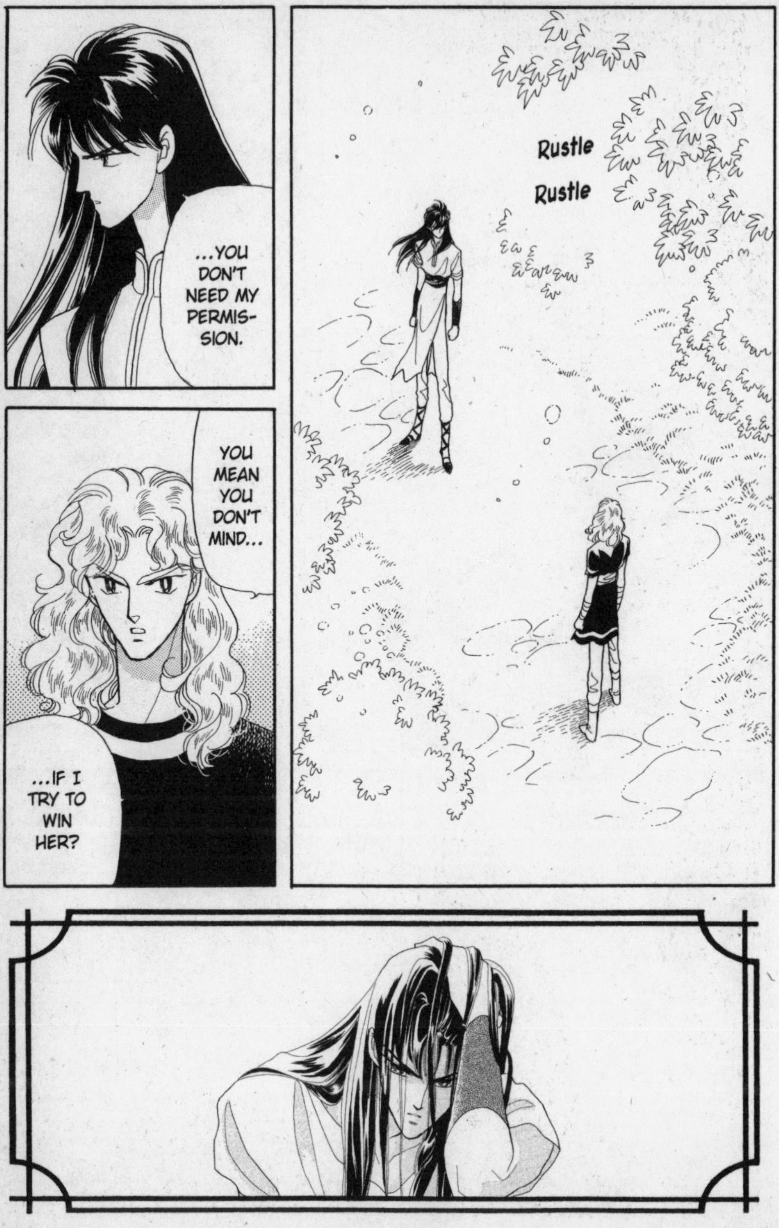
Rustle
Rustle
...YOU DON'T NEED MY PERMIS-SION.
YOU MEAN YOU DON'T MIND...
...IF I TRY TO WIN HER?

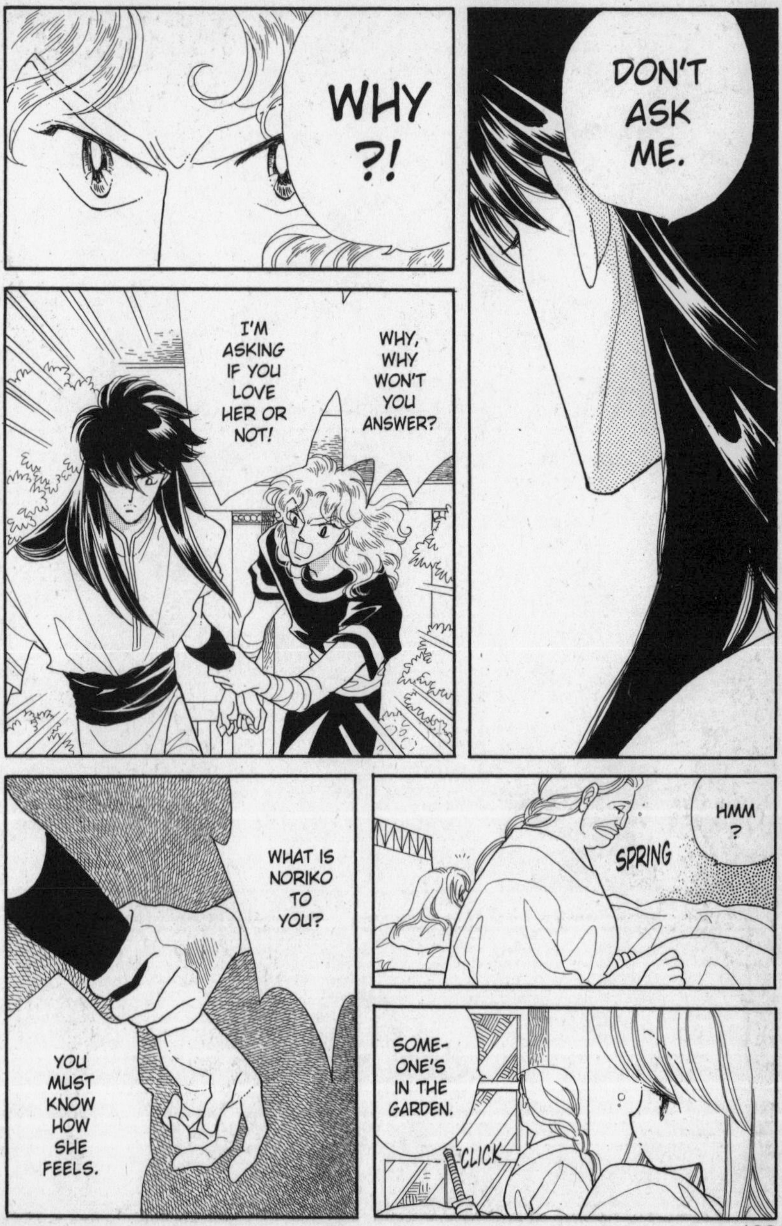
DON'T ASK ME.
WHY ?!
WHY, WHY WON'T YOU ANSWER?
I'M ASKING IF YOU LOVE HER OR NOT!
HMM ?
SPRING
SOME-ONE'S IN THE GARDEN.
CLICK
WHAT IS NORIKO TO YOU?
YOU MUST KNOW HOW SHE FEELS.

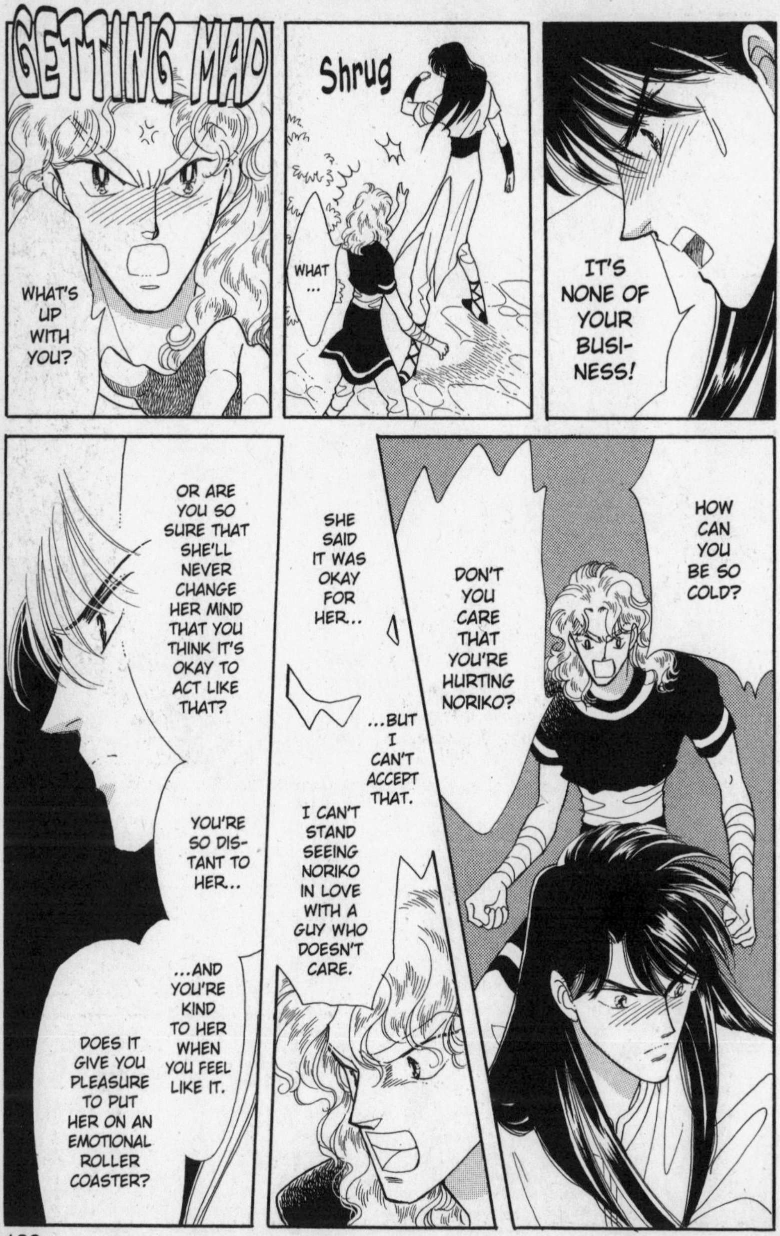
IT'S NONE OF YOUR BUSINESS!
Shrug
WHAT ...
GETTING MAD
WHAT'S UP WITH YOU?
HOW CAN YOU BE SO COLD?
DON'T YOU CARE THAT YOU'RE HURTING NORIKO?
SHE SAID IT WAS OKAY FOR HER...
...BUT I CAN'T ACCEPT THAT.
I CAN'T STAND SEEING NORIKO IN LOVE WITH A GUY WHO DOESN'T CARE.
OR ARE YOU SO SURE THAT SHE'LL NEVER CHANGE HER MIND THAT YOU THINK IT'S OKAY TO ACT LIKE THAT?
YOU'RE SO DISTANT TO HER...
...AND YOU'RE KIND TO HER WHEN YOU FEEL LIKE IT.
DOES IT GIVE YOU PLEASURE TO PUT HER ON AN EMOTIONAL ROLLER COASTER?

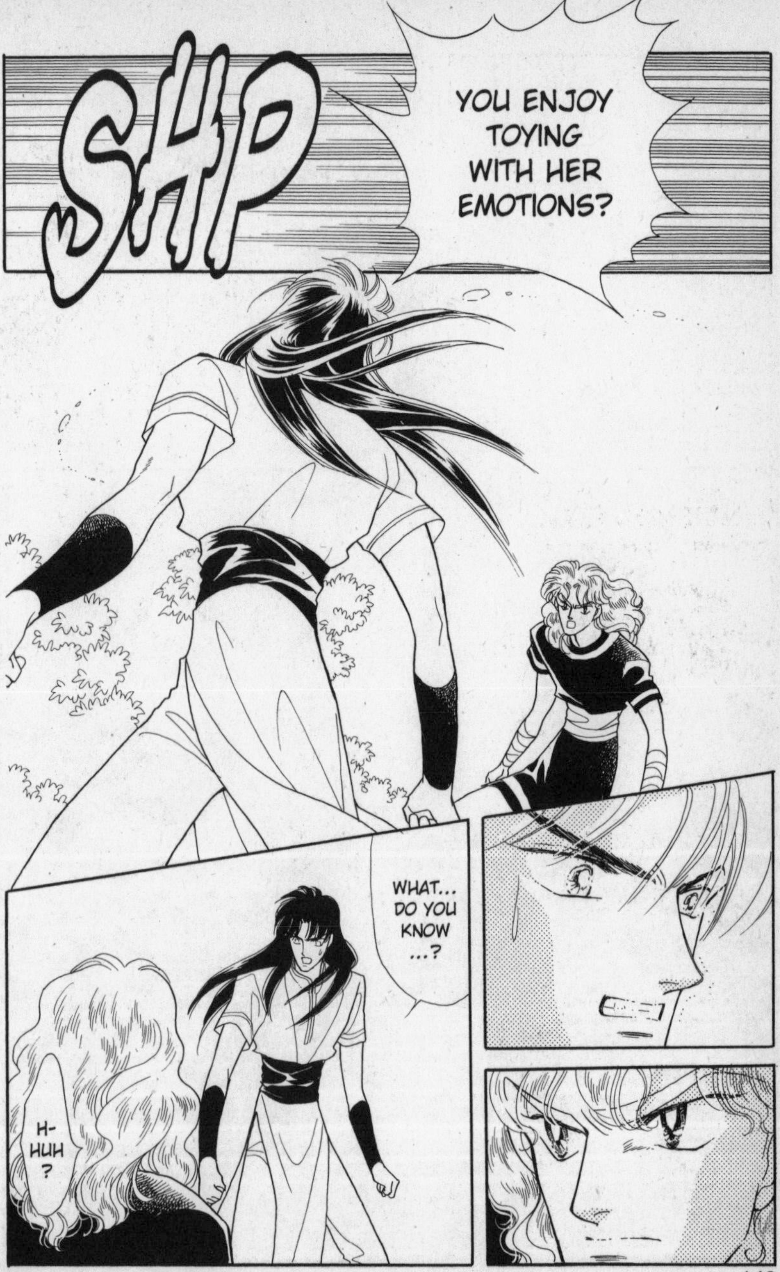
YOU ENJOY TOYING WITH HER EMOTIONS?
SHP
WHAT... DO YOU KNOW ...?
H-HUH ?

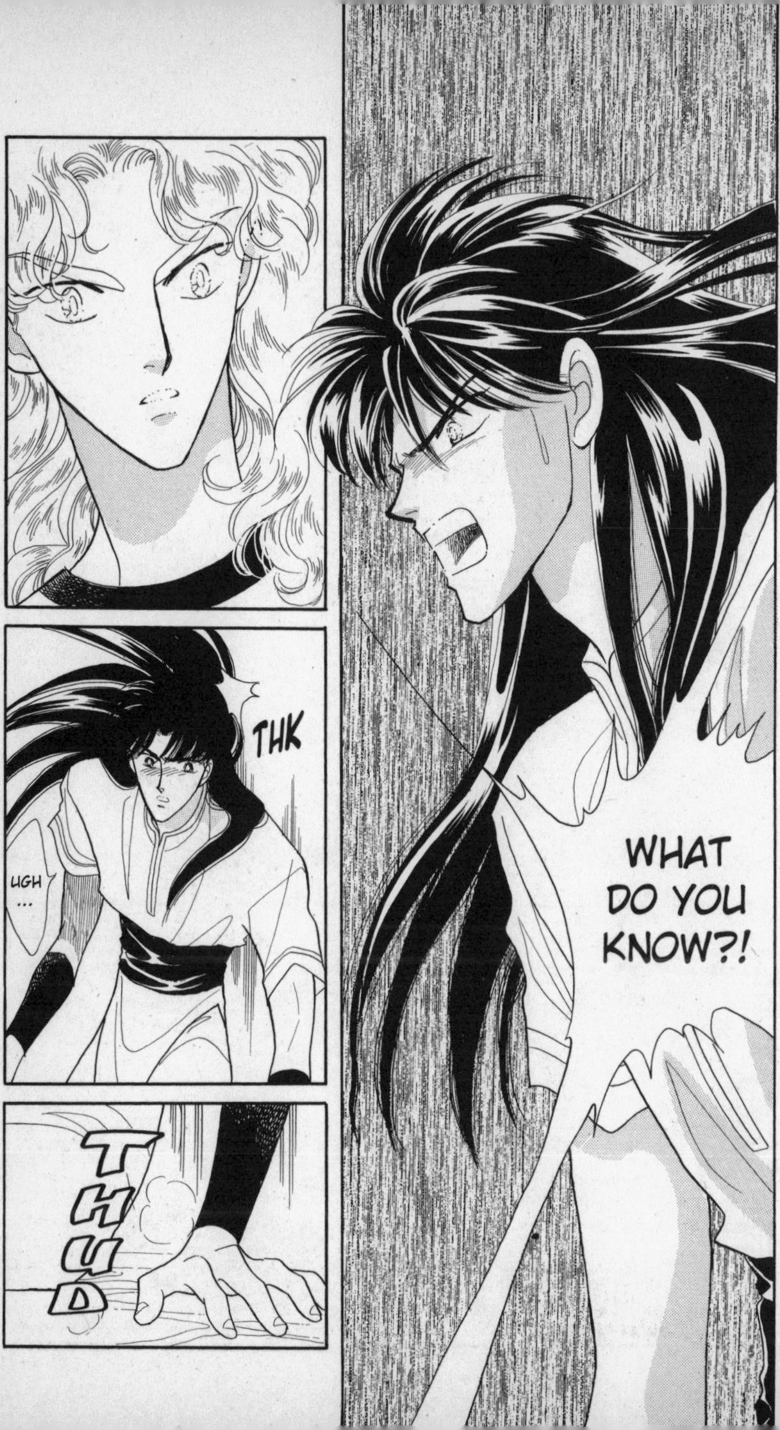
WHAT DO YOU KNOW?!
THK
UGH ...
THUD

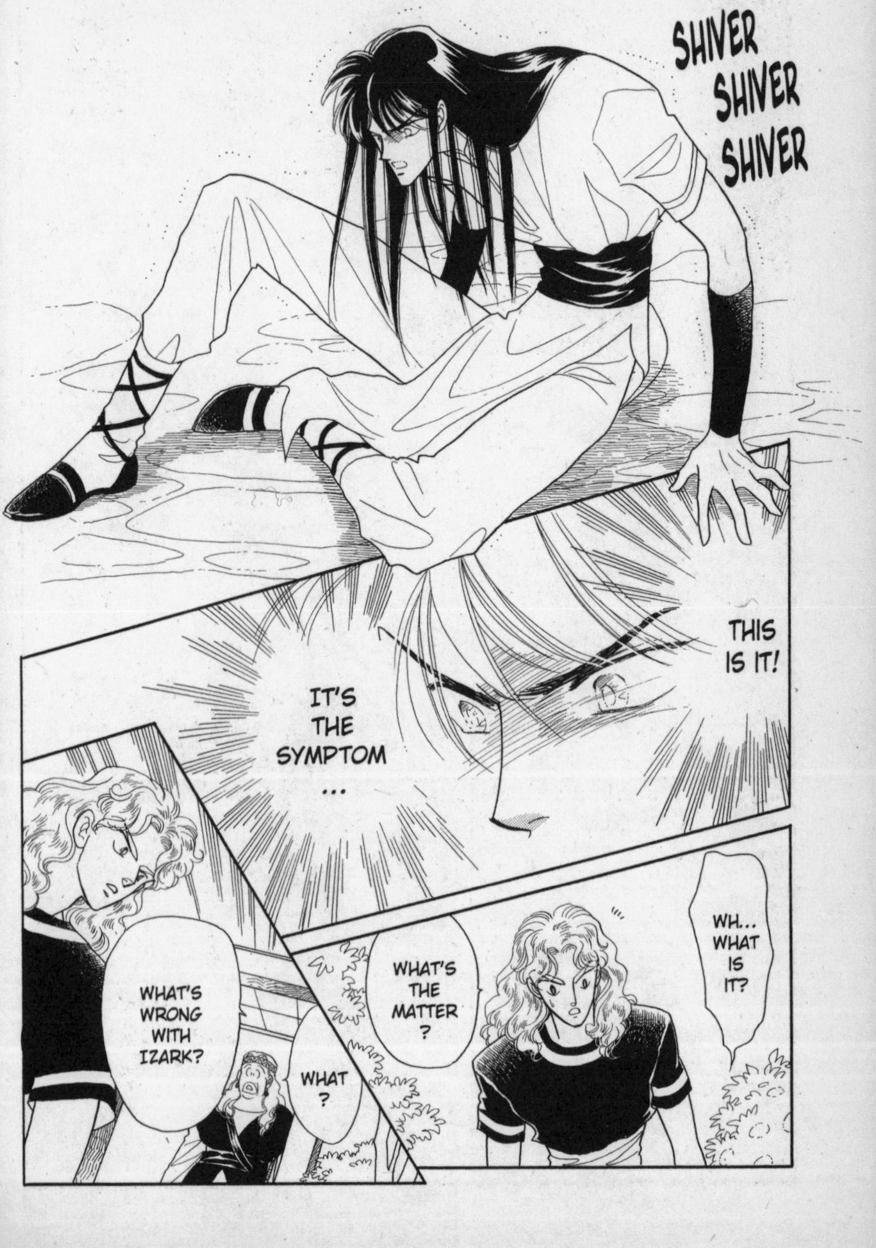
SHIVER SHIVER SHIVER
THIS IS IT!
IT'S THE SYMPTOM ...
WH... WHAT IS IT?
WHAT'S THE MATTER?
WHAT?
WHAT'S WRONG WITH IZARK?

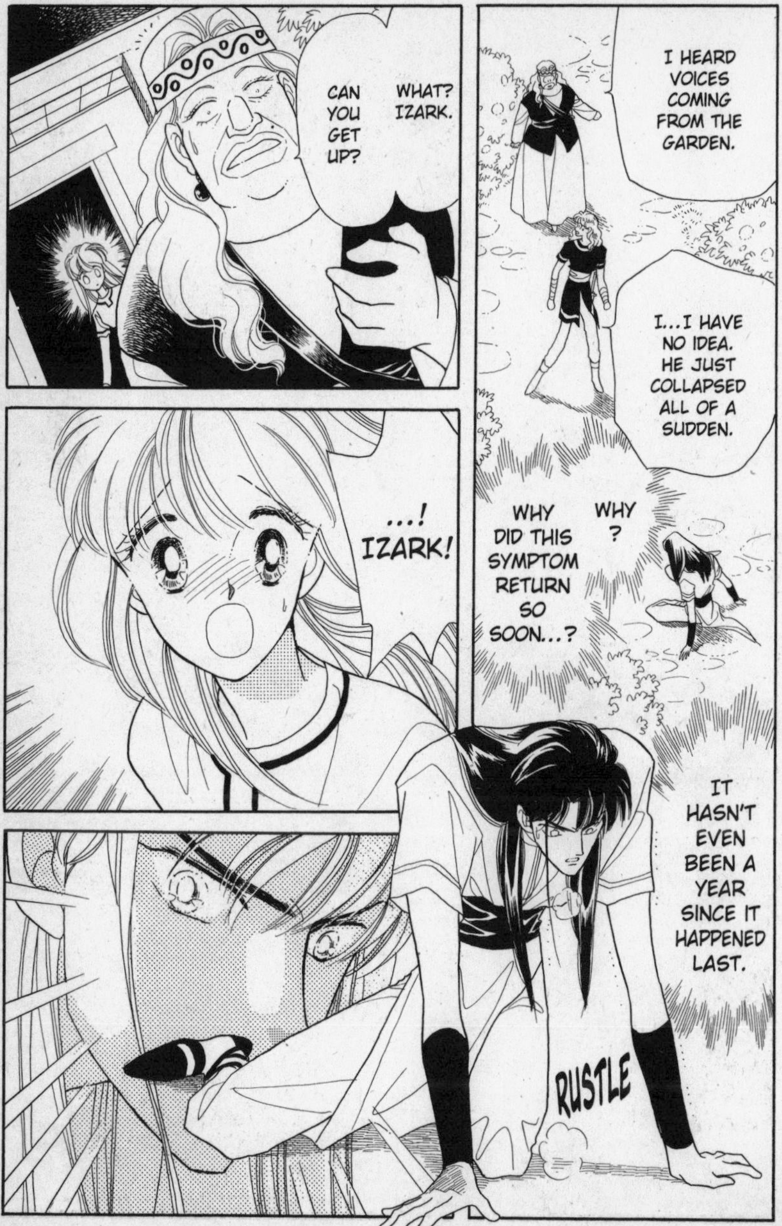
I HEARD VOICES COMING FROM THE GARDEN.
I...I HAVE NO IDEA. HE JUST COLLAPSED ALL OF A SUDDEN.
WHY?
WHY DID THIS SYMPTOM RETURN SO SOON...?
IT HASN'T EVEN BEEN A YEAR SINCE IT HAPPENED LAST.
RUSTLE
WHAT? IZARK.
CAN YOU GET UP?
...! IZARK!

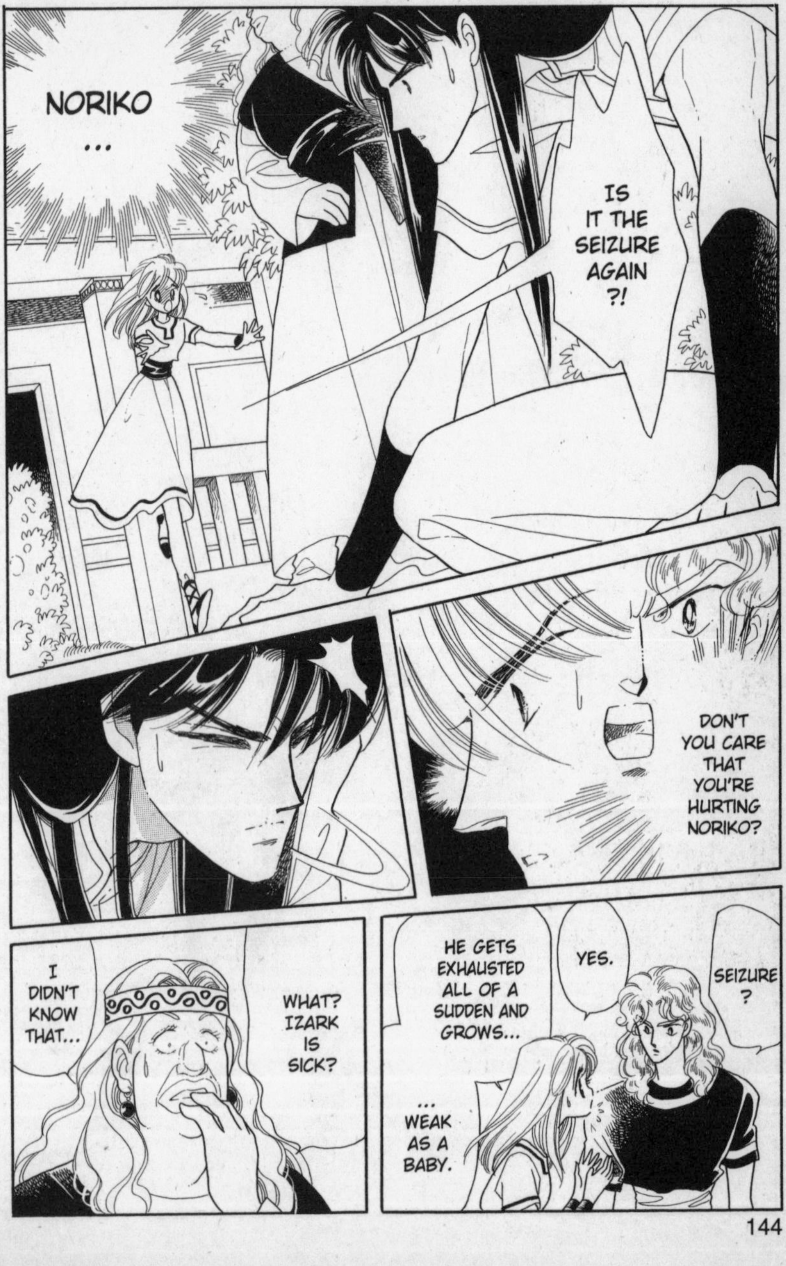
IS IT THE SEIZURE AGAIN ?!
NORIKO ...
DON'T YOU CARE THAT YOU'RE HURTING NORIKO?
SEIZURE ?
YES.
HE GETS EXHAUSTED ALL OF A SUDDEN AND GROWS...
... WEAK AS A BABY.
WHAT? IZARK IS SICK?
I DIDN'T KNOW THAT...

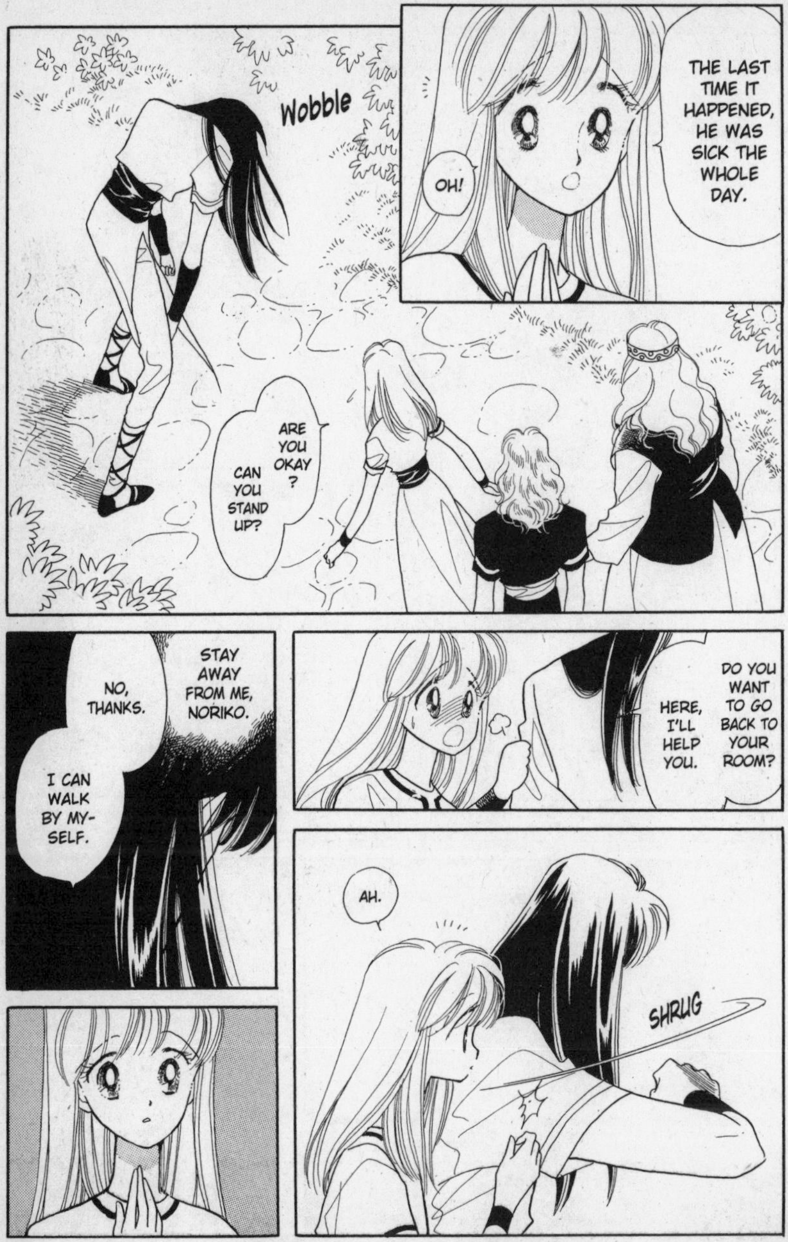
THE LAST TIME IT HAPPENED, HE WAS SICK THE WHOLE DAY.
OH!
Wobble
ARE YOU OKAY?
CAN YOU STAND UP?
DO YOU WANT TO GO BACK TO YOUR ROOM?
HERE, I'LL HELP YOU.
AH.
SHRUG
STAY AWAY FROM ME, NORIKO.
NO, THANKS.
I CAN WALK BY MY-SELF.

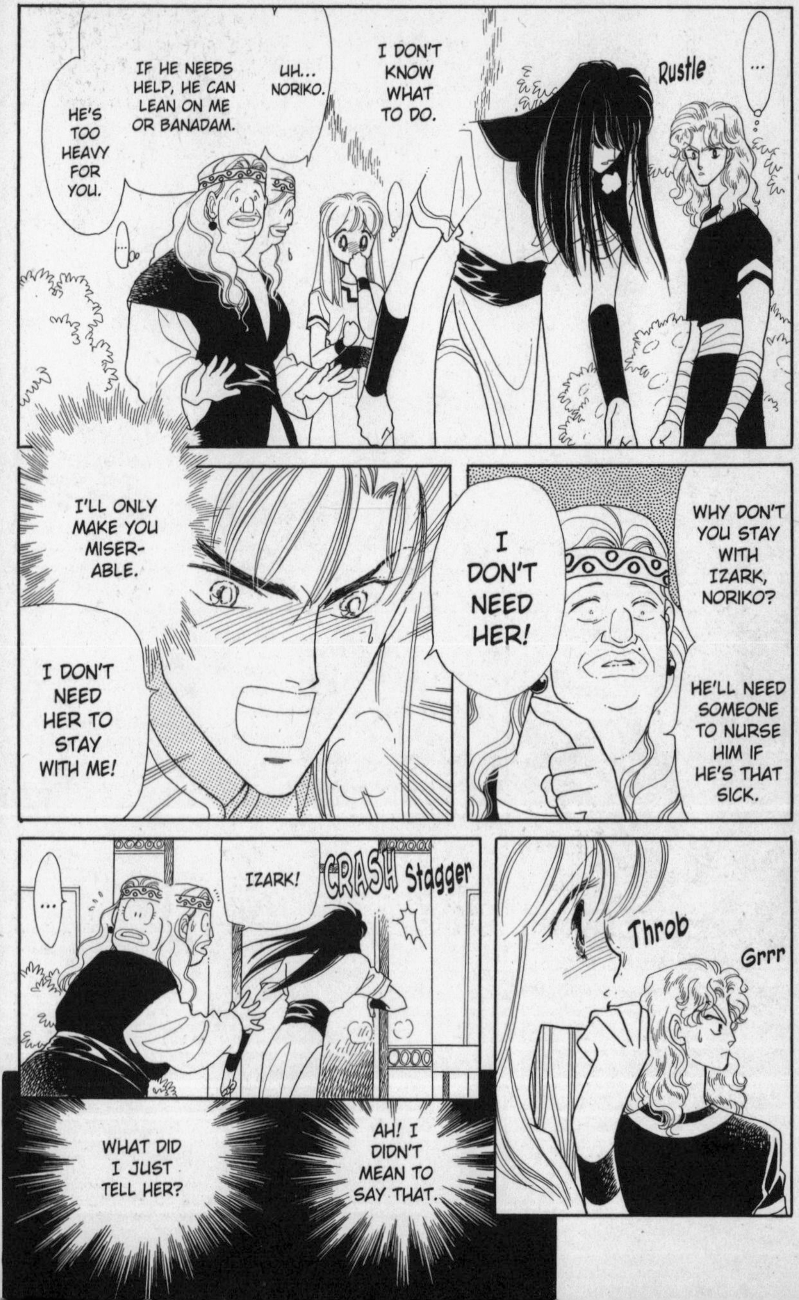
...
Rustle
I DON'T KNOW WHAT TO DO.
UH... NORIKO.
IF HE NEEDS HELP, HE CAN LEAN ON ME OR BANADAM.
HE'S TOO HEAVY FOR YOU.
...
...
WHY DON'T YOU STAY WITH IZARK, NORIKO?
HE'LL NEED SOMEONE TO NURSE HIM IF HE'S THAT SICK.
I DON'T NEED HER!
I'LL ONLY MAKE YOU MISER-ABLE.
I DON'T NEED HER TO STAY WITH ME!
Throb
Grrr
Stagger
CRASH
IZARK!
...
AH! I DIDN'T MEAN TO SAY THAT.
WHAT DID I JUST TELL HER?

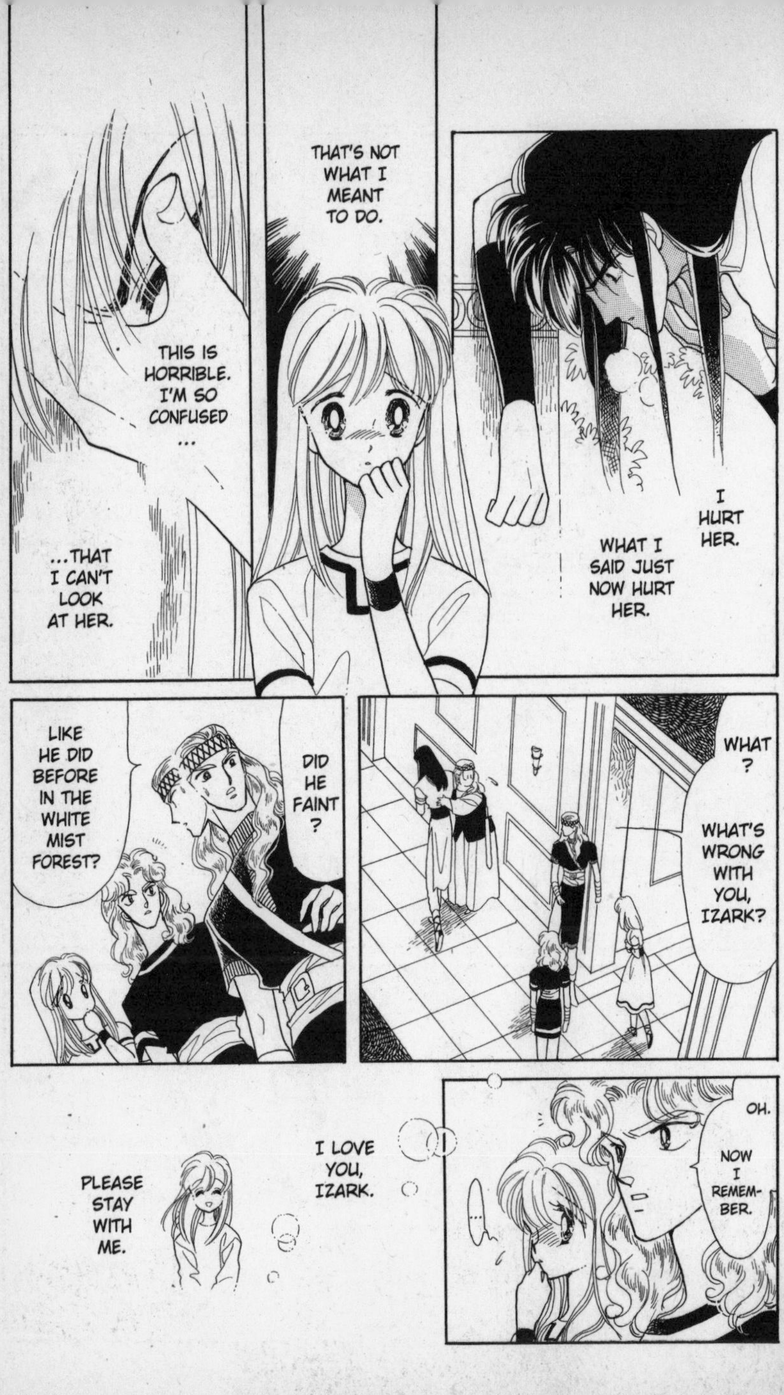
I HURT HER.
WHAT I SAID JUST NOW HURT HER.
THAT'S NOT WHAT I MEANT TO DO.
THIS IS HORRIBLE. I'M SO CONFUSED ...
...THAT I CAN'T LOOK AT HER.
WHAT?
WHAT'S WRONG WITH YOU, IZARK?
DID HE FAINT?
LIKE HE DID BEFORE IN THE WHITE MIST FOREST?
OH.
NOW I REMEMBER.
...
I LOVE YOU, IZARK.
PLEASE STAY WITH ME.

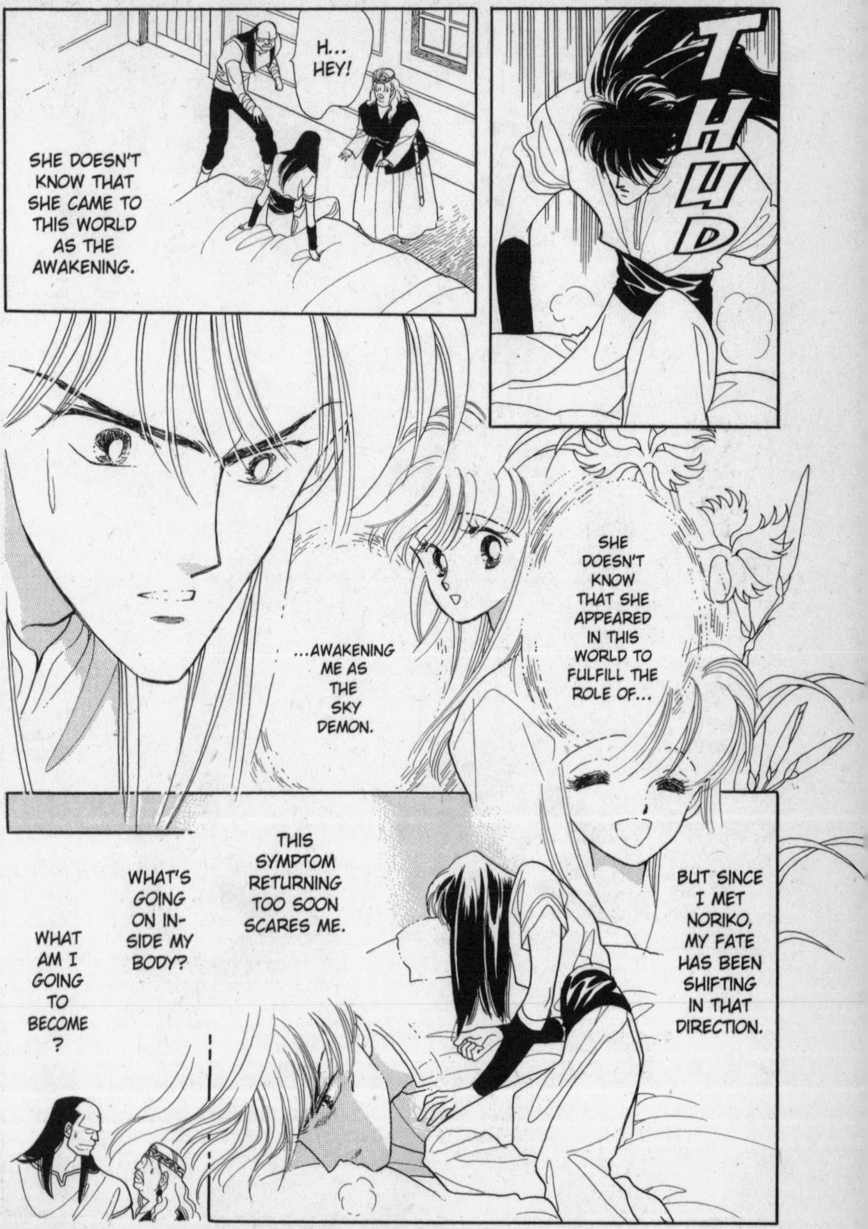
THUD
H... HEY!
SHE DOESN'T KNOW THAT SHE CAME TO THIS WORLD AS THE AWAKENING.
SHE DOESN'T KNOW THAT SHE APPEARED IN THIS WORLD TO FULFILL THE ROLE OF...
...AWAKENING ME AS THE SKY DEMON.
BUT SINCE I MET NORIKO, MY FATE HAS BEEN SHIFTING IN THAT DIRECTION.
THIS SYMPTOM RETURNING TOO SOON SCARES ME.
WHAT'S GOING ON IN-SIDE MY BODY?
WHAT AM I GOING TO BECOME ?

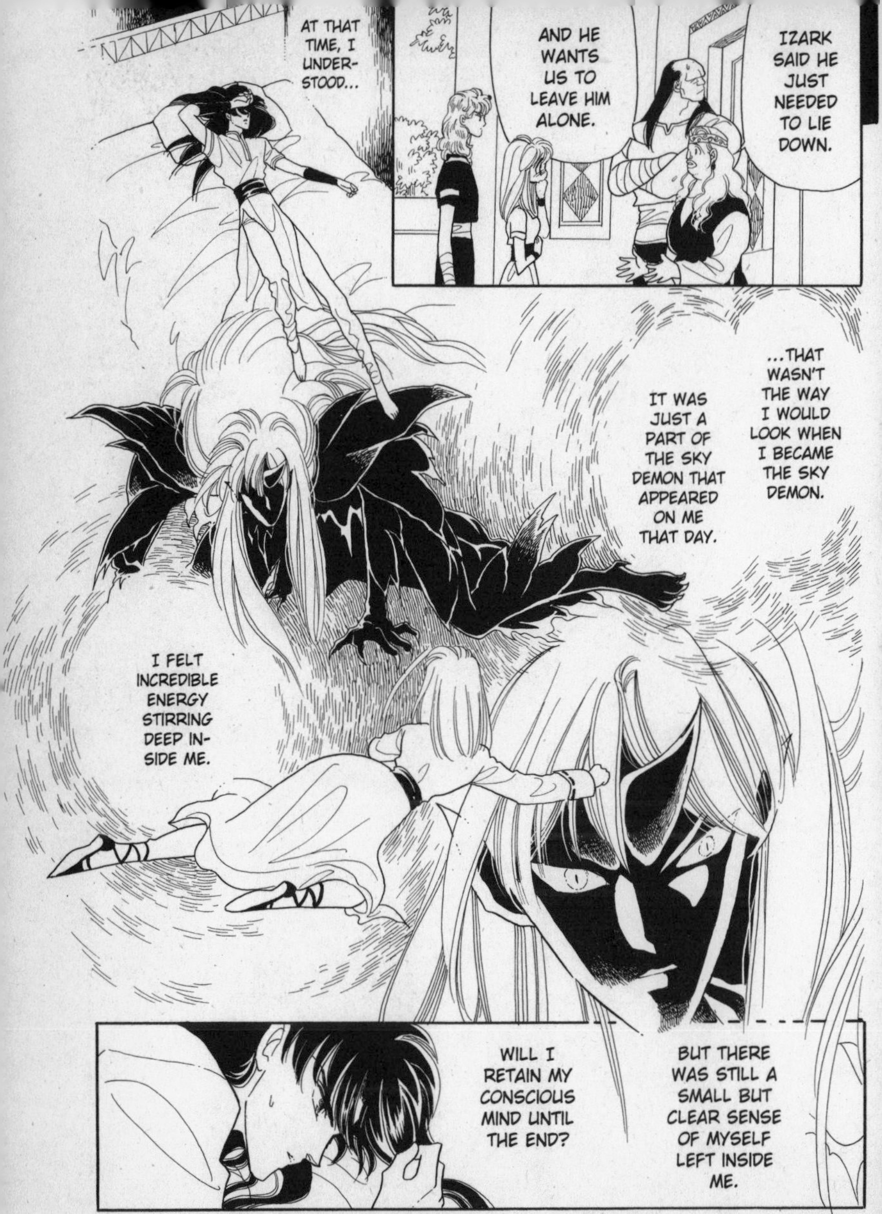
IZARK SAID HE JUST NEEDED TO LIE DOWN.
AND HE WANTS US TO LEAVE HIM ALONE.
AT THAT TIME, I UNDER-STOOD...
...THAT WASN'T THE WAY I WOULD LOOK WHEN I BECAME THE SKY DEMON.
IT WAS JUST A PART OF THE SKY DEMON THAT APPEARED ON ME THAT DAY.
I FELT INCREDIBLE ENERGY STIRRING DEEP IN-SIDE ME.
BUT THERE WAS STILL A SMALL BUT CLEAR SENSE OF MYSELF LEFT INSIDE ME.
WILL I RETAIN MY CONSCIOUS MIND UNTIL THE END?

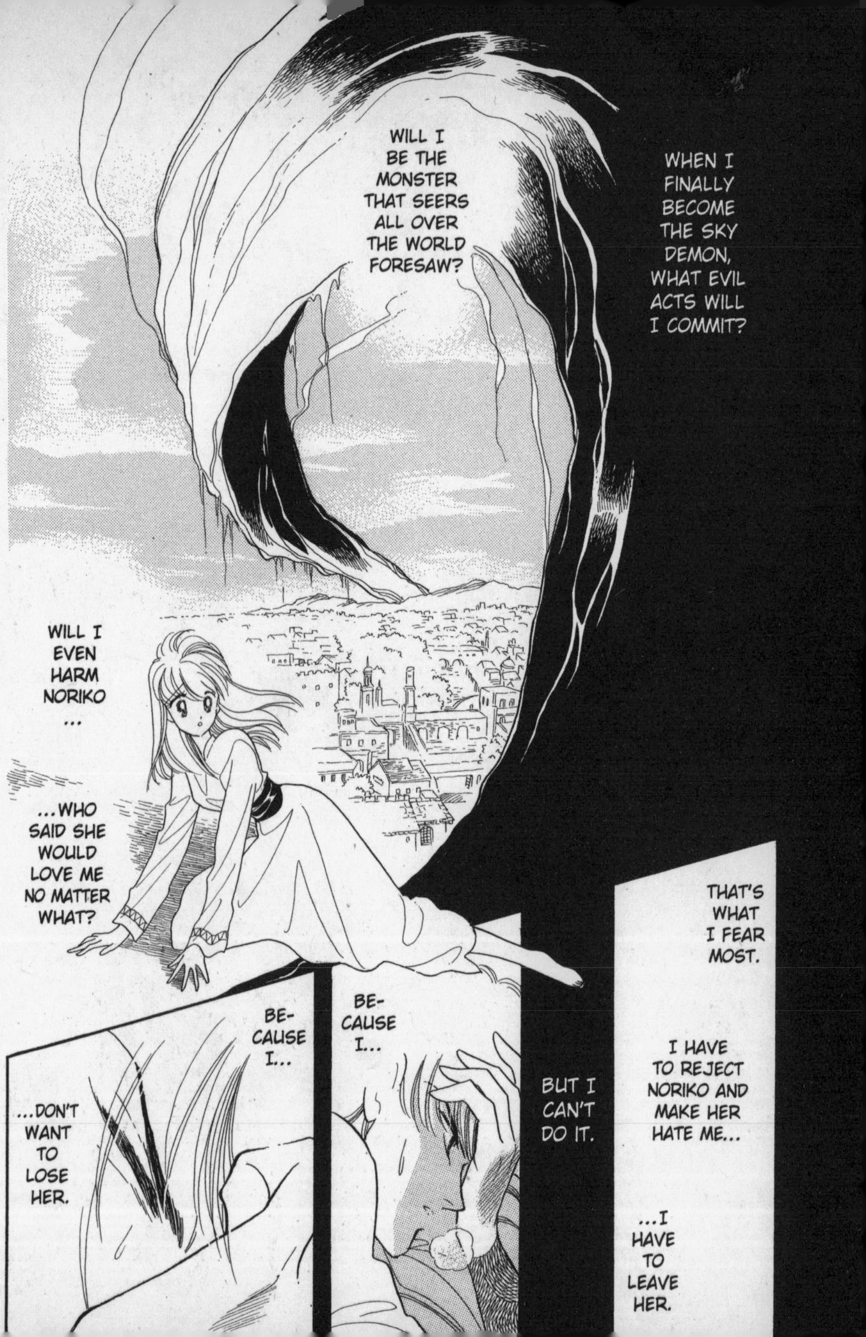
WHEN I FINALLY BECOME THE SKY DEMON, WHAT EVIL ACTS WILL I COMMIT?
WILL I BE THE MONSTER THAT SEERS ALL OVER THE WORLD FORESAW?
WILL I EVEN HARM NORIKO ...
...WHO SAID SHE WOULD LOVE ME NO MATTER WHAT?
THAT'S WHAT I FEAR MOST.
I HAVE TO REJECT NORIKO AND MAKE HER HATE ME...
...I HAVE TO LEAVE HER.
BUT I CAN'T DO IT.
BE-CAUSE I...
BE-CAUSE I...
...DON'T WANT TO LOSE HER.

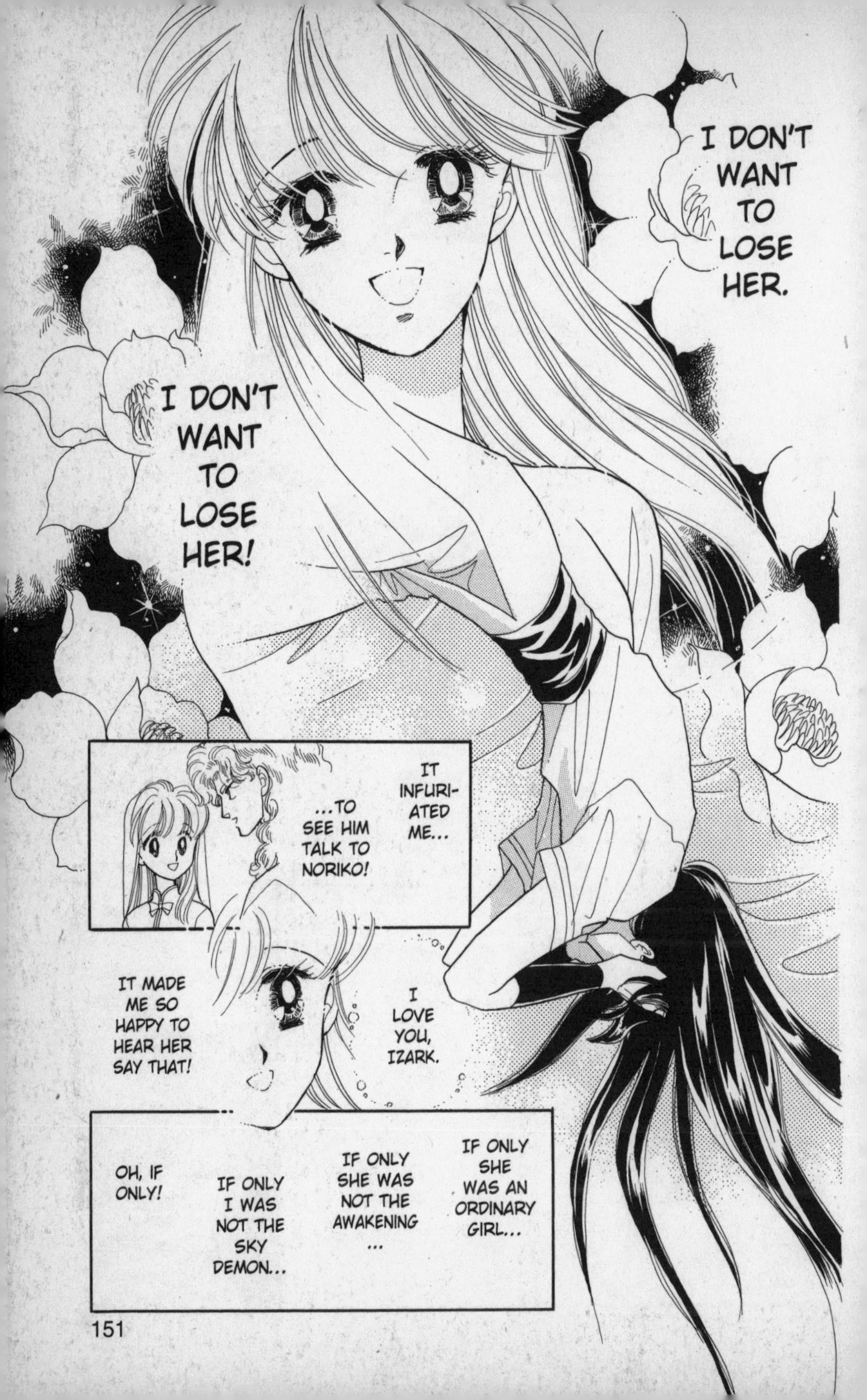
I DON'T WANT TO LOSE HER.
I DON'T WANT TO LOSE HER!
IT INFURIATED ME...
...TO SEE HIM TALK TO NORIKO!
I LOVE YOU, IZARK.
IT MADE ME SO HAPPY TO HEAR HER SAY THAT!
IF ONLY SHE WAS AN ORDINARY GIRL...
IF ONLY SHE WAS NOT THE AWAKENING ...
IF ONLY I WAS NOT THE SKY DEMON...
OH, IF ONLY!

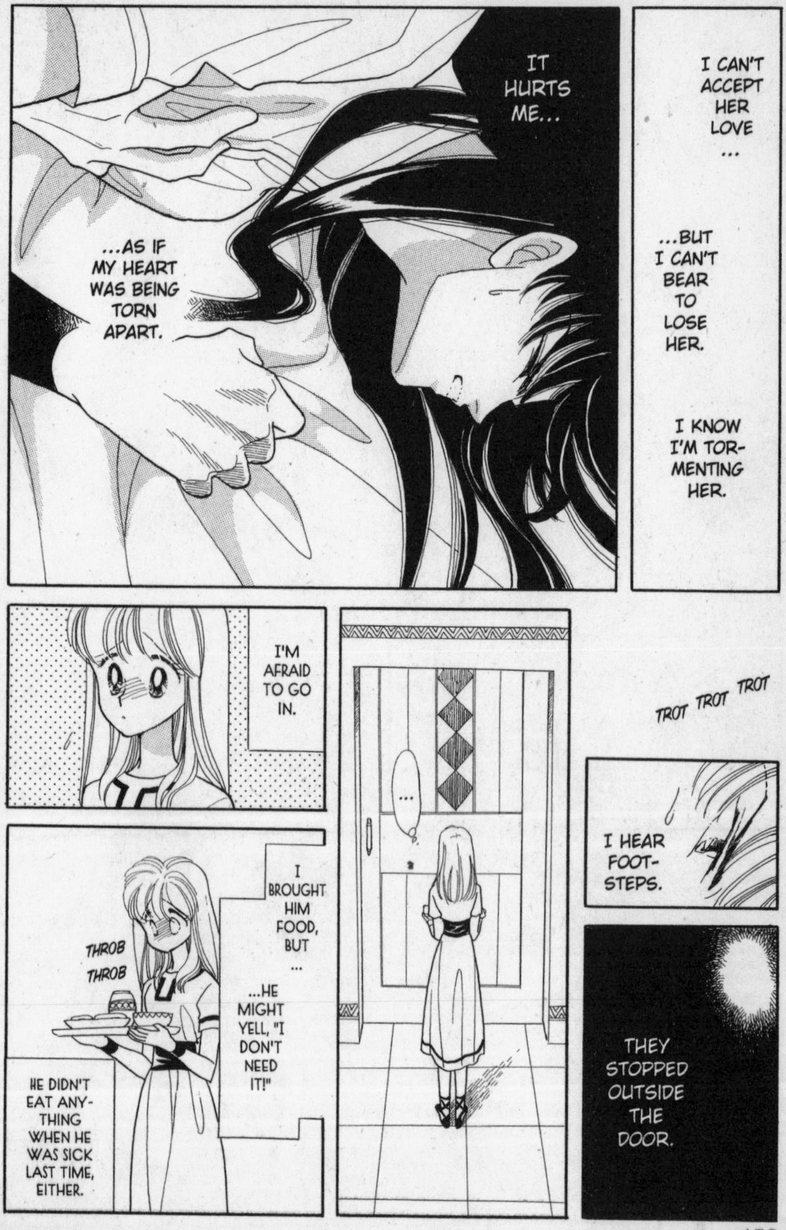
I CAN'T ACCEPT HER LOVE ...
...BUT I CAN'T BEAR TO LOSE HER.
I KNOW I'M TOR-MENTING HER.
IT HURTS ME...
...AS IF MY HEART WAS BEING TORN APART.
TROT TROT TROT
I HEAR FOOT-STEPS.
THEY STOPPED OUTSIDE THE DOOR.
...
I'M AFRAID TO GO IN.
I BROUGHT HIM FOOD, BUT ...
...HE MIGHT YELL, "I DON'T NEED IT!"
THROB THROB
HE DIDN'T EAT ANY-THING WHEN HE WAS SICK LAST TIME, EITHER.

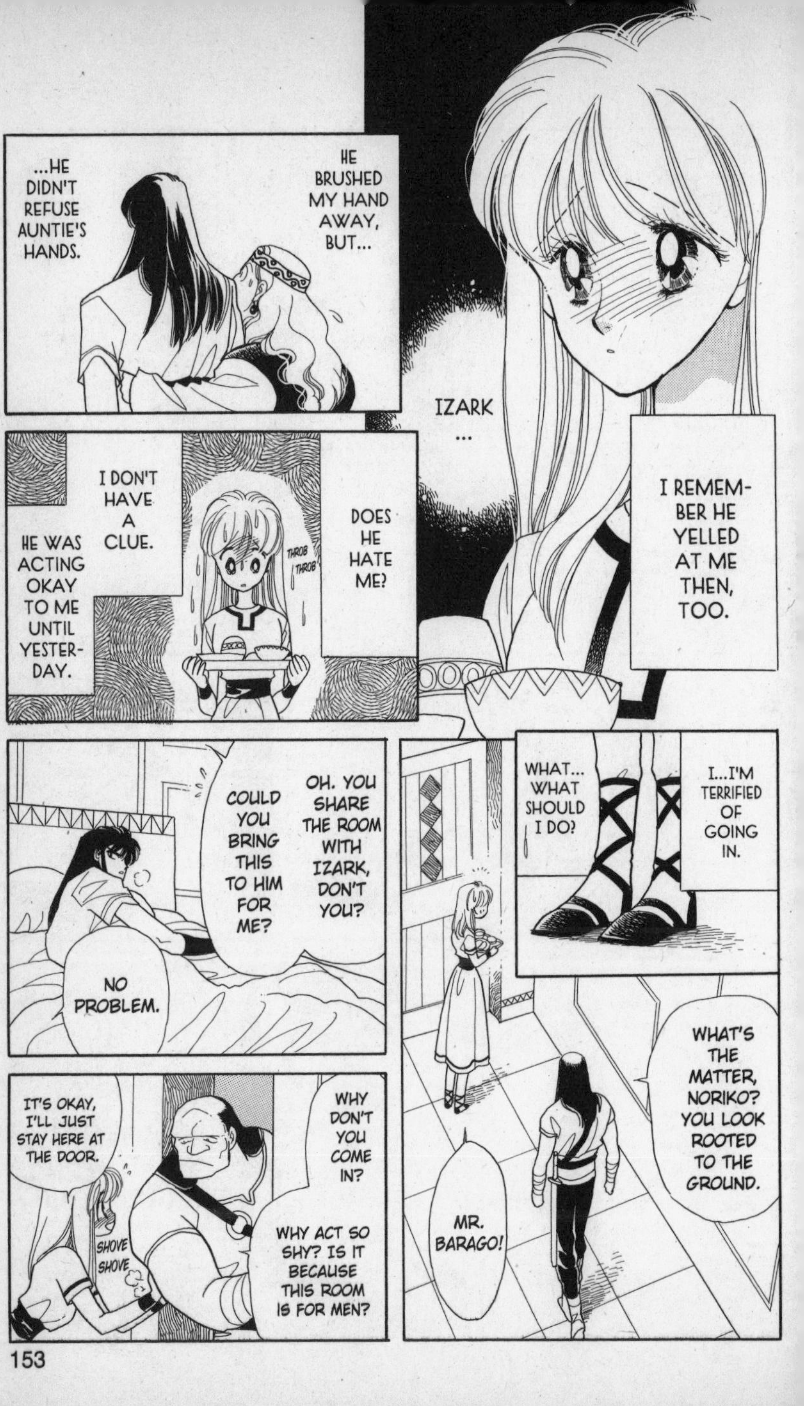
IZARK ...
I REMEMBER HE YELLED AT ME THEN, TOO.
HE BRUSHED MY HAND AWAY, BUT...
...HE DIDN'T REFUSE AUNTIE'S HANDS.
DOES HE HATE ME?
I DON'T HAVE A CLUE.
THROB THROB
HE WAS ACTING OKAY TO ME UNTIL YESTERDAY.
I...I'M TERRIFIED OF GOING IN.
WHAT... WHAT SHOULD I DO?
WHAT'S THE MATTER, NORIKO? YOU LOOK ROOTED TO THE GROUND.
MR. BARAGO!
OH. YOU SHARE THE ROOM WITH IZARK, DON'T YOU?
COULD YOU BRING THIS TO HIM FOR ME?
NO PROBLEM.
WHY DON'T YOU COME IN?
WHY ACT SO SHY? IS IT BECAUSE THIS ROOM IS FOR MEN?
IT'S OKAY, I'LL JUST STAY HERE AT THE DOOR.
SHOVE SHOVE

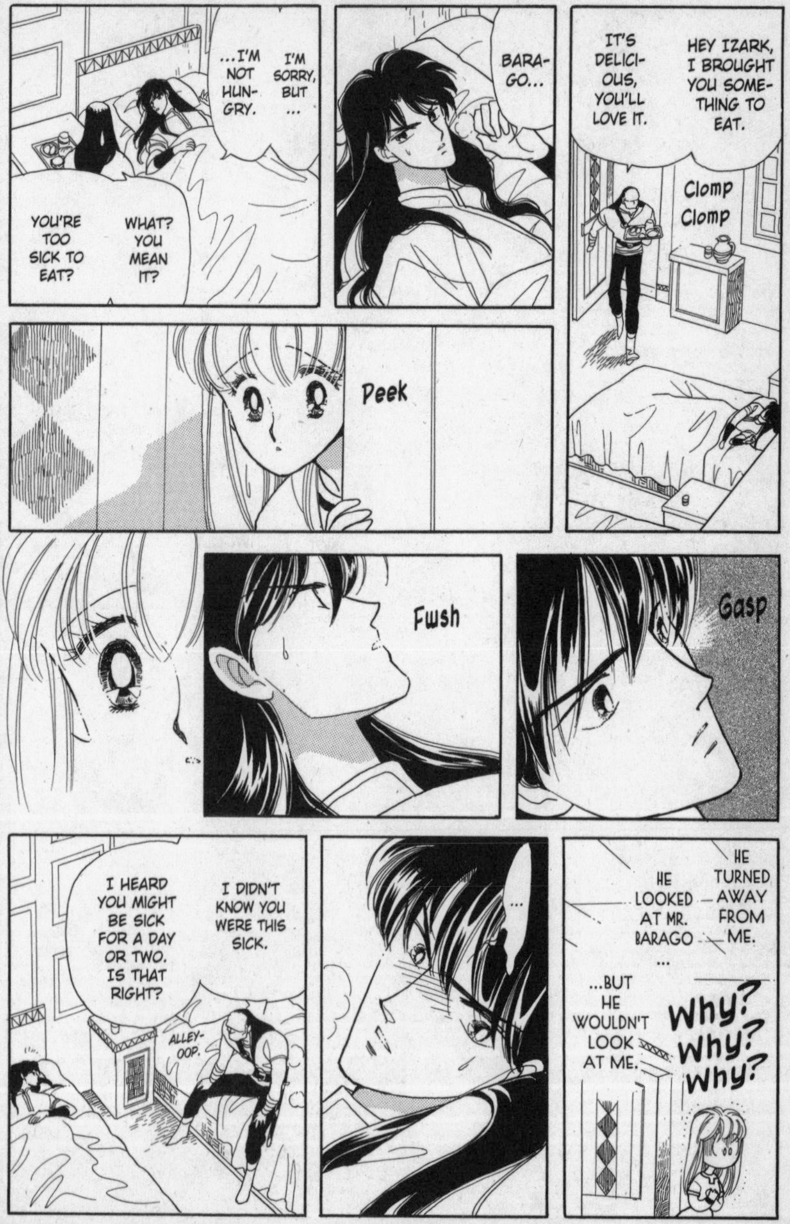
HEY IZARK, I BROUGHT YOU SOMETHING TO EAT.
IT'S DELICIOUS, YOU'LL LOVE IT.
Clomp Clomp
BARAGO...
I'M SORRY, BUT ...
...I'M NOT HUNGRY.
WHAT? YOU MEAN IT?
YOU'RE TOO SICK TO EAT?
Peek
Gasp
Fwsh
HE TURNED AWAY FROM ME.
HE LOOKED AT MR. BARAGO ...
...BUT HE WOULDN'T LOOK AT ME.
Why? Why? Why?
...
I DIDN'T KNOW YOU WERE THIS SICK.
I HEARD YOU MIGHT BE SICK FOR A DAY OR TWO. IS THAT RIGHT?
ALLEY-OOP.

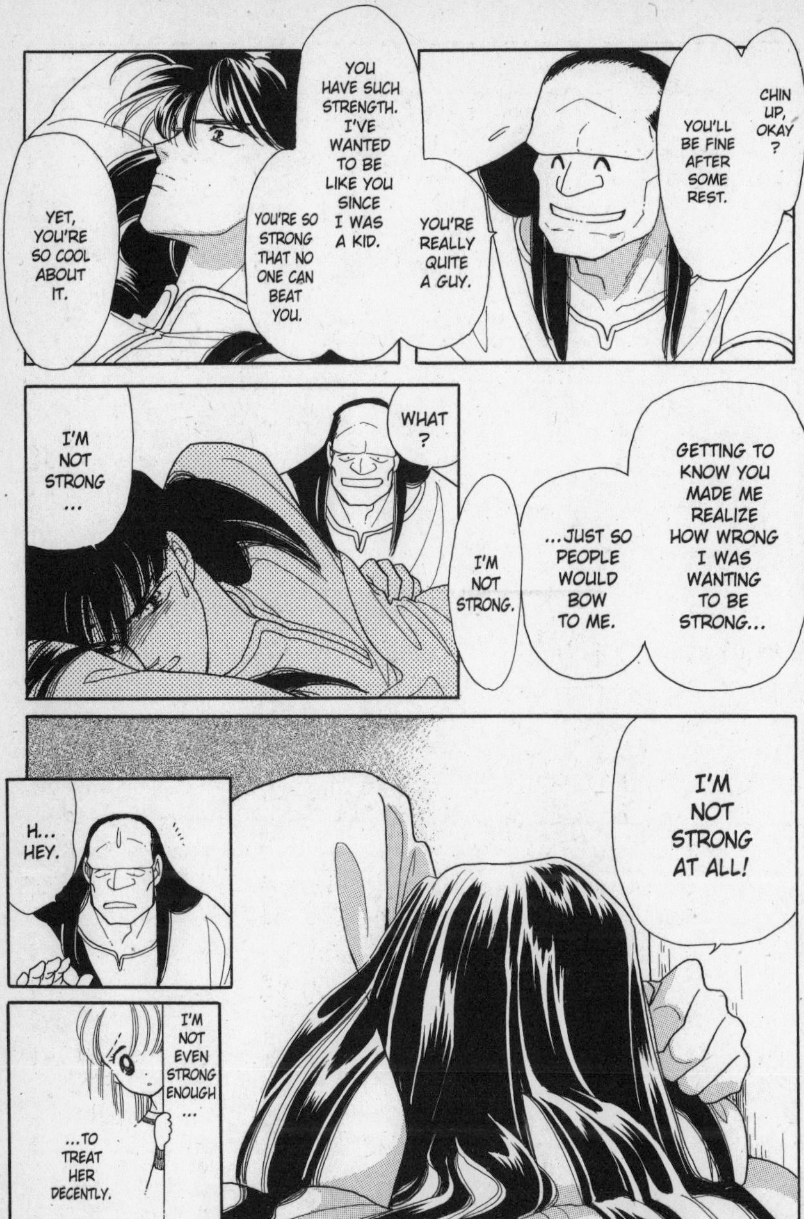
CHIN UP, OKAY?
YOU'LL BE FINE AFTER SOME REST.
YOU'RE REALLY QUITE A GUY.
YOU HAVE SUCH STRENGTH. I'VE WANTED TO BE LIKE YOU SINCE I WAS A KID.
YOU'RE SO STRONG THAT NO ONE CAN BEAT YOU.
YET, YOU'RE SO COOL ABOUT IT.
GETTING TO KNOW YOU MADE ME REALIZE HOW WRONG I WAS WANTING TO BE STRONG...
...JUST SO PEOPLE WOULD BOW TO ME.
I'M NOT STRONG.
WHAT?
I'M NOT STRONG...
I'M NOT STRONG AT ALL!
H... HEY.
I'M NOT EVEN STRONG ENOUGH...
...TO TREAT HER DECENTLY.

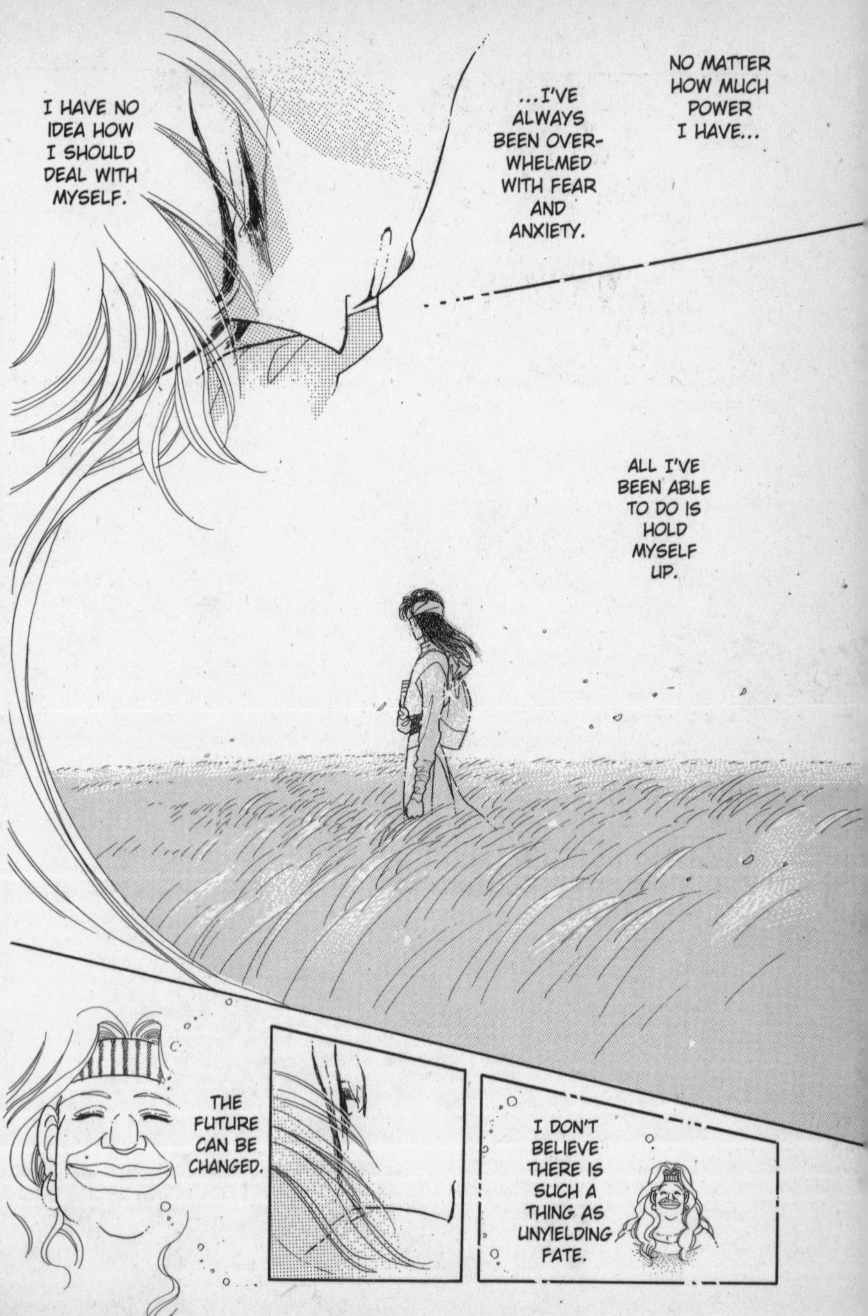
NO MATTER HOW MUCH POWER I HAVE...
...I'VE ALWAYS BEEN OVER-WHELMED WITH FEAR AND ANXIETY.
I HAVE NO IDEA HOW I SHOULD DEAL WITH MYSELF.
ALL I'VE BEEN ABLE TO DO IS HOLD MYSELF UP.
I DON'T BELIEVE THERE IS SUCH A THING AS UNYIELDING FATE.
THE FUTURE CAN BE CHANGED.

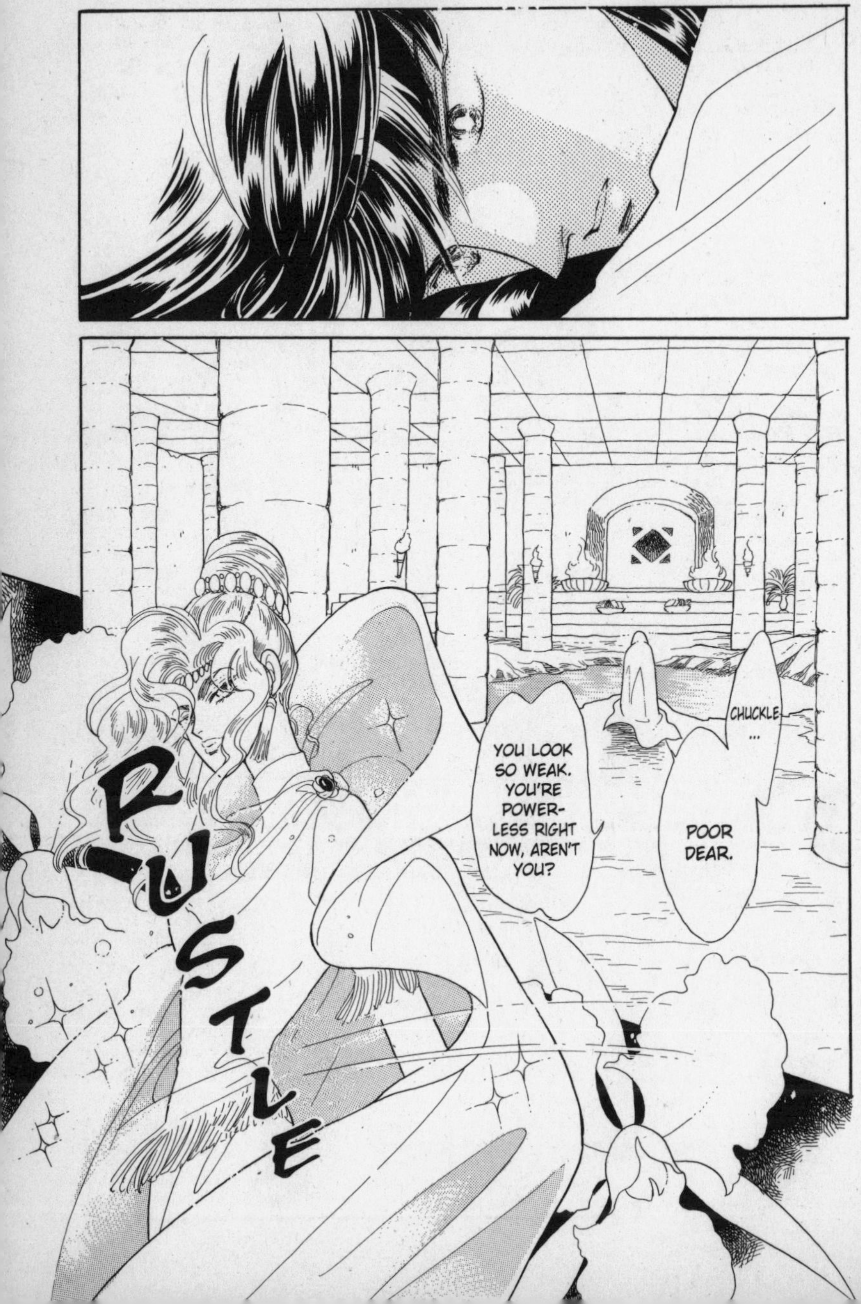
CHUCKLE ...
POOR DEAR.
YOU LOOK SO WEAK. YOU'RE POWER-LESS RIGHT NOW, AREN'T YOU?
RUSTLE

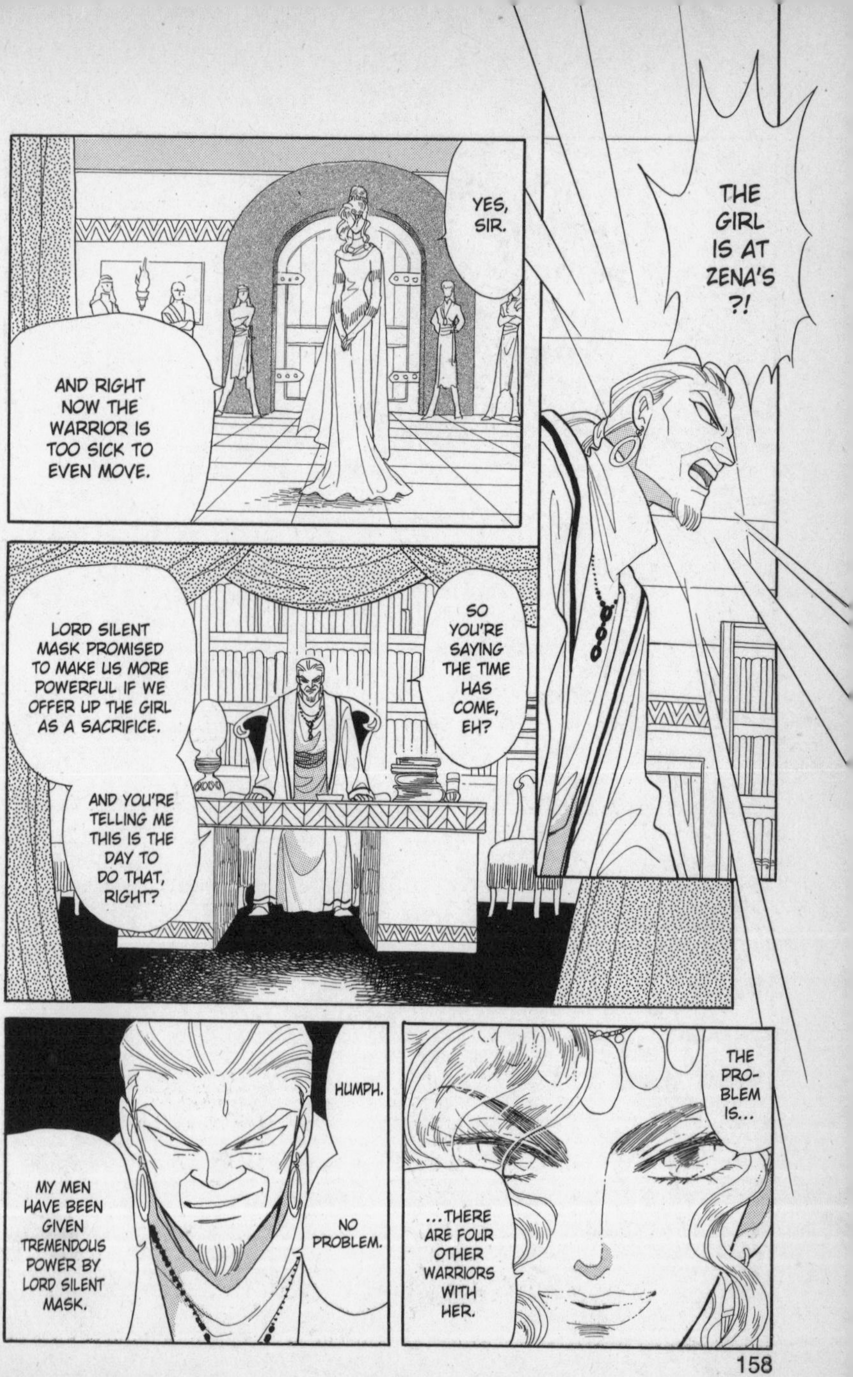
THE GIRL IS AT ZENA'S?!
YES, SIR.
AND RIGHT NOW THE WARRIOR IS TOO SICK TO EVEN MOVE.
SO YOU'RE SAYING THE TIME HAS COME, EH?
LORD SILENT MASK PROMISED TO MAKE US MORE POWERFUL IF WE OFFER UP THE GIRL AS A SACRIFICE.
AND YOU'RE TELLING ME THIS IS THE DAY TO DO THAT, RIGHT?
THE PROBLEM IS...
...THERE ARE FOUR OTHER WARRIORS WITH HER.
HUMPH.
NO PROBLEM.
MY MEN HAVE BEEN GIVEN TREMENDOUS POWER BY LORD SILENT MASK.

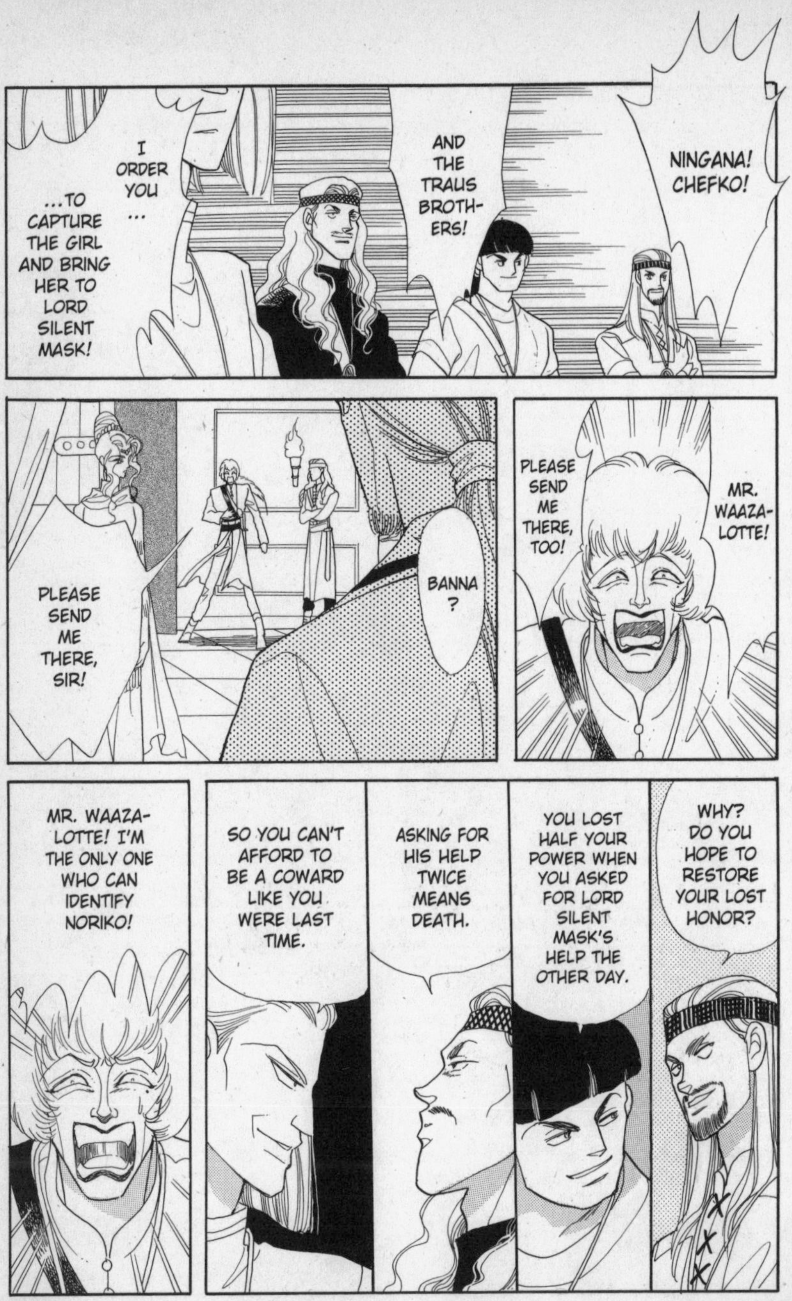
NINGANA! CHEFKO!
AND THE TRAUS BROTHERS!
I ORDER YOU ...
...TO CAPTURE THE GIRL AND BRING HER TO LORD SILENT MASK!
MR. WAAZA-LOTTE!
PLEASE SEND ME THERE, TOO!
BANNA?
PLEASE SEND ME THERE, SIR!
WHY? DO YOU HOPE TO RESTORE YOUR LOST HONOR?
YOU LOST HALF YOUR POWER WHEN YOU ASKED FOR LORD SILENT MASK'S HELP THE OTHER DAY.
ASKING FOR HIS HELP TWICE MEANS DEATH.
SO YOU CAN'T AFFORD TO BE A COWARD LIKE YOU WERE LAST TIME.
MR. WAAZA-LOTTE! I'M THE ONLY ONE WHO CAN IDENTIFY NORIKO!

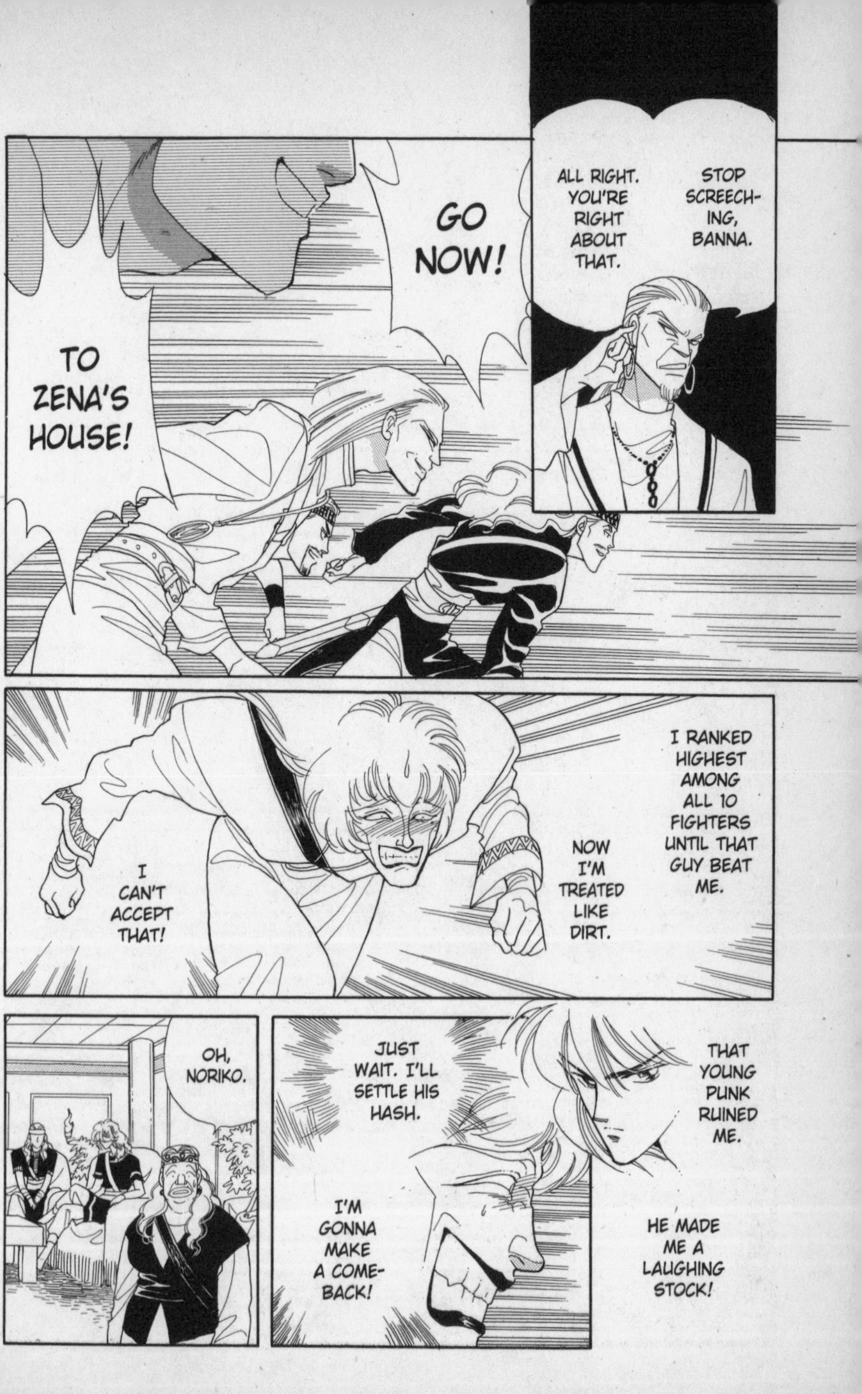
STOP SCREECHING, BANNA.
ALL RIGHT. YOU'RE RIGHT ABOUT THAT.
GO NOW!
TO ZENA'S HOUSE!
I RANKED HIGHEST AMONG ALL 10 FIGHTERS UNTIL THAT GUY BEAT ME.
NOW I'M TREATED LIKE DIRT.
I CAN'T ACCEPT THAT!
THAT YOUNG PUNK RUINED ME.
JUST WAIT. I'LL SETTLE HIS HASH.
HE MADE ME A LAUGHING STOCK!
I'M GONNA MAKE A COME-BACK!
OH, NORIKO.

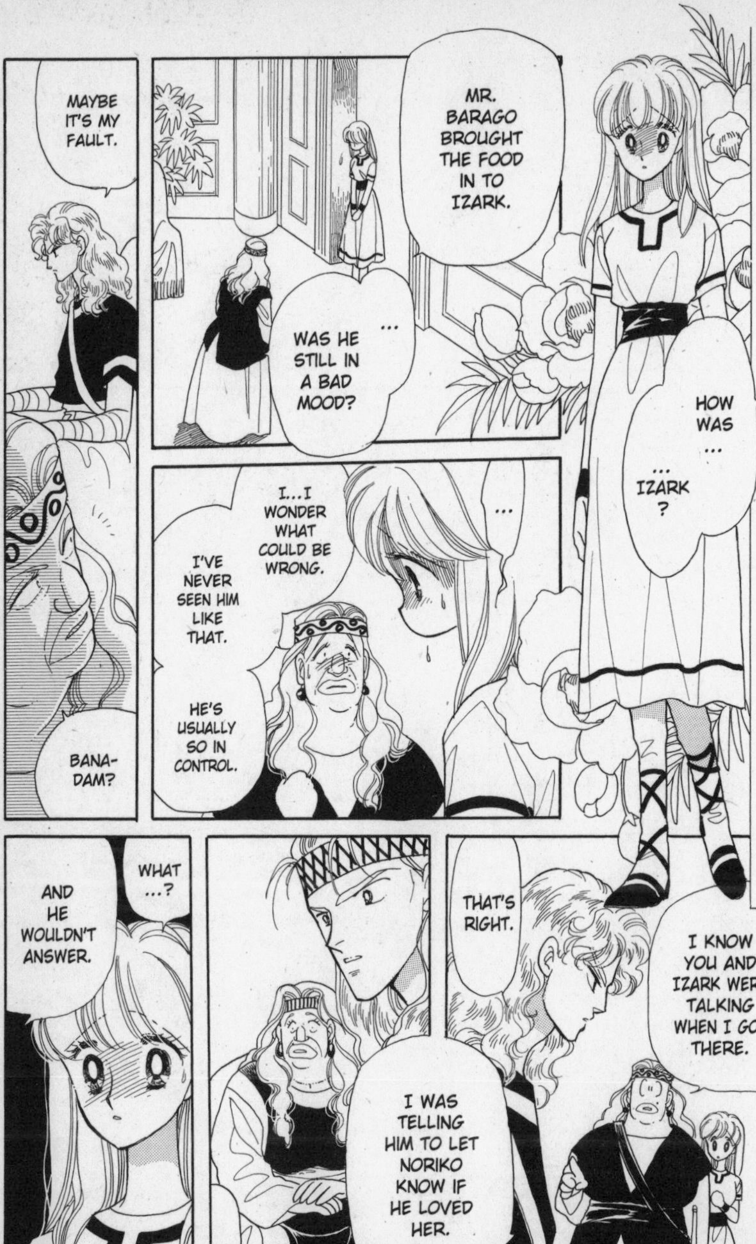
HOW WAS ... ... IZARK ?
MR. BARAGO BROUGHT THE FOOD IN TO IZARK.
... WAS HE STILL IN A BAD MOOD?
...
I...I WONDER WHAT COULD BE WRONG.
I'VE NEVER SEEN HIM LIKE THAT.
HE'S USUALLY SO IN CONTROL.
MAYBE IT'S MY FAULT.
BANA-DAM?
I KNOW YOU AND IZARK WERE TALKING WHEN I GOT THERE.
THAT'S RIGHT.
I WAS TELLING HIM TO LET NORIKO KNOW IF HE LOVED HER.
WHAT ...?
AND HE WOULDN'T ANSWER.

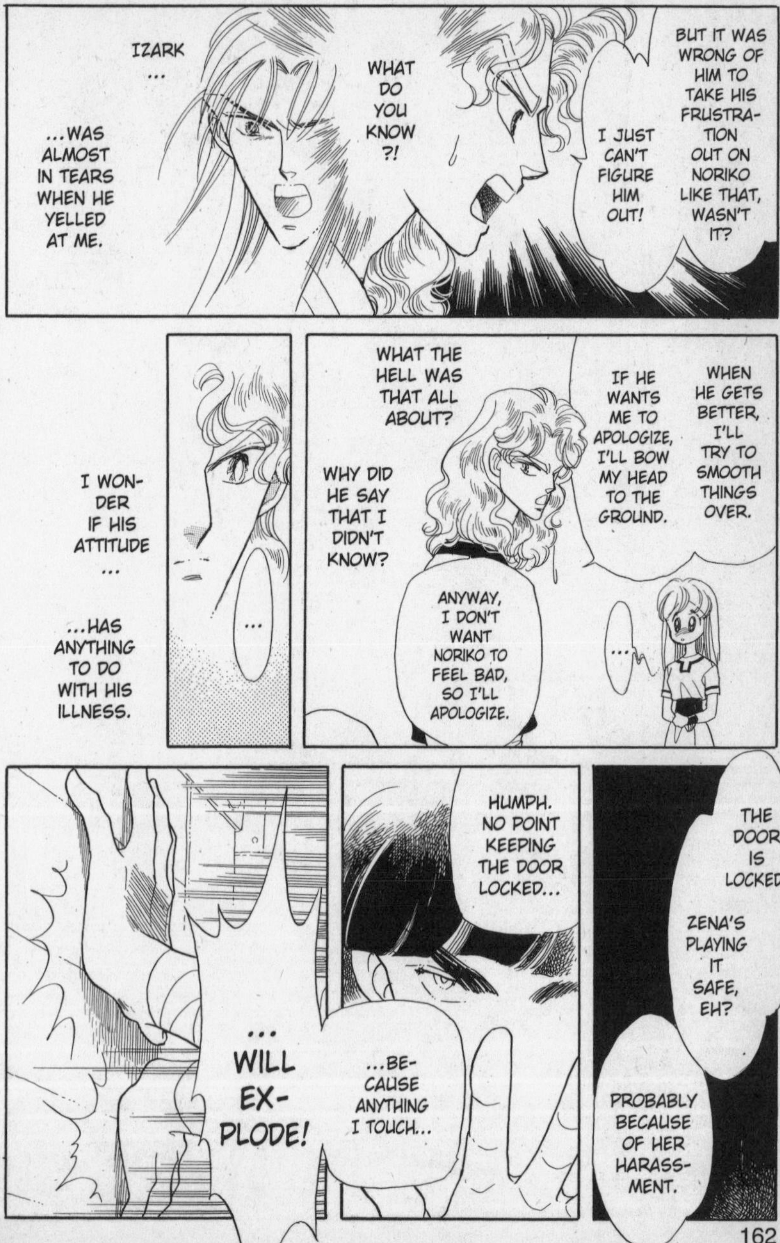
BUT IT WAS WRONG OF HIM TO TAKE HIS FRUSTRATION OUT ON NORIKO LIKE THAT, WASN'T IT?
I JUST CAN'T FIGURE HIM OUT!
WHAT DO YOU KNOW?!
IZARK...
...WAS ALMOST IN TEARS WHEN HE YELLED AT ME.
WHEN HE GETS BETTER, I'LL TRY TO SMOOTH THINGS OVER.
IF HE WANTS ME TO APOLOGIZE, I'LL BOW MY HEAD TO THE GROUND.
WHAT THE HELL WAS THAT ALL ABOUT?
WHY DID HE SAY THAT I DIDN'T KNOW?
...
ANYWAY, I DON'T WANT NORIKO TO FEEL BAD, SO I'LL APOLOGIZE.
I WONDER IF HIS ATTITUDE...
...
...HAS ANYTHING TO DO WITH HIS ILLNESS.
THE DOOR IS LOCKED.
ZENA'S PLAYING IT SAFE, EH?
PROBABLY BECAUSE OF HER HARASSMENT.
HUMPH. NO POINT KEEPING THE DOOR LOCKED...
...BECAUSE ANYTHING I TOUCH...
...WILL EXPLODE!

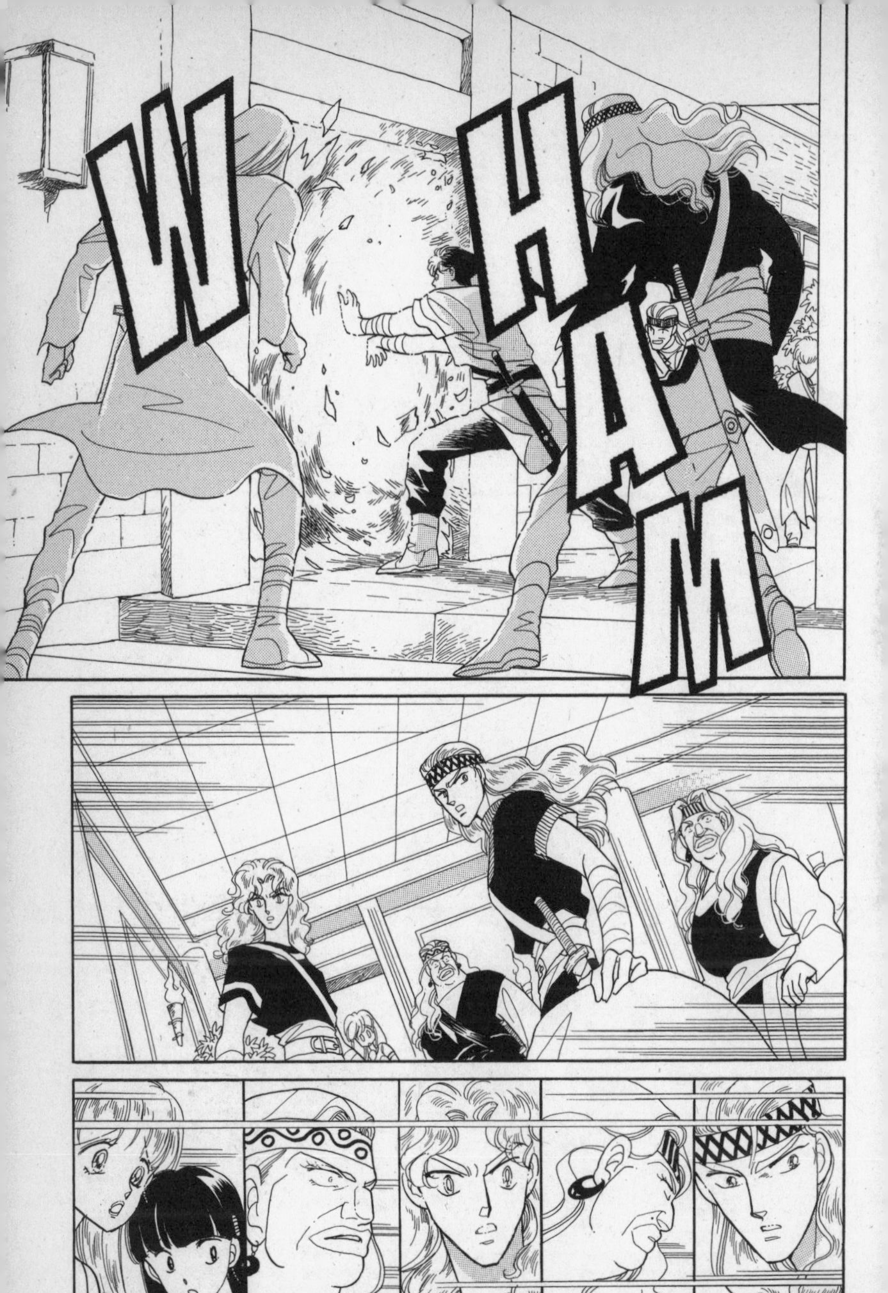
WHAM

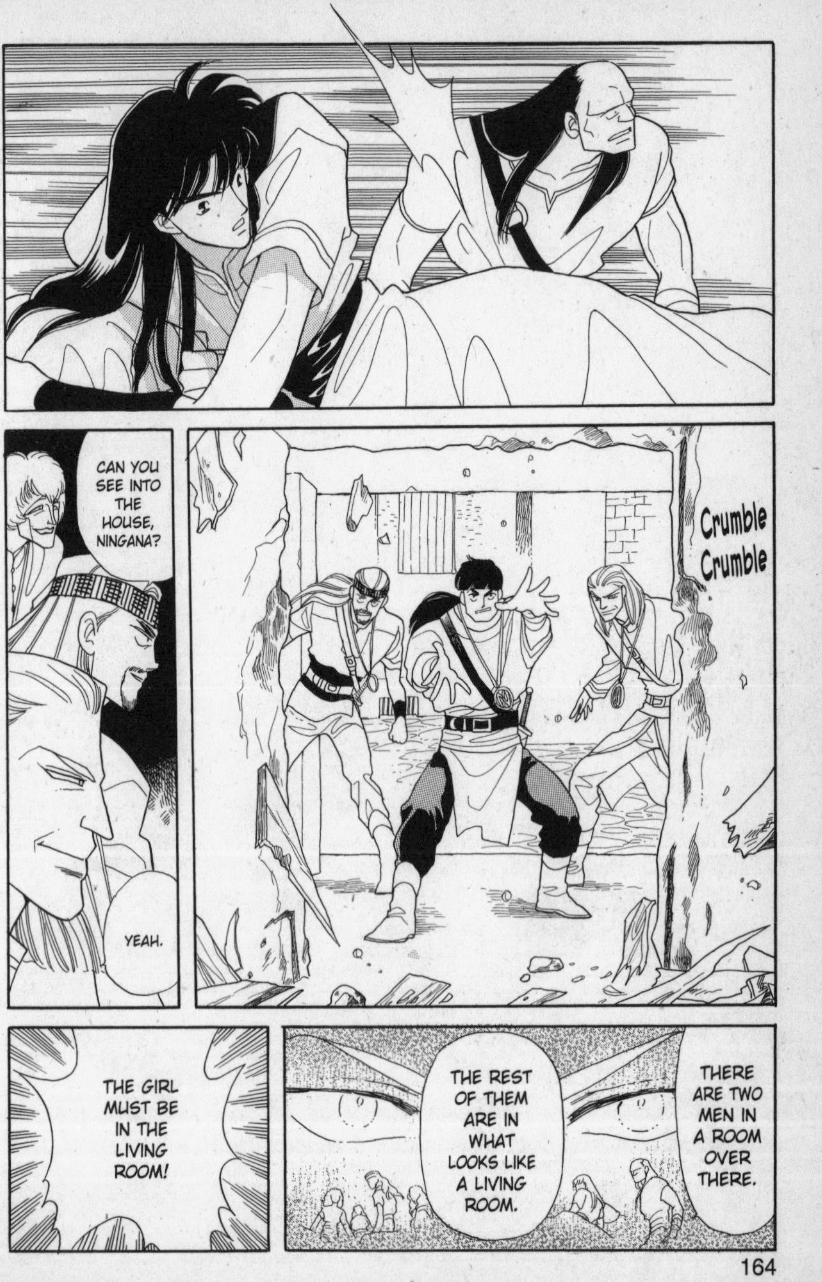
Crumble Crumble
CAN YOU SEE INTO THE HOUSE, NINGANA?
YEAH.
THERE ARE TWO MEN IN A ROOM OVER THERE.
THE REST OF THEM ARE IN WHAT LOOKS LIKE A LIVING ROOM.
THE GIRL MUST BE IN THE LIVING ROOM!

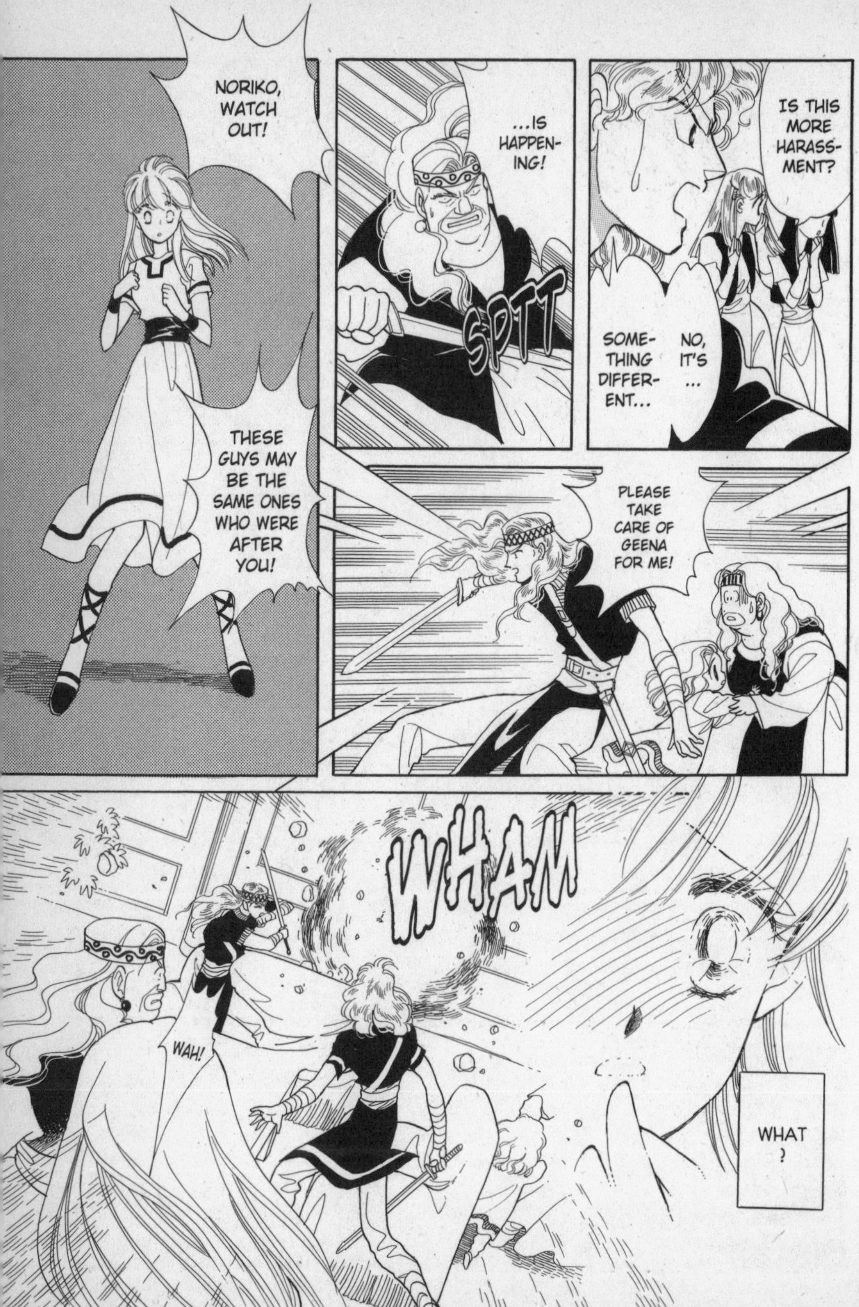
IS THIS MORE HARASS-MENT?
NO, IT'S...
SOME-THING DIFFER-ENT...
...IS HAPPEN-ING!
SPTT
PLEASE TAKE CARE OF GEENA FOR ME!
NORIKO, WATCH OUT!
THESE GUYS MAY BE THE SAME ONES WHO WERE AFTER YOU!
WHAT?
WHAM
WAH!

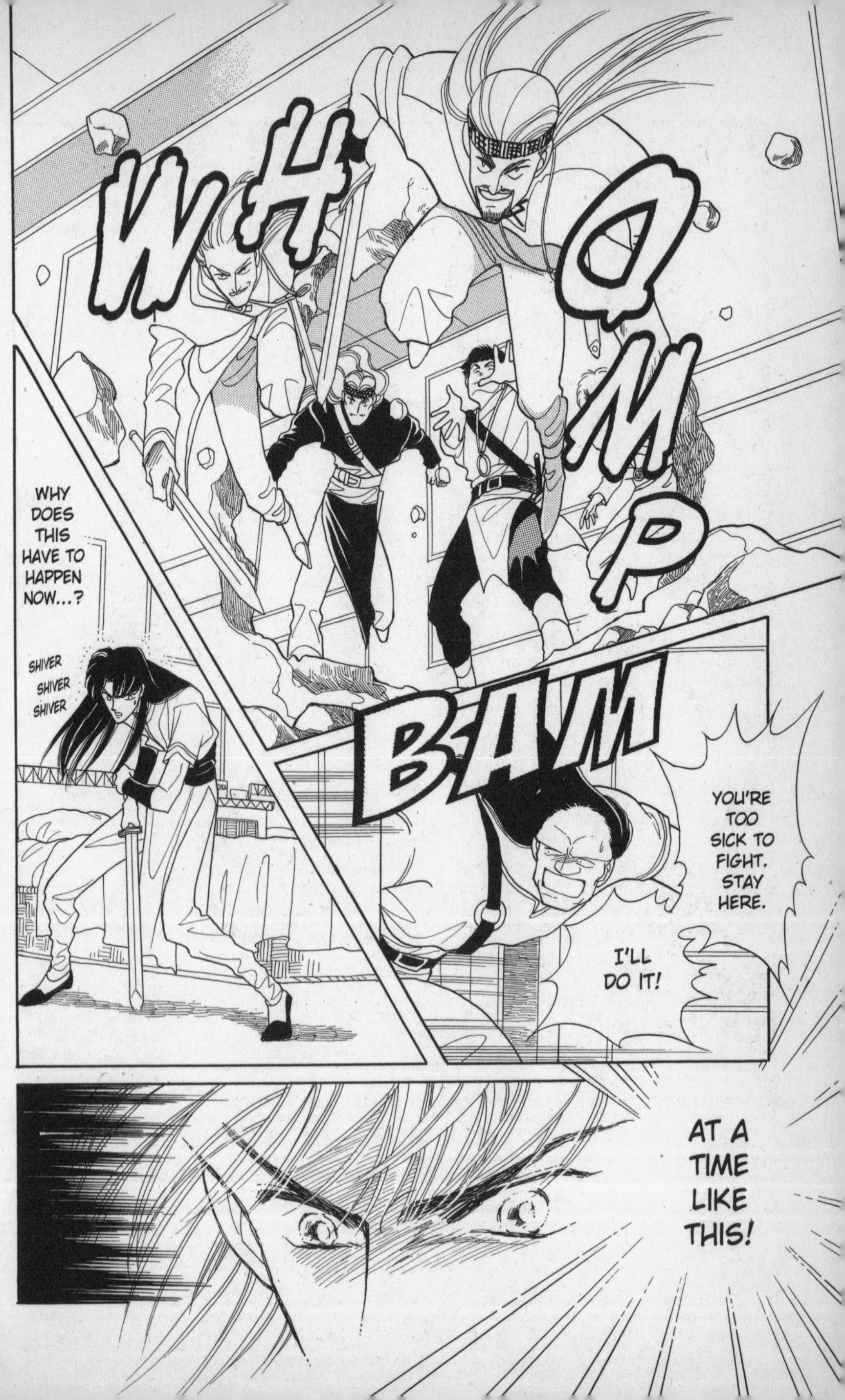

WHOMP
BAM
YOU'RE TOO SICK TO FIGHT. STAY HERE.
I'LL DO IT!
WHY DOES THIS HAVE TO HAPPEN NOW...?
SHIVER SHIVER SHIVER
AT A TIME LIKE THIS!

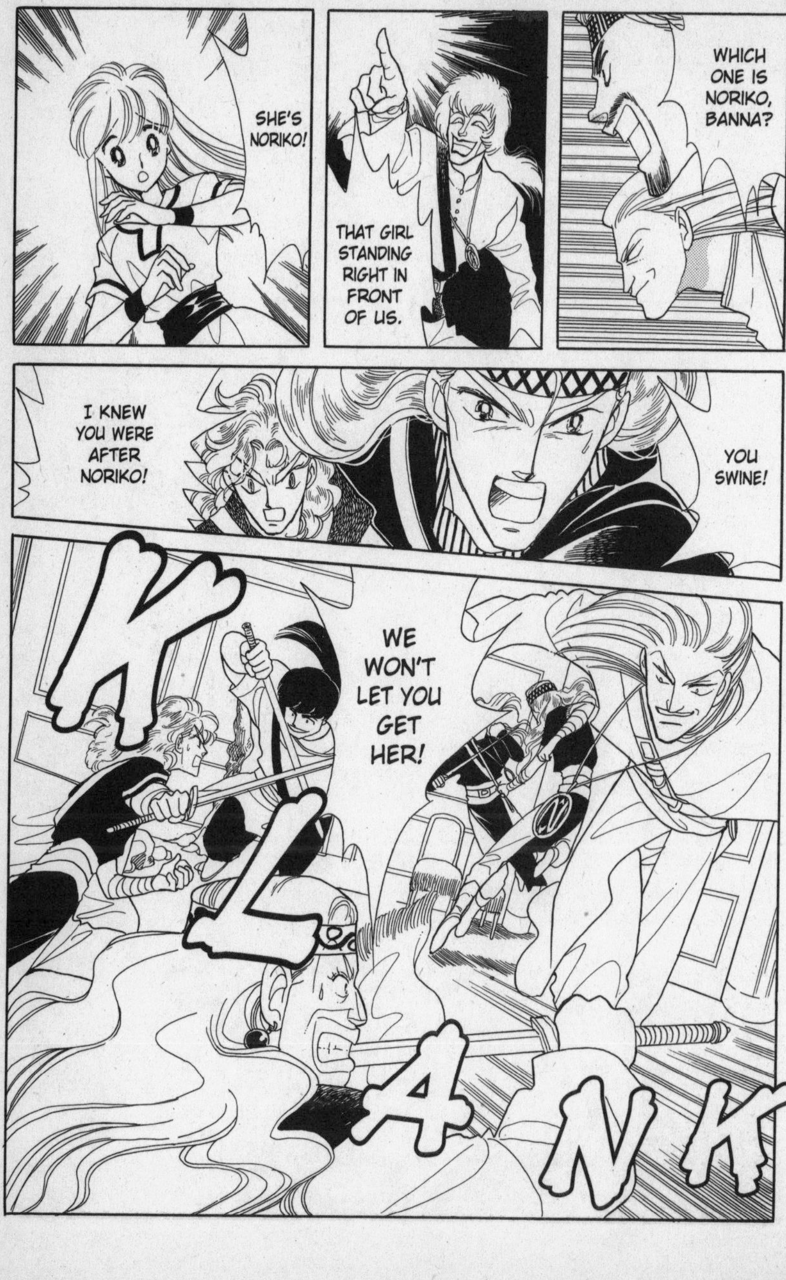
WHICH ONE IS NORIKO, BANNA?
THAT GIRL STANDING RIGHT IN FRONT OF US.
SHE'S NORIKO!
YOU SWINE!
I KNEW YOU WERE AFTER NORIKO!
WE WON'T LET YOU GET HER!
KLANK

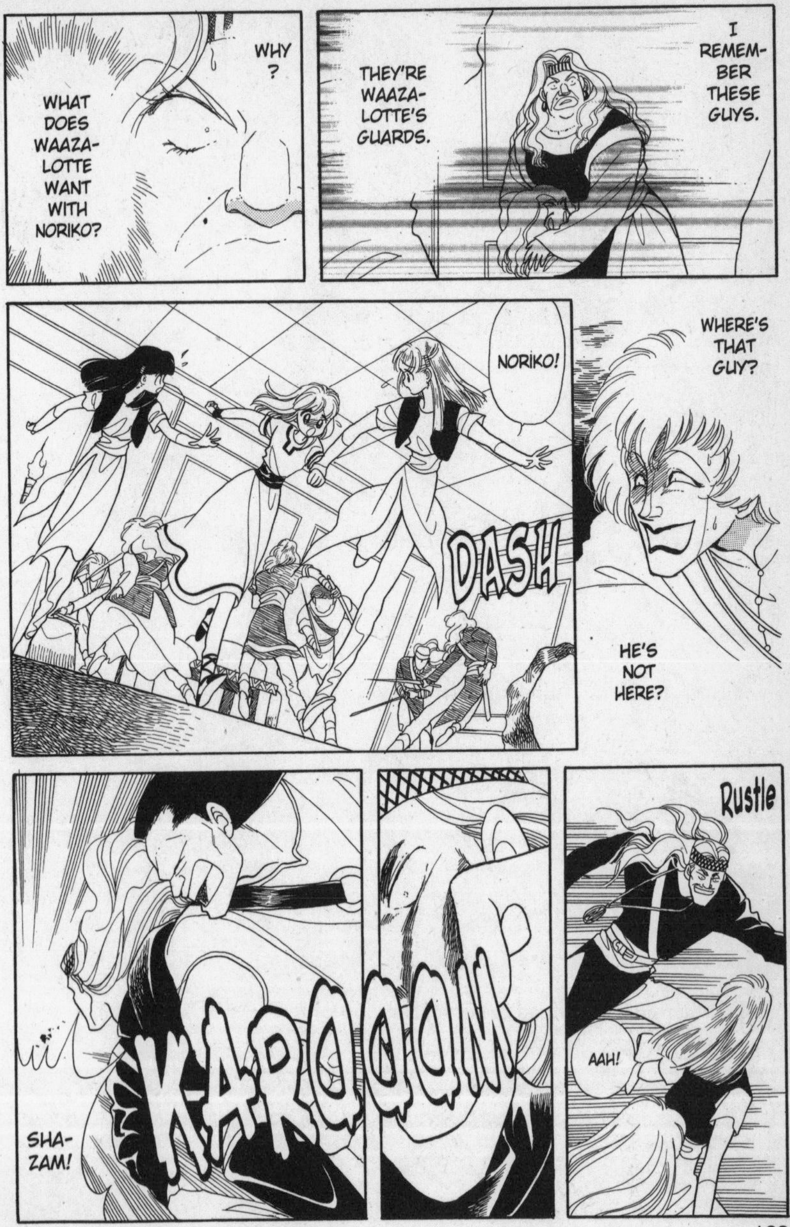
I REMEMBER THESE GUYS.
THEY'RE WAAZALOTTE'S GUARDS.
WHY?
WHAT DOES WAAZALOTTE WANT WITH NORIKO?
WHERE'S THAT GUY?
HE'S NOT HERE?
NORIKO!
DASH
Rustle
AAH!
KAROOOM
SHA-ZAM!

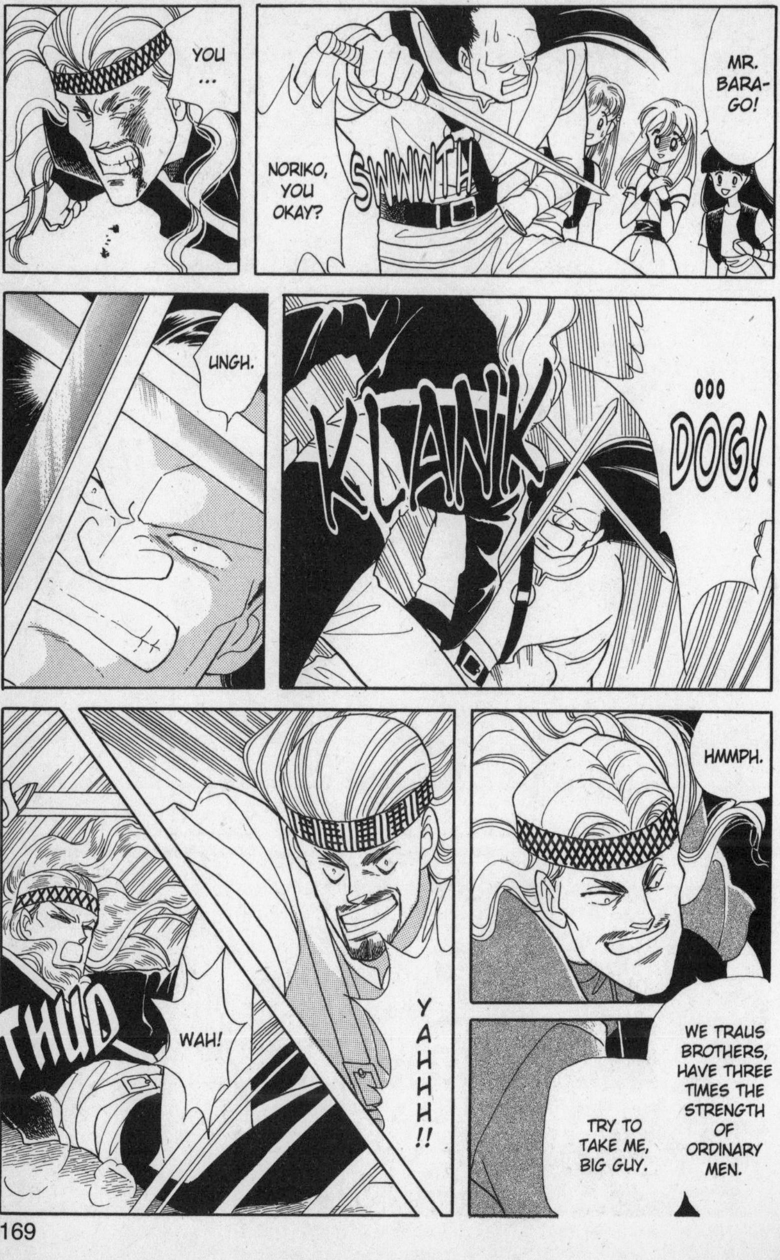
MR. BARA-GO!
SWWWTH
NORIKO, YOU OKAY?
YOU ...
... DOG!
KLANK
UNGH.
HMMPH.
WE TRAUS BROTHERS, HAVE THREE TIMES THE STRENGTH OF ORDINARY MEN.
TRY TO TAKE ME, BIG GUY.
YAHHHH!!
WAH!
THUD

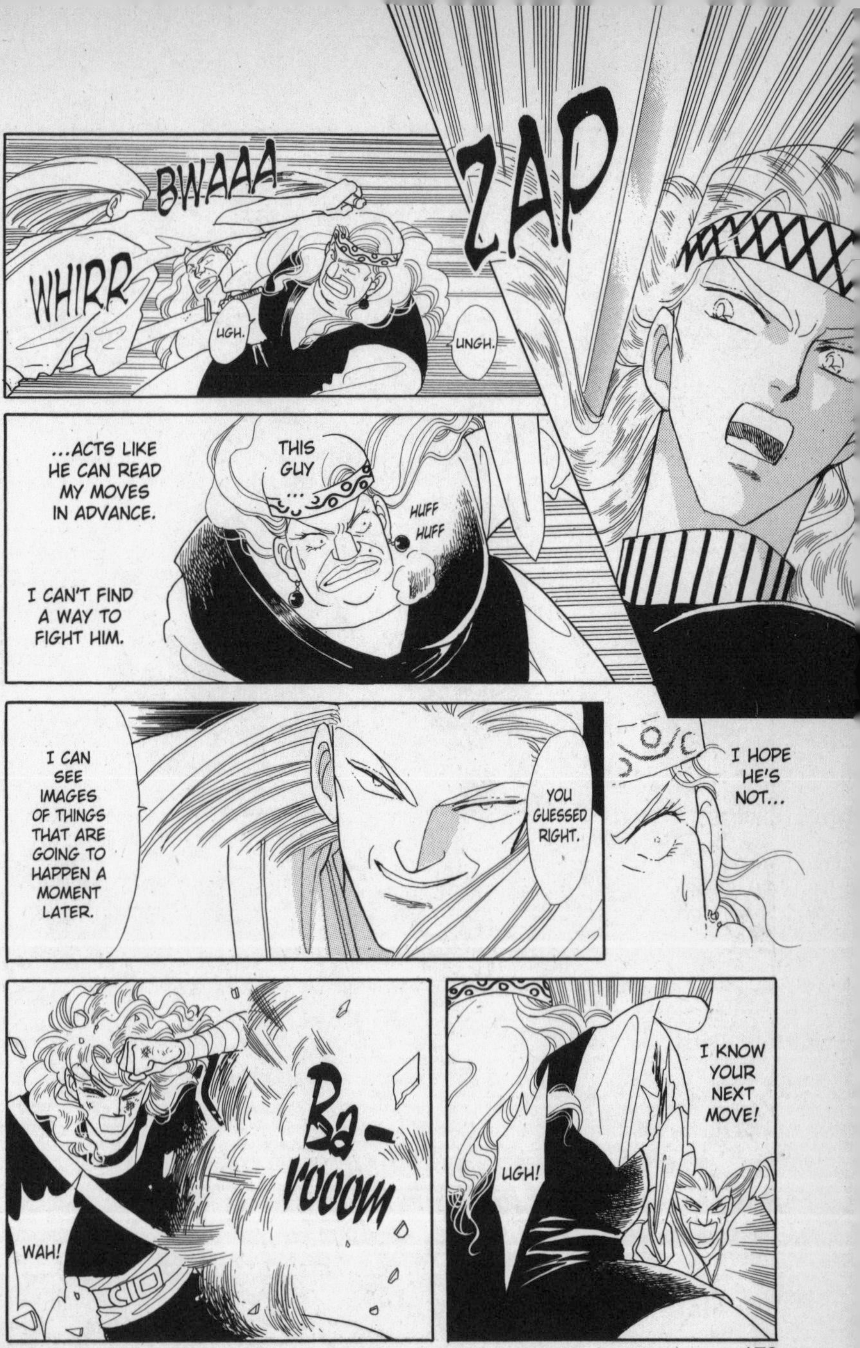
ZAP
UNGH.
BWAAA
UGH.
WHIRR
THIS GUY ...
HUFF HUFF
...ACTS LIKE HE CAN READ MY MOVES IN ADVANCE.
I CAN'T FIND A WAY TO FIGHT HIM.
I HOPE HE'S NOT...
YOU GUESSED RIGHT.
I CAN SEE IMAGES OF THINGS THAT ARE GOING TO HAPPEN A MOMENT LATER.
I KNOW YOUR NEXT MOVE!
UGH!
Ba-rooom
WAH!

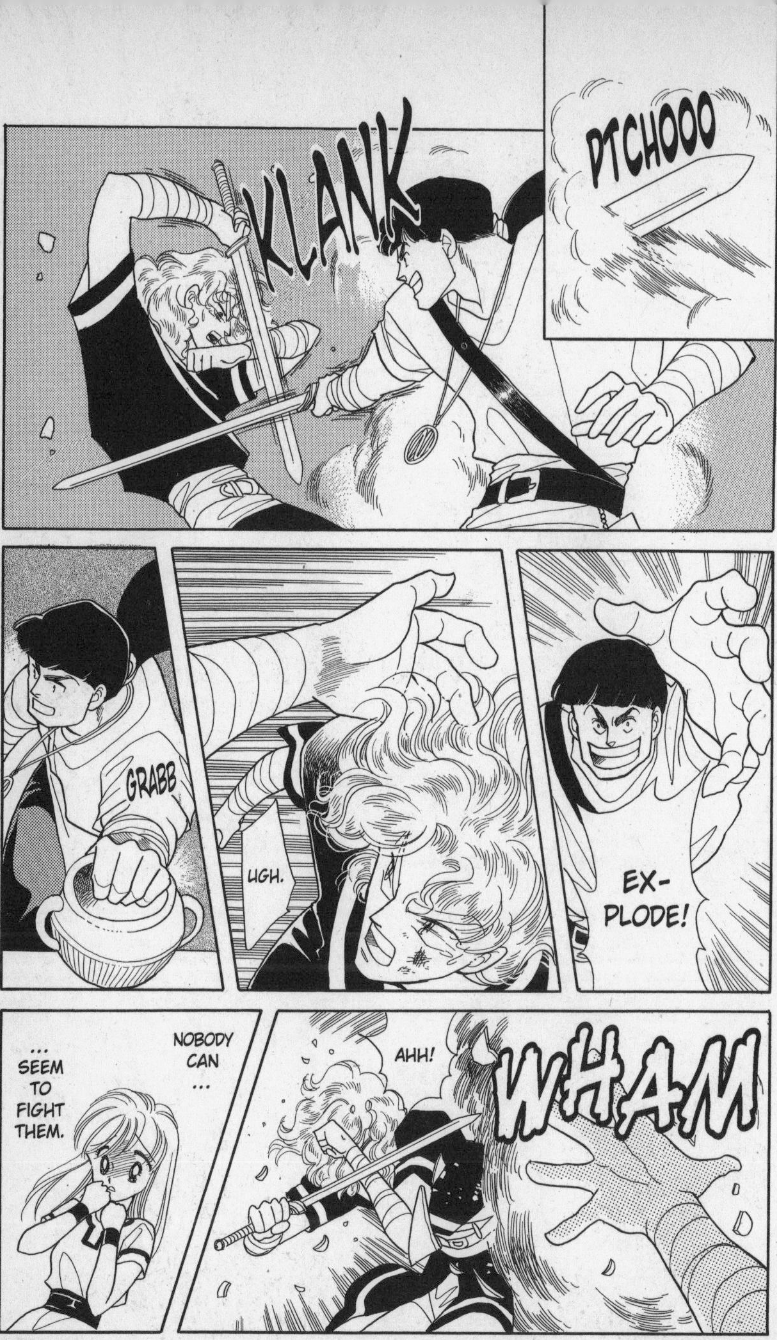
DTCHOOO
KLANK
EX- PLODE!
UGH.
GRABB
AHH!
WHAM
NOBODY CAN ...
... SEEM TO FIGHT THEM.

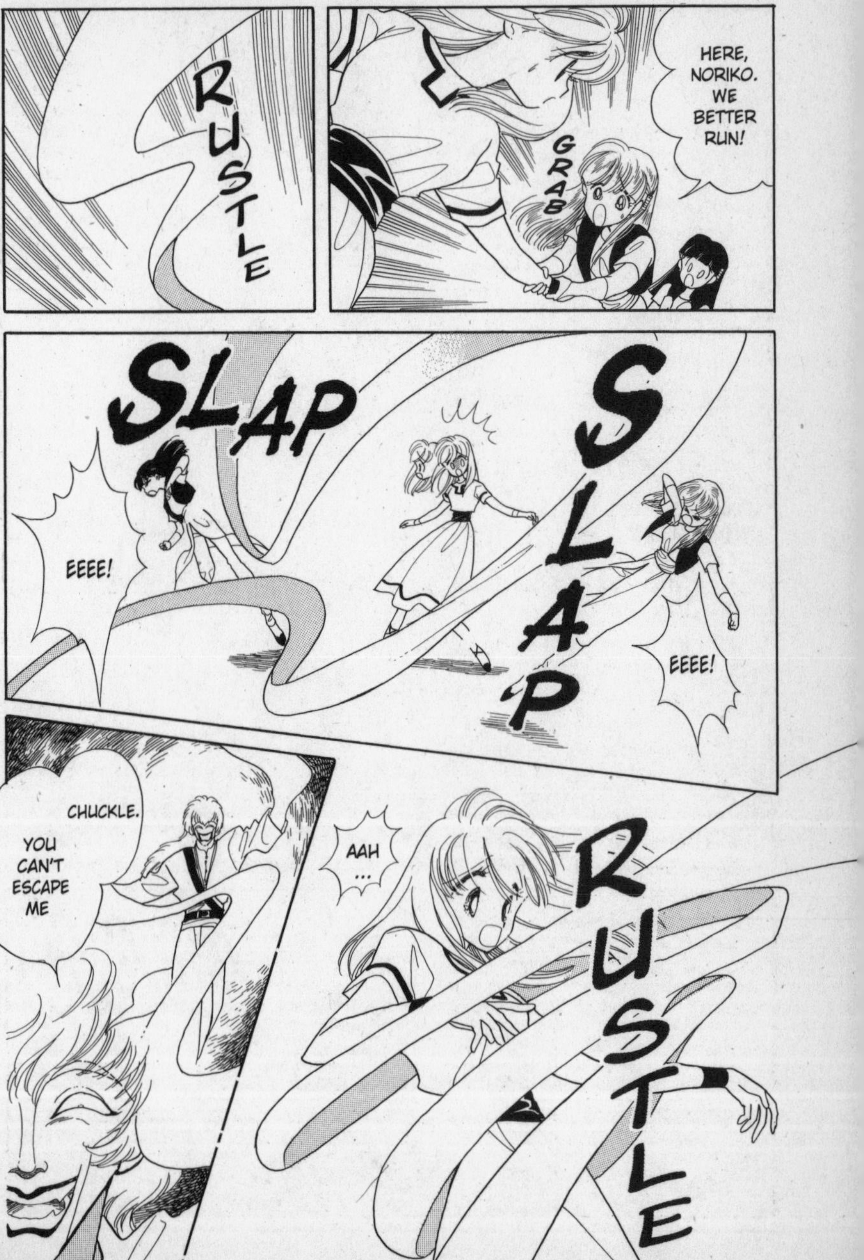
HERE, NORIKO. WE BETTER RUN!
GRAB
RUSTLE
SLAP
EEEE!
SLAP
EEEE!
RUSTLE
AAH ...
CHUCKLE.
YOU CAN'T ESCAPE ME

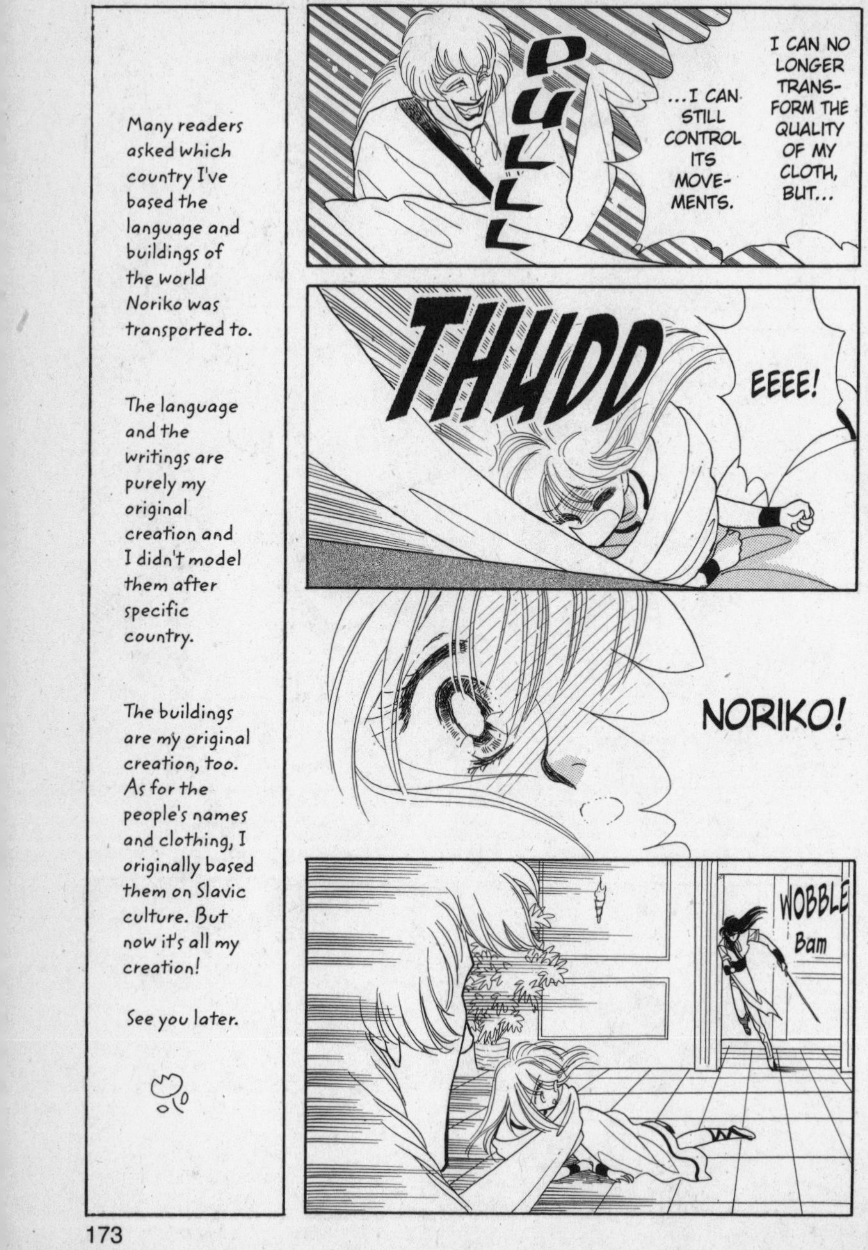
I CAN NO LONGER TRANS-FORM THE QUALITY OF MY CLOTH, BUT...
...I CAN STILL CONTROL ITS MOVE-MENTS.
PULLL
THUDD
EEEE!
NORIKO!
WOBBLE
Bam

Many readers asked which country I've based the language and buildings of the world Noriko was transported to.

The language and the writings are purely my original creation and I didn't model them after specific country.

The buildings are my original creation, too. As for the people's names and clothing, I originally based them on Slavic culture. But now it's all my creation!

See you later.

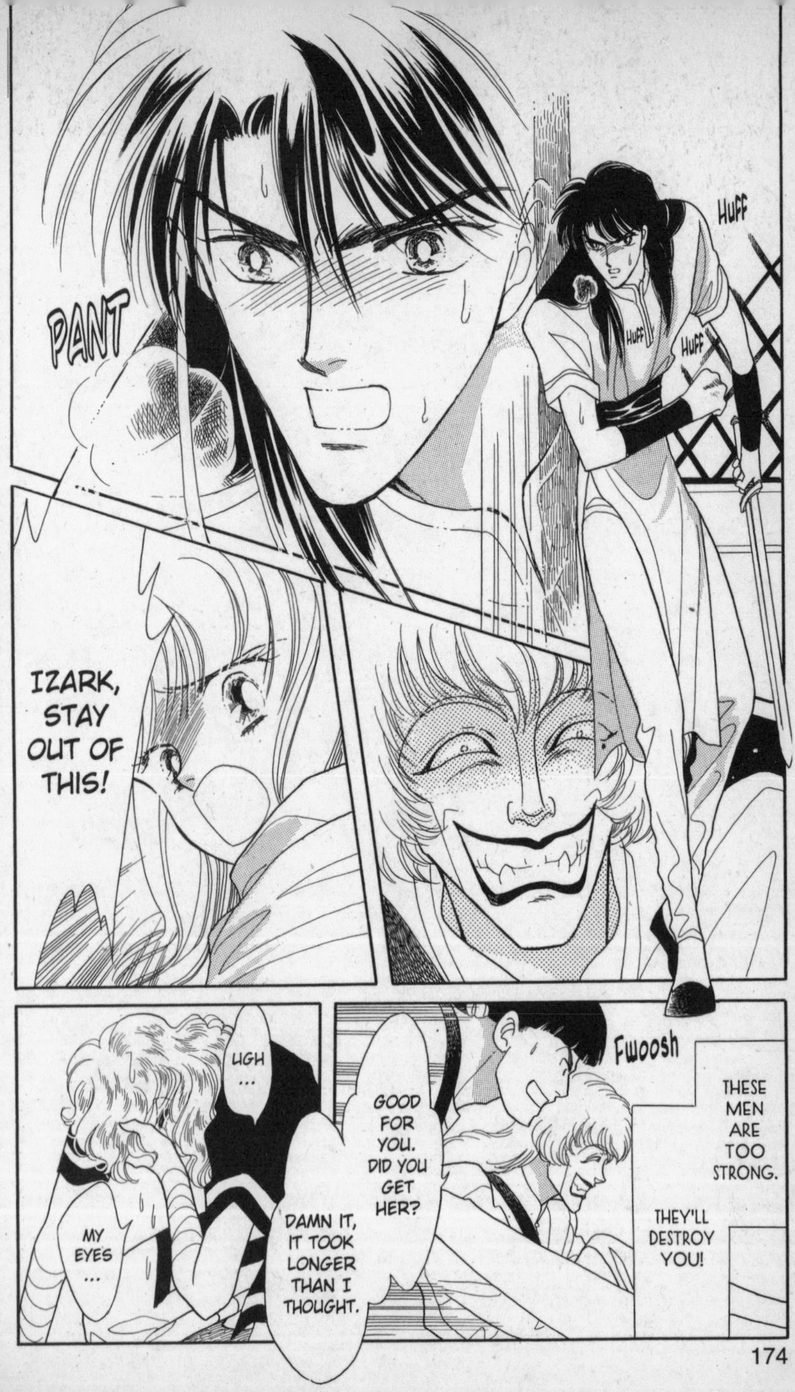
Huff
Huff
Huff
PANT
IZARK, STAY OUT OF THIS!
Fwoosh
THESE MEN ARE TOO STRONG.
THEY'LL DESTROY YOU!
GOOD FOR YOU. DID YOU GET HER?
DAMN IT, IT TOOK LONGER THAN I THOUGHT.
UGH ...
MY EYES ...

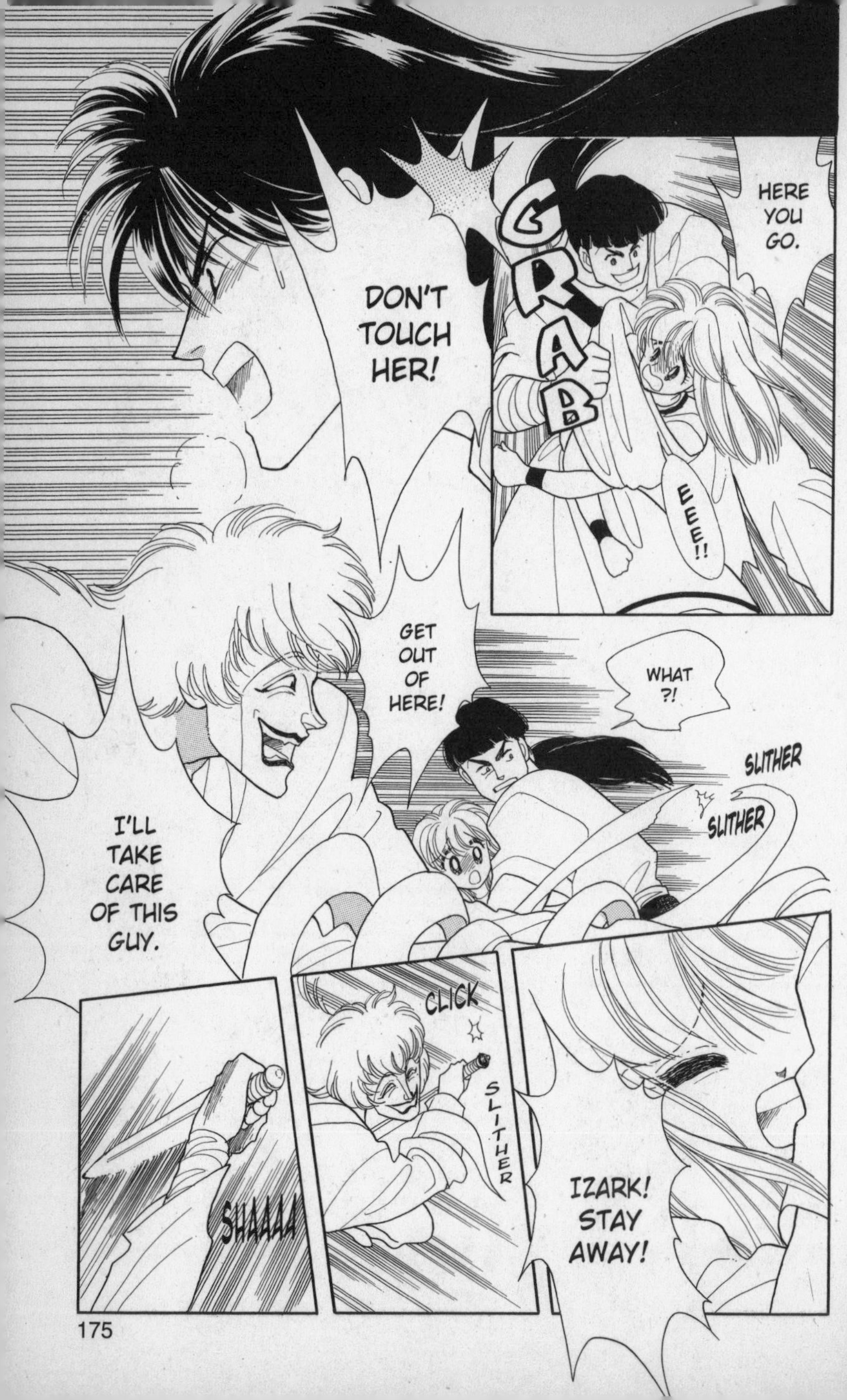
HERE YOU GO.
GRAB
EEE!!
DON'T TOUCH HER!
WHAT?!
SLITHER
SLITHER
GET OUT OF HERE!
I'LL TAKE CARE OF THIS GUY.
IZARK! STAY AWAY!
CLICK
SLITHER
SHAAAA

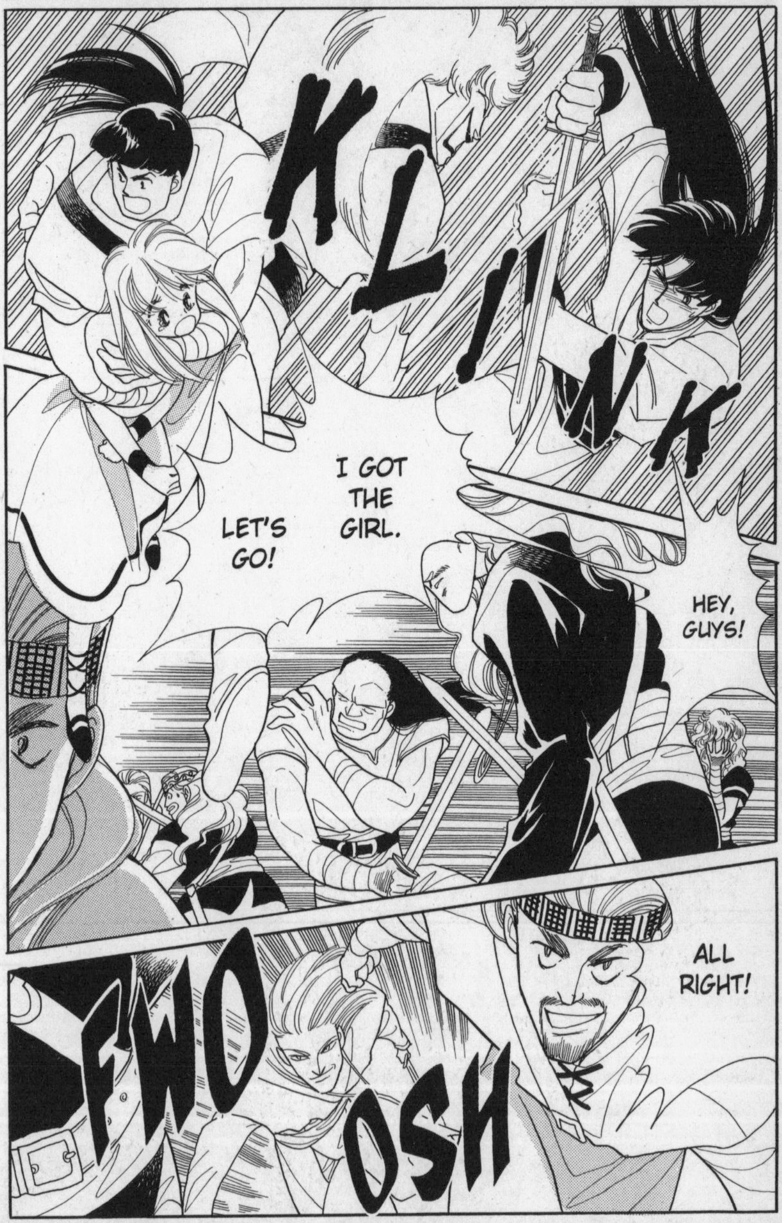
KLINK
I GOT THE GIRL.
LET'S GO!
HEY, GUYS!
ALL RIGHT!
FWOOSH

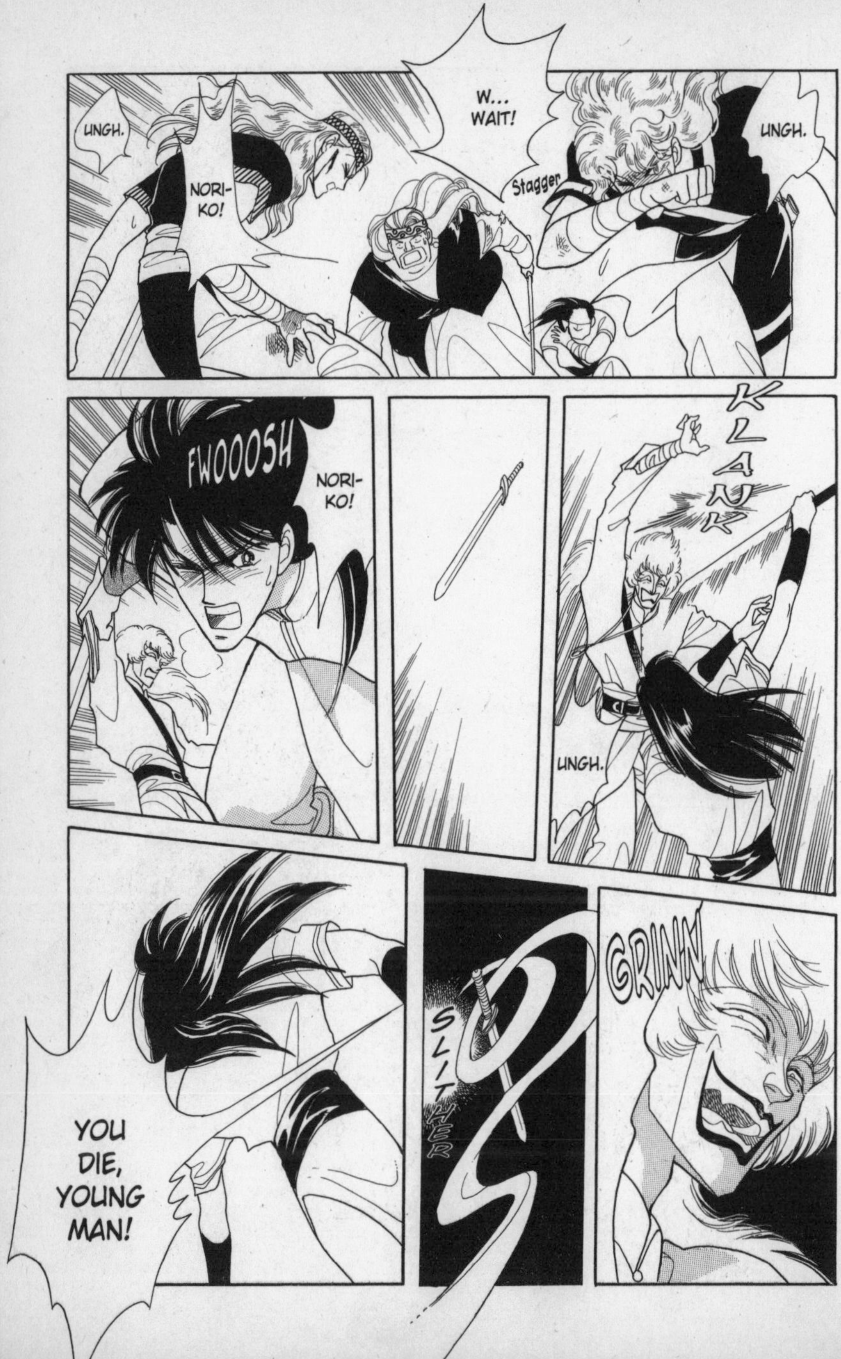
UNGH.
W... WAIT!
Stagger
NORI-KO!
UNGH.
KLANK
UNGH.
FWOOOSH
NORI-KO!
GRINN
SLITHER
YOU DIE, YOUNG MAN!

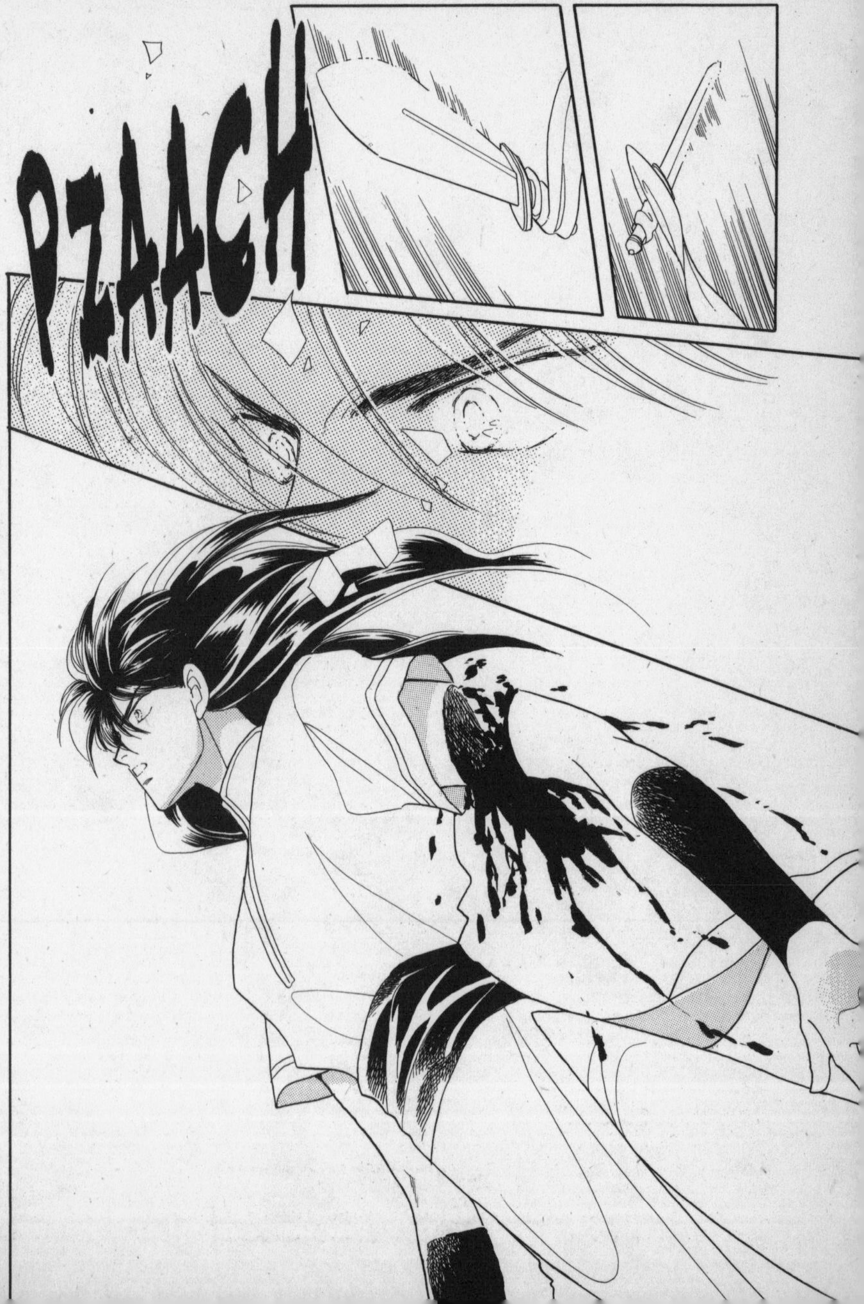
PZAACH

From Far Aw
Vol
Shôjo Editi

Story and Art
Kyoko Hika

English Adaptation/Trina Robbi
Translation/Yuko Sawa
Touch-Up Art & Lettering/Walden Wo
Cover & Graphic Design/Andrea Ri
Editor/Eric Searlem

Managing Editor/Annette Rom
Director of Production/Noboru Watana
Vice President of Publishing/Alvin
Sr. Director of Acquisitions/Rika Inou
Vice President of Sales & Marketing/Liza Coppo
Publisher/Hyoe Nar

Printed in Cana

Published by VIZ Media, L
P.O. Box 770
San Francisco, CA 941

Shôjo Editi
10 9 8 7 6 5 4 3 2
First printing, August 20

www.viz.com

PARENTAL ADVISORY
FROM FAR AWAY is rated T for Teen and is recommended for ages 13 and up. This volume contains fantasy violence.

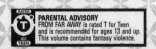

store.viz.co

EDITOR RECOMMENDATIONS

Did you enjoy this volume of ***FROM FAR AWAY***? If so, here are three more titles the editor thinks you'd like.

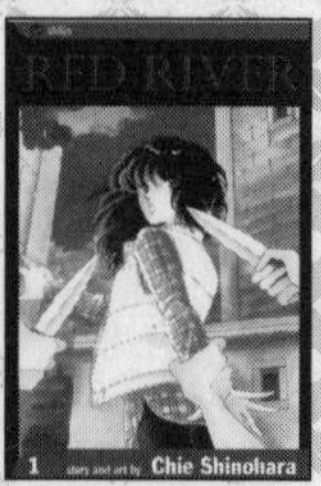
RED RIVER
1
Chie Shinohara

RED RIVER by Chie Shinohara: All Yuri wants to do is go to high school and fall in love. Her life changes dramatically when she suddenly gets whisked away to a magical Middle-Eastern village. Added bonus: lots of sex and romance!

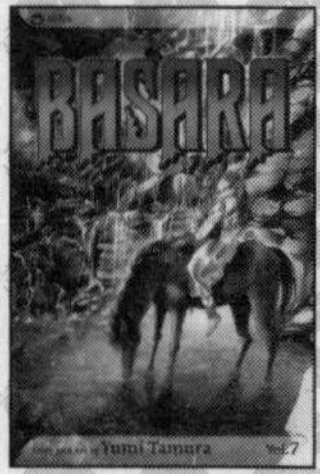
BASARA
Yumi Tamura

BASARA by Yumi Tamura: Into Japan's post-apocalyptic future walks a child of destiny. An epic tale of hope and salvation. Highly recommended!

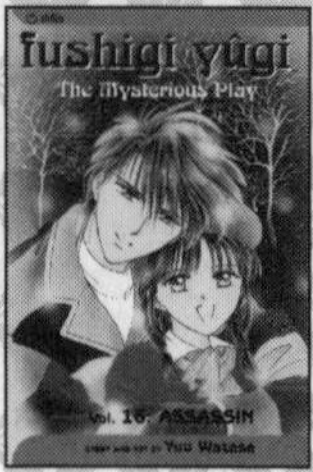
fushigi yûgi
The Mysterious Play
ASSASSIN
Yuu Watase

FUSHIGI YÛGI by Yuu Watase: Myth and reality come together when a Japanese teenager plunges into the world of ancient China. If she's not careful, young Miaka might change the course of history forever!

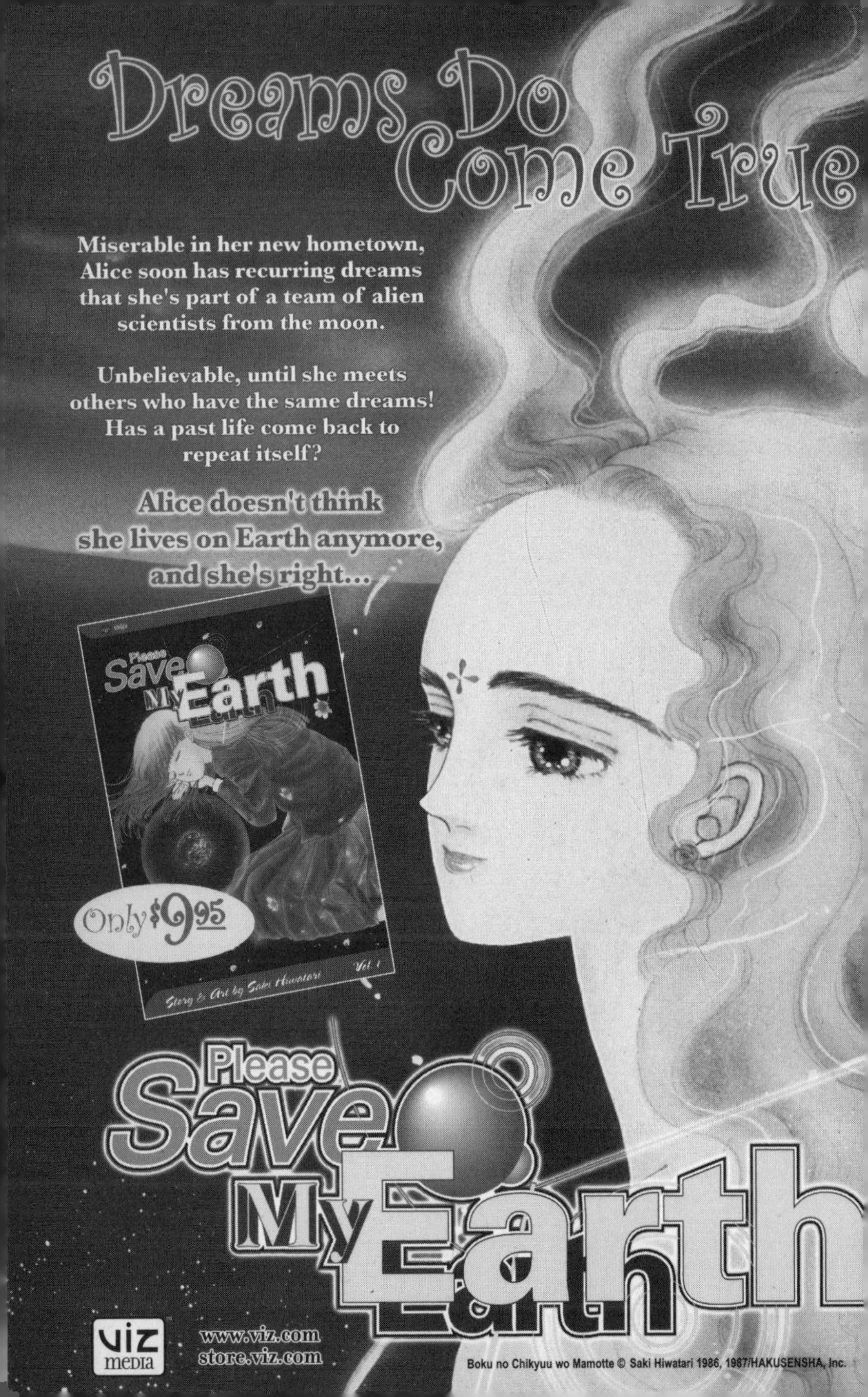
Dreams Do Come True
Miserable in her new hometown, Alice soon has recurring dreams that she's part of a team of alien scientists from the moon.
Unbelievable, until she meets others who have the same dreams! Has a past life come back to repeat itself?
Alice doesn't think she lives on Earth anymore, and she's right...
Please Save My Earth
Vol. 1
Story & Art by Saki Hiwatari
Only $9.95
Please Save My Earth
viz media
www.viz.com
store.viz.com
Boku no Chikyuu wo Mamotte © Saki Hiwatari 1986, 1987/HAKUSENSHA, Inc.

LOVE SHOJO? LET US KNOW!

☐ Please do NOT send me information about VIZ Media products, news and events, special offers, or other information.

☐ Please do NOT send me information from VIZ' trusted business partners.

Name: _____

Address: _____

City: _____ State: _____ Zip: _____

E-mail: _____

☐ Male ☐ Female   Date of Birth (mm/dd/yyyy): ___/___/___   (Under 13? Parental consent required)

What race/ethnicity do you consider yourself? (check all that apply)

☐ White/Caucasian ☐ Black/African American ☐ Hispanic/Latino

☐ Asian/Pacific Islander ☐ Native American/Alaskan Native ☐ Other: _____

What VIZ shojo title(s) did you purchase? (indicate title(s) purchased)

_____

What other shojo titles from other publishers do you own? _____

_____

Reason for purchase: (check all that apply)

☐ Special offer ☐ Favorite title / author / artist / genre

☐ Gift ☐ Recommendation ☐ Collection

☐ Read excerpt in VIZ manga sampler ☐ Other _____

Where did you make your purchase? (please check one)

☐ Comic store ☐ Bookstore ☐ Mass/Grocery Store

☐ Newsstand ☐ Video/Video Game Store

☐ Online (site:_____) ☐ Other _____

How many shojo titles have you purchased in the last year? How many were VIZ shojo titles?
(please check one from each column)

SHOJO MANGA	VIZ SHOJO MANGA
☐ None	☐ None
☐ 1 – 4	☐ 1 – 4
☐ 5 – 10	☐ 5 – 10
☐ 11+	☐ 11+

What do you like most about shojo graphic novels? (check all that apply)

☐ Romance ☐ Drama / conflict ☐ Fantasy

☐ Comedy ☐ Real-life storylines ☐ Relatable characters

☐ Other ______________________________

Do you purchase every volume of your favorite shojo series?

☐ Yes! Gotta have 'em as my own

☐ No. Please explain: ______________________________

Who are your favorite shojo authors / artists? ______________________________

____

What shojo titles would like you translated and sold in English? ______________________________

____

THANK YOU! Please send the completed form to:

VIZ media™

NJW Research
ATTN: VIZ Media Shojo Survey
42 Catharine Street
Poughkeepsie, NY 12601

Your privacy is very important to us. All information provided will be used for internal purposes only and will not be sold or otherwise divulged.